13

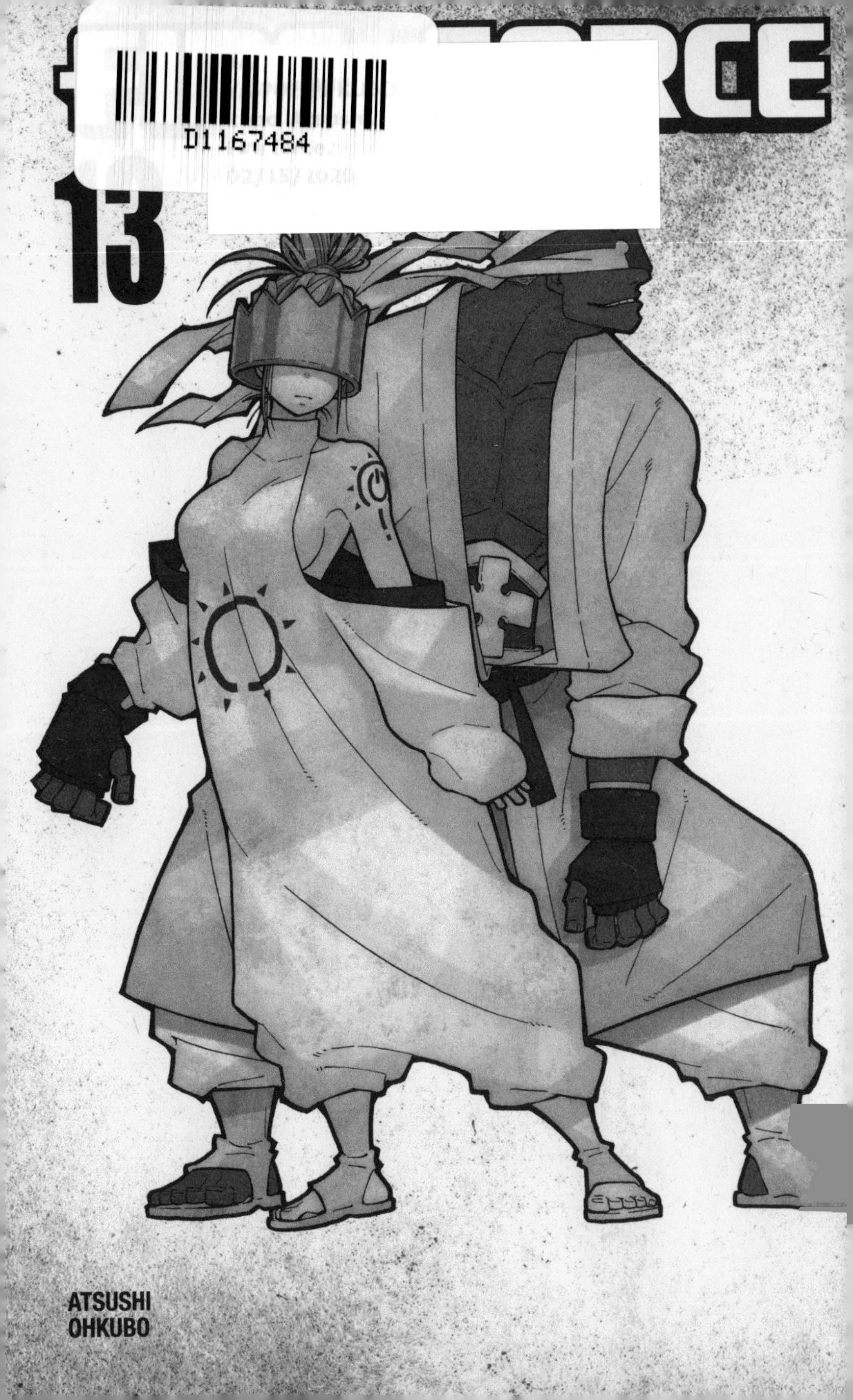

ATSUSHI
OHKUBO

world... the great deep.

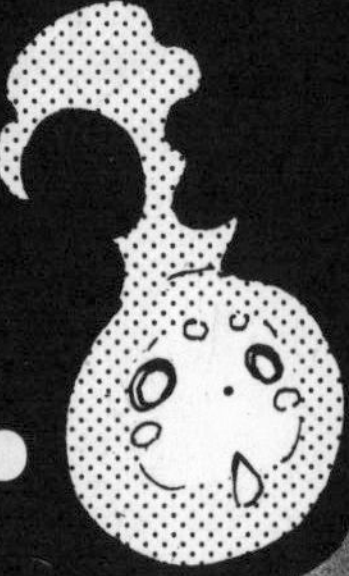

VOL. 13

ATSUSHI OHKUBO

To a new
Across
fiery

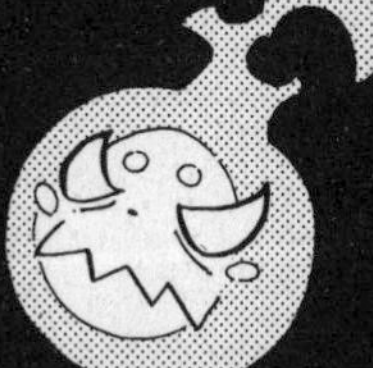

FIRE
FORCE

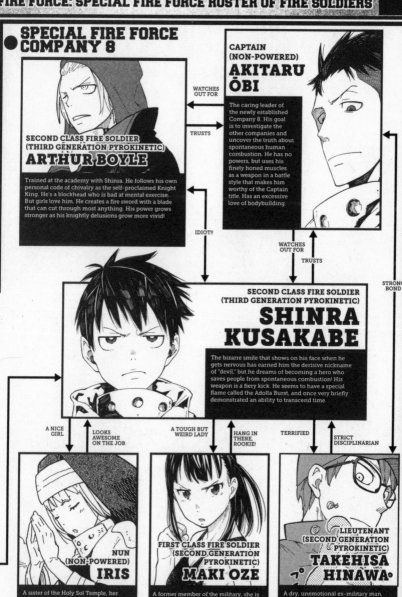

SPECIAL FIRE FORCE COMPANY 8

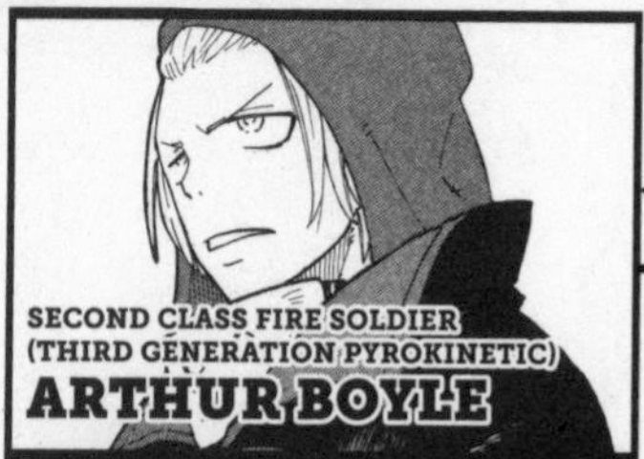

SECOND CLASS FIRE SOLDIER
(THIRD GENERATION PYROKINETIC)
ARTHUR BOYLE

Trained at the academy with Shinra. He follows his own personal code of chivalry as the self-proclaimed Knight King. He's a blockhead who is bad at mental exercise. But girls love him. He creates a fire sword with a blade that can cut through most anything. His power grows stronger as his knightly delusions grow more vivid!

WATCHES OUT FOR

TRUSTS

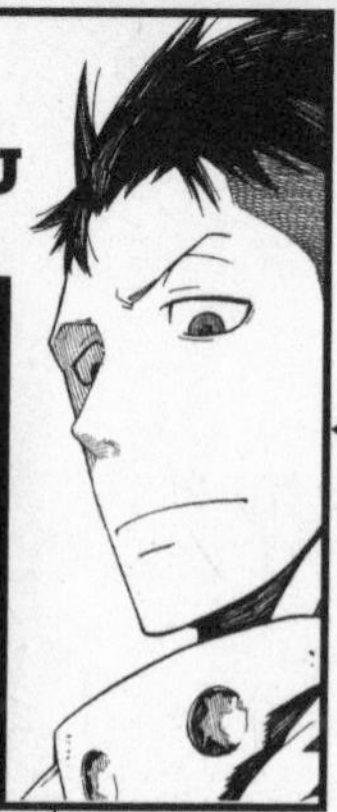

CAPTAIN
(NON-POWERED)
AKITARU ŌBI

The caring leader of the newly established Company 8. His goal is to investigate the other companies and uncover the truth about spontaneous human combustion. He has no powers, but uses his finely honed muscles as a weapon in a battle style that makes him worthy of the Captain title. Has an excessive love of bodybuilding.

IDIOT!!

WATCHES OUT FOR

TRUSTS

STRONG BOND

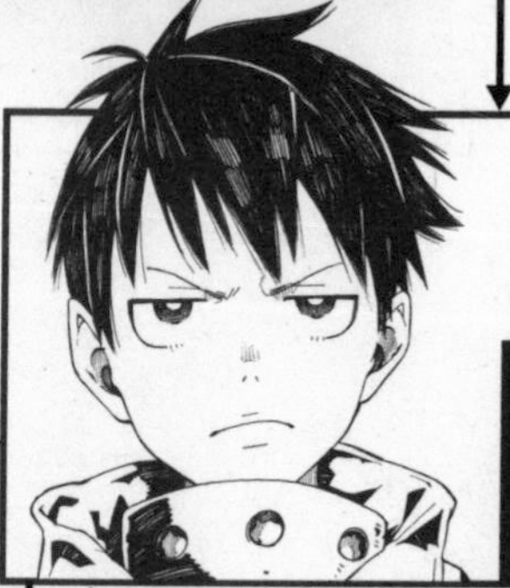

SECOND CLASS FIRE SOLDIER
(THIRD GENERATION PYROKINETIC)
SHINRA KUSAKABE

The bizarre smile that shows on his face when he gets nervous has earned him the derisive nickname of "devil," but he dreams of becoming a hero who saves people from spontaneous combustion! His weapon is a fiery kick. He seems to have a special flame called the Adolla Burst, and once very briefly demonstrated an ability to transcend time.

A NICE GIRL

LOOKS AWESOME ON THE JOB

A TOUGH BUT WEIRD LADY

HANG IN THERE, ROOKIE!

TERRIFIED

STRICT DISCIPLINARIAN

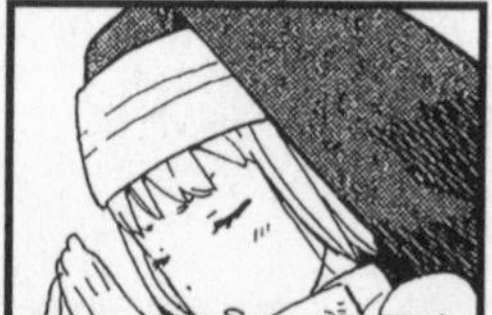

NUN
(NON-POWERED)
IRIS

A sister of the Holy Sol Temple, her prayers are an indispensable part of extinguishing Infernals. Personality-wise, she is no less than an angel. Her boobs are big. Very big. Since reconciling with Captain Hibana from Company 5, they have been as close as real sisters.

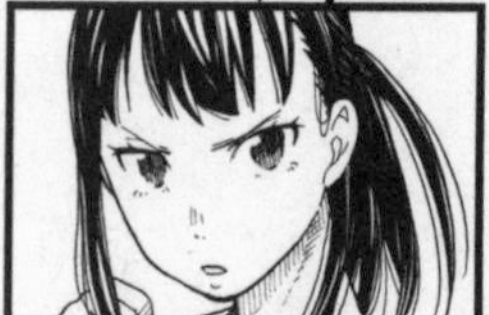

FIRST CLASS FIRE SOLDIER
(SECOND GENERATION PYROKINETIC)
MAKI OZE

A former member of the military, she is an excellent fighter who controls fire. She's a cool lady, but is mad about love stories, and her beauty is overshadowed by her "head full of flowers and wedding bells." She's friendly, but goes berserk when anyone comments on her muscles. Apparently she used to be slender.

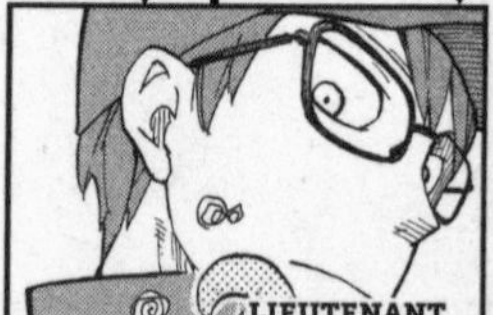

LIEUTENANT
(SECOND GENERATION PYROKINETIC)
TAKEHISA HINAWA

A dry, unemotional ex-military man, whose stern discipline is feared among the new recruits. He helped Ōbi to found Company 8. He never allows the soldiers to play with fire. The gun he uses is a cherished memento from his friend who became an Infernal.

THE GIRLS' CLUB

RESPECTS

A NEW ADOLLA BURST

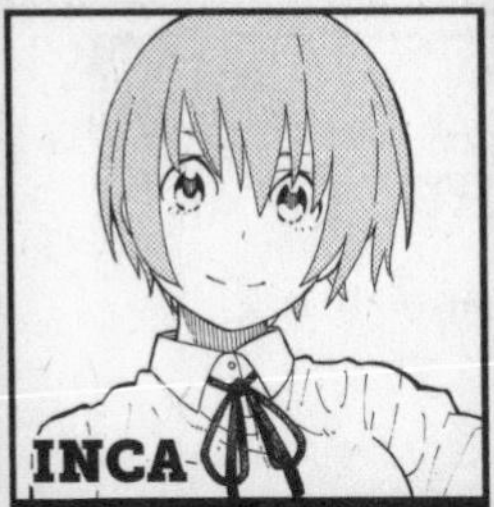

INCA

The Fifth Pillar, who gained her Adolla Burst powers in the Great Fire, which sparked her ability to predict what a fire will do. She is currently the target of the Evangelist's minions. She abhors boredom!

FOLLOWERS OF THE EVANGELIST

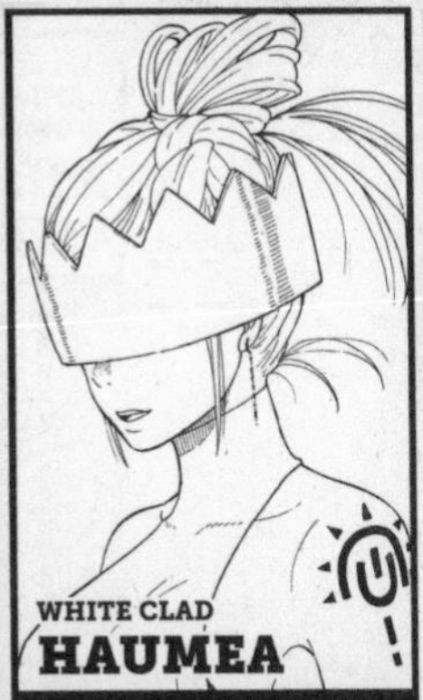

WHITE CLAD
HAUMEA

One of the Evangelist's white-clad combatants. She is a troublesome opponent who can control others with her mind-jacking powers, and she has a foul mouth.

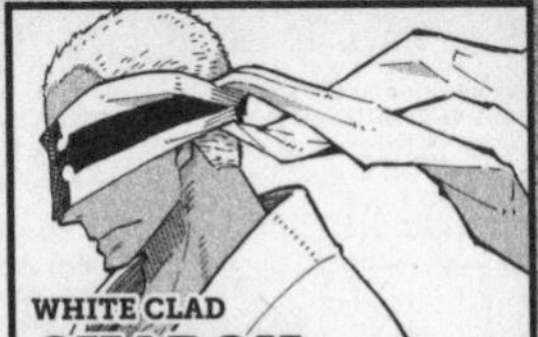

WHITE CLAD
CHARON

A talkative man who specializes in question barrages. He boasts explosive offensive power and overwhelming endurance that renders Shinra's attacks virtually useless.

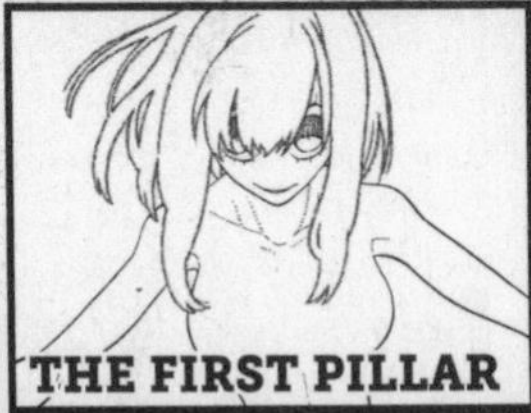

THE FIRST PILLAR

A mysterious woman who has used an Adolla Link to take over Shinra's mind.

SOLDIERS OF EACH COMPANY

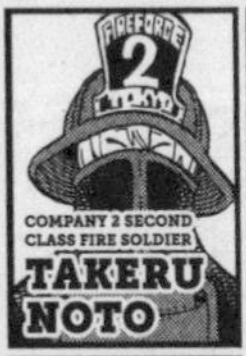

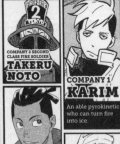

COMPANY 2 SECOND CLASS FIRE SOLDIER
TAKERU NOTO

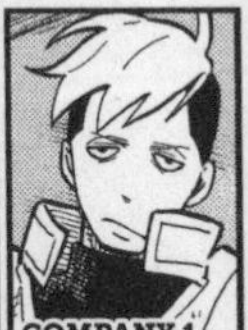

COMPANY 1
KARIM

An able pyrokinetic who can turn fire into ice.

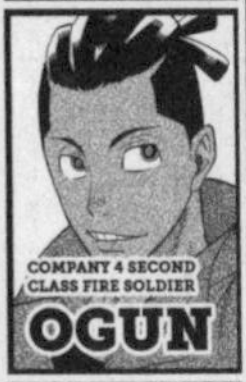

COMPANY 4 SECOND CLASS FIRE SOLDIER
OGUN

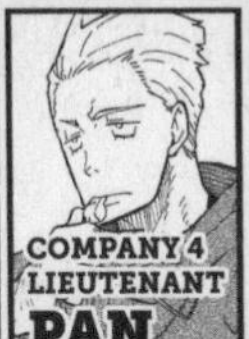

COMPANY 4 LIEUTENANT
PAN

Shinra's instructor from his days in the Academy. Specializes in status enhancements.

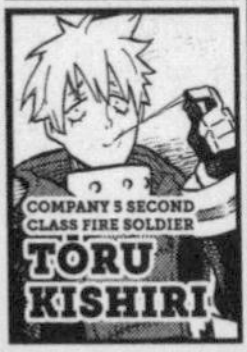

COMPANY 5 SECOND CLASS FIRE SOLDIER
TŌRU KISHIRI

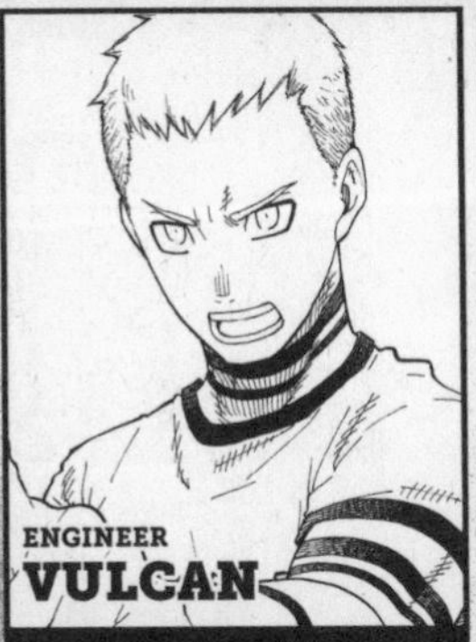

ENGINEER
VULCAN

The greatest engineer of the day, renowned as the God of Fire and the Forge. The weapons he created have increased Company 8's powers immensely. His excessively rock-and-roll designs are Ōbi-approved!

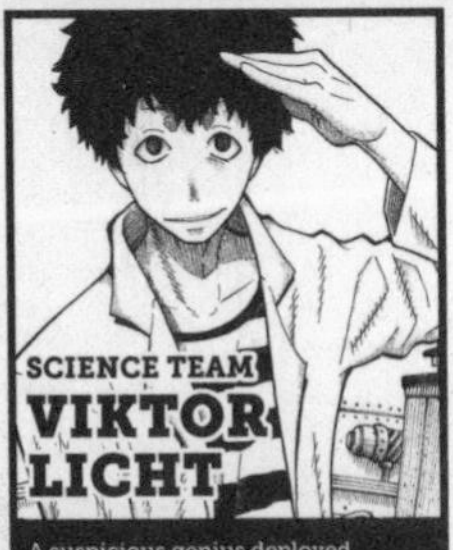

SCIENCE TEAM
VIKTOR LICHT

A suspicious genius deployed from Haijima Industries to fill the vacancy in Company 8's science department. Working to analyze the scene of the fire.

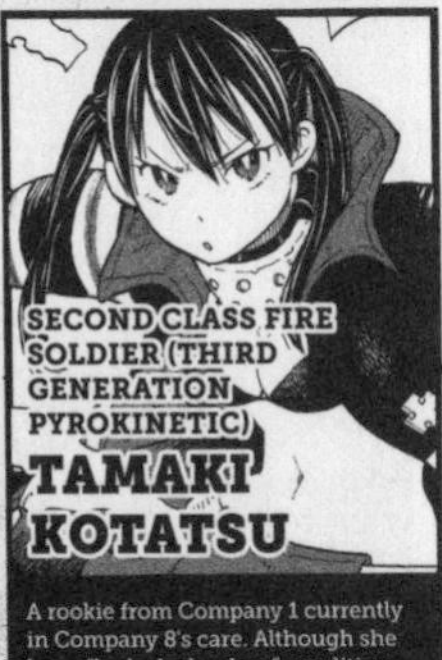

SECOND CLASS FIRE SOLDIER (THIRD GENERATION PYROKINETIC)
TAMAKI KOTATSU

A rookie from Company 1 currently in Company 8's care. Although she has a "lucky lecher lure" condition, she nevertheless has a pure heart. In the big fire, she is working as a nun to put souls to rest.

SUMMARY...

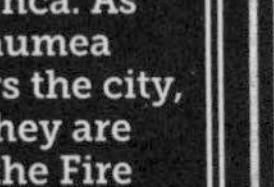
SPUTT
SPUTT

Informed of the coming appearance of a new Adolla Burst by a girl known as the First Pillar, Shinra and his friends engage in a fight with the Evangelist's followers over the Fifth Pillar, a girl named Inca. As Company 8 combats fierce attacks led by Haumea and Charon, as well as a large fire that covers the city, and even the appearance of a new demon, they are joined by other Fire Force Companies! Can the Fire Force guard Inca from the Evangelist and take her to safety?!

FIRE FORCE 13
CONTENTS

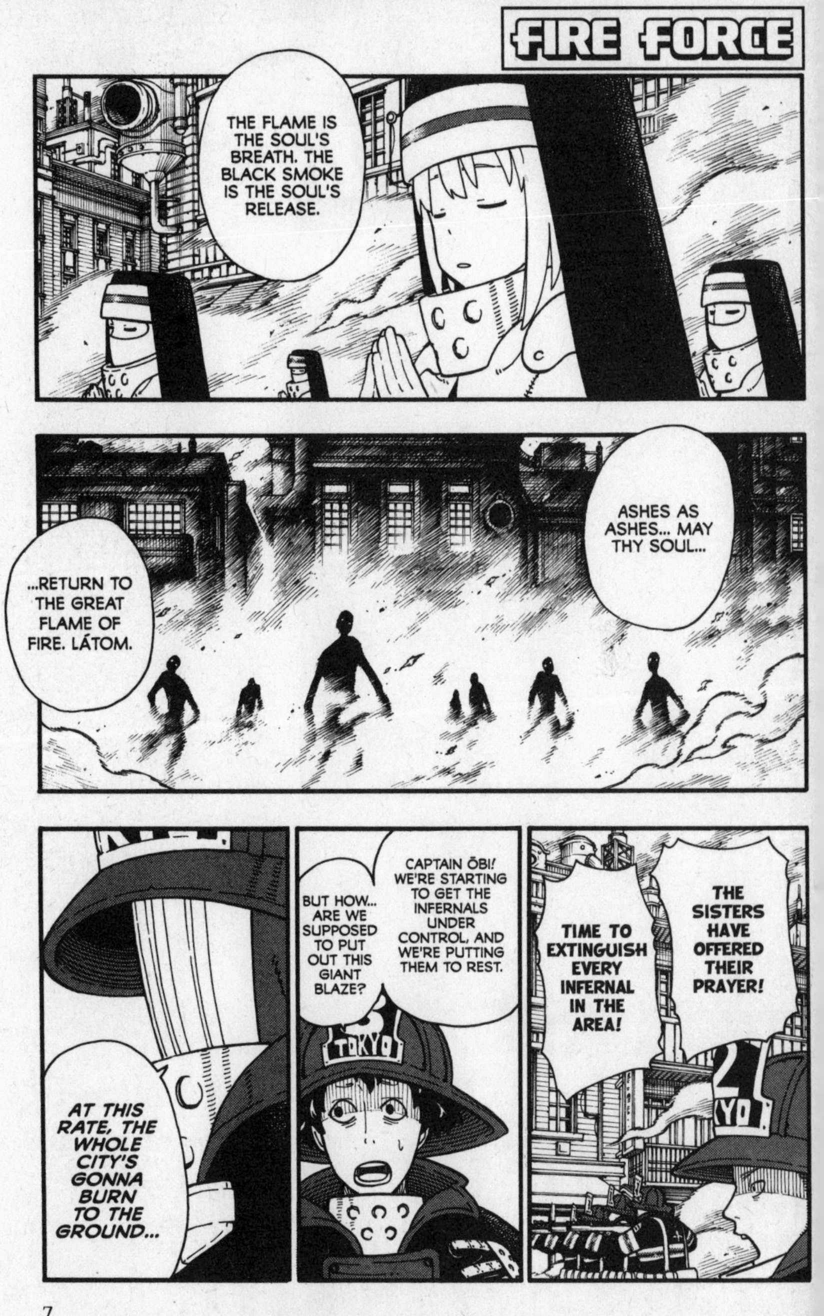
THE FLAME IS THE SOUL'S BREATH. THE BLACK SMOKE IS THE SOUL'S RELEASE.
ASHES AS ASHES... MAY THY SOUL...
...RETURN TO THE GREAT FLAME OF FIRE. LÁTOM.
THE SISTERS HAVE OFFERED THEIR PRAYER!
TIME TO EXTINGUISH EVERY INFERNAL IN THE AREA!
CAPTAIN ŌBI! WE'RE STARTING TO GET THE INFERNALS UNDER CONTROL, AND WE'RE PUTTING THEM TO REST.
BUT HOW... ARE WE SUPPOSED TO PUT OUT THIS GIANT BLAZE?
AT THIS RATE, THE WHOLE CITY'S GONNA BURN TO THE GROUND...

CHAPTER CVI: SECOND GENERATION

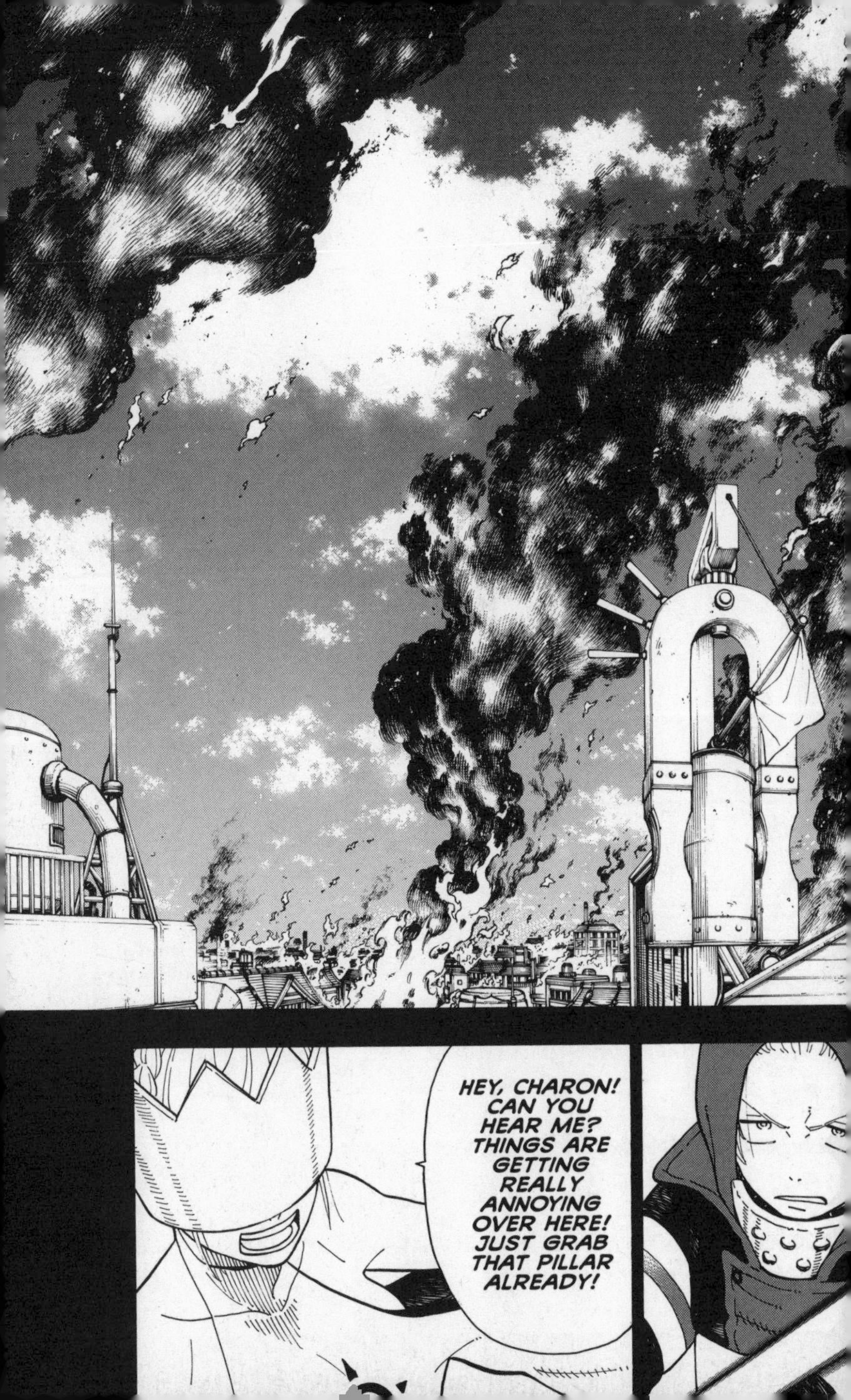
HEY, CHARON! CAN YOU HEAR ME? THINGS ARE GETTING REALLY ANNOYING OVER HERE! JUST GRAB THAT PILLAR ALREADY!

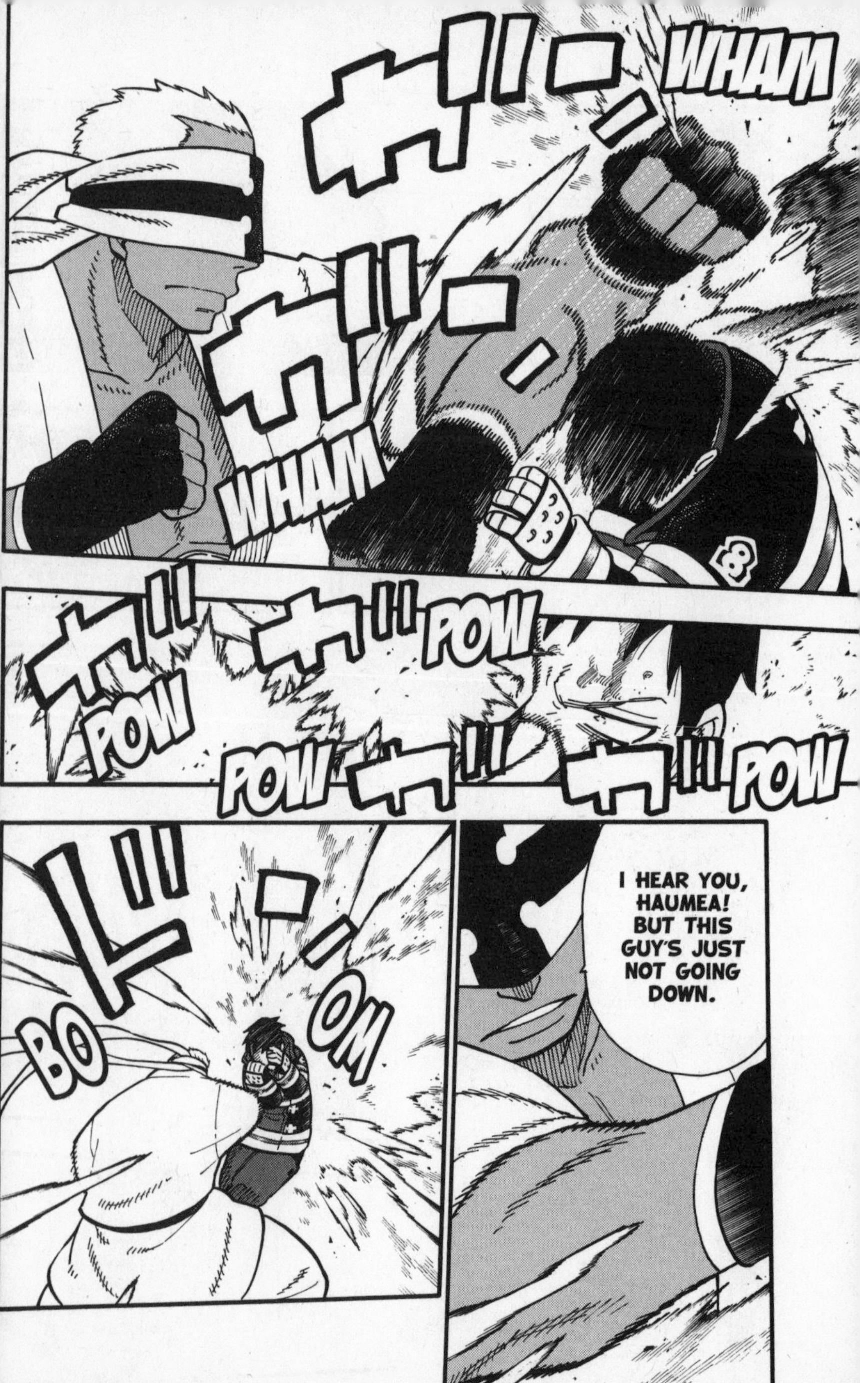
WHAM
WHAM
POW
POW
POW
POW
I HEAR YOU, HAUMEA! BUT THIS GUY'S JUST NOT GOING DOWN.
BO
OM

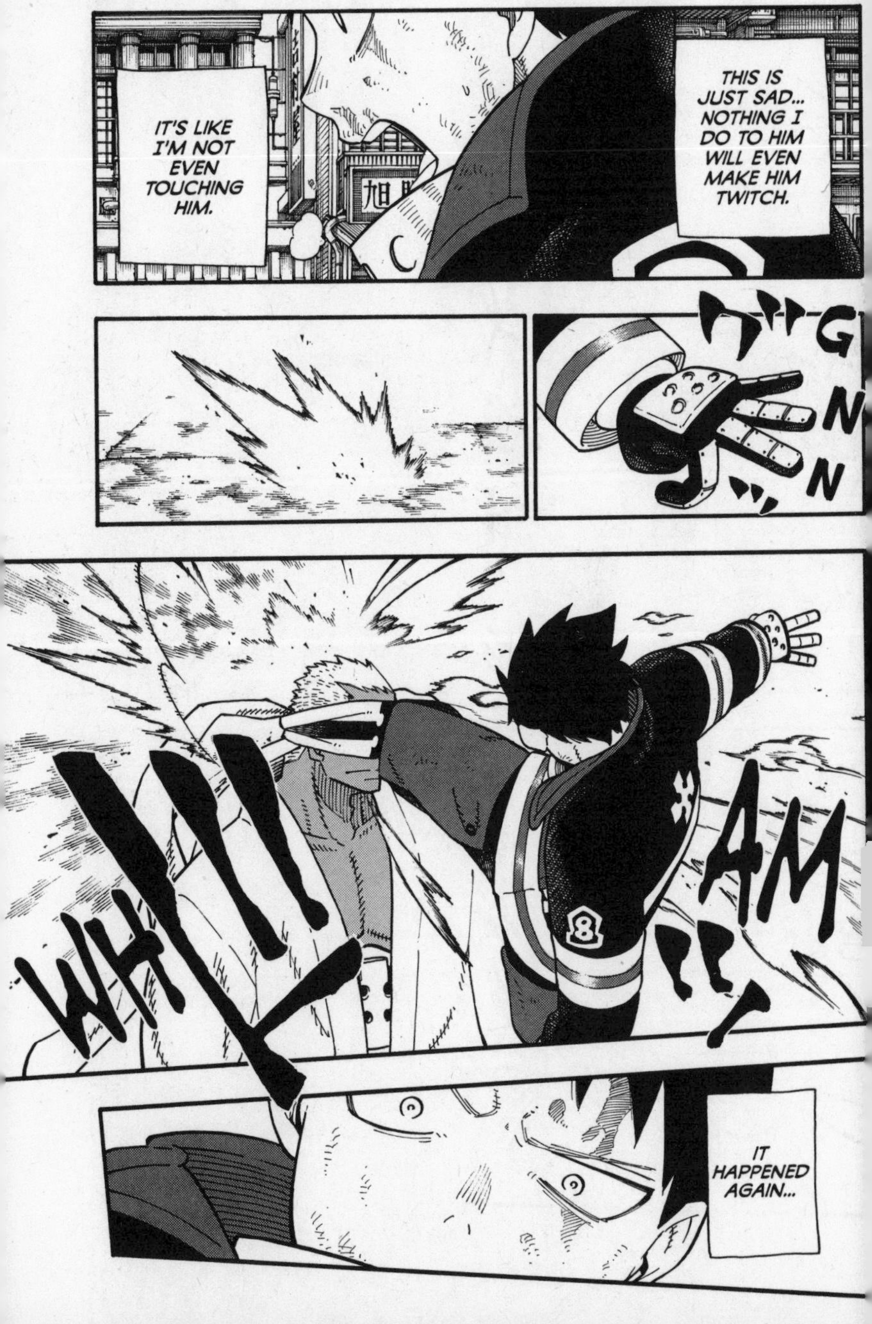
THIS IS JUST SAD... NOTHING I DO TO HIM WILL EVEN MAKE HIM TWITCH.
IT'S LIKE I'M NOT EVEN TOUCHING HIM.
GNN
WHAM
IT HAPPENED AGAIN...

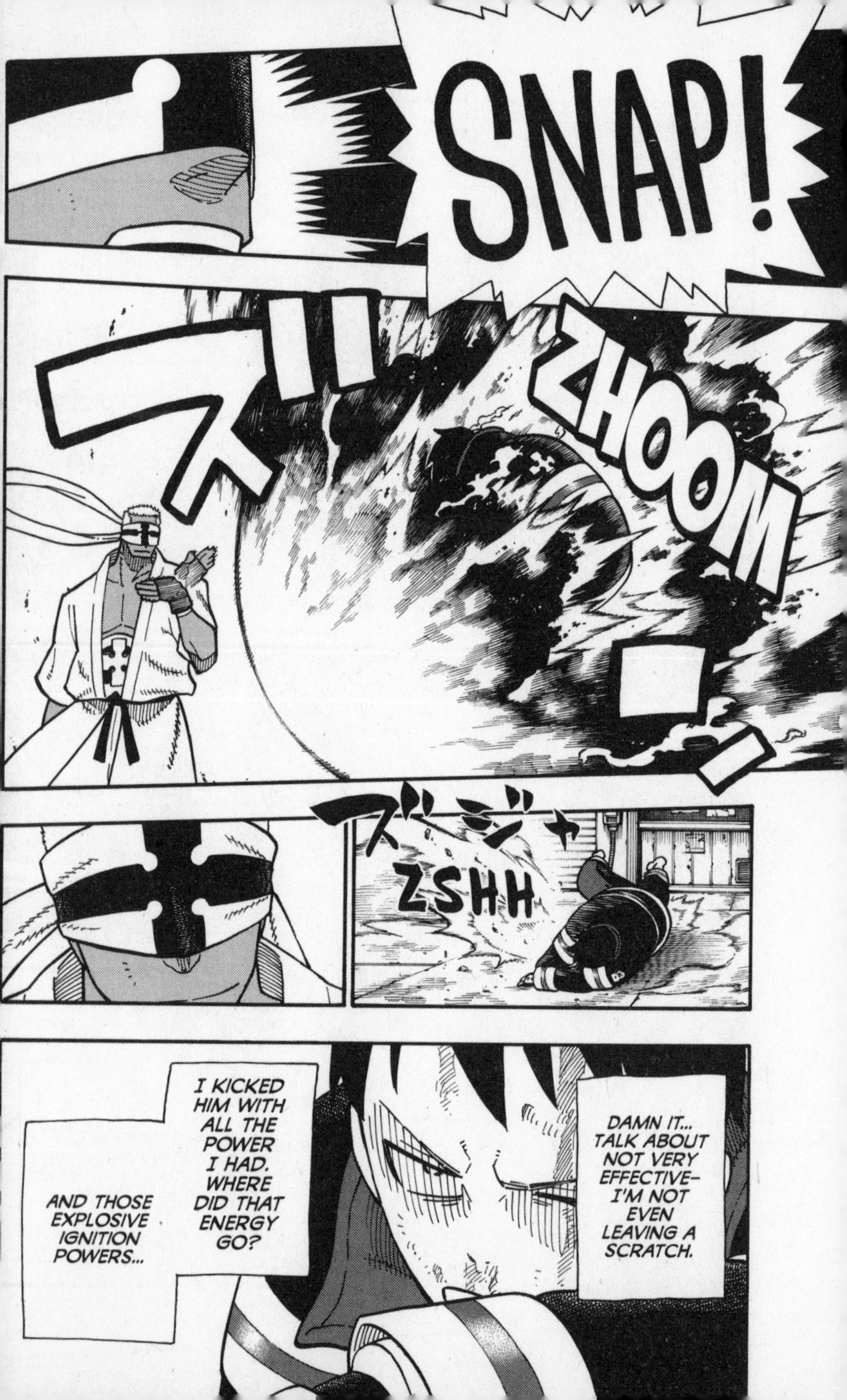
SNAP!
ZHOOM
ZSHH
DAMN IT... TALK ABOUT NOT VERY EFFECTIVE— I'M NOT EVEN LEAVING A SCRATCH.
I KICKED HIM WITH ALL THE POWER I HAD. WHERE DID THAT ENERGY GO?
AND THOSE EXPLOSIVE IGNITION POWERS...

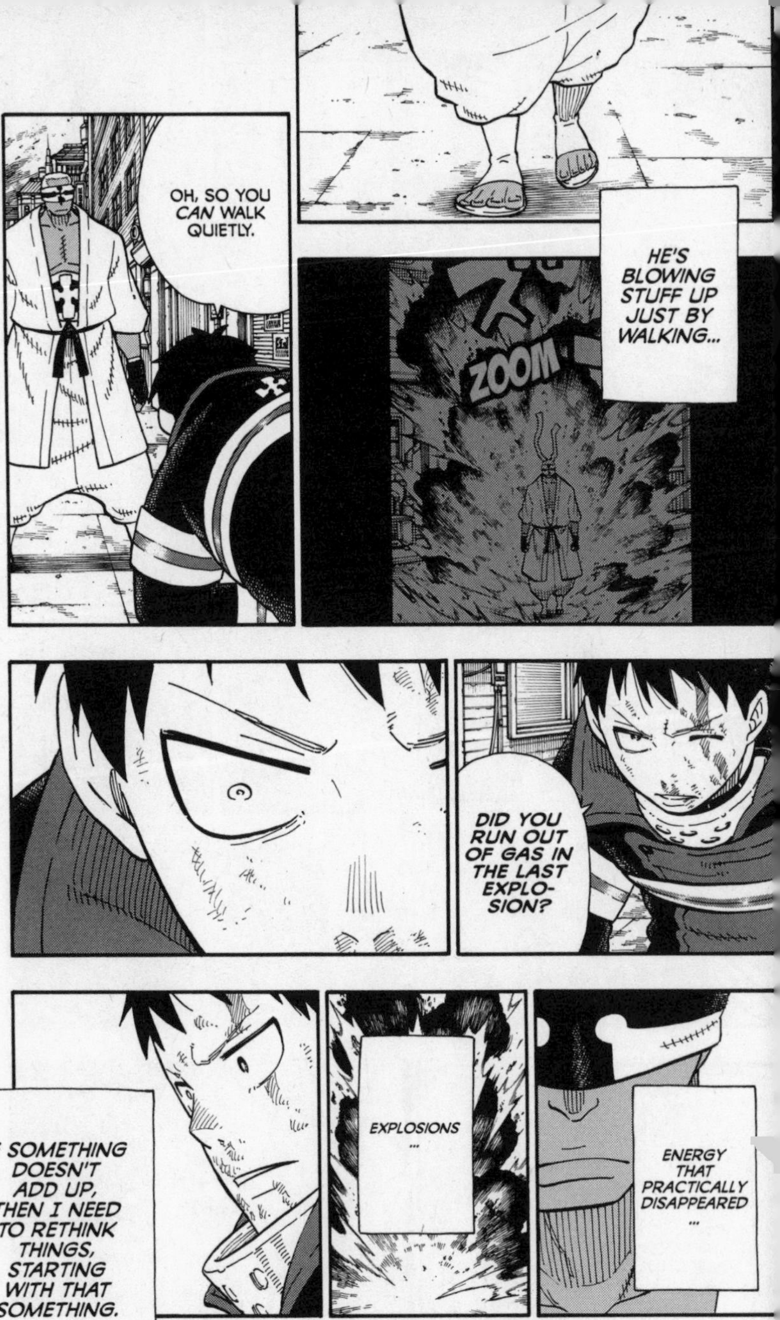
HE'S BLOWING STUFF UP JUST BY WALKING...
ZOOM
OH, SO YOU *CAN* WALK QUIETLY.
DID YOU RUN OUT OF GAS IN THE LAST EXPLO-SION?
ENERGY THAT PRACTICALLY DISAPPEARED ...
EXPLOSIONS ...
IF SOMETHING DOESN'T ADD UP, THEN I NEED TO RETHINK THINGS, STARTING WITH THAT SOMETHING.

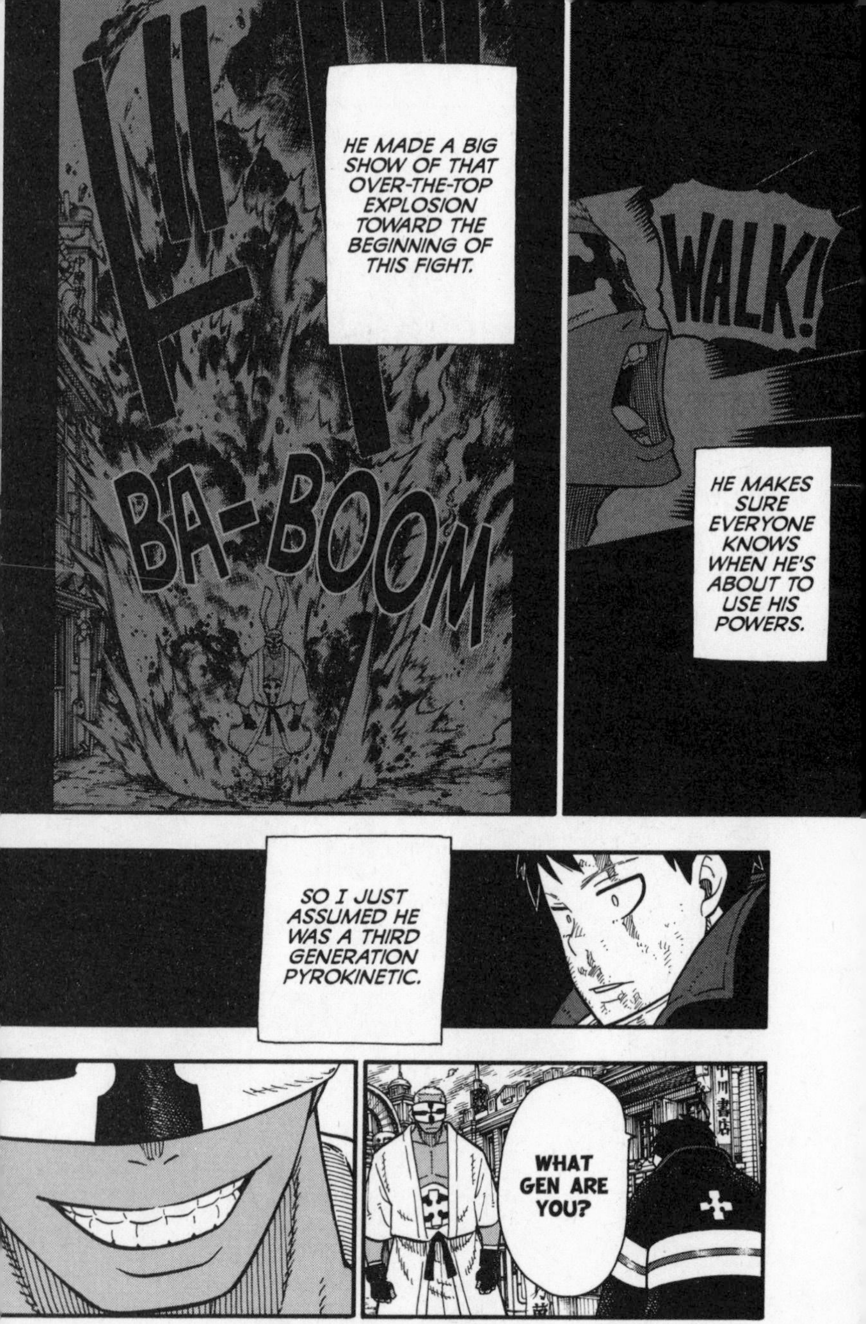
WALK!
HE MAKES SURE EVERYONE KNOWS WHEN HE'S ABOUT TO USE HIS POWERS.
HE MADE A BIG SHOW OF THAT OVER-THE-TOP EXPLOSION TOWARD THE BEGINNING OF THIS FIGHT.
BA-BOOM
SO I JUST ASSUMED HE WAS A THIRD GENERATION PYROKINETIC.
WHAT GEN ARE YOU?

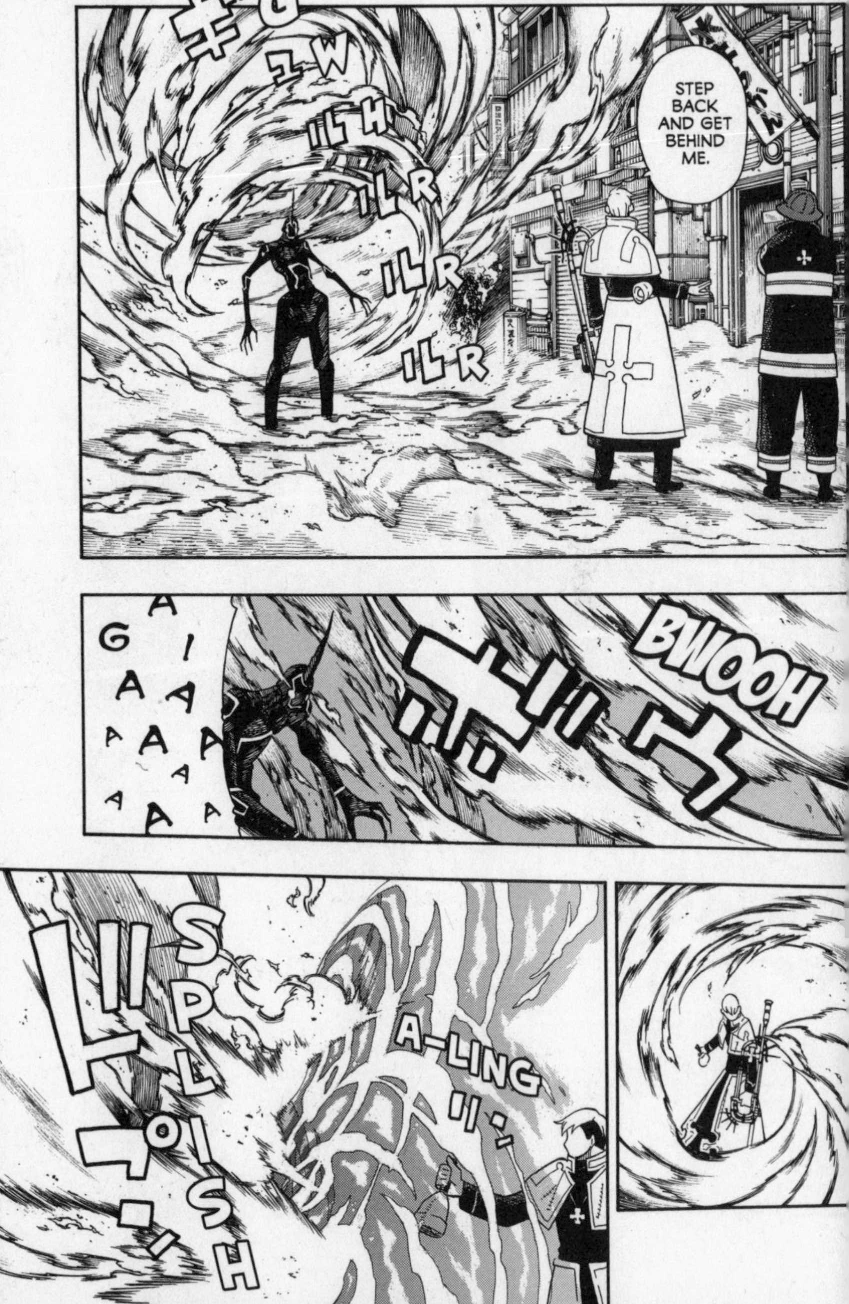
GWHRRR
STEP BACK AND GET BEHIND ME.
BWOOH
GAAAAAAAAA
A-LING
SPLISH

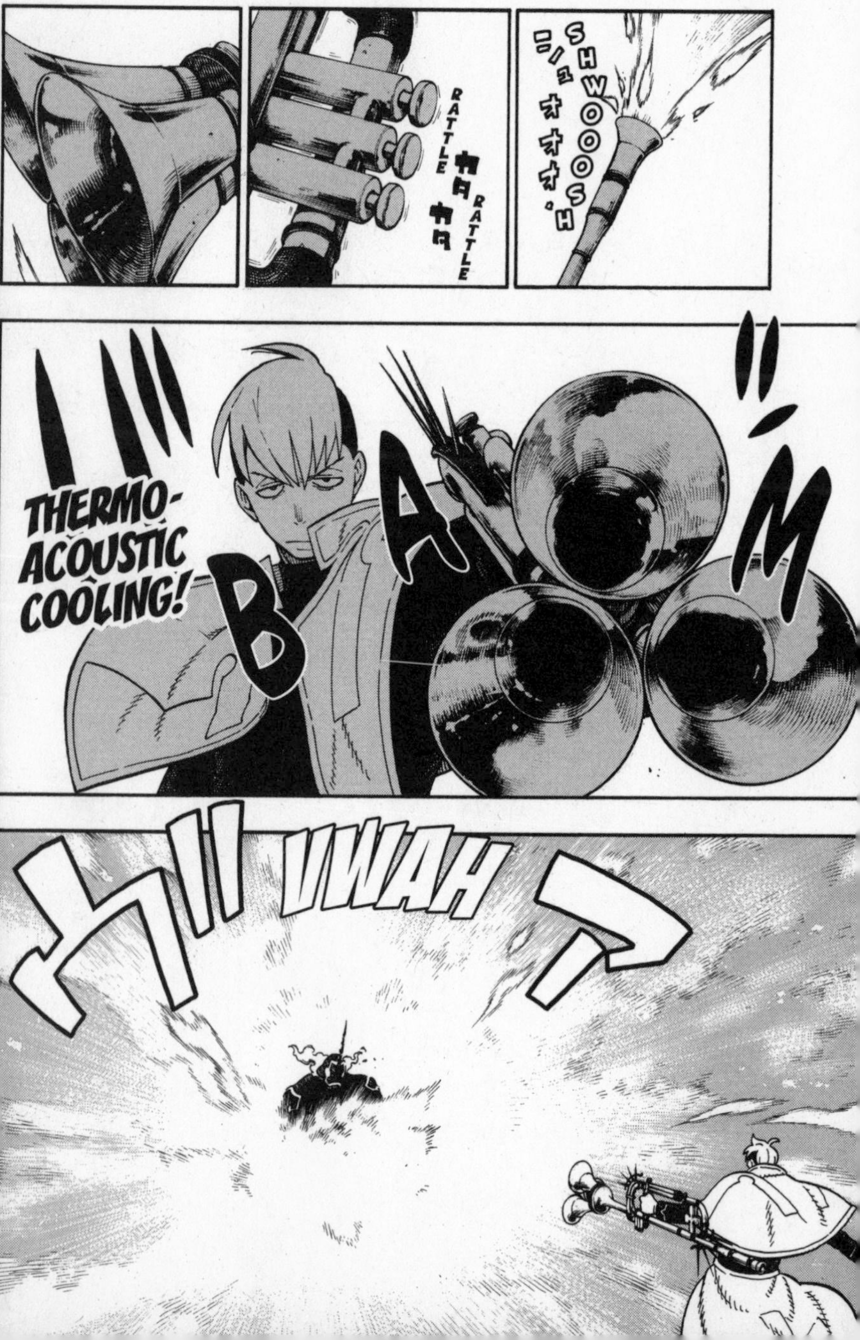
SHWOOOSH
RATTLE RATTLE
BAM
THERMO-ACOUSTIC COOLING!
VWAH

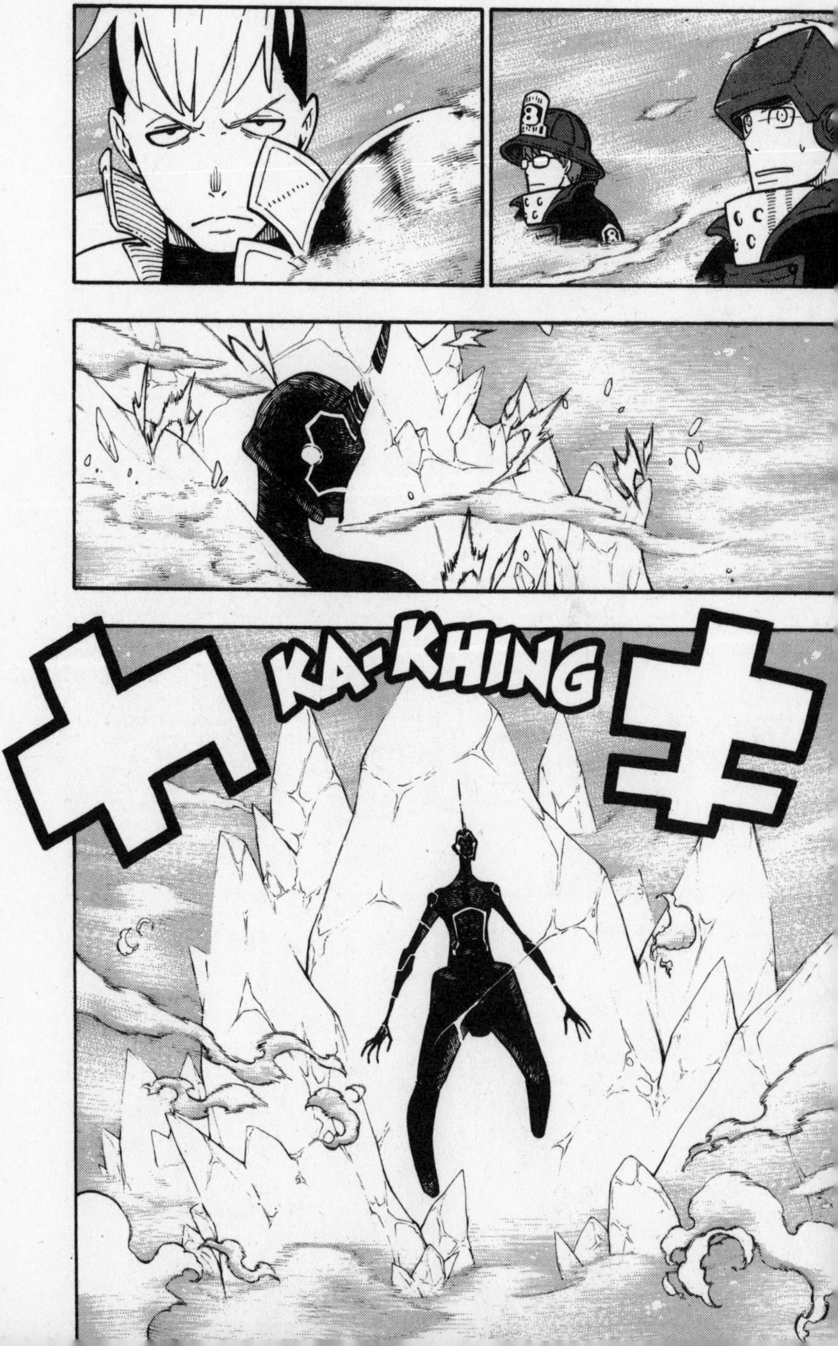
KA-KHING

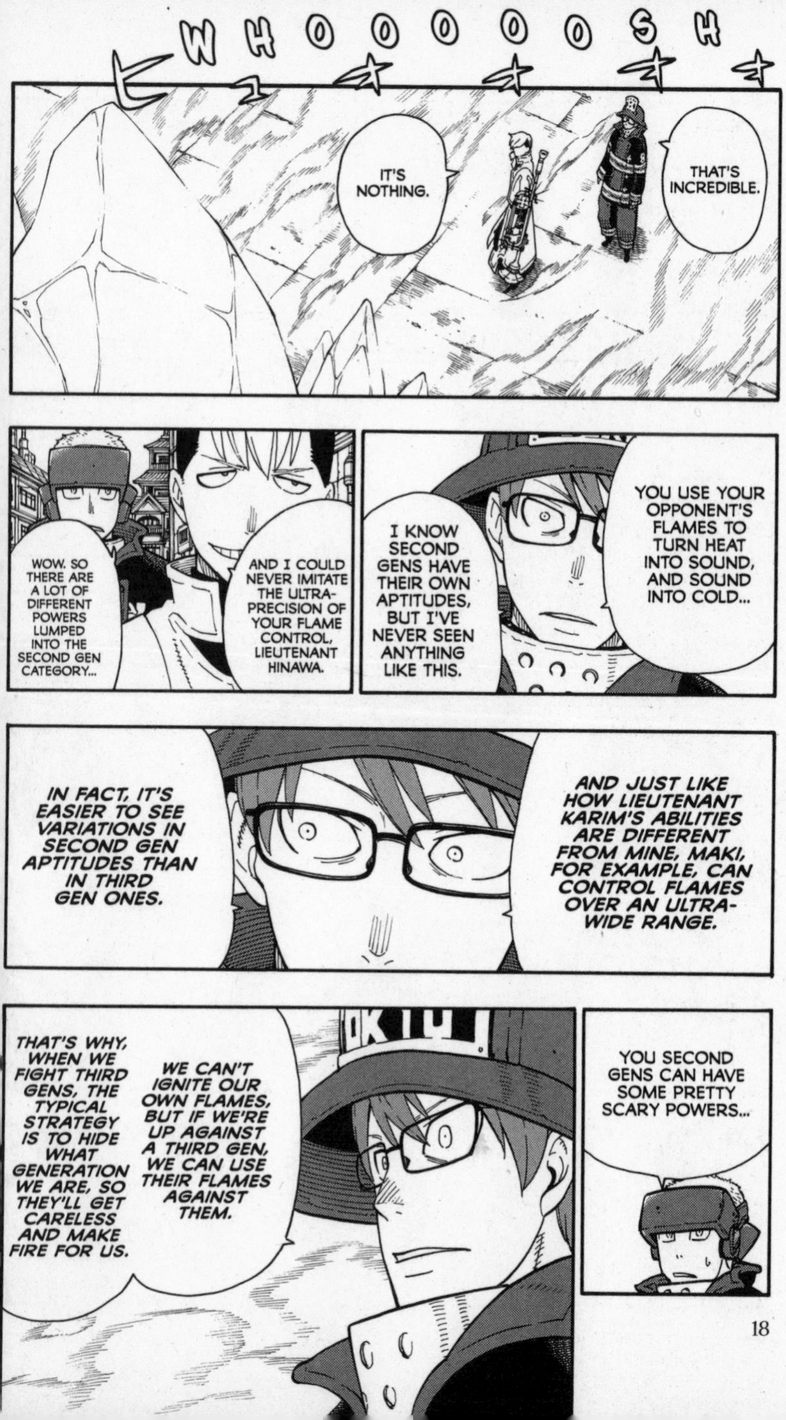
WHOOOOOSH
THAT'S INCREDIBLE.
IT'S NOTHING.
YOU USE YOUR OPPONENT'S FLAMES TO TURN HEAT INTO SOUND, AND SOUND INTO COLD...
I KNOW SECOND GENS HAVE THEIR OWN APTITUDES, BUT I'VE NEVER SEEN ANYTHING LIKE THIS.
AND I COULD NEVER IMITATE THE ULTRA-PRECISION OF YOUR FLAME CONTROL, LIEUTENANT HINAWA.
WOW. SO THERE ARE A LOT OF DIFFERENT POWERS LUMPED INTO THE SECOND GEN CATEGORY...
AND JUST LIKE HOW LIEUTENANT KARIM'S ABILITIES ARE DIFFERENT FROM MINE, MAKI, FOR EXAMPLE, CAN CONTROL FLAMES OVER AN ULTRA-WIDE RANGE.
IN FACT, IT'S EASIER TO SEE VARIATIONS IN SECOND GEN APTITUDES THAN IN THIRD GEN ONES.
YOU SECOND GENS CAN HAVE SOME PRETTY SCARY POWERS...
WE CAN'T IGNITE OUR OWN FLAMES, BUT IF WE'RE UP AGAINST A THIRD GEN, WE CAN USE THEIR FLAMES AGAINST THEM.
THAT'S WHY, WHEN WE FIGHT THIRD GENS, THE TYPICAL STRATEGY IS TO HIDE WHAT GENERATION WE ARE, SO THEY'LL GET CARELESS AND MAKE FIRE FOR US.

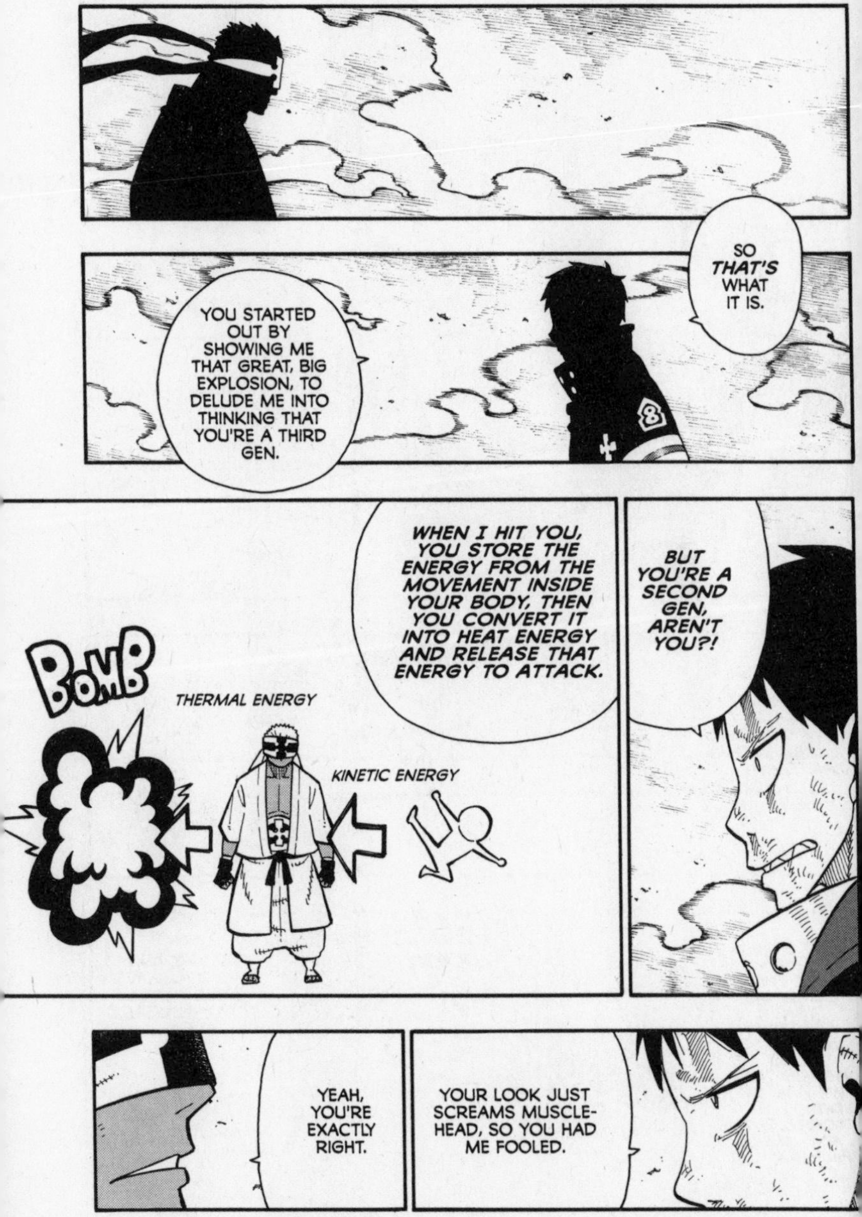
SO *THAT'S* WHAT IT IS.
YOU STARTED OUT BY SHOWING ME THAT GREAT, BIG EXPLOSION, TO DELUDE ME INTO THINKING THAT YOU'RE A THIRD GEN.
BUT YOU'RE A SECOND GEN, AREN'T YOU?!
WHEN I HIT YOU, YOU STORE THE ENERGY FROM THE MOVEMENT INSIDE YOUR BODY, THEN YOU CONVERT IT INTO HEAT ENERGY AND RELEASE THAT ENERGY TO ATTACK.
BOMP
THERMAL ENERGY
KINETIC ENERGY
YOUR LOOK JUST SCREAMS MUSCLE-HEAD, SO YOU HAD ME FOOLED.
YEAH, YOU'RE EXACTLY RIGHT.

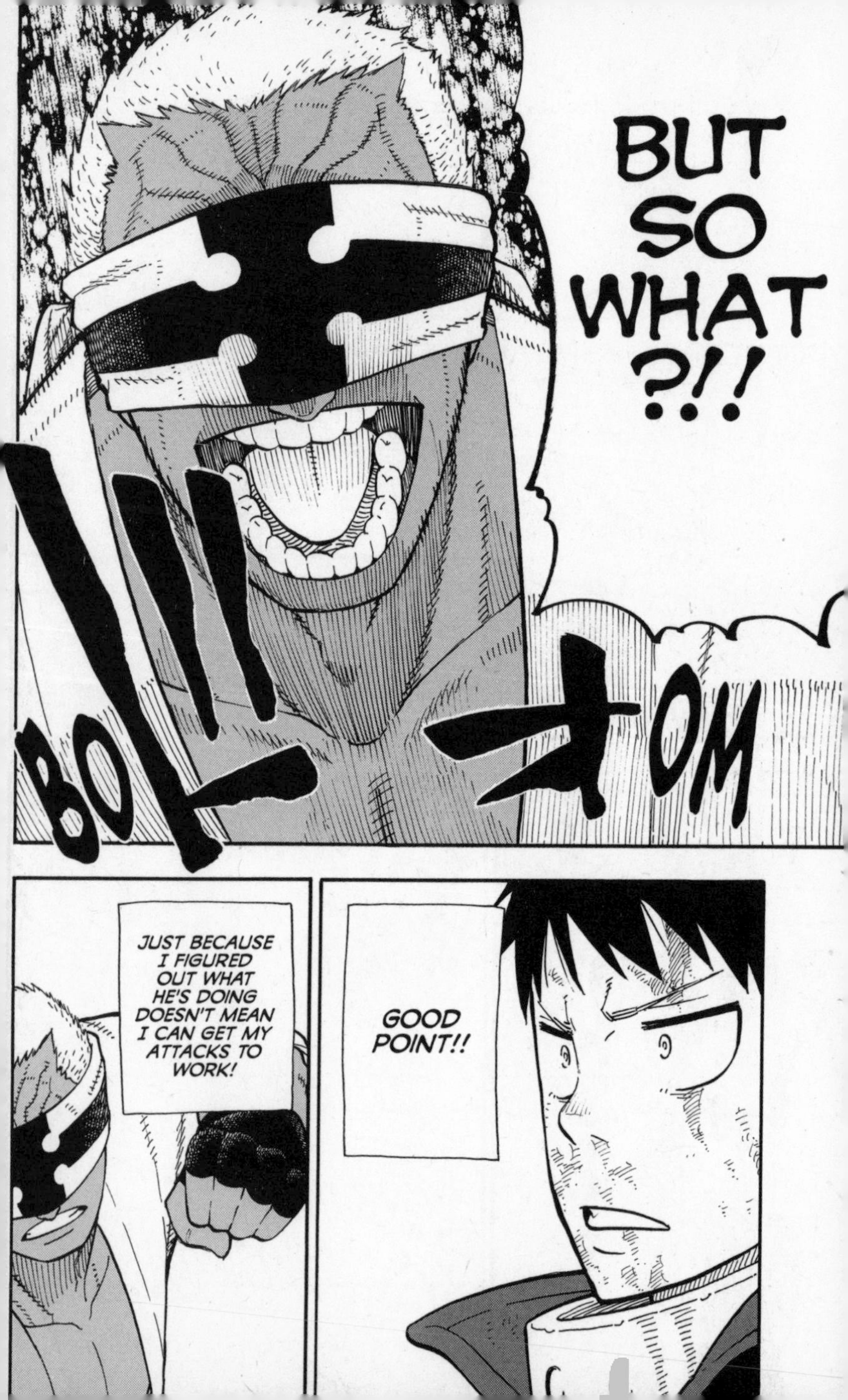
BUT SO WHAT?!!
BOOM
GOOD POINT!!
JUST BECAUSE I FIGURED OUT WHAT HE'S DOING DOESN'T MEAN I CAN GET MY ATTACKS TO WORK!

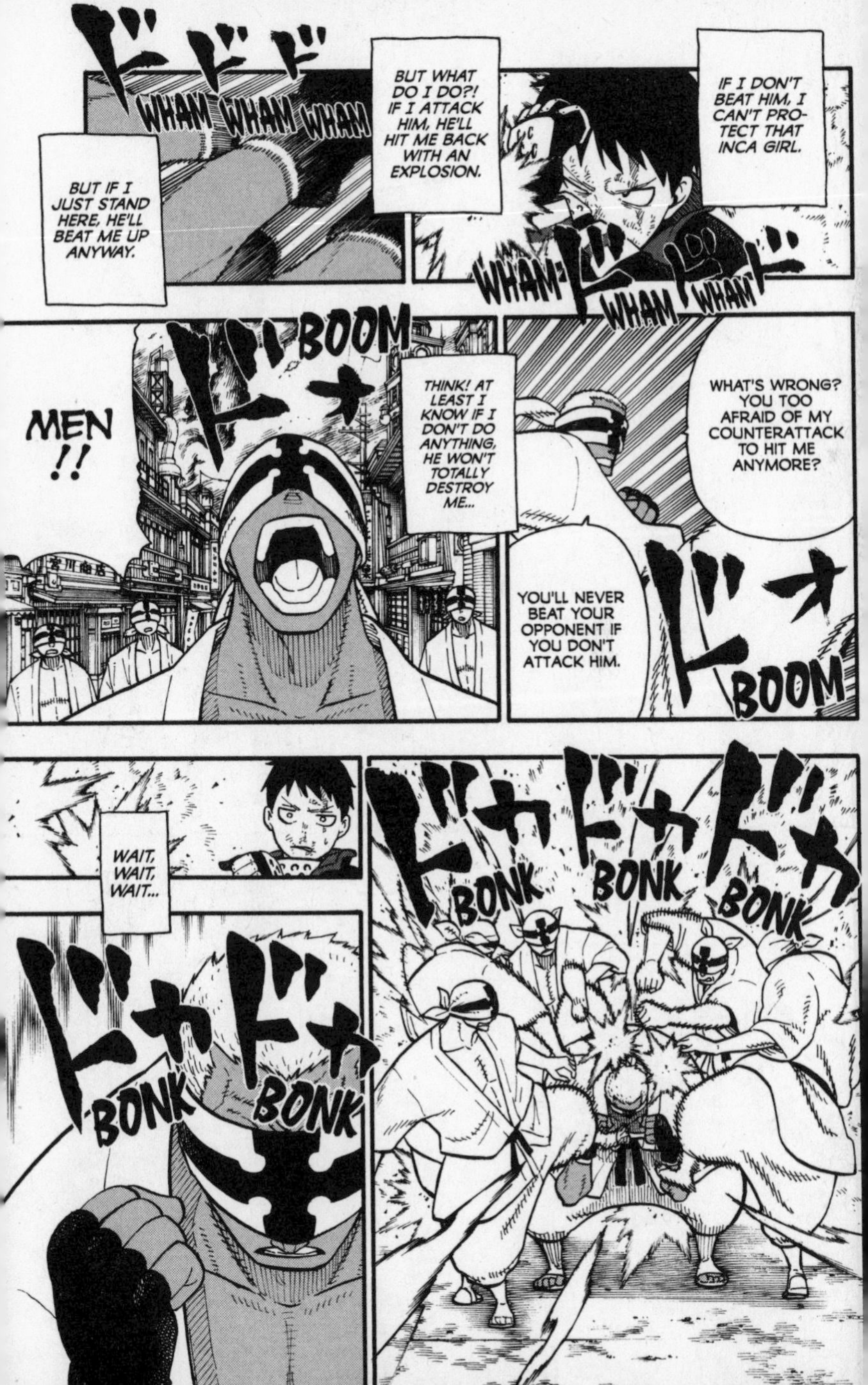
IF I DON'T BEAT HIM, I CAN'T PROTECT THAT INCA GIRL.
BUT WHAT DO I DO?! IF I ATTACK HIM, HE'LL HIT ME BACK WITH AN EXPLOSION.
WHAM WHAM WHAM
WHAM WHAM WHAM
BUT IF I JUST STAND HERE, HE'LL BEAT ME UP ANYWAY.
WHAT'S WRONG? YOU TOO AFRAID OF MY COUNTERATTACK TO HIT ME ANYMORE?
YOU'LL NEVER BEAT YOUR OPPONENT IF YOU DON'T ATTACK HIM.
BOOM
THINK! AT LEAST I KNOW IF I DON'T DO ANYTHING, HE WON'T TOTALLY DESTROY ME...
BOOM
MEN!!
BONK BONK BONK
WAIT, WAIT, WAIT...
BONK BONK

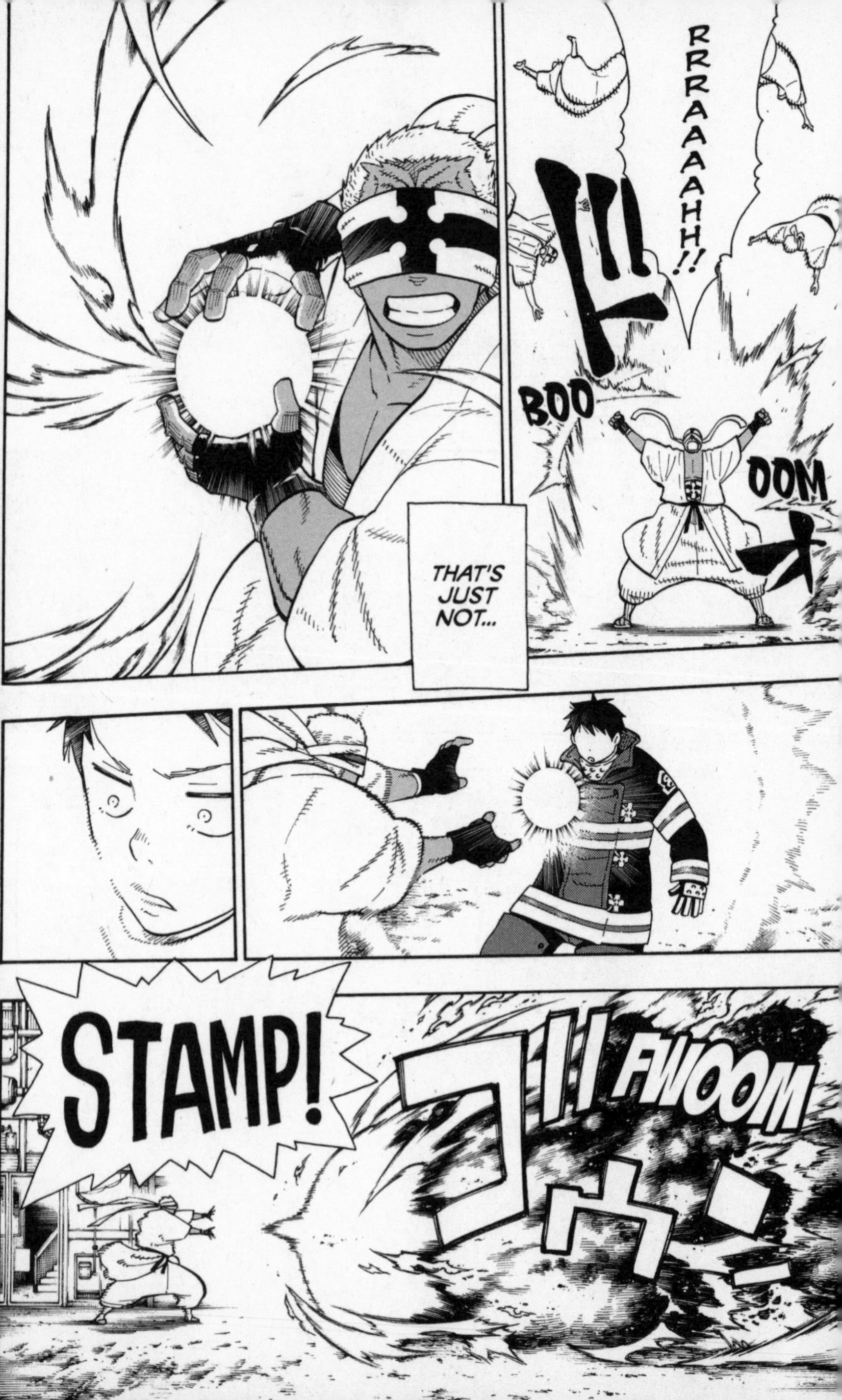
RRRAAAAHH!!
BOO
OOM
THAT'S JUST NOT...
FWOOM
STAMP!

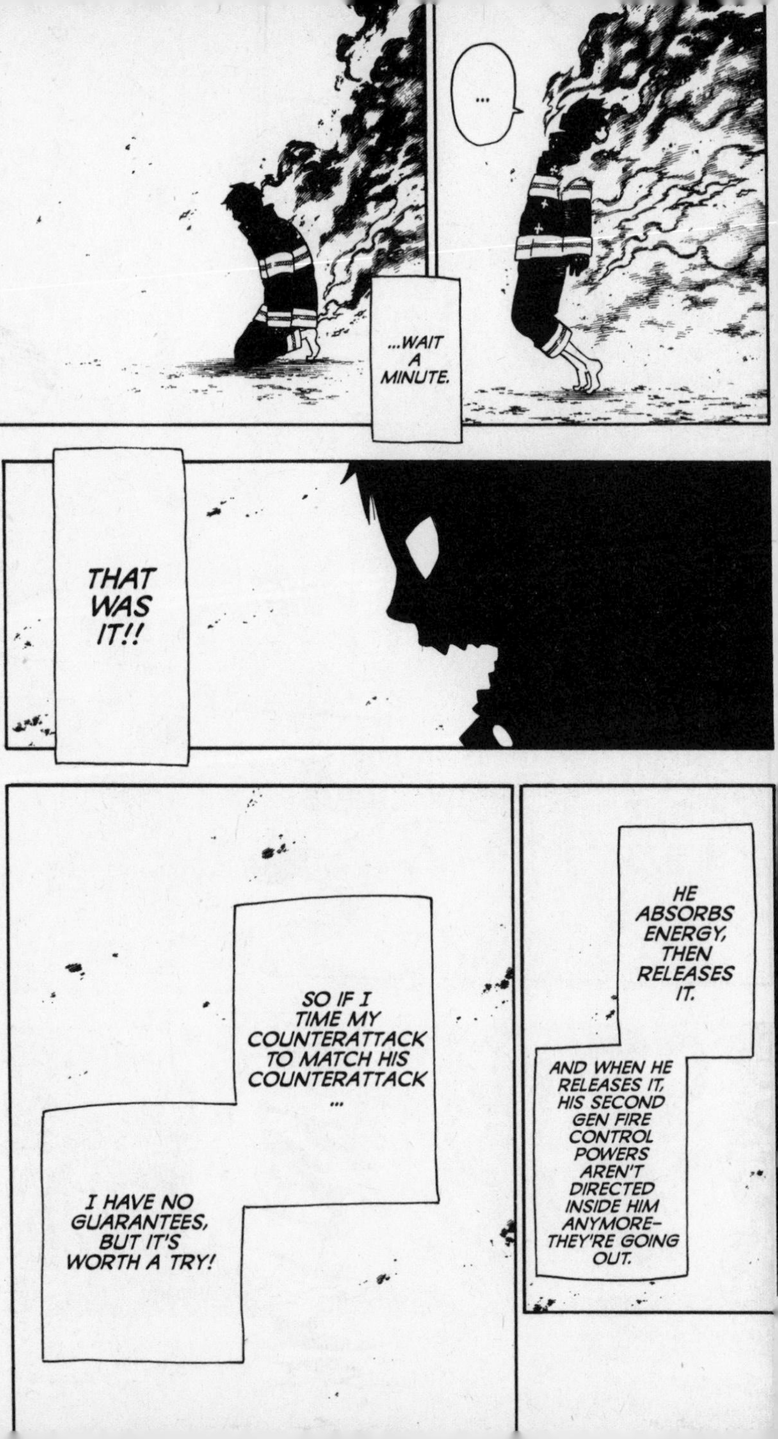
...
...WAIT A MINUTE.
THAT WAS IT!!
HE ABSORBS ENERGY, THEN RELEASES IT.
AND WHEN HE RELEASES IT, HIS SECOND GEN FIRE CONTROL POWERS AREN'T DIRECTED INSIDE HIM ANYMORE— THEY'RE GOING OUT.
SO IF I TIME MY COUNTERATTACK TO MATCH HIS COUNTERATTACK ...
I HAVE NO GUARANTEES, BUT IT'S WORTH A TRY!

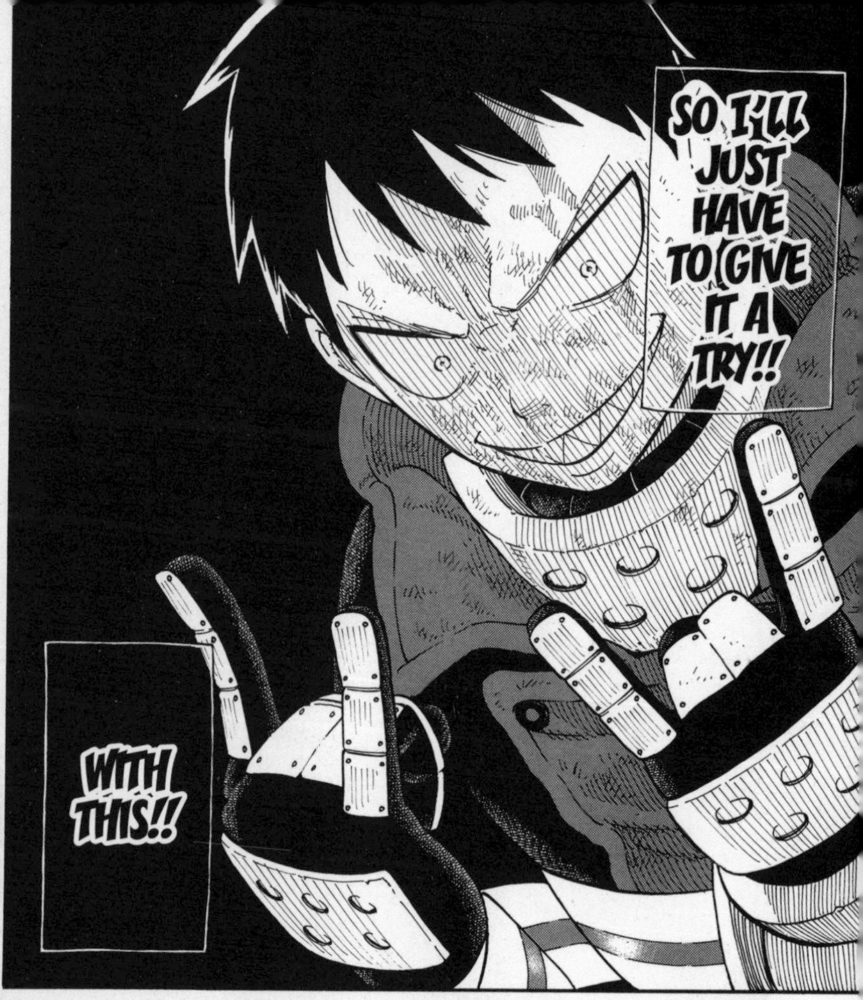
SO I'LL JUST HAVE TO GIVE IT A TRY!!
WITH THIS!!

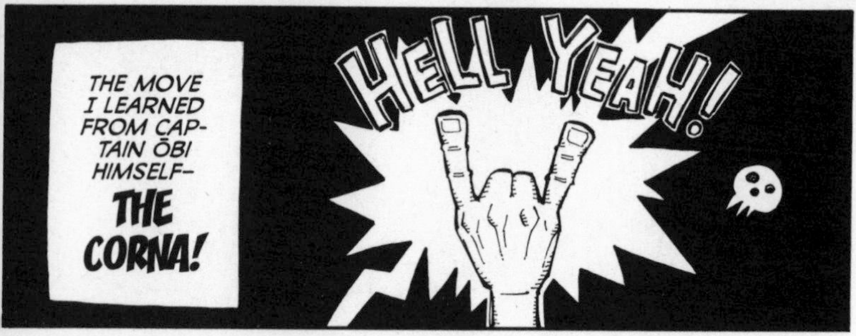
HELL YEAH!
THE MOVE I LEARNED FROM CAP-TAIN ŌBI HIMSELF– THE CORNA!

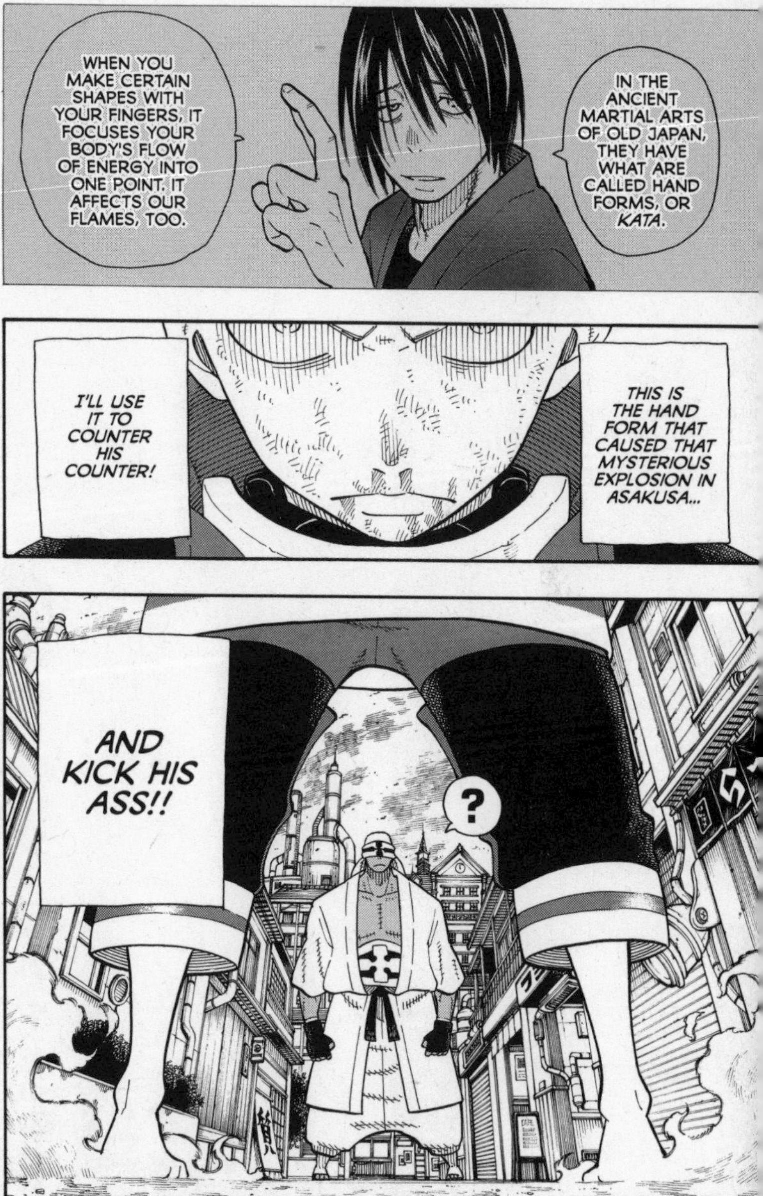
IN THE ANCIENT MARTIAL ARTS OF OLD JAPAN, THEY HAVE WHAT ARE CALLED HAND FORMS, OR *KATA*.
WHEN YOU MAKE CERTAIN SHAPES WITH YOUR FINGERS, IT FOCUSES YOUR BODY'S FLOW OF ENERGY INTO ONE POINT. IT AFFECTS OUR FLAMES, TOO.
THIS IS THE HAND FORM THAT CAUSED THAT MYSTERIOUS EXPLOSION IN ASAKUSA...
I'LL USE IT TO COUNTER HIS COUNTER!
AND KICK HIS ASS!!
?

FIRE FORCE

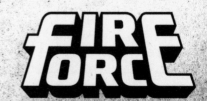

CHAPTER CVII:
THE CORNA

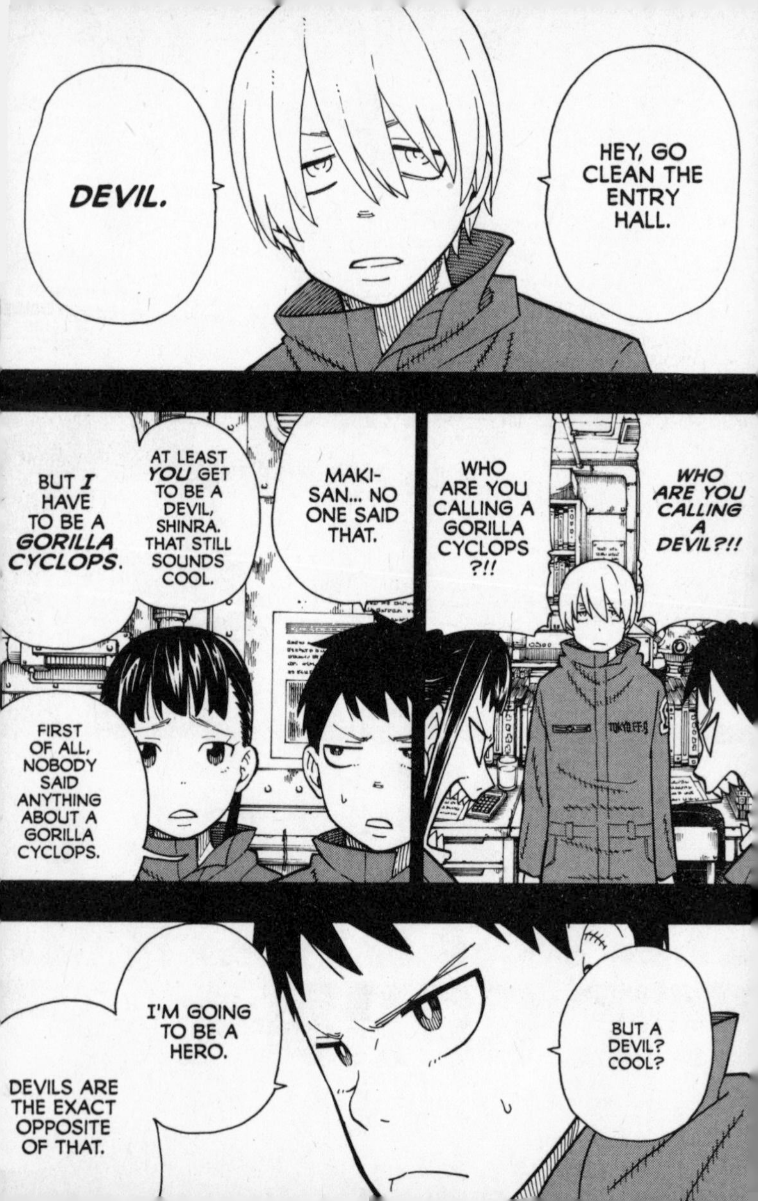
HEY, GO CLEAN THE ENTRY HALL.
DEVIL.
WHO ARE YOU CALLING A DEVIL?!!
WHO ARE YOU CALLING A GORILLA CYCLOPS ?!!
MAKI-SAN... NO ONE SAID THAT.
AT LEAST *YOU* GET TO BE A DEVIL, SHINRA. THAT STILL SOUNDS COOL.
BUT *I* HAVE TO BE A *GORILLA CYCLOPS*.
FIRST OF ALL, NOBODY SAID ANYTHING ABOUT A GORILLA CYCLOPS.
BUT A DEVIL? COOL?
I'M GOING TO BE A HERO.
DEVILS ARE THE EXACT OPPOSITE OF THAT.

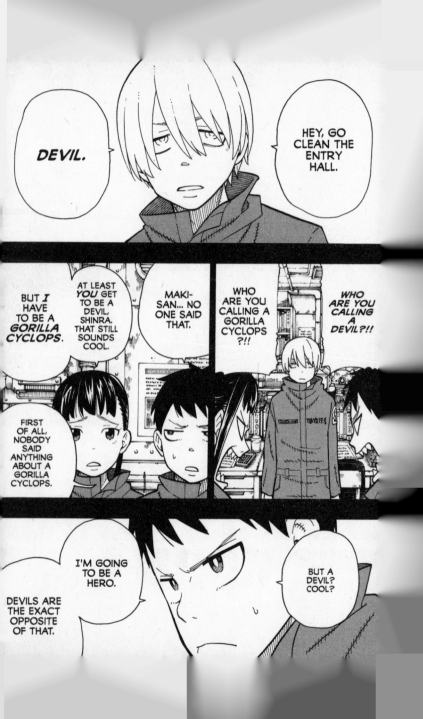

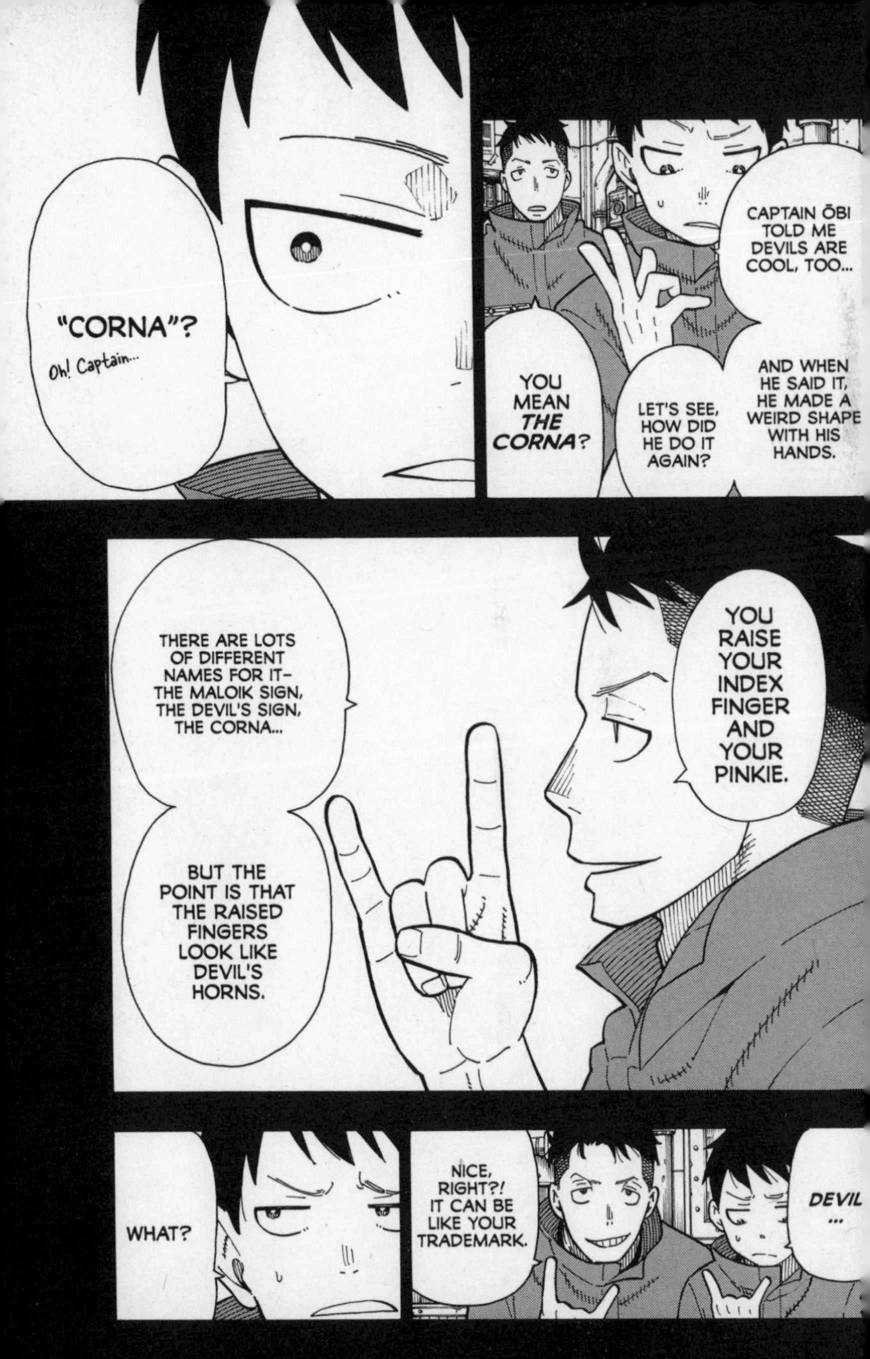
CAPTAIN ŌBI TOLD ME DEVILS ARE COOL, TOO...
AND WHEN HE SAID IT, HE MADE A WEIRD SHAPE WITH HIS HANDS.
LET'S SEE, HOW DID HE DO IT AGAIN?
YOU MEAN *THE CORNA*?
"CORNA"?
Oh! Captain...
YOU RAISE YOUR INDEX FINGER AND YOUR PINKIE.
THERE ARE LOTS OF DIFFERENT NAMES FOR IT– THE MALOIK SIGN, THE DEVIL'S SIGN, THE CORNA...
BUT THE POINT IS THAT THE RAISED FINGERS LOOK LIKE DEVIL'S HORNS.
DEVIL ...
NICE, RIGHT?! IT CAN BE LIKE YOUR TRADEMARK.
WHAT?

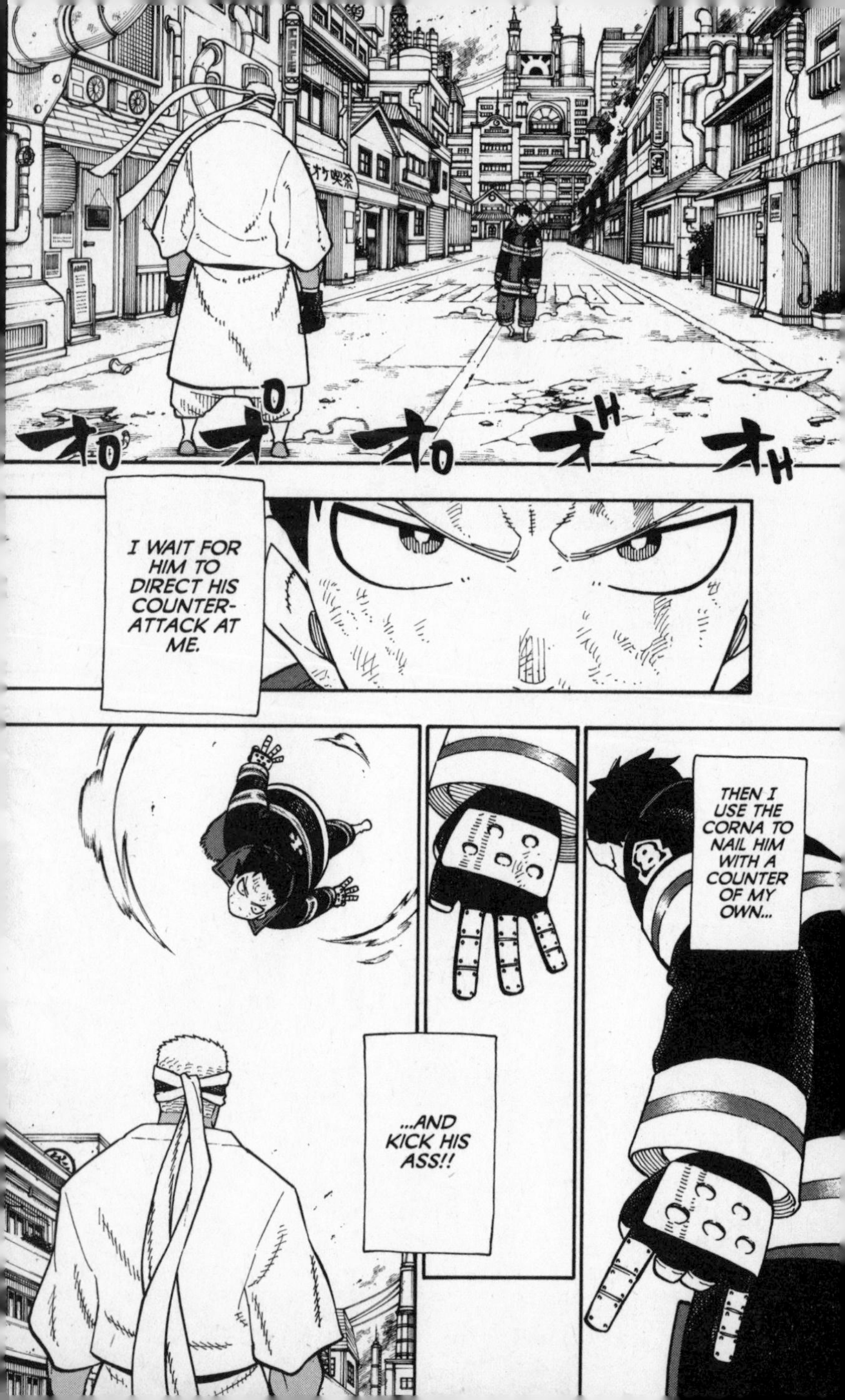

オH
オH
オO
オO
オO
I WAIT FOR HIM TO DIRECT HIS COUNTER-ATTACK AT ME.
THEN I USE THE CORNA TO NAIL HIM WITH A COUNTER OF MY OWN...
...AND KICK HIS ASS!!

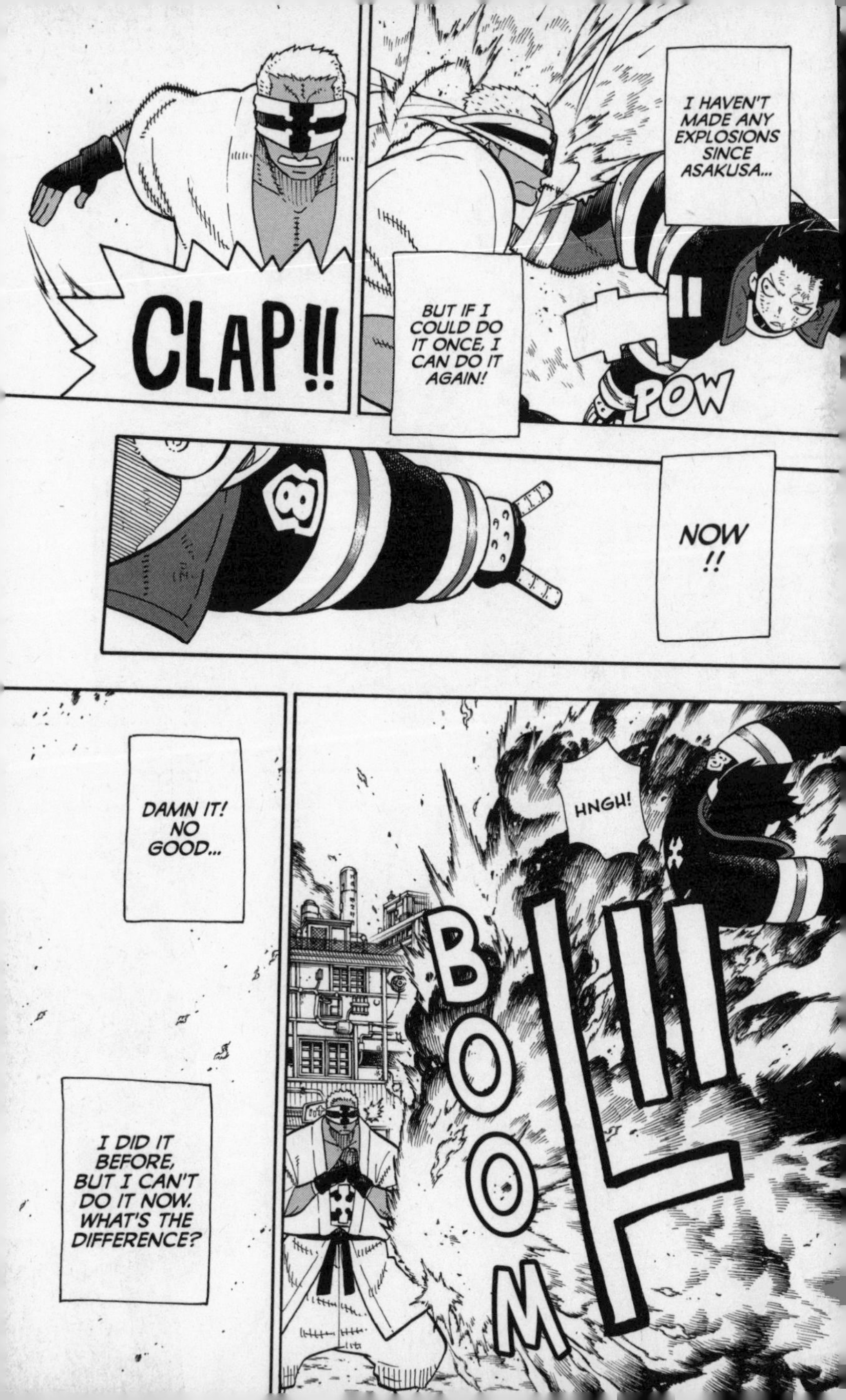
I HAVEN'T MADE ANY EXPLOSIONS SINCE ASAKUSA...
BUT IF I COULD DO IT ONCE, I CAN DO IT AGAIN!
POW
CLAP!!
NOW!!
HNGH!
BOOOM!!!
DAMN IT! NO GOOD...
I DID IT BEFORE, BUT I CAN'T DO IT NOW. WHAT'S THE DIFFERENCE?

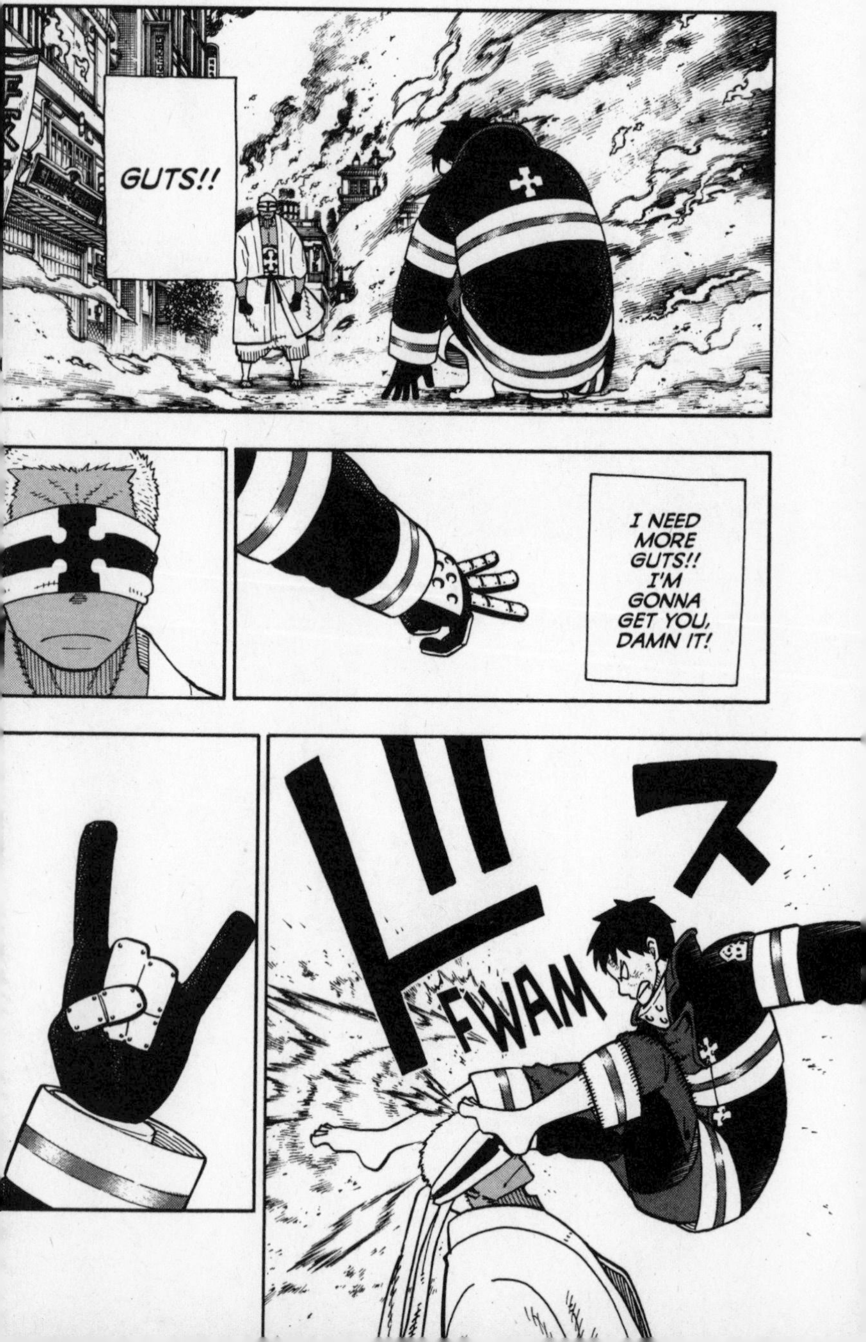
GUTS!!
I NEED MORE GUTS!! I'M GONNA GET YOU, DAMN IT!
FWAM

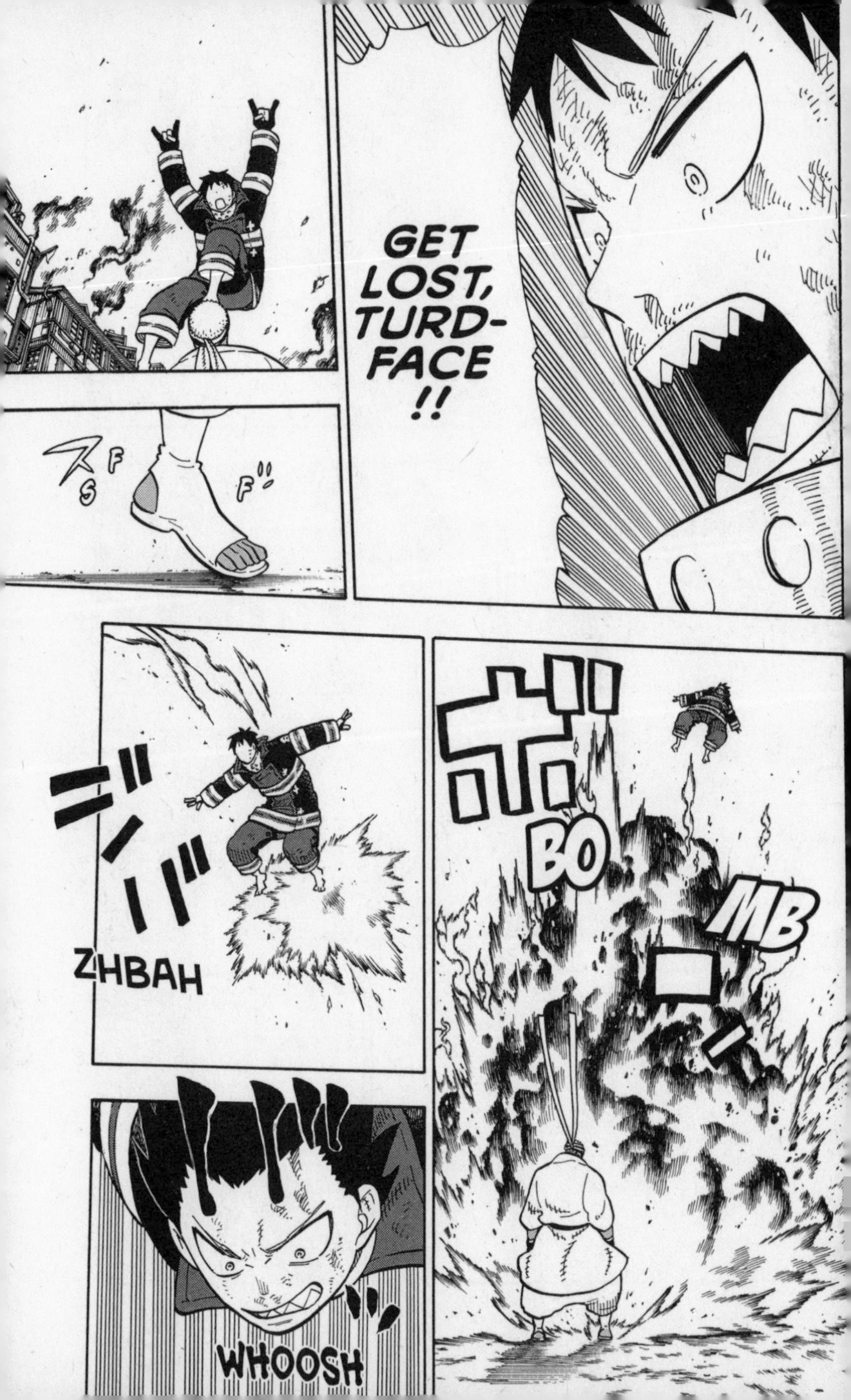
GET LOST, TURD-FACE!!
F
S
F
BO
MB
ZHBAH
WHOOSH

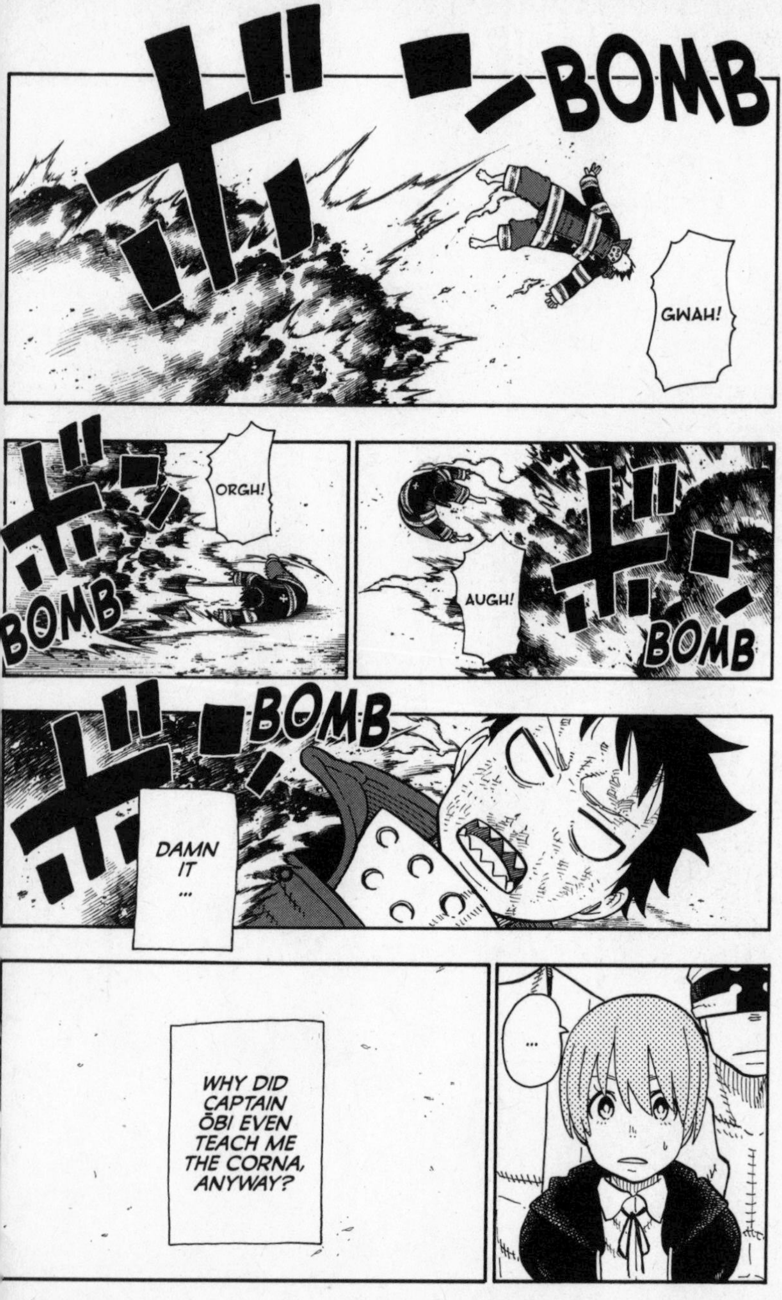
BOMB
GWAH!
AUGH!
BOMB
ORGH!
BOMB
BOMB
DAMN IT ...
...
WHY DID CAPTAIN ŌBI EVEN TEACH ME THE CORNA, ANYWAY?

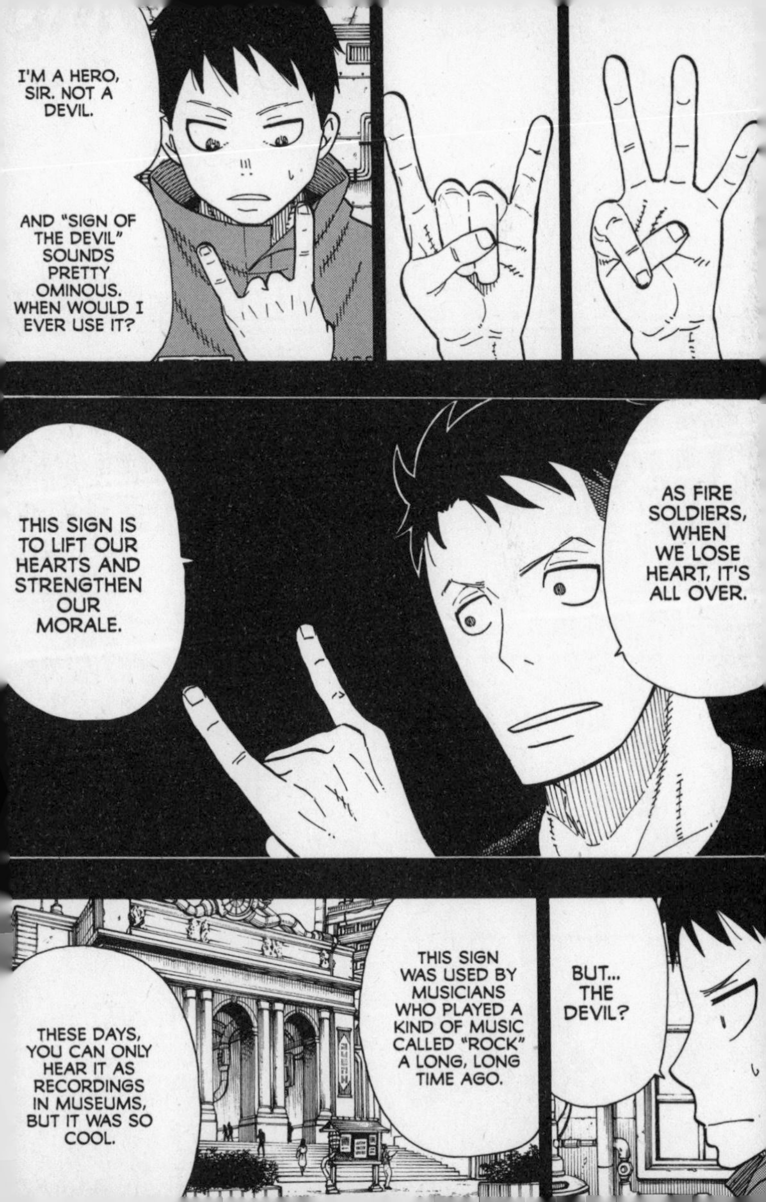
I'M A HERO, SIR. NOT A DEVIL.
AND "SIGN OF THE DEVIL" SOUNDS PRETTY OMINOUS. WHEN WOULD I EVER USE IT?
AS FIRE SOLDIERS, WHEN WE LOSE HEART, IT'S ALL OVER.
THIS SIGN IS TO LIFT OUR HEARTS AND STRENGTHEN OUR MORALE.
BUT... THE DEVIL?
THIS SIGN WAS USED BY MUSICIANS WHO PLAYED A KIND OF MUSIC CALLED "ROCK" A LONG, LONG TIME AGO.
THESE DAYS, YOU CAN ONLY HEAR IT AS RECORDINGS IN MUSEUMS, BUT IT WAS SO COOL.

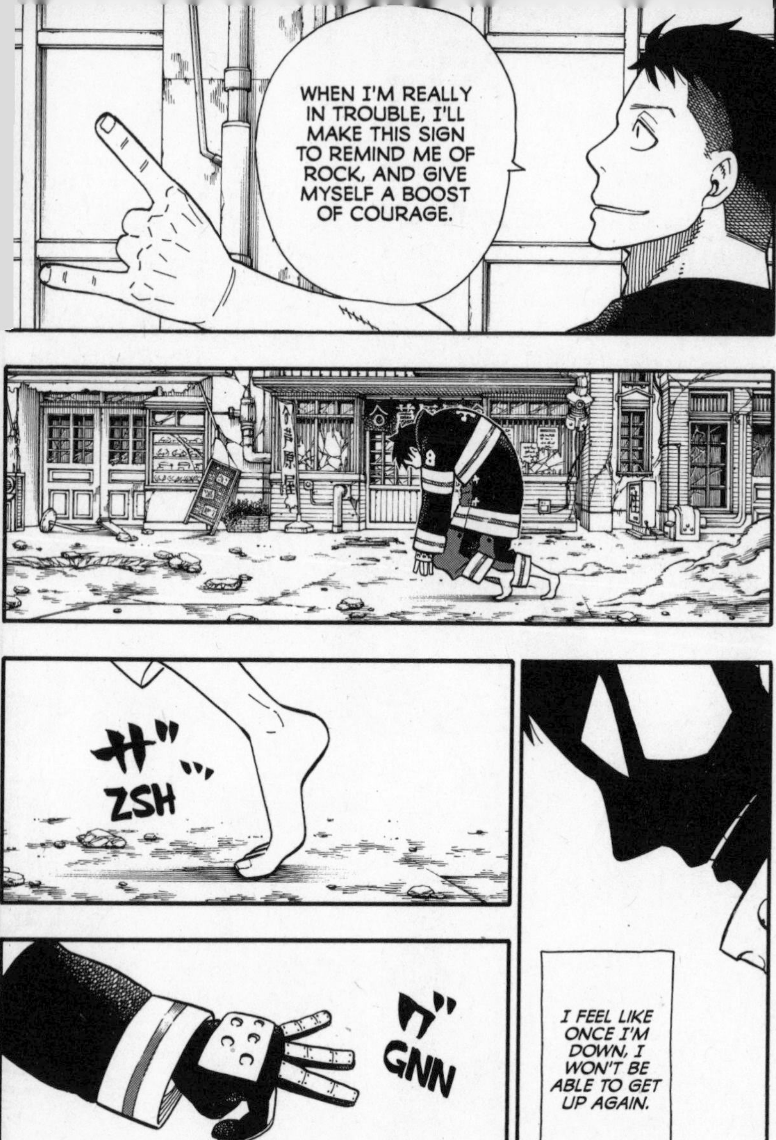
WHEN I'M REALLY IN TROUBLE, I'LL MAKE THIS SIGN TO REMIND ME OF ROCK, AND GIVE MYSELF A BOOST OF COURAGE.
I FEEL LIKE ONCE I'M DOWN, I WON'T BE ABLE TO GET UP AGAIN.
ZSH
GNN

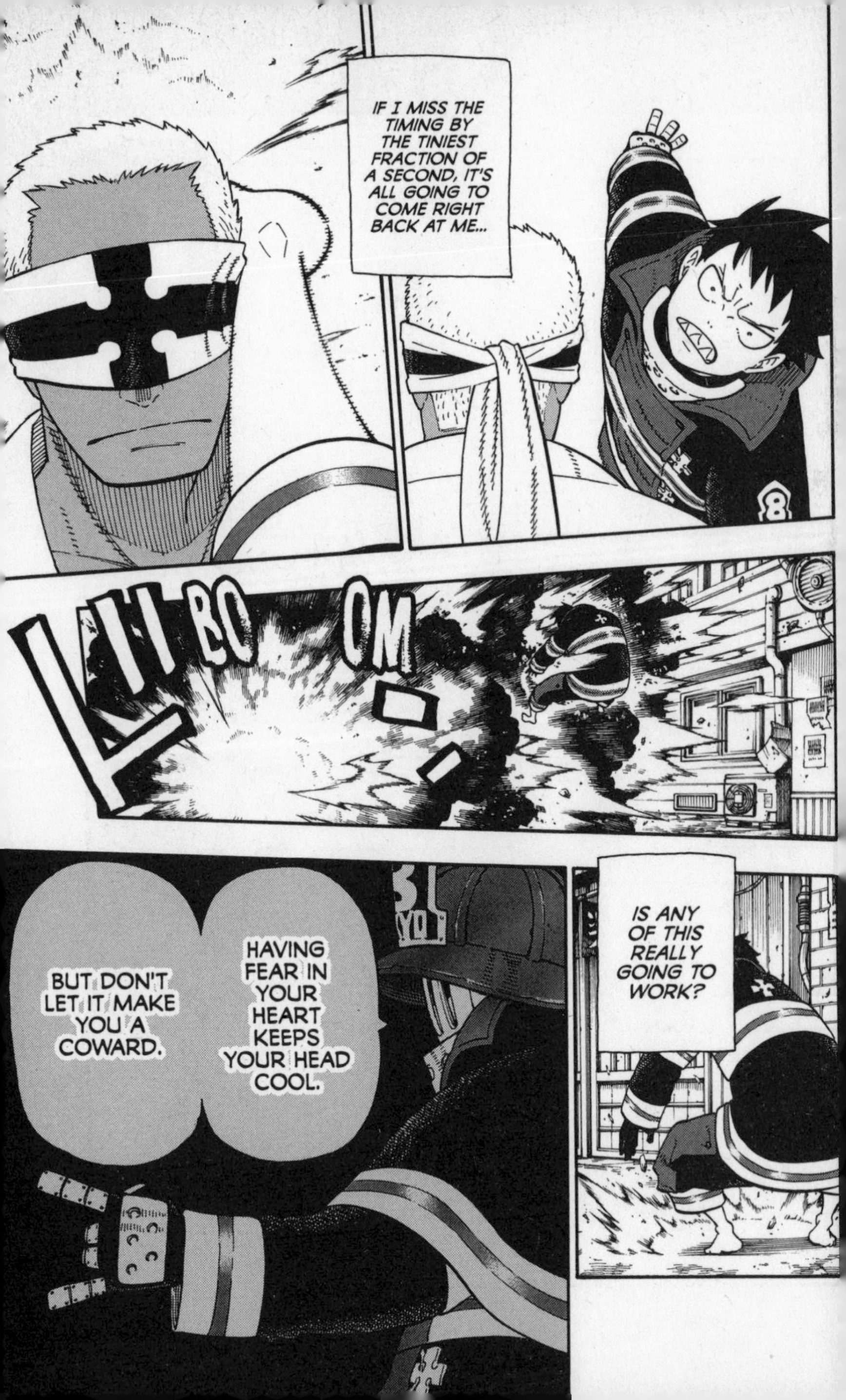
IF I MISS THE TIMING BY THE TINIEST FRACTION OF A SECOND, IT'S ALL GOING TO COME RIGHT BACK AT ME...
BOOM
IS ANY OF THIS REALLY GOING TO WORK?
HAVING FEAR IN YOUR HEART KEEPS YOUR HEAD COOL.
BUT DON'T LET IT MAKE YOU A COWARD.

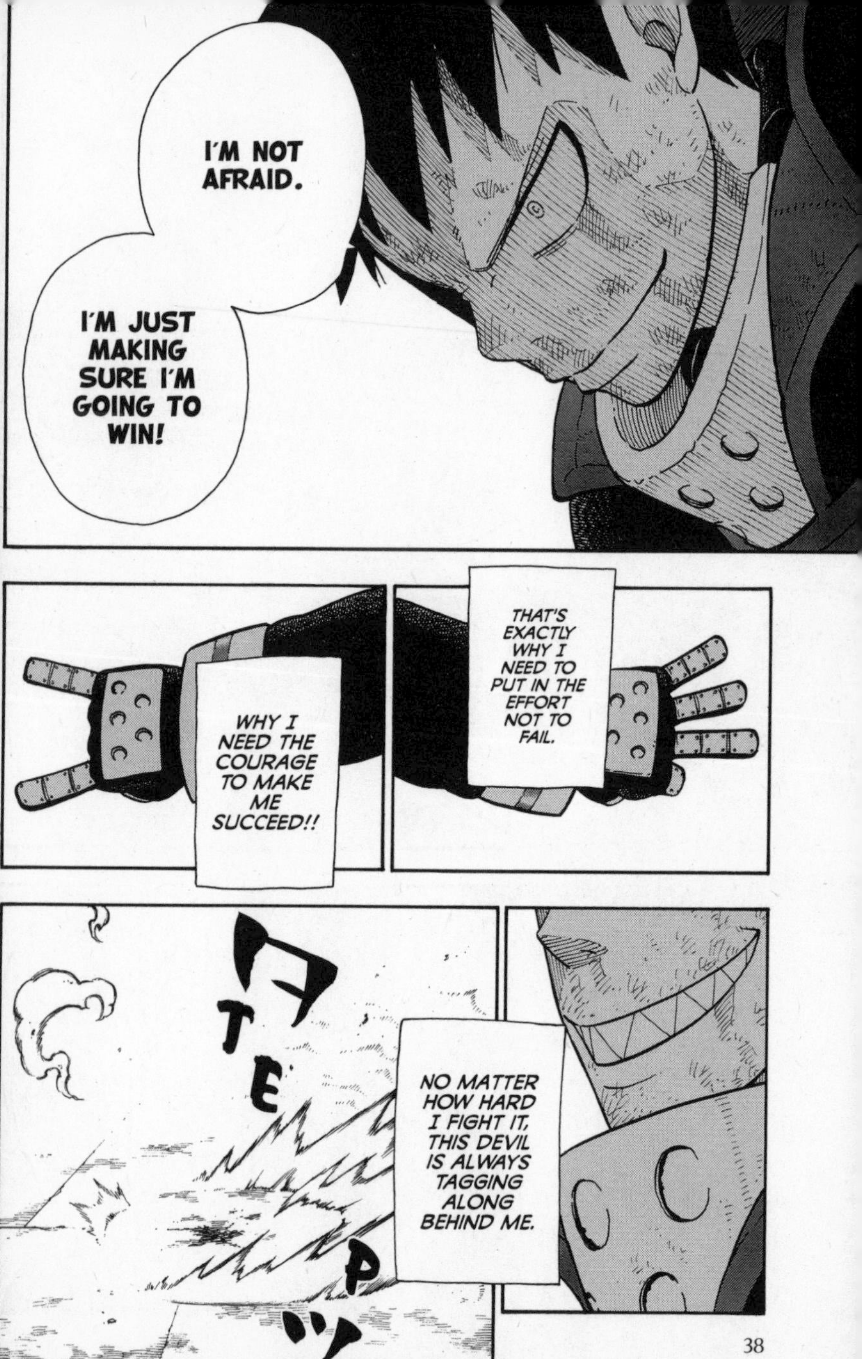
I'M NOT AFRAID.
I'M JUST MAKING SURE I'M GOING TO WIN!
THAT'S EXACTLY WHY I NEED TO PUT IN THE EFFORT NOT TO FAIL.
WHY I NEED THE COURAGE TO MAKE ME SUCCEED!!
NO MATTER HOW HARD I FIGHT IT, THIS DEVIL IS ALWAYS TAGGING ALONG BEHIND ME.
TEP

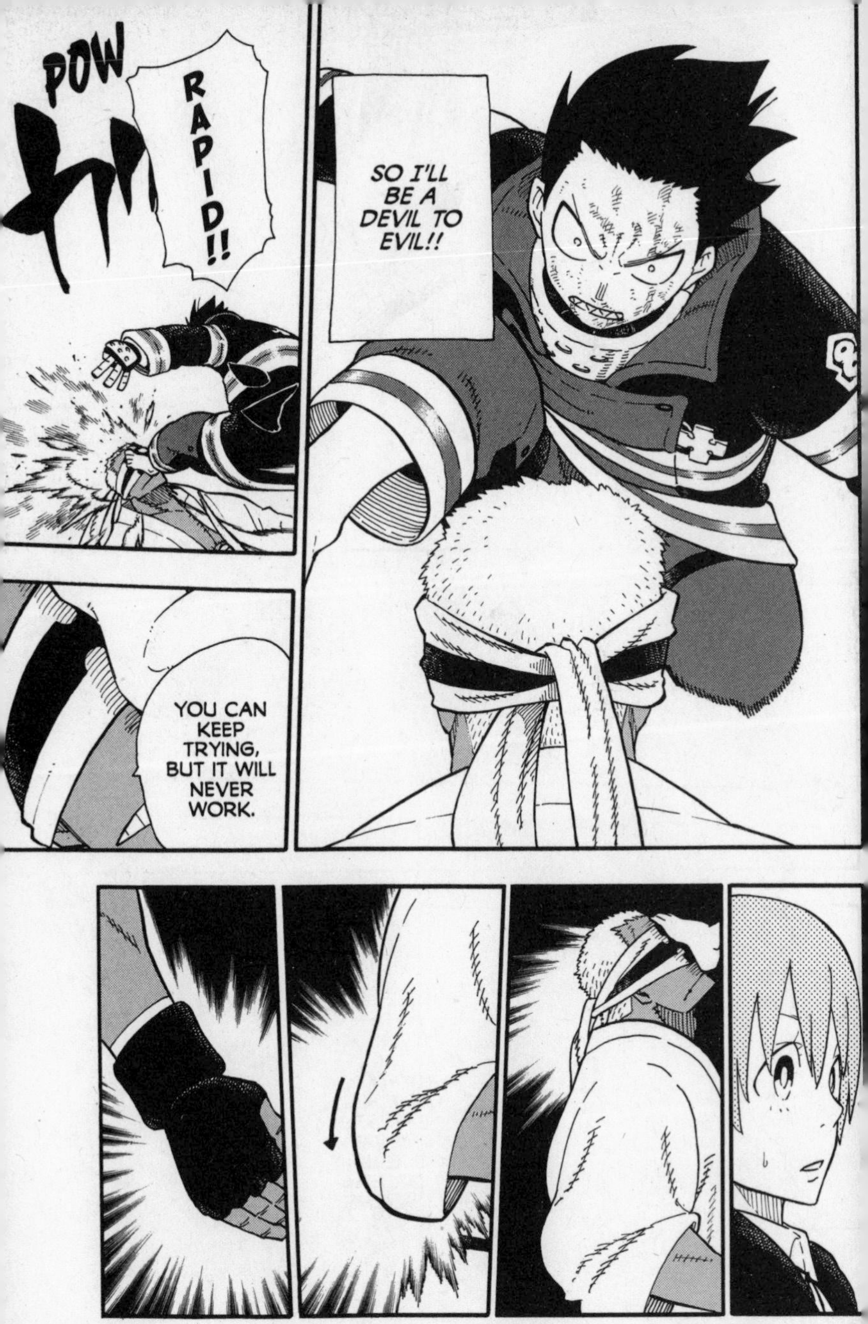
SO I'LL BE A DEVIL TO EVIL!!
POW
RAPID!!
YOU CAN KEEP TRYING, BUT IT WILL NEVER WORK.

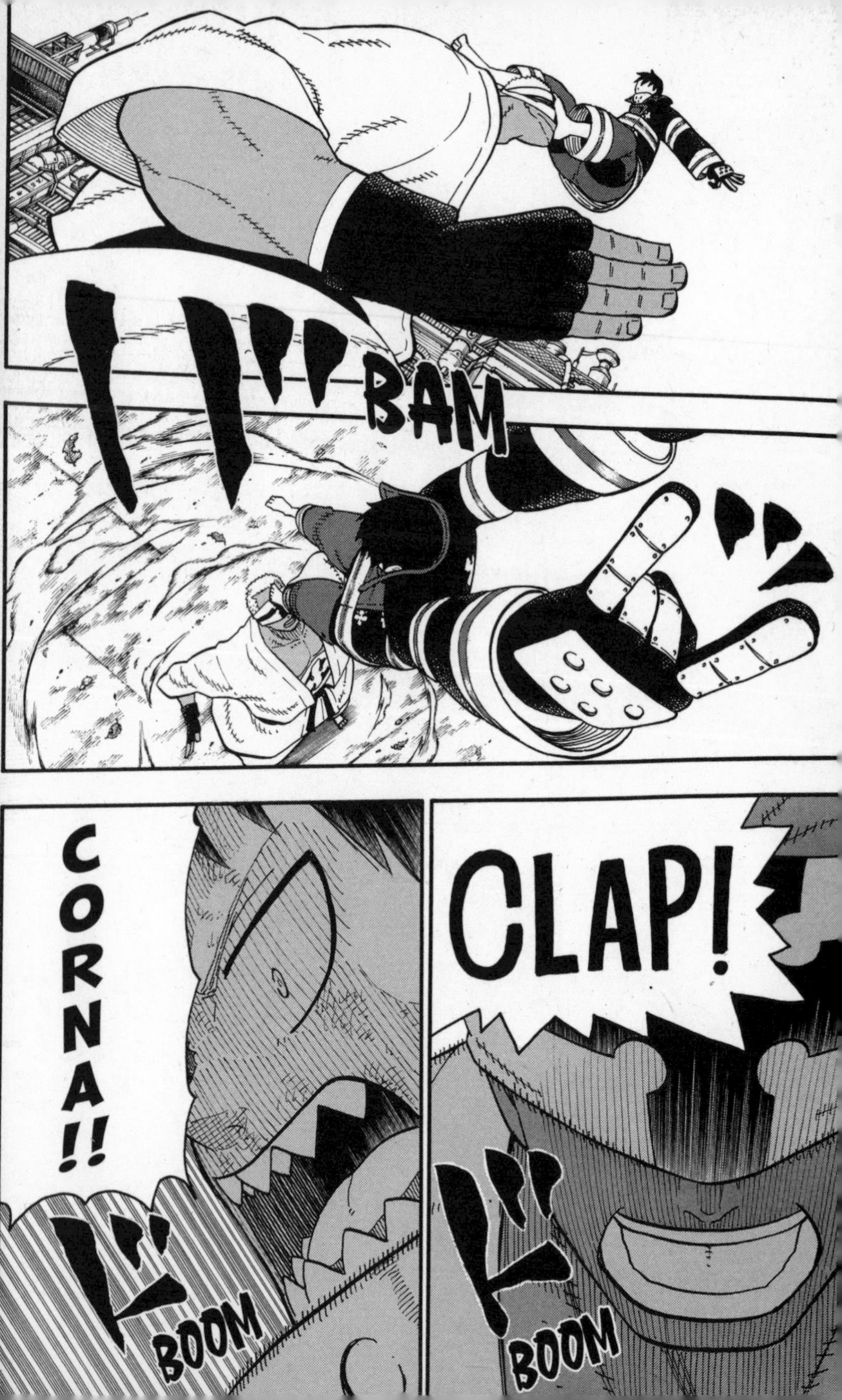
BAM
CLAP!
BOOM
CORNA!!
BOOM

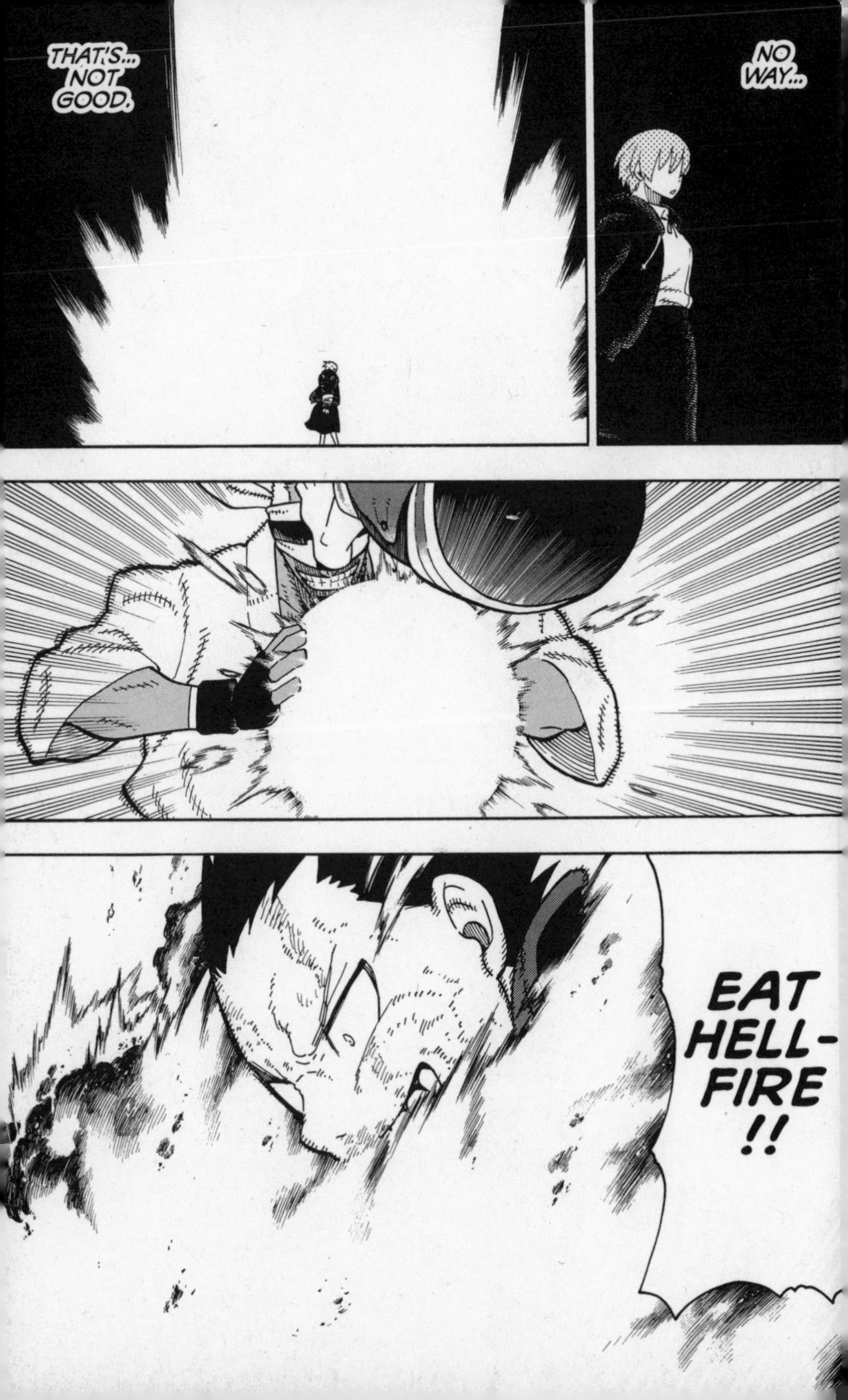
NO WAY...
THAT'S... NOT GOOD.
EAT HELL-FIRE!!

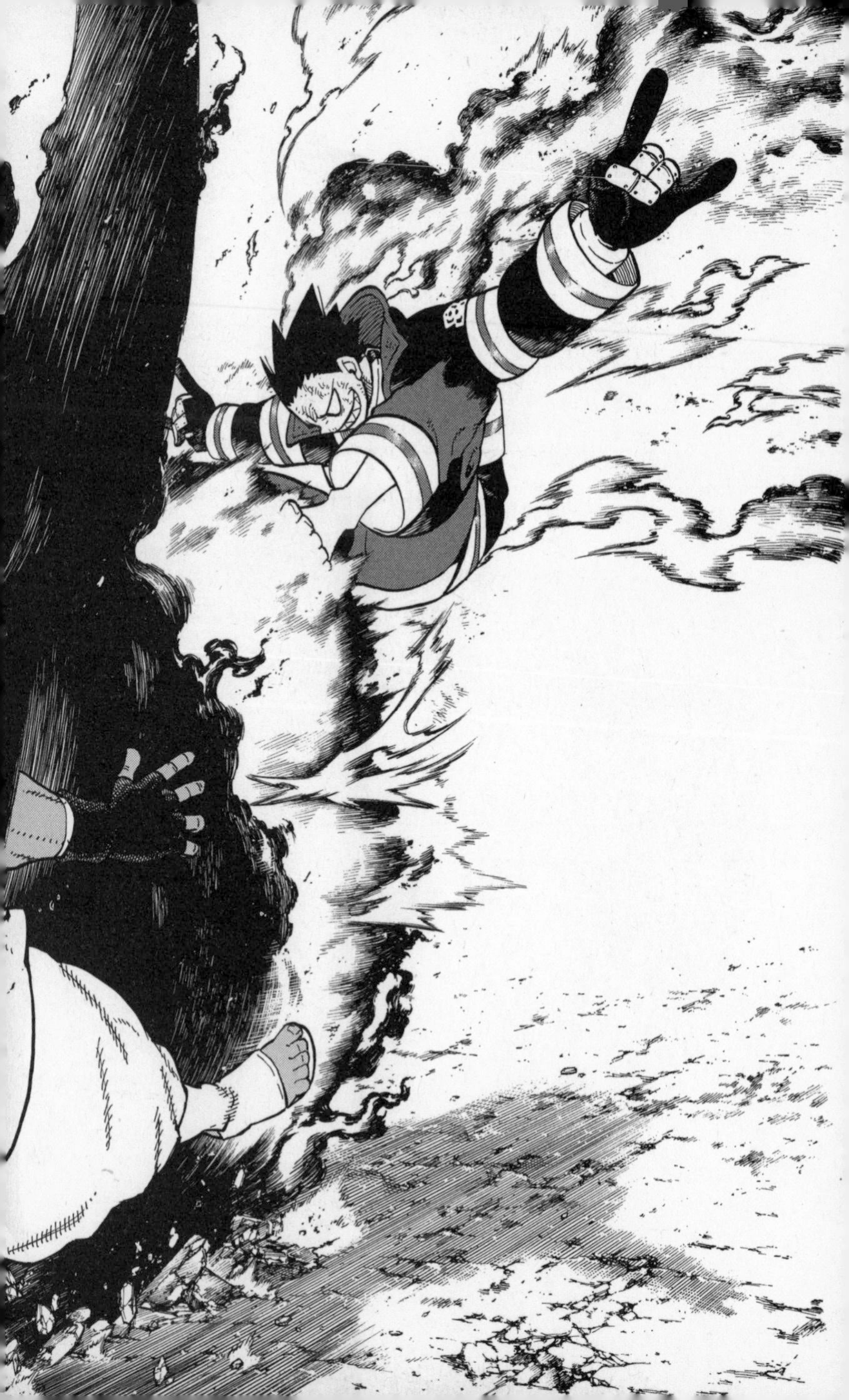

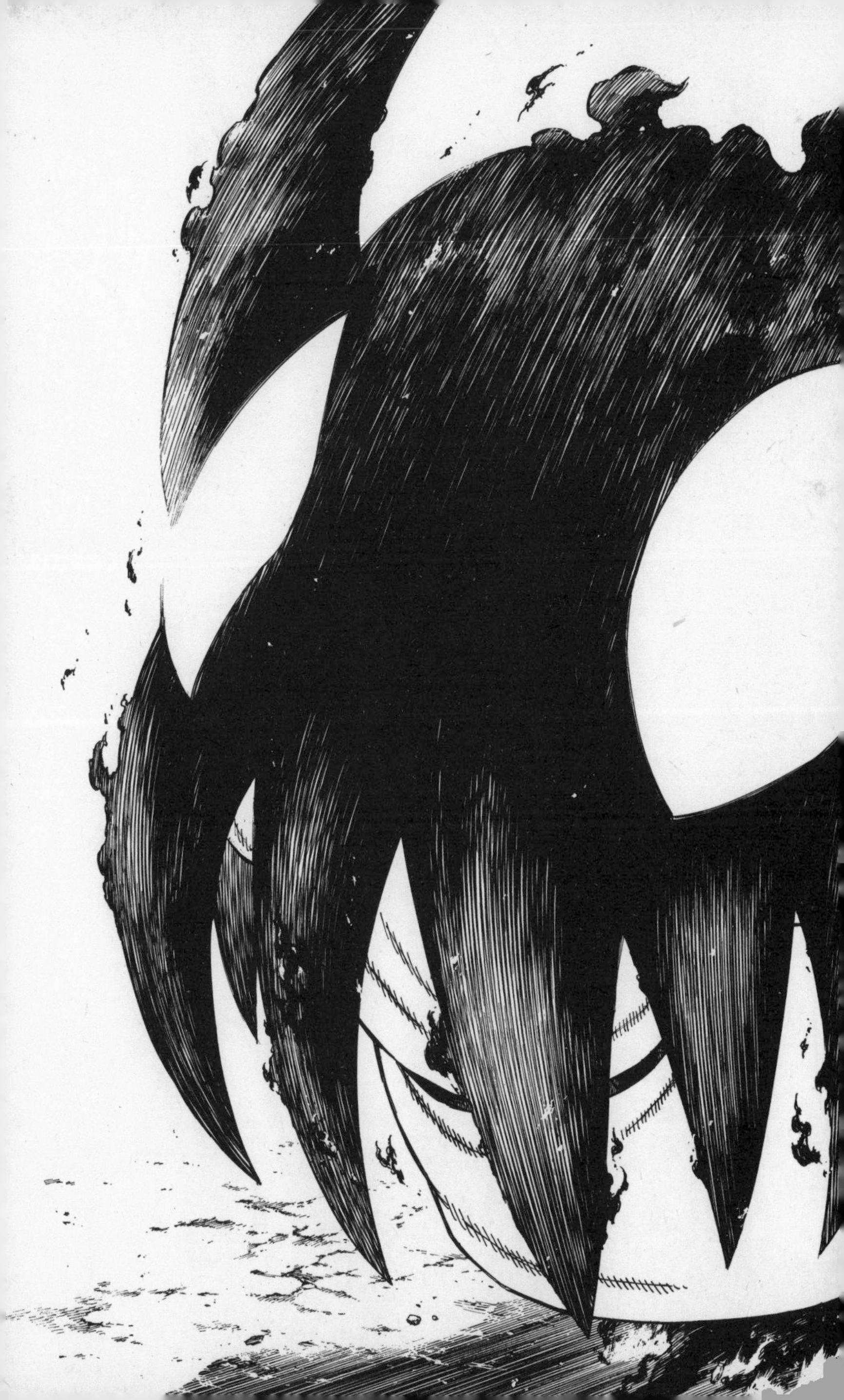

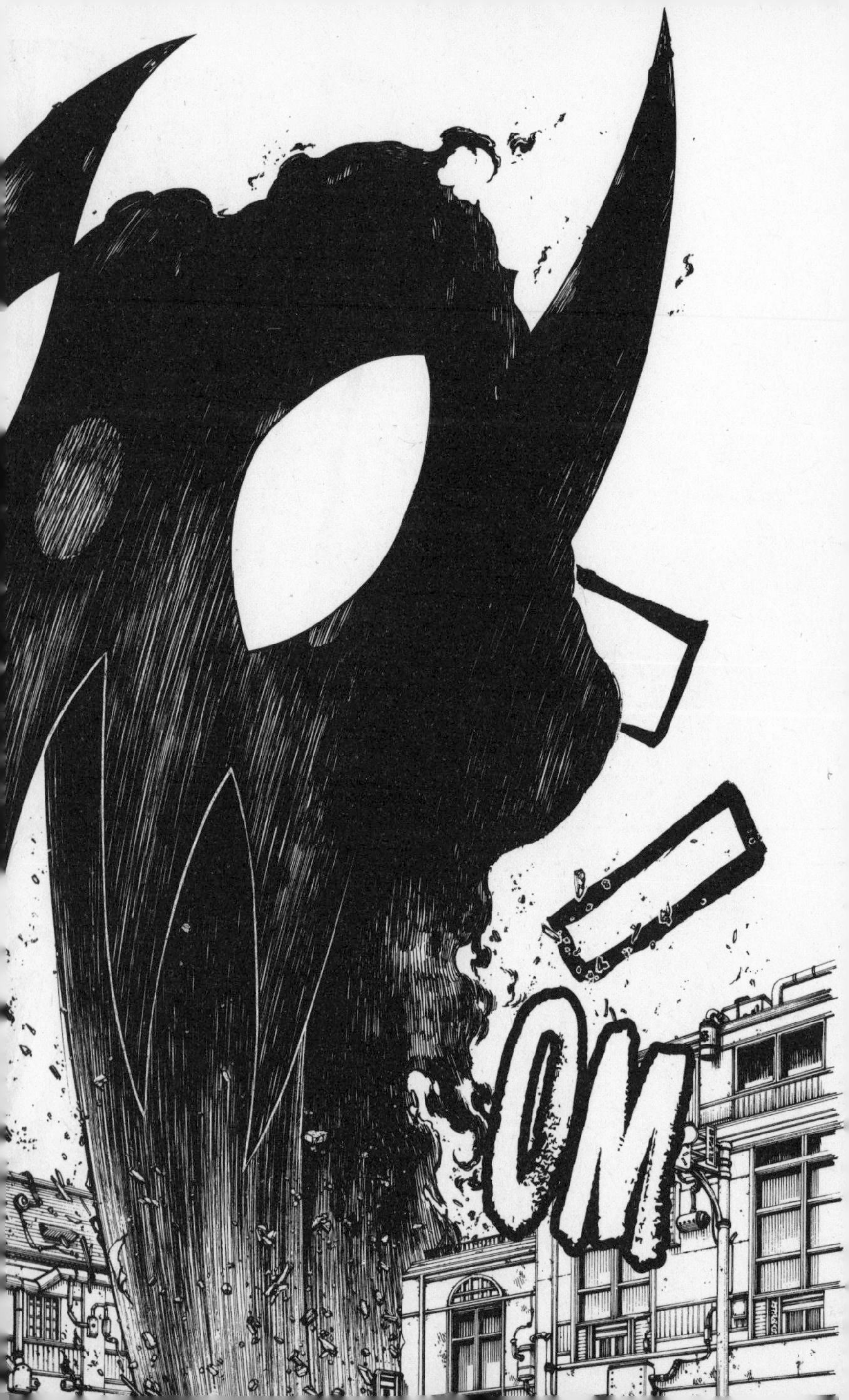
OM

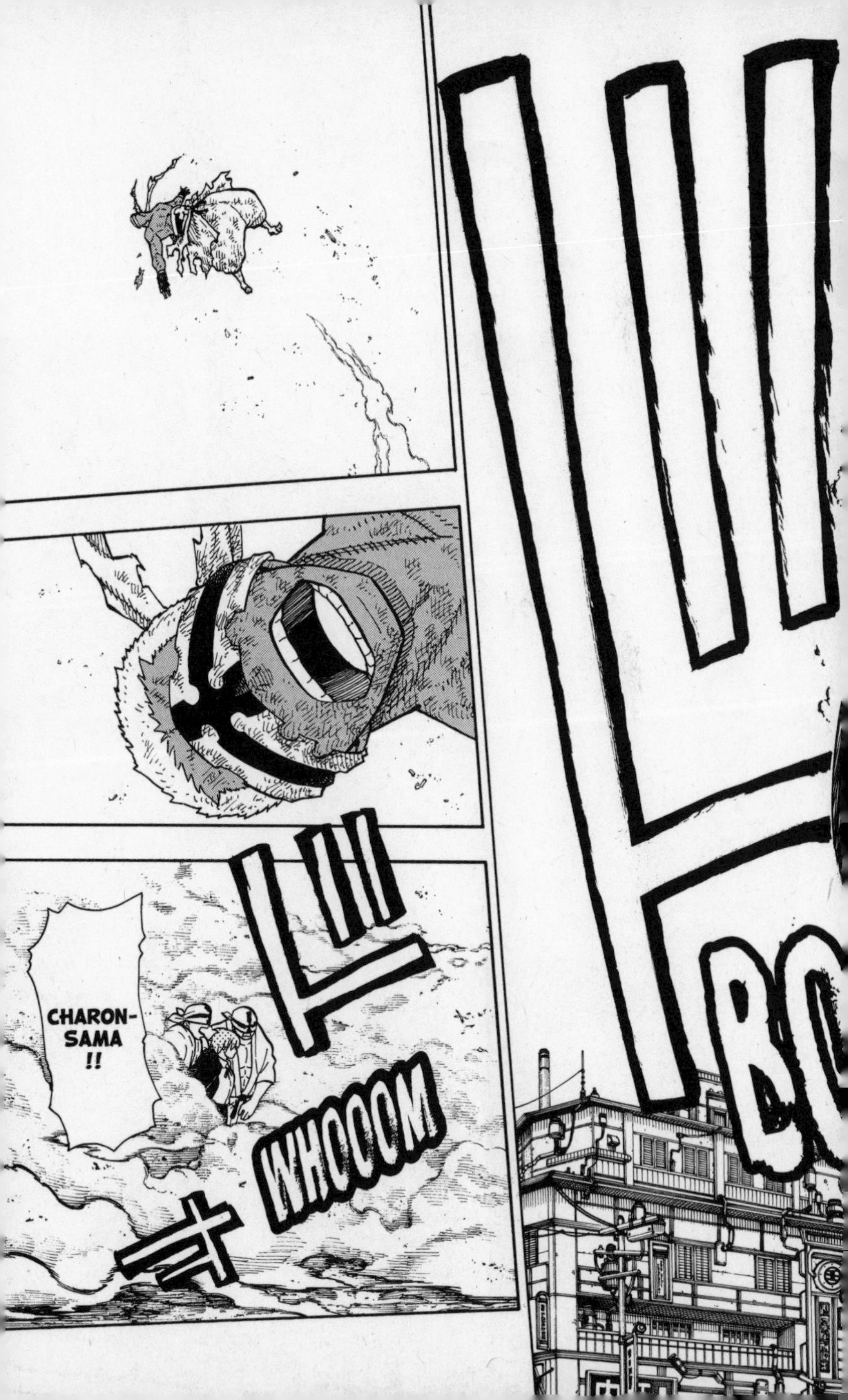
CHARON-SAMA !!
WHOOOM

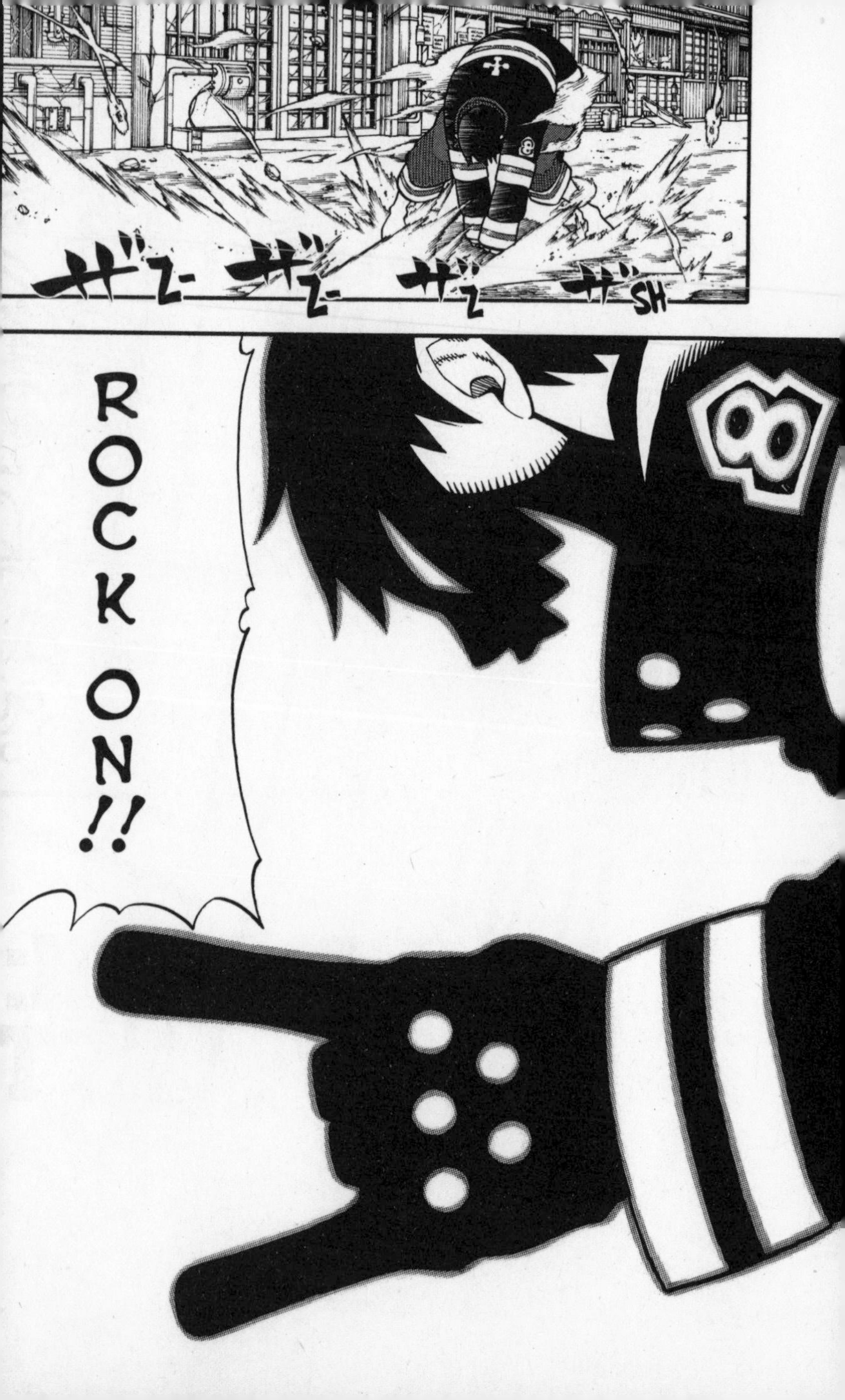
ザZ- ザZ- ザZ ザSH
ROCK ON!!

CHAPTER CVIII: LICHT'S SECRET PLAN

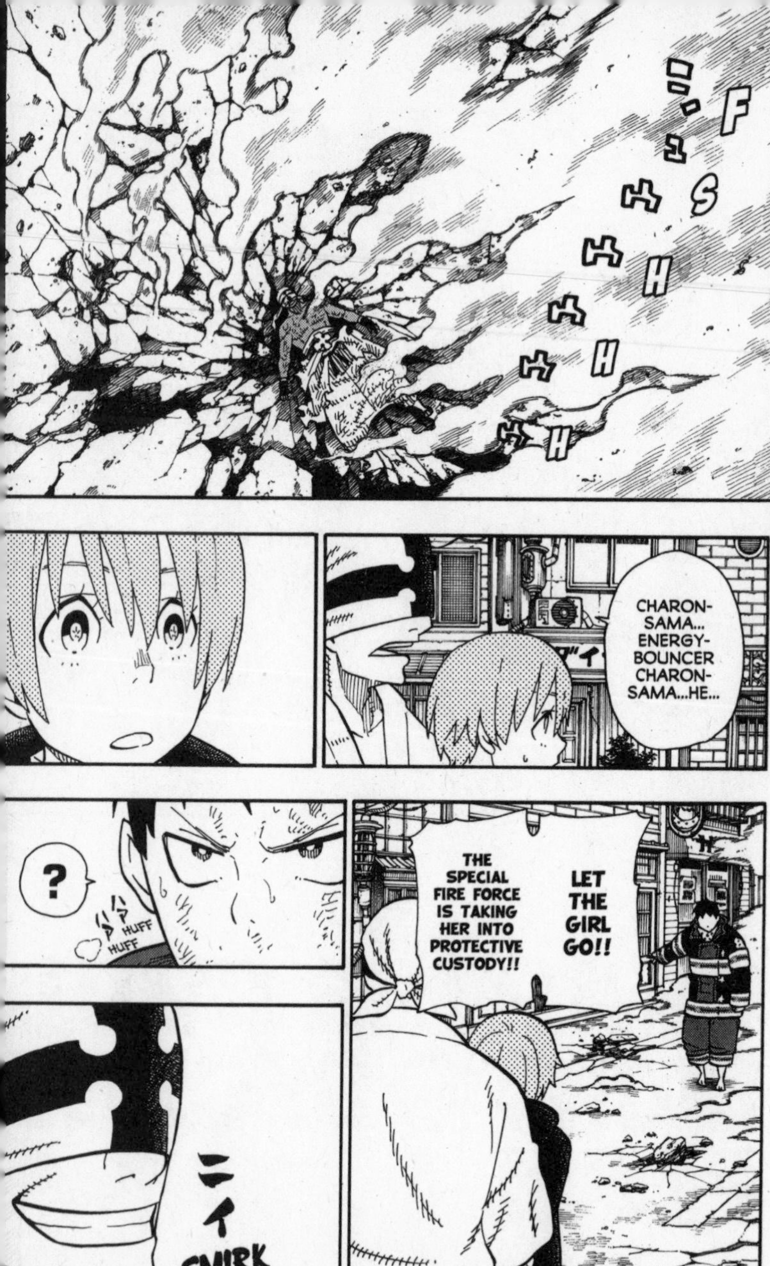
FSHHHH
CHARON-SAMA... ENERGY-BOUNCER CHARON-SAMA...HE...
LET THE GIRL GO!!
THE SPECIAL FIRE FORCE IS TAKING HER INTO PROTECTIVE CUSTODY!!
?
HUFF HUFF
ニイ
SMIRK

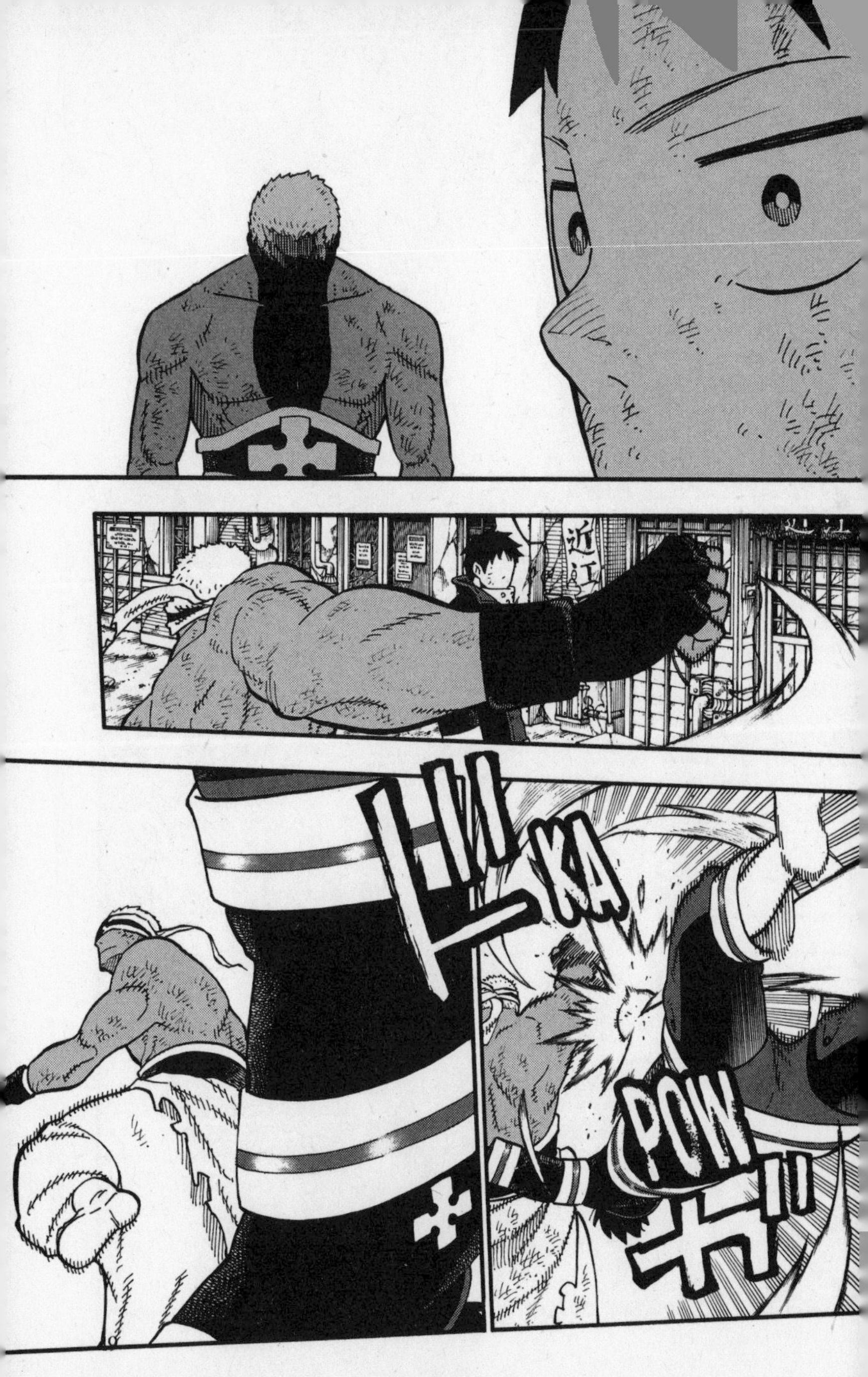
KA
POW

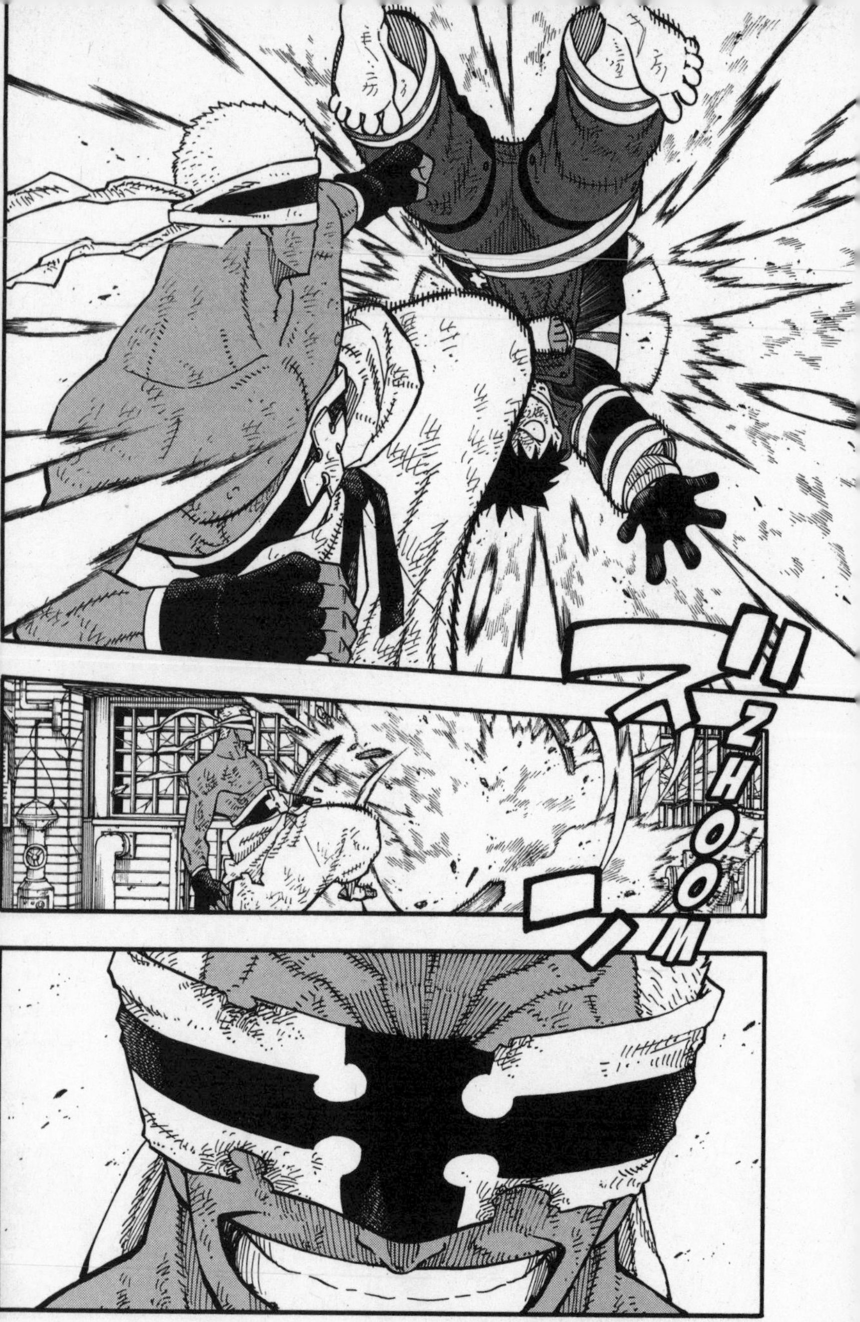
ZHOOOM

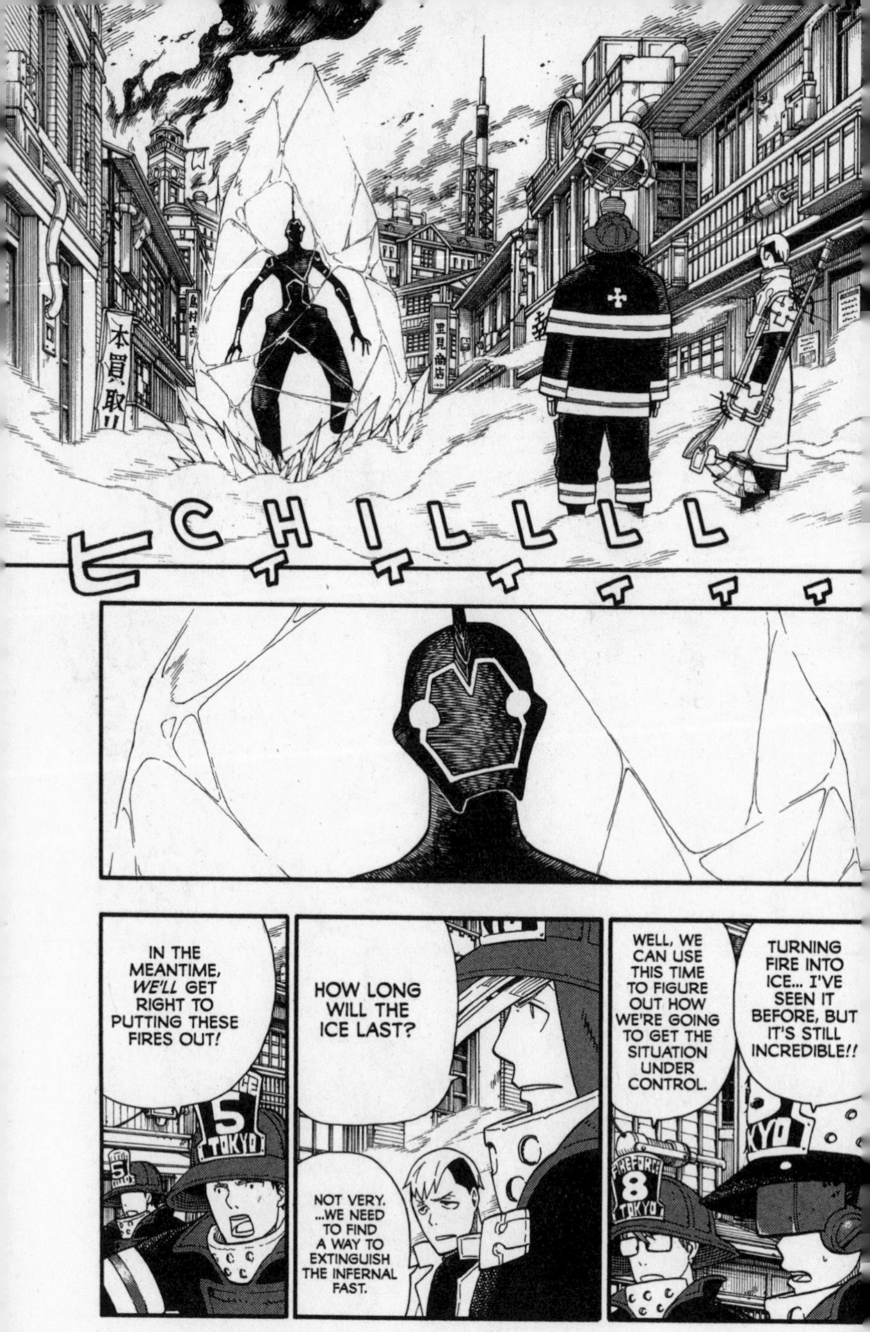
CHILLLL
TURNING FIRE INTO ICE... I'VE SEEN IT BEFORE, BUT IT'S STILL INCREDIBLE!!
WELL, WE CAN USE THIS TIME TO FIGURE OUT HOW WE'RE GOING TO GET THE SITUATION UNDER CONTROL.
HOW LONG WILL THE ICE LAST?
NOT VERY. ...WE NEED TO FIND A WAY TO EXTINGUISH THE INFERNAL FAST.
IN THE MEANTIME, *WE'LL* GET RIGHT TO PUTTING THESE FIRES OUT!

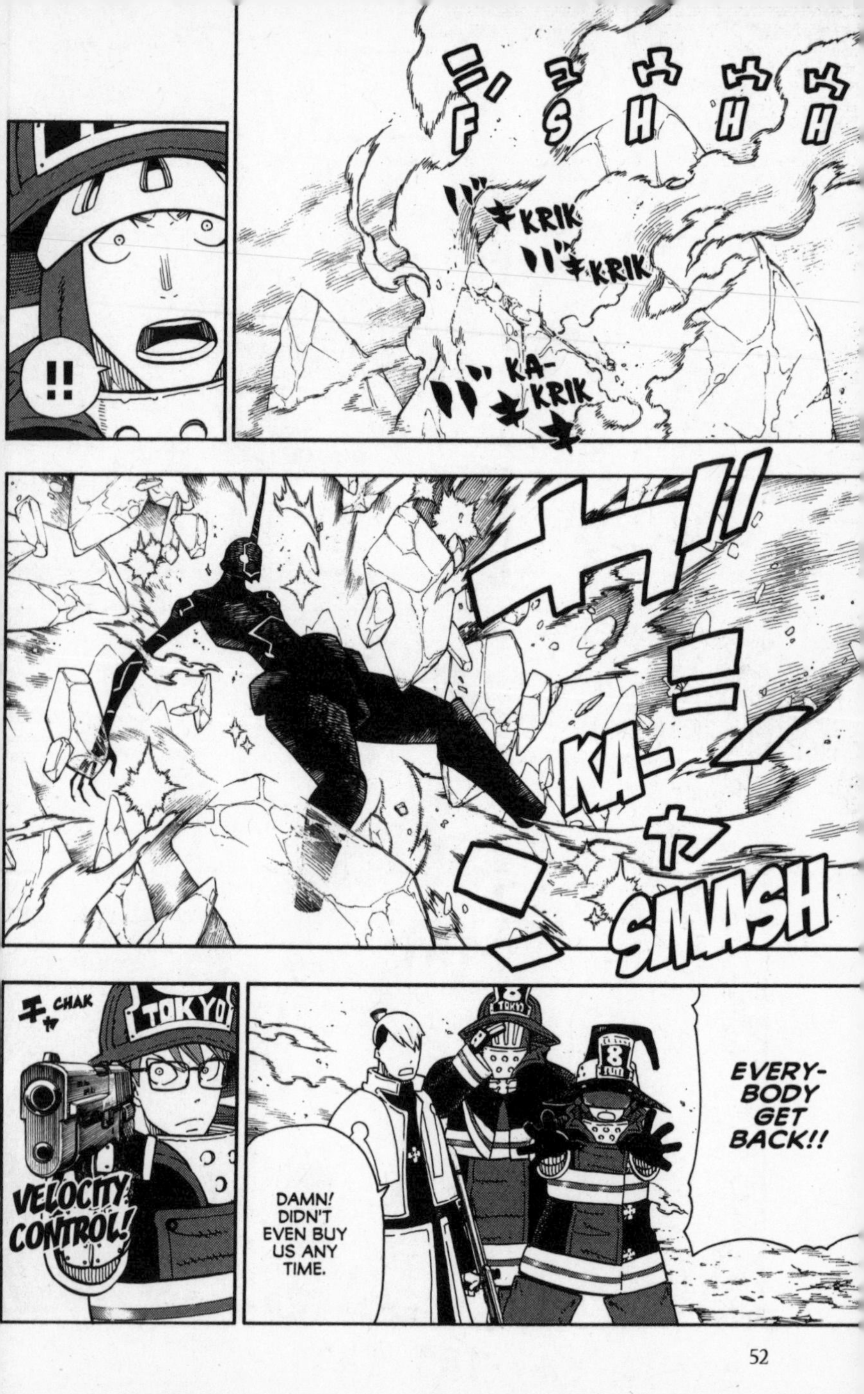
F S H H H
KRIK
KRIK
KA-KRIK
!!
KA-SMASH
EVERY-BODY GET BACK!!
DAMN! DIDN'T EVEN BUY US ANY TIME.
CHAK
VELOCITY CONTROL!

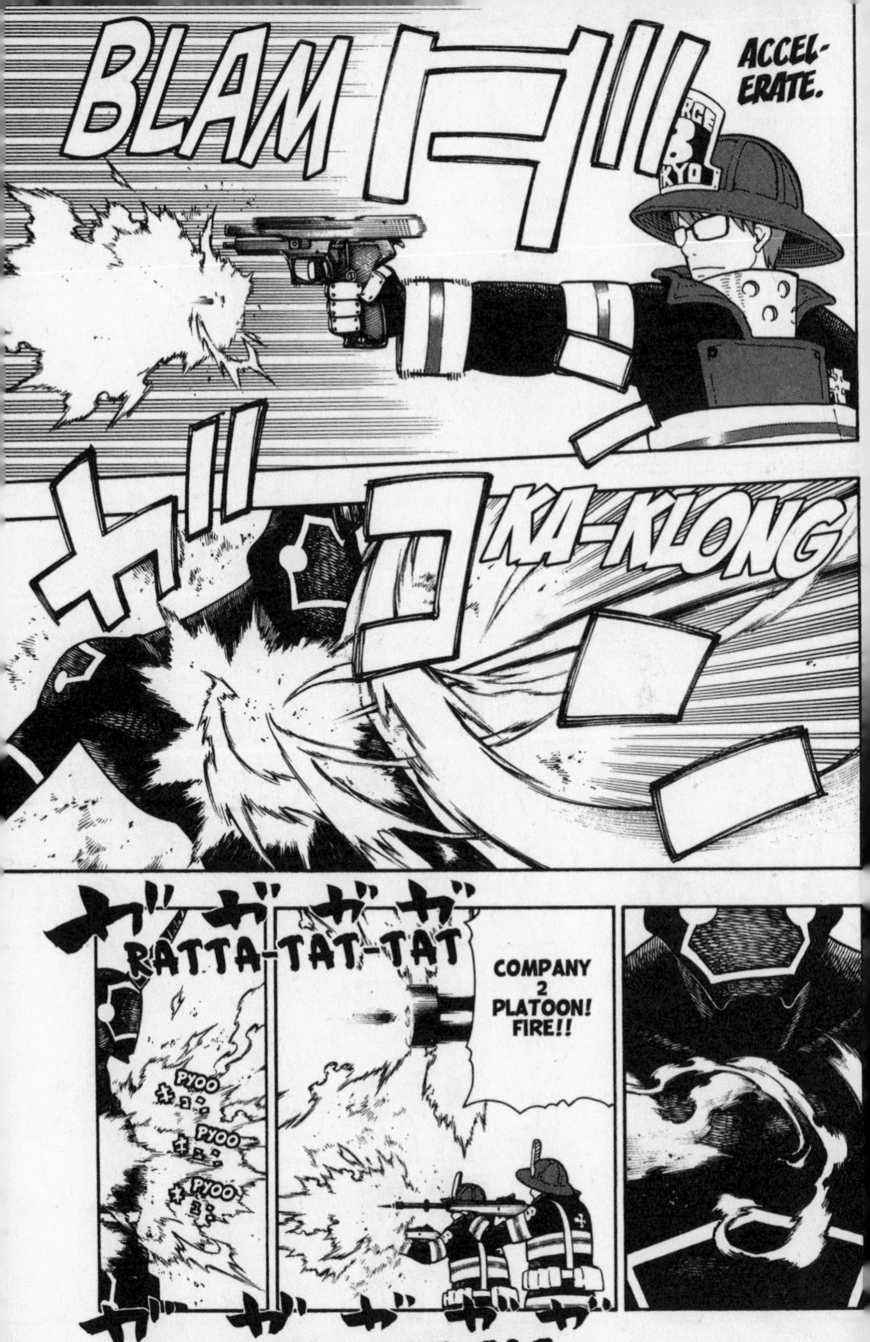
ACCEL-
ERATE.
BLAM
KA-KLONG
COMPANY 2 PLATOON! FIRE!!
RATTA-TAT-TAT
PYOO
PYOO
PYOO
RATTA-TAT-TAT-TAT

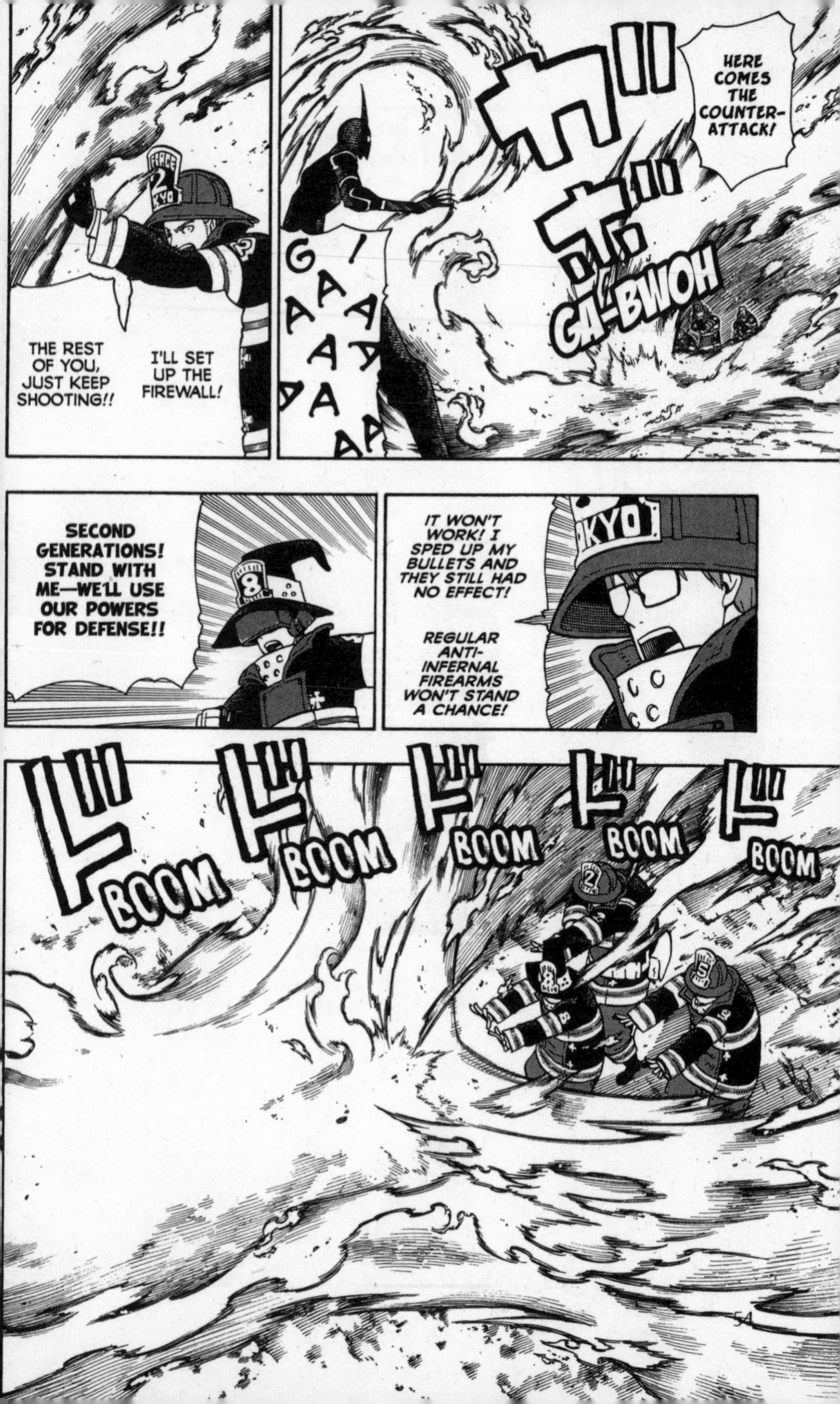
HERE COMES THE COUNTER-ATTACK!
GA-BWOH
GAAAAAA
I'LL SET UP THE FIREWALL!
THE REST OF YOU, JUST KEEP SHOOTING!!
IT WON'T WORK! I SPED UP MY BULLETS AND THEY STILL HAD NO EFFECT!
REGULAR ANTI-INFERNAL FIREARMS WON'T STAND A CHANCE!
SECOND GENERATIONS! STAND WITH ME—WE'LL USE OUR POWERS FOR DEFENSE!!
BOOM
BOOM
BOOM
BOOM
BOOM

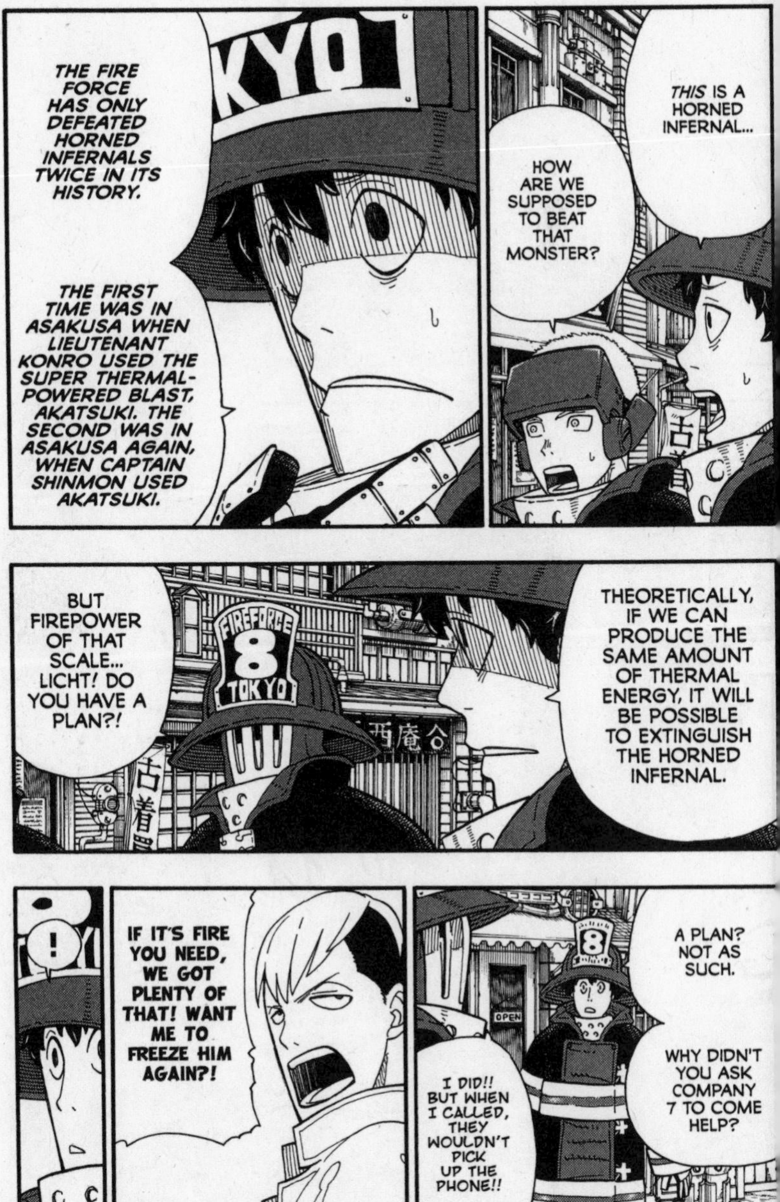
THIS IS A HORNED INFERNAL...
HOW ARE WE SUPPOSED TO BEAT THAT MONSTER?
THE FIRE FORCE HAS ONLY DEFEATED HORNED INFERNALS TWICE IN ITS HISTORY.
THE FIRST TIME WAS IN ASAKUSA WHEN LIEUTENANT KONRO USED THE SUPER THERMAL-POWERED BLAST, AKATSUKI. THE SECOND WAS IN ASAKUSA AGAIN, WHEN CAPTAIN SHINMON USED AKATSUKI.
THEORETICALLY, IF WE CAN PRODUCE THE SAME AMOUNT OF THERMAL ENERGY, IT WILL BE POSSIBLE TO EXTINGUISH THE HORNED INFERNAL.
BUT FIREPOWER OF THAT SCALE... LICHT! DO YOU HAVE A PLAN?!
A PLAN? NOT AS SUCH.
WHY DIDN'T YOU ASK COMPANY 7 TO COME HELP?
I DID!! BUT WHEN I CALLED, THEY WOULDN'T PICK UP THE PHONE!!
IF IT'S FIRE YOU NEED, WE GOT PLENTY OF THAT! WANT ME TO FREEZE HIM AGAIN?!
!

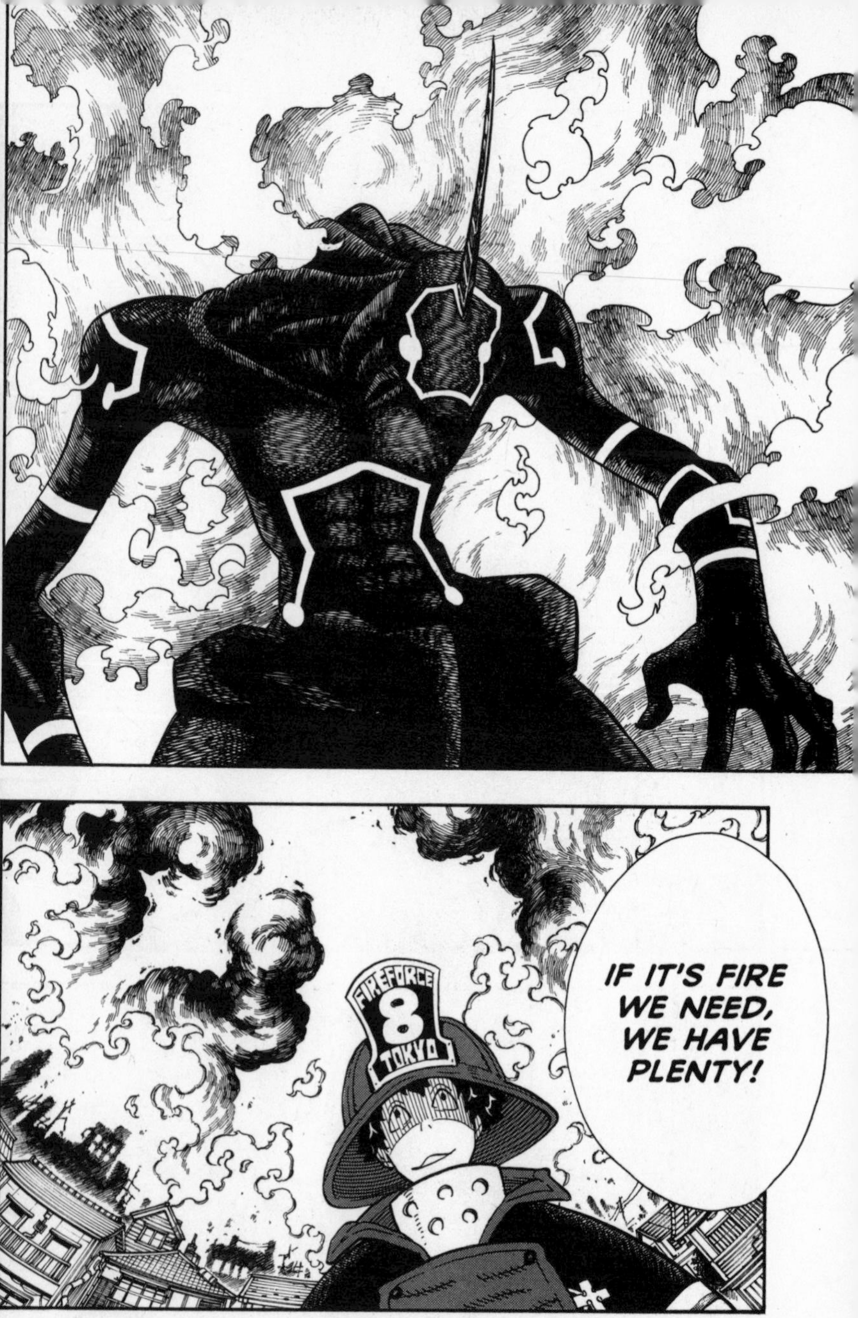
IF IT'S FIRE WE NEED, WE HAVE PLENTY!
FIREFORCE
8
TOKYO

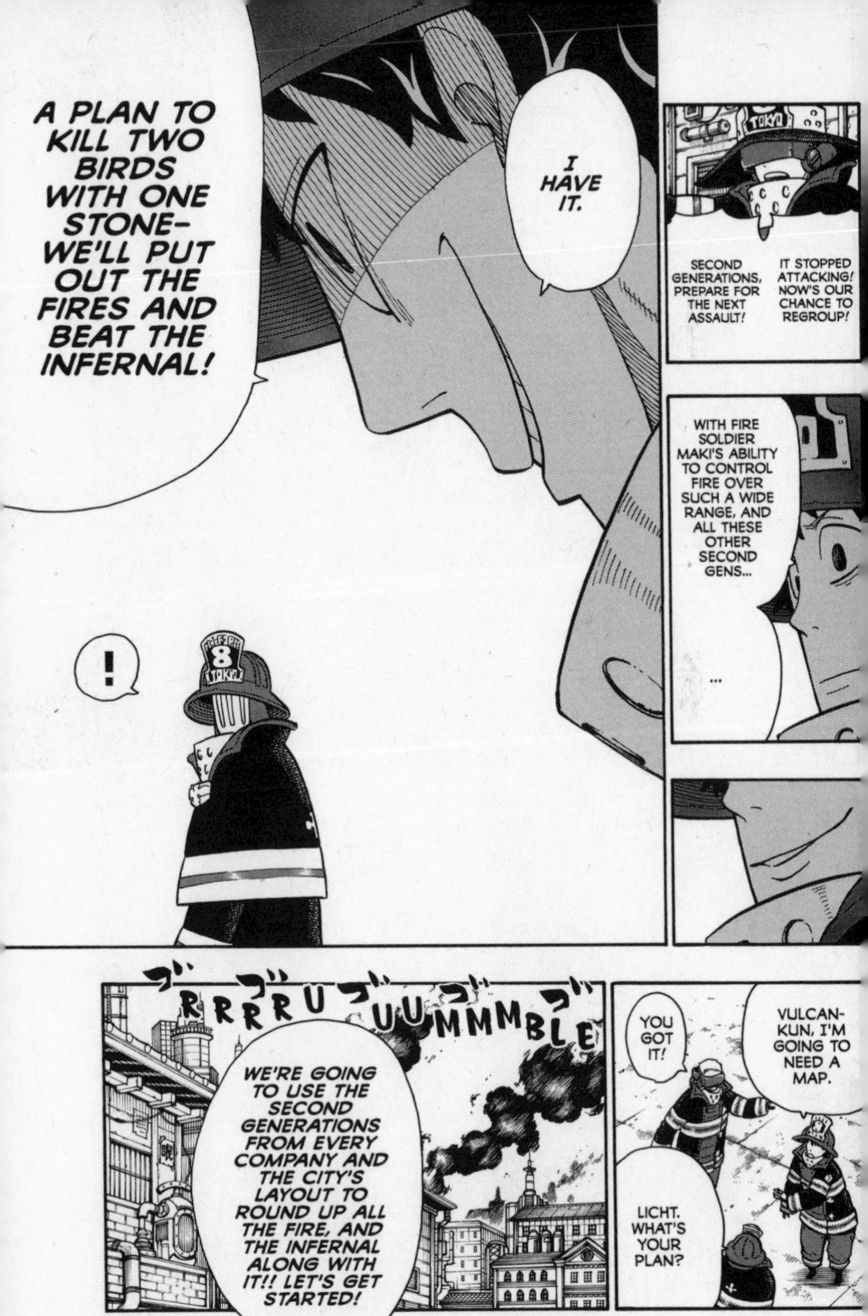
IT STOPPED ATTACKING! NOW'S OUR CHANCE TO REGROUP!
SECOND GENERATIONS, PREPARE FOR THE NEXT ASSAULT!
WITH FIRE SOLDIER MAKI'S ABILITY TO CONTROL FIRE OVER SUCH A WIDE RANGE, AND ALL THESE OTHER SECOND GENS...
...
I HAVE IT.
A PLAN TO KILL TWO BIRDS WITH ONE STONE- WE'LL PUT OUT THE FIRES AND BEAT THE INFERNAL!
!
VULCAN-KUN, I'M GOING TO NEED A MAP.
YOU GOT IT!
LICHT. WHAT'S YOUR PLAN?
RRRRUUMMMBLE
WE'RE GOING TO USE THE SECOND GENERATIONS FROM EVERY COMPANY AND THE CITY'S LAYOUT TO ROUND UP ALL THE FIRE, AND THE INFERNAL ALONG WITH IT!! LET'S GET STARTED!

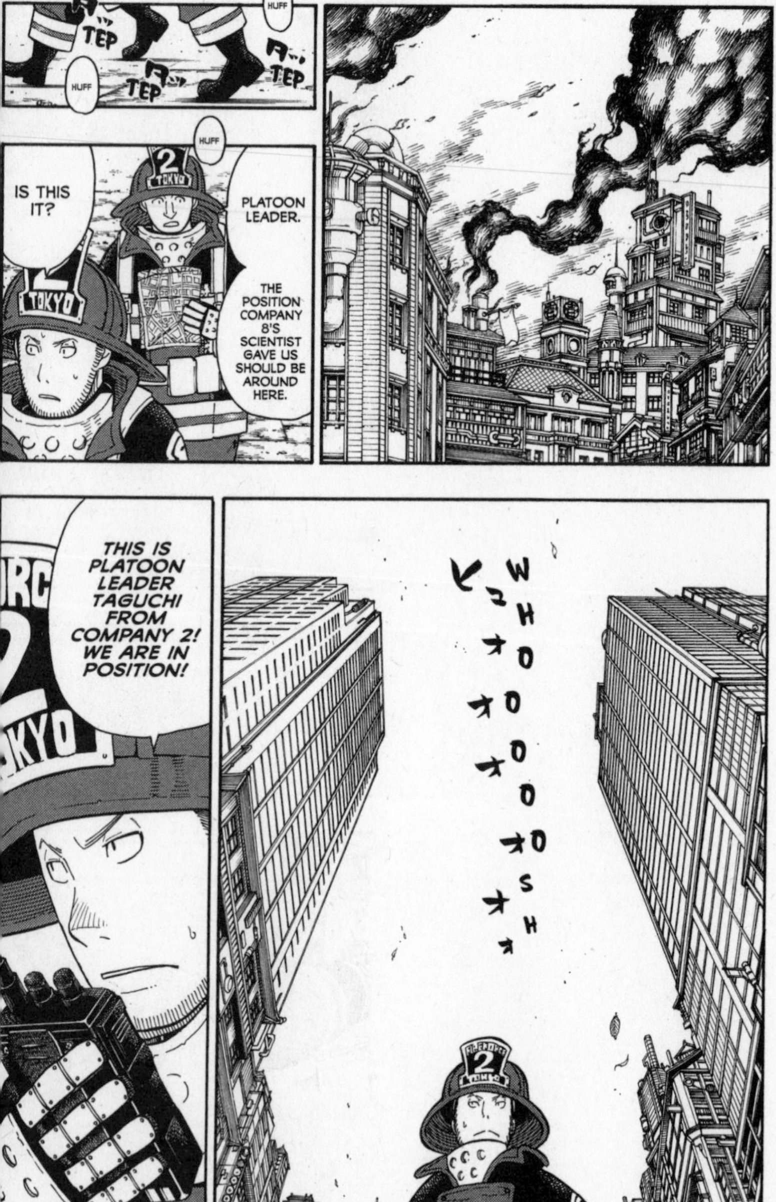
HUFF
TEP
TEP
HUFF
TEP
TEP
HUFF
PLATOON LEADER.
THE POSITION COMPANY 8'S SCIENTIST GAVE US SHOULD BE AROUND HERE.
IS THIS IT?
WHOOOOOOSH
THIS IS PLATOON LEADER TAGUCHI FROM COMPANY 2! WE ARE IN POSITION!

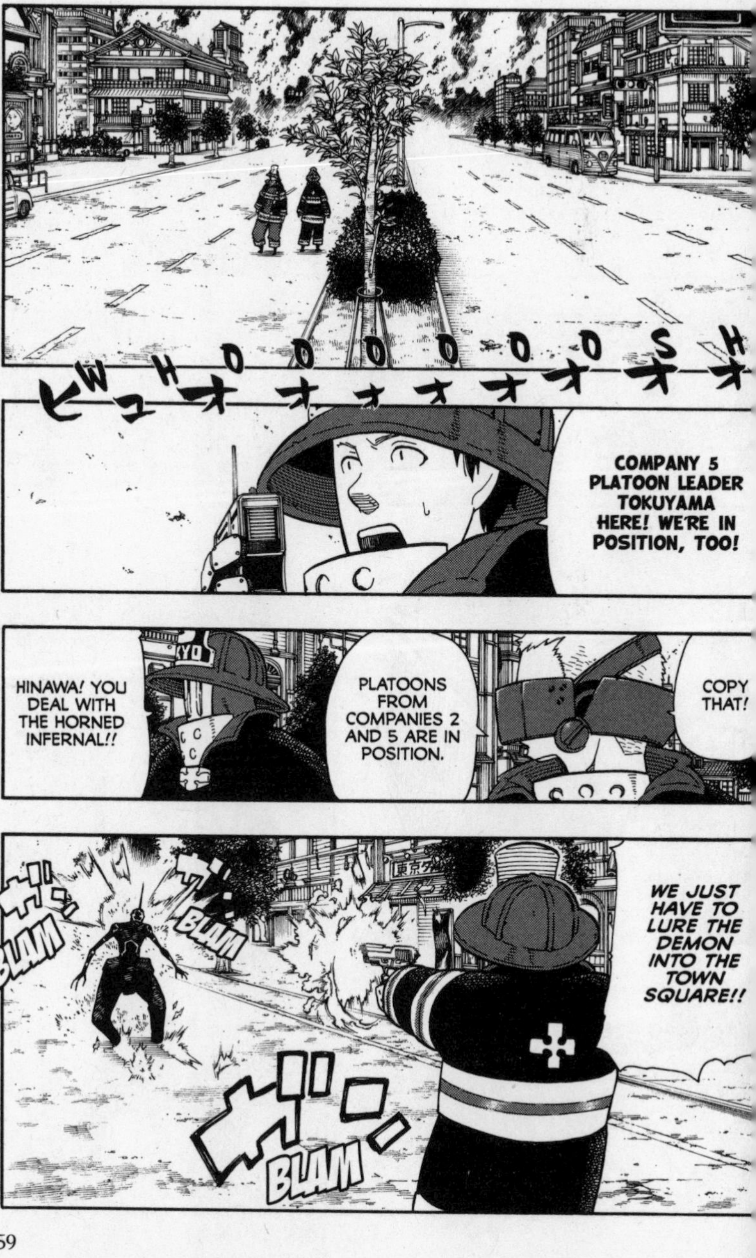

WHOOOOOOSH
COMPANY 5 PLATOON LEADER TOKUYAMA HERE! WE'RE IN POSITION, TOO!
COPY THAT!
PLATOONS FROM COMPANIES 2 AND 5 ARE IN POSITION.
HINAWA! YOU DEAL WITH THE HORNED INFERNAL!!
WE JUST HAVE TO LURE THE DEMON INTO THE TOWN SQUARE!!
BLAM
BLAM
BLAM

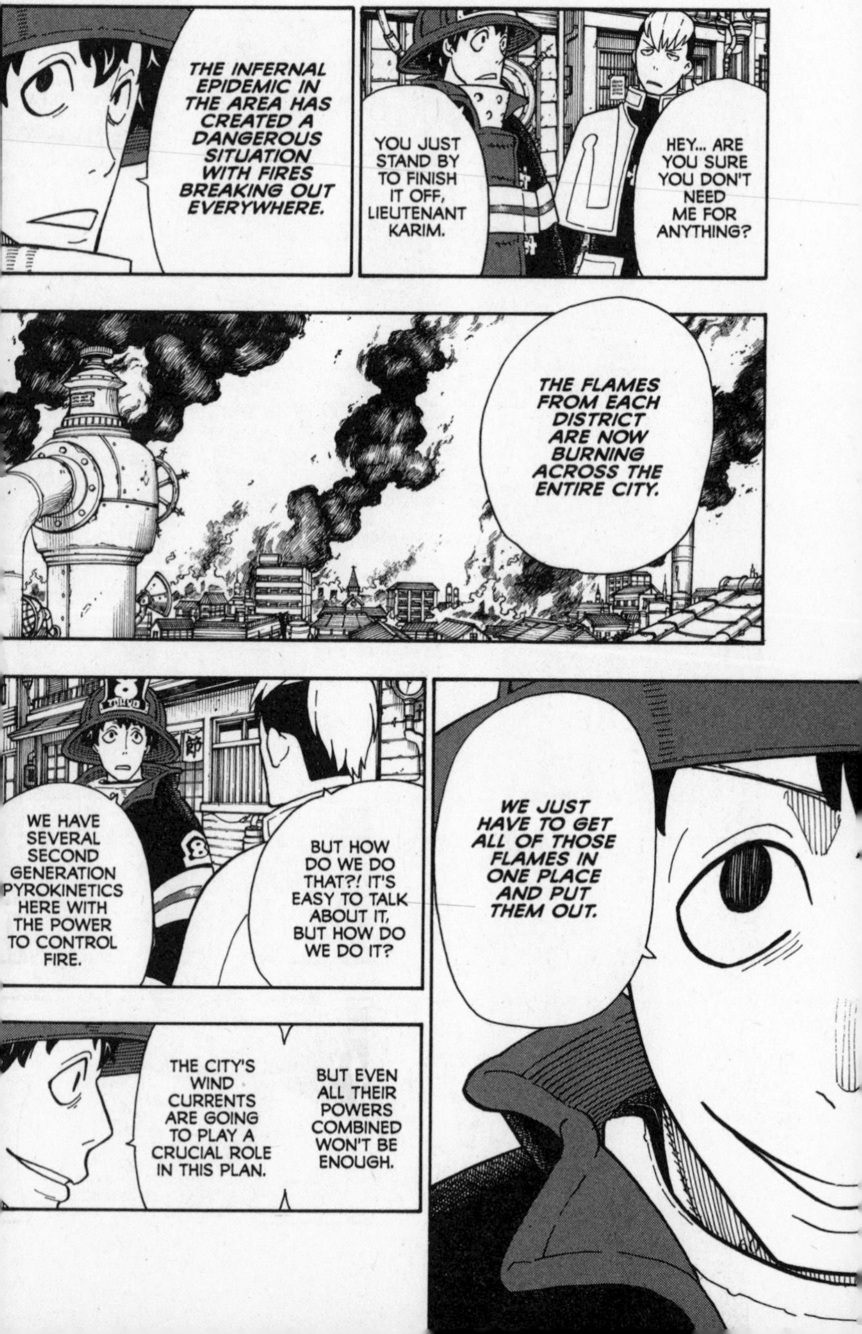
HEY... ARE YOU SURE YOU DON'T NEED ME FOR ANYTHING?
YOU JUST STAND BY TO FINISH IT OFF, LIEUTENANT KARIM.
THE INFERNAL EPIDEMIC IN THE AREA HAS CREATED A DANGEROUS SITUATION WITH FIRES BREAKING OUT EVERYWHERE.
THE FLAMES FROM EACH DISTRICT ARE NOW BURNING ACROSS THE ENTIRE CITY.
WE JUST HAVE TO GET ALL OF THOSE FLAMES IN ONE PLACE AND PUT THEM OUT.
BUT HOW DO WE DO THAT?! IT'S EASY TO TALK ABOUT IT, BUT HOW DO WE DO IT?
WE HAVE SEVERAL SECOND GENERATION PYROKINETICS HERE WITH THE POWER TO CONTROL FIRE.
BUT EVEN ALL THEIR POWERS COMBINED WON'T BE ENOUGH.
THE CITY'S WIND CURRENTS ARE GOING TO PLAY A CRUCIAL ROLE IN THIS PLAN.

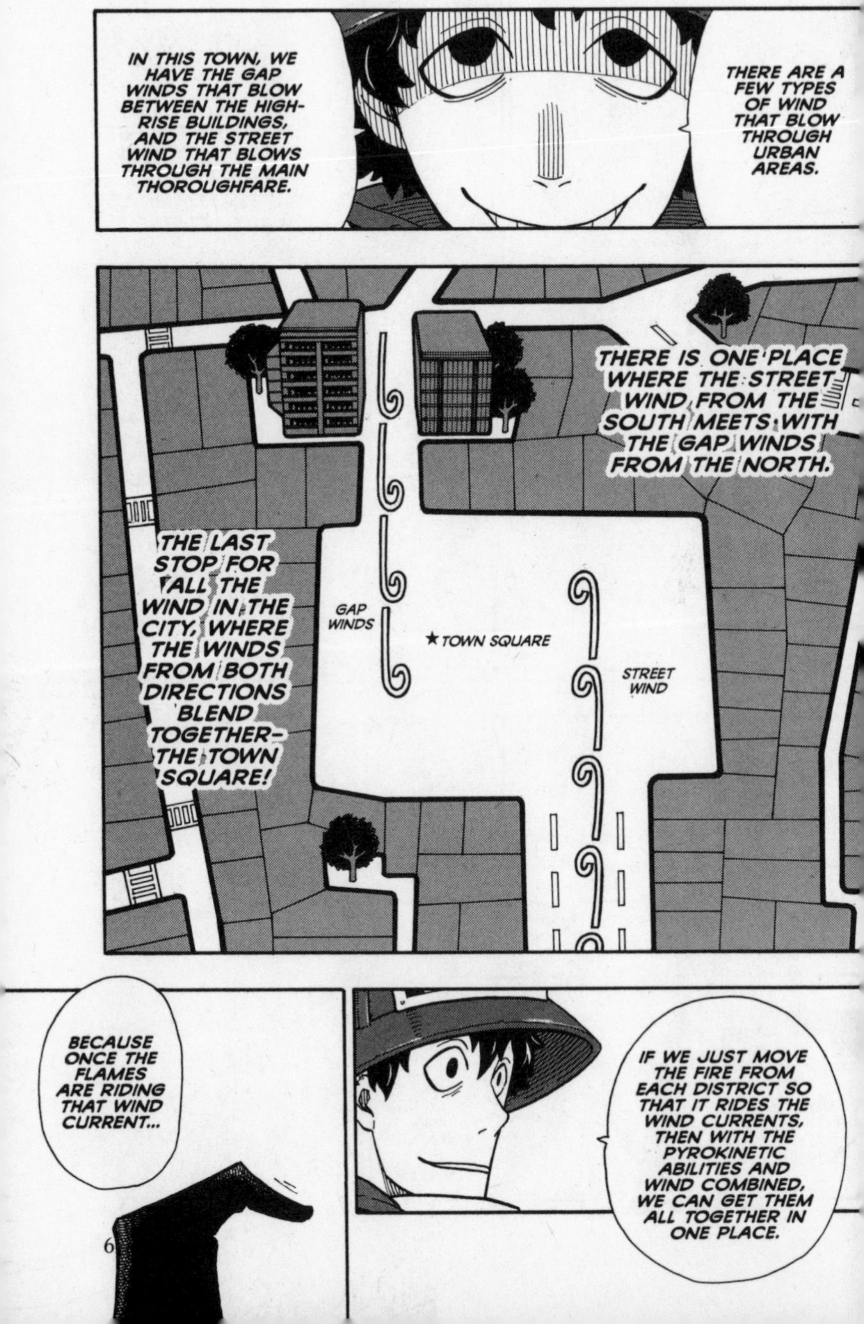
THERE ARE A FEW TYPES OF WIND THAT BLOW THROUGH URBAN AREAS.
IN THIS TOWN, WE HAVE THE GAP WINDS THAT BLOW BETWEEN THE HIGH-RISE BUILDINGS, AND THE STREET WIND THAT BLOWS THROUGH THE MAIN THOROUGHFARE.
THERE IS ONE PLACE WHERE THE STREET WIND FROM THE SOUTH MEETS WITH THE GAP WINDS FROM THE NORTH.
THE LAST STOP FOR ALL THE WIND IN THE CITY, WHERE THE WINDS FROM BOTH DIRECTIONS BLEND TOGETHER– THE TOWN SQUARE!
GAP WINDS
★TOWN SQUARE
STREET WIND
IF WE JUST MOVE THE FIRE FROM EACH DISTRICT SO THAT IT RIDES THE WIND CURRENTS, THEN WITH THE PYROKINETIC ABILITIES AND WIND COMBINED, WE CAN GET THEM ALL TOGETHER IN ONE PLACE.
BECAUSE ONCE THE FLAMES ARE RIDING THAT WIND CURRENT...

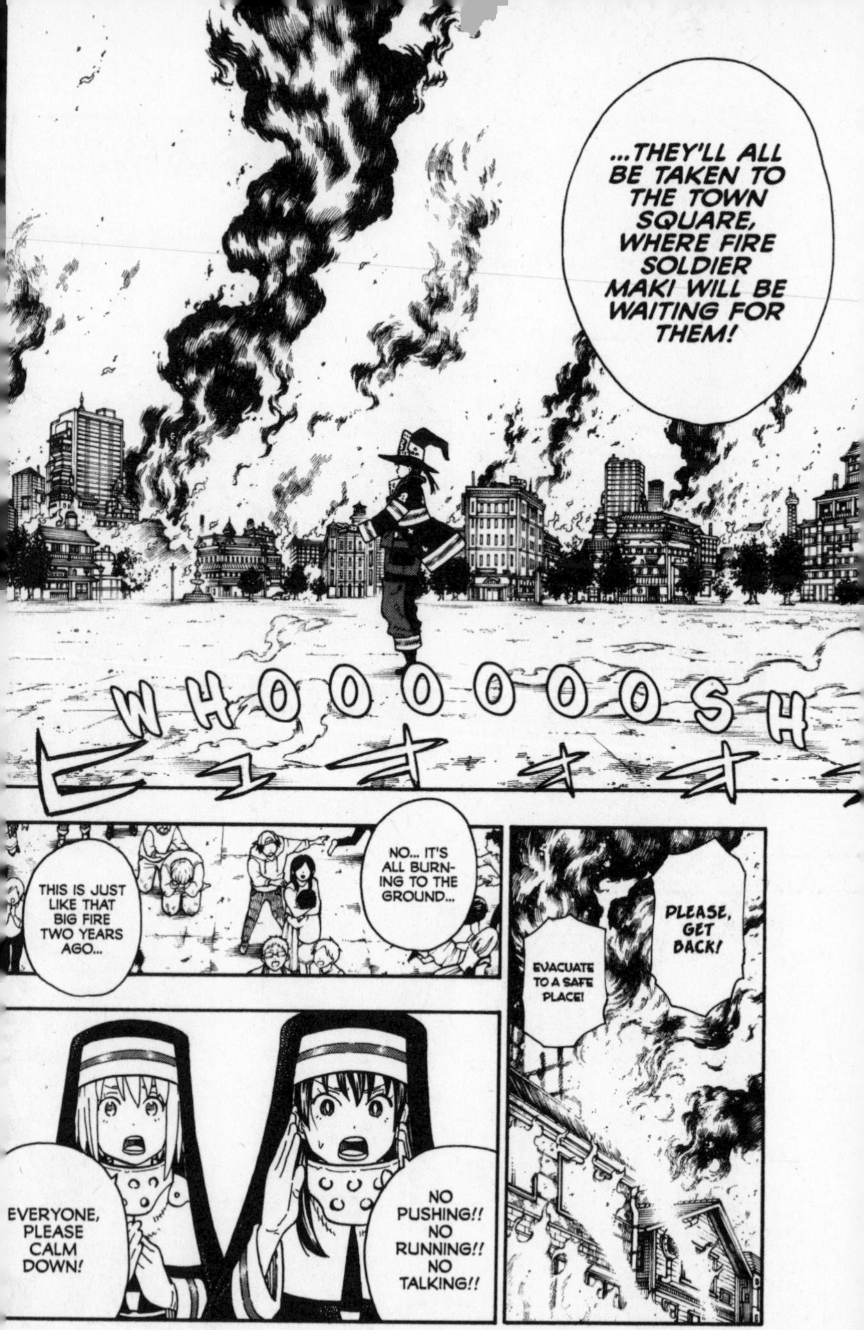
...THEY'LL ALL BE TAKEN TO THE TOWN SQUARE, WHERE FIRE SOLDIER MAKI WILL BE WAITING FOR THEM!
WHOOOOOOOSH
PLEASE, GET BACK!
EVACUATE TO A SAFE PLACE!
NO... IT'S ALL BURNING TO THE GROUND...
THIS IS JUST LIKE THAT BIG FIRE TWO YEARS AGO...
NO PUSHING!! NO RUNNING!! NO TALKING!!
EVERYONE, PLEASE CALM DOWN!

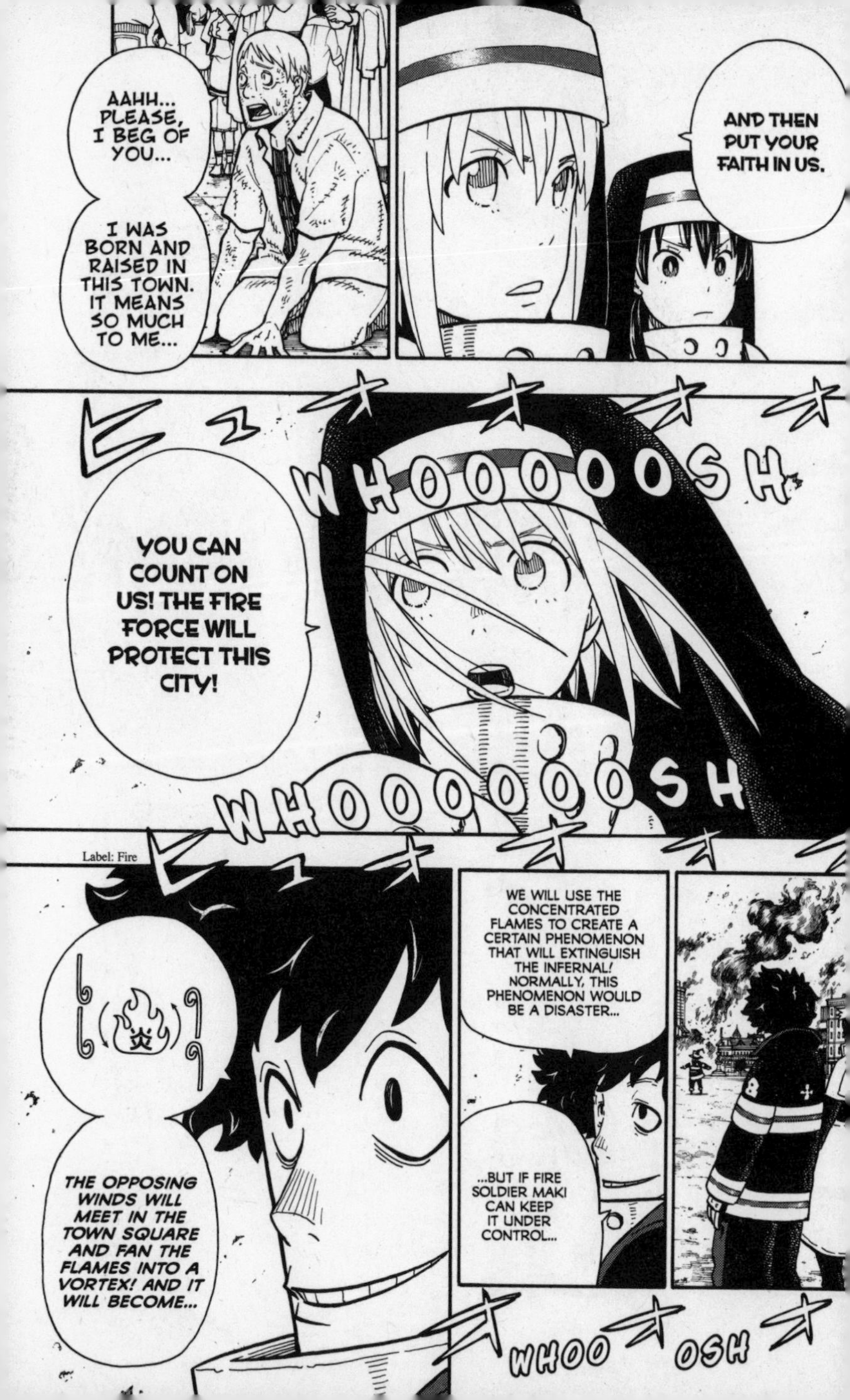
AND THEN PUT YOUR FAITH IN US.
AAHH... PLEASE, I BEG OF YOU...
I WAS BORN AND RAISED IN THIS TOWN. IT MEANS SO MUCH TO ME...
WHOOOOOSH
YOU CAN COUNT ON US! THE FIRE FORCE WILL PROTECT THIS CITY!
WHOOOOOOOSH
Label: Fire
WE WILL USE THE CONCENTRATED FLAMES TO CREATE A CERTAIN PHENOMENON THAT WILL EXTINGUISH THE INFERNAL! NORMALLY, THIS PHENOMENON WOULD BE A DISASTER...
...BUT IF FIRE SOLDIER MAKI CAN KEEP IT UNDER CONTROL...
炎
THE OPPOSING WINDS WILL MEET IN THE TOWN SQUARE AND FAN THE FLAMES INTO A VORTEX! AND IT WILL BECOME...
WHOO OSH

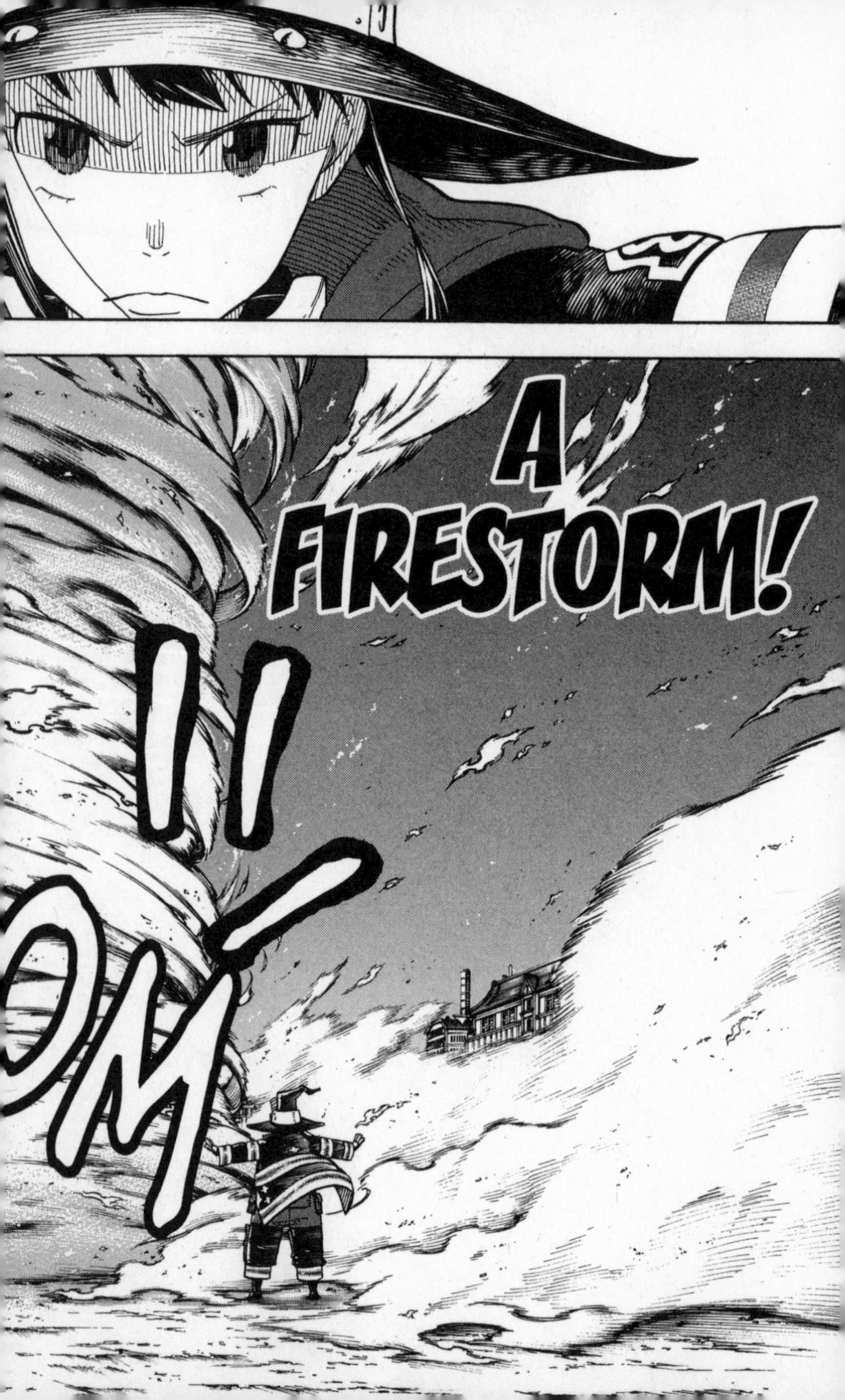
A FIRESTORM!

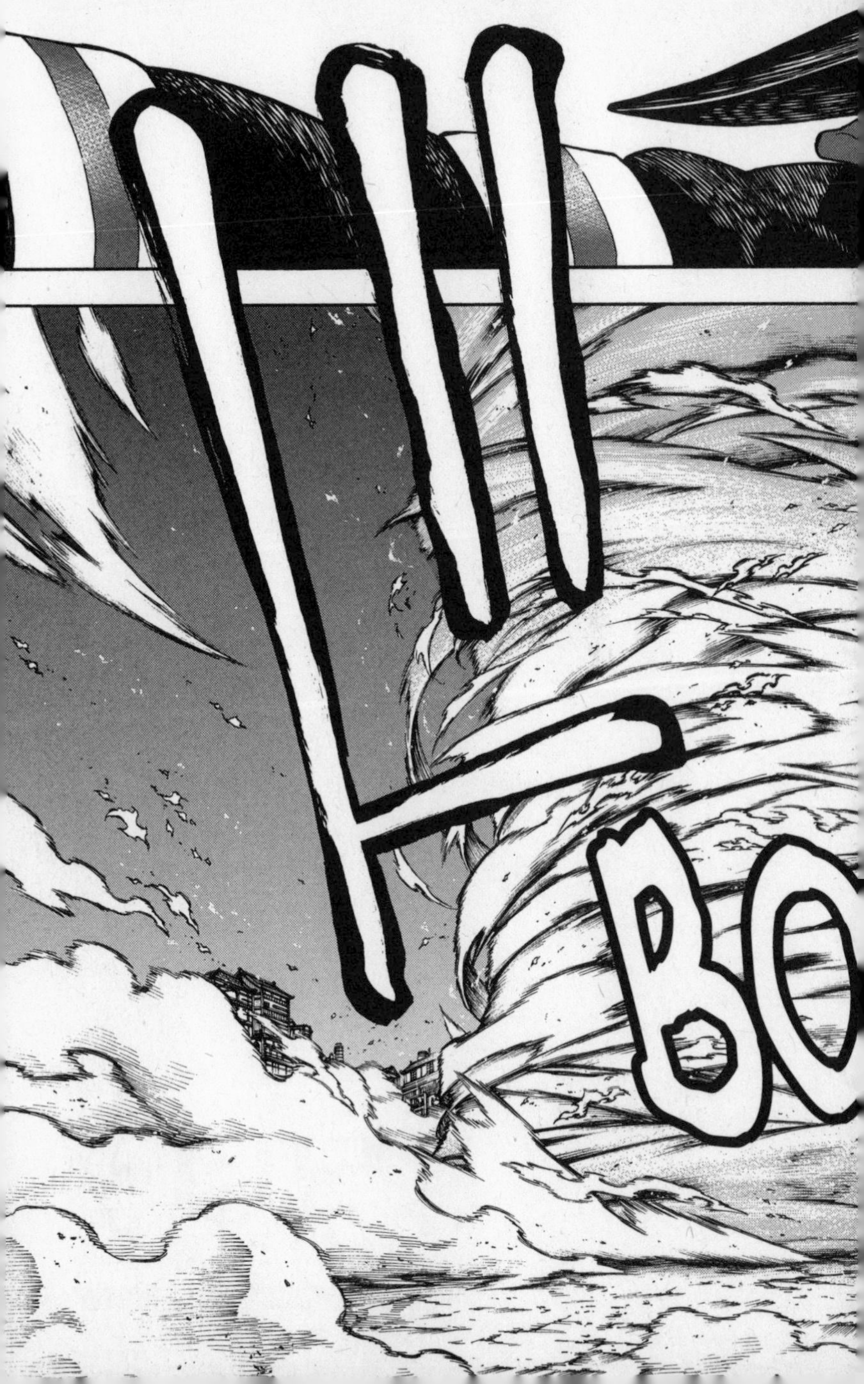
BO

FIRE FORCE

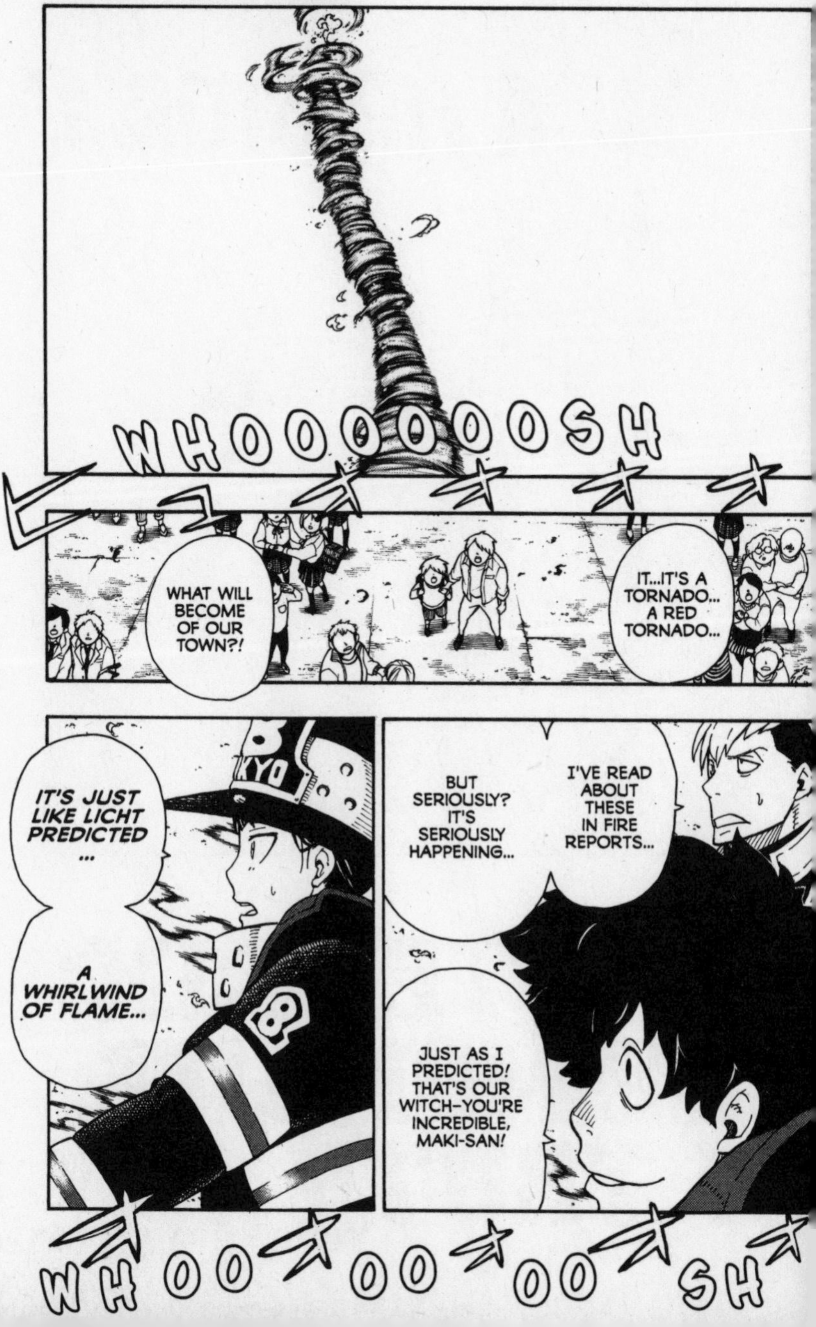
WHOOOOOOSH
IT...IT'S A TORNADO... A RED TORNADO...
WHAT WILL BECOME OF OUR TOWN?!
I'VE READ ABOUT THESE IN FIRE REPORTS...
BUT SERIOUSLY? IT'S SERIOUSLY HAPPENING...
JUST AS I PREDICTED! THAT'S OUR WITCH—YOU'RE INCREDIBLE, MAKI-SAN!
IT'S JUST LIKE LICHT PREDICTED...
A WHIRLWIND OF FLAME...
WHOOOOOOSH

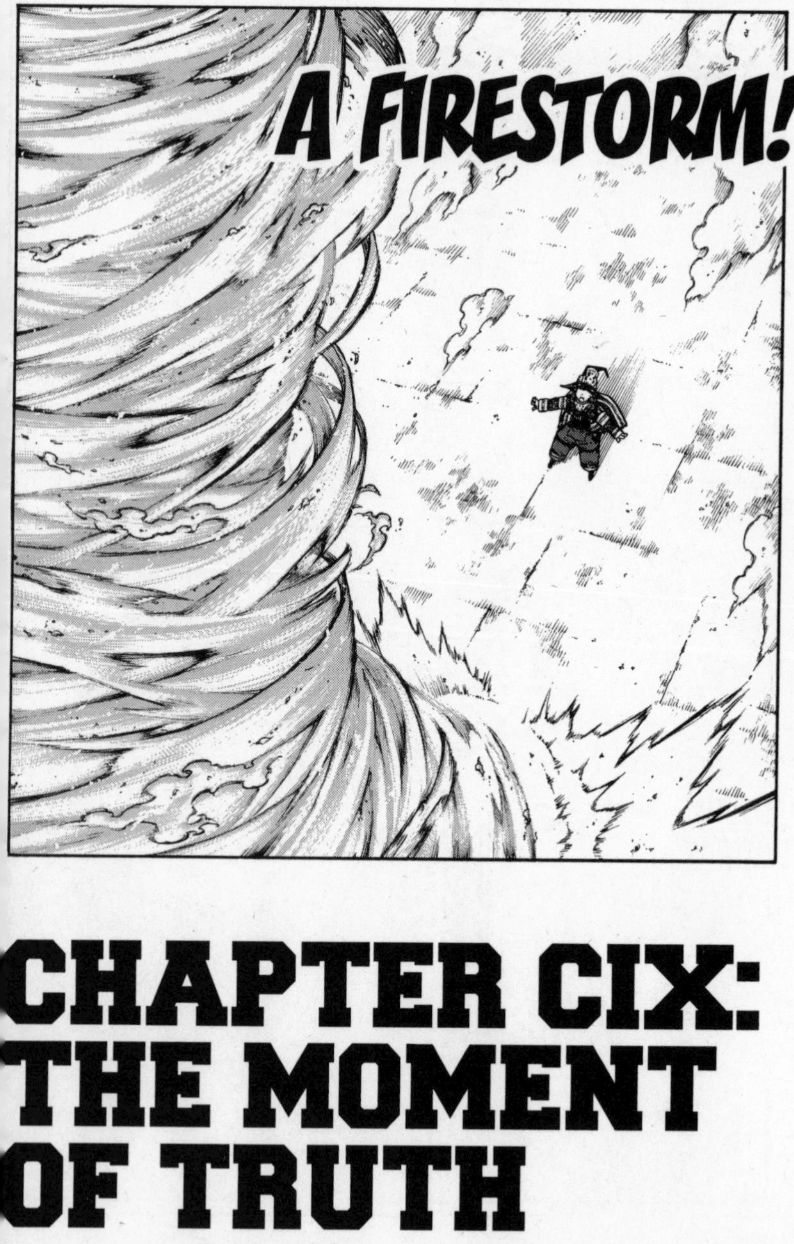
A FIRESTORM!

CHAPTER CIX: THE MOMENT OF TRUTH

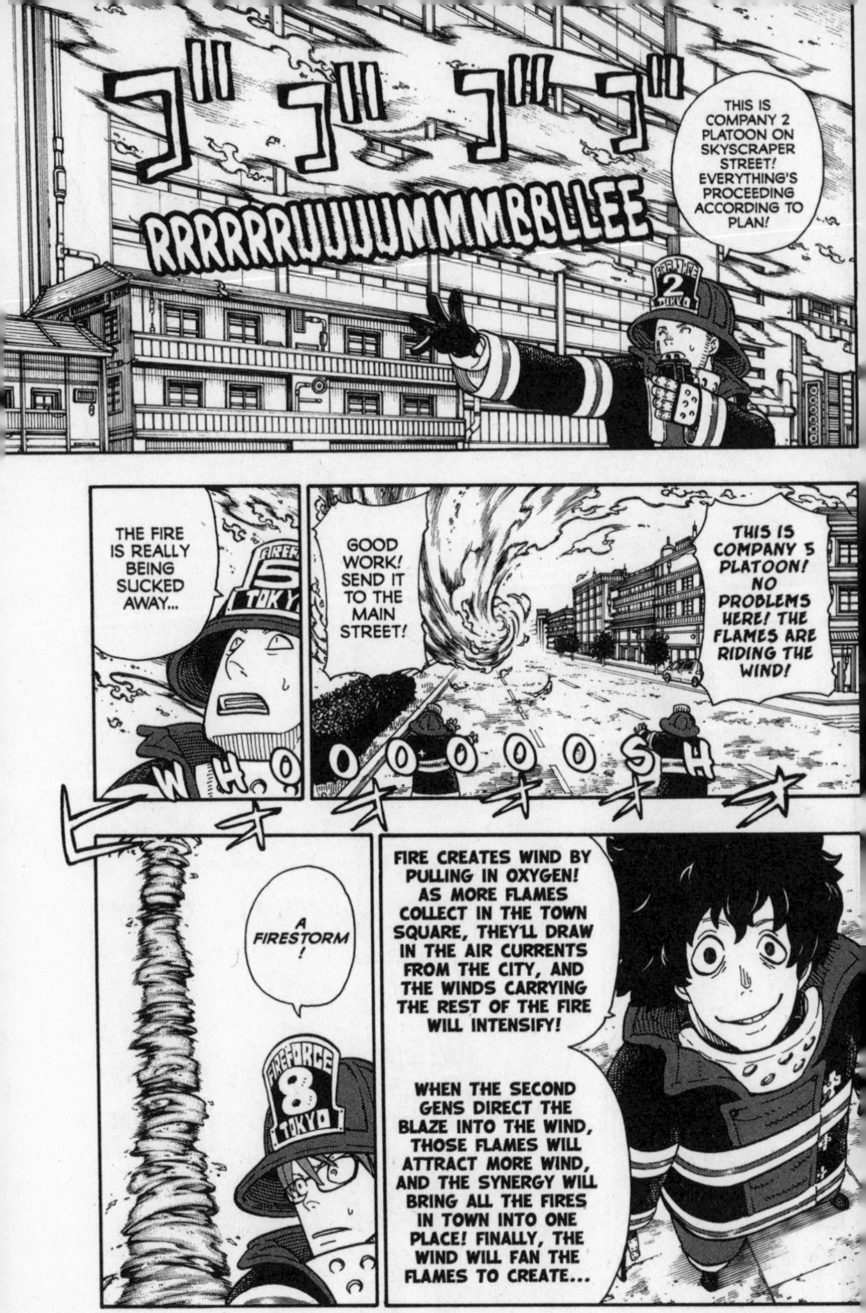

ゴゴゴゴ
RRRRRUUUUMMMBBLLEE
THIS IS COMPANY 2 PLATOON ON SKYSCRAPER STREET! EVERYTHING'S PROCEEDING ACCORDING TO PLAN!
THIS IS COMPANY 5 PLATOON! NO PROBLEMS HERE! THE FLAMES ARE RIDING THE WIND!
GOOD WORK! SEND IT TO THE MAIN STREET!
WHOOOOOSH
THE FIRE IS REALLY BEING SUCKED AWAY...
FIRE CREATES WIND BY PULLING IN OXYGEN! AS MORE FLAMES COLLECT IN THE TOWN SQUARE, THEY'LL DRAW IN THE AIR CURRENTS FROM THE CITY, AND THE WINDS CARRYING THE REST OF THE FIRE WILL INTENSIFY!
WHEN THE SECOND GENS DIRECT THE BLAZE INTO THE WIND, THOSE FLAMES WILL ATTRACT MORE WIND, AND THE SYNERGY WILL BRING ALL THE FIRES IN TOWN INTO ONE PLACE! FINALLY, THE WIND WILL FAN THE FLAMES TO CREATE...
A FIRESTORM!

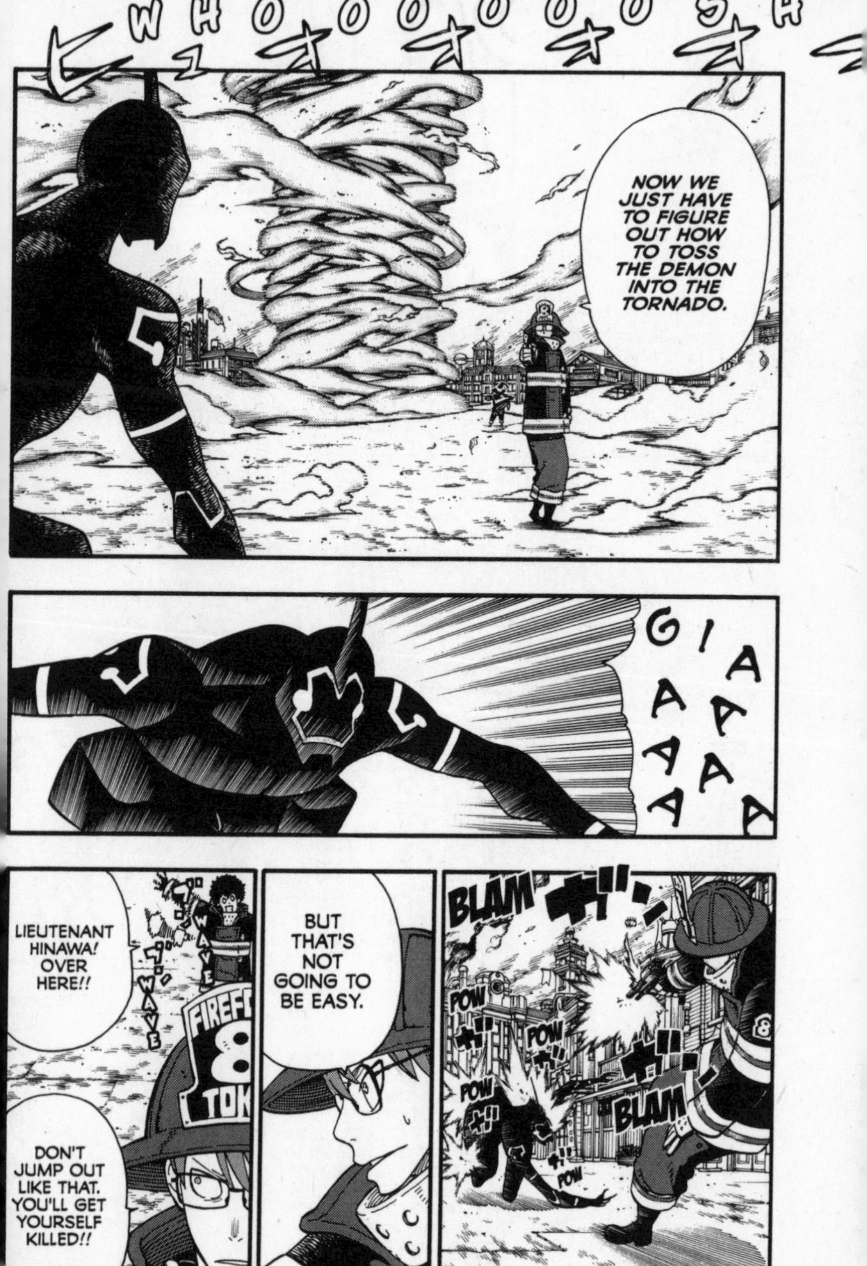
WHOOOOOOSH
NOW WE JUST HAVE TO FIGURE OUT HOW TO TOSS THE DEMON INTO THE TORNADO.
GIAAAAAAA
BLAM
POW
POW
POW
BLAM
POW
BUT THAT'S NOT GOING TO BE EASY.
LIEUTENANT HINAWA! OVER HERE!!
WAVE
WAVE
FIREF
8
TOK
DON'T JUMP OUT LIKE THAT. YOU'LL GET YOURSELF KILLED!!

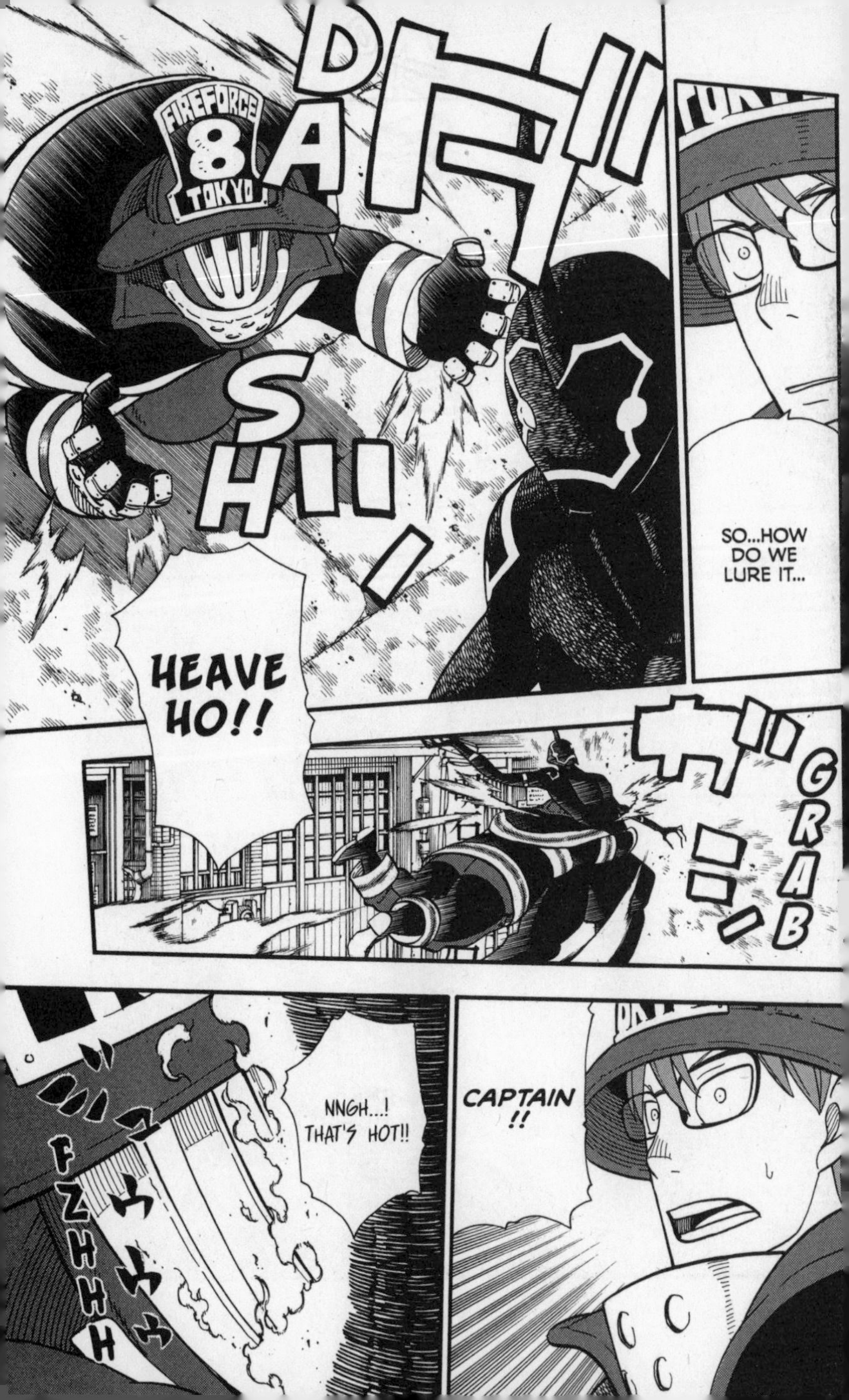
SO...HOW DO WE LURE IT...
FIREFORCE 8 TOKYO
DASH
HEAVE HO!!
GRAB
CAPTAIN !!
NNGH...! THAT'S HOT!!
FZHHHH

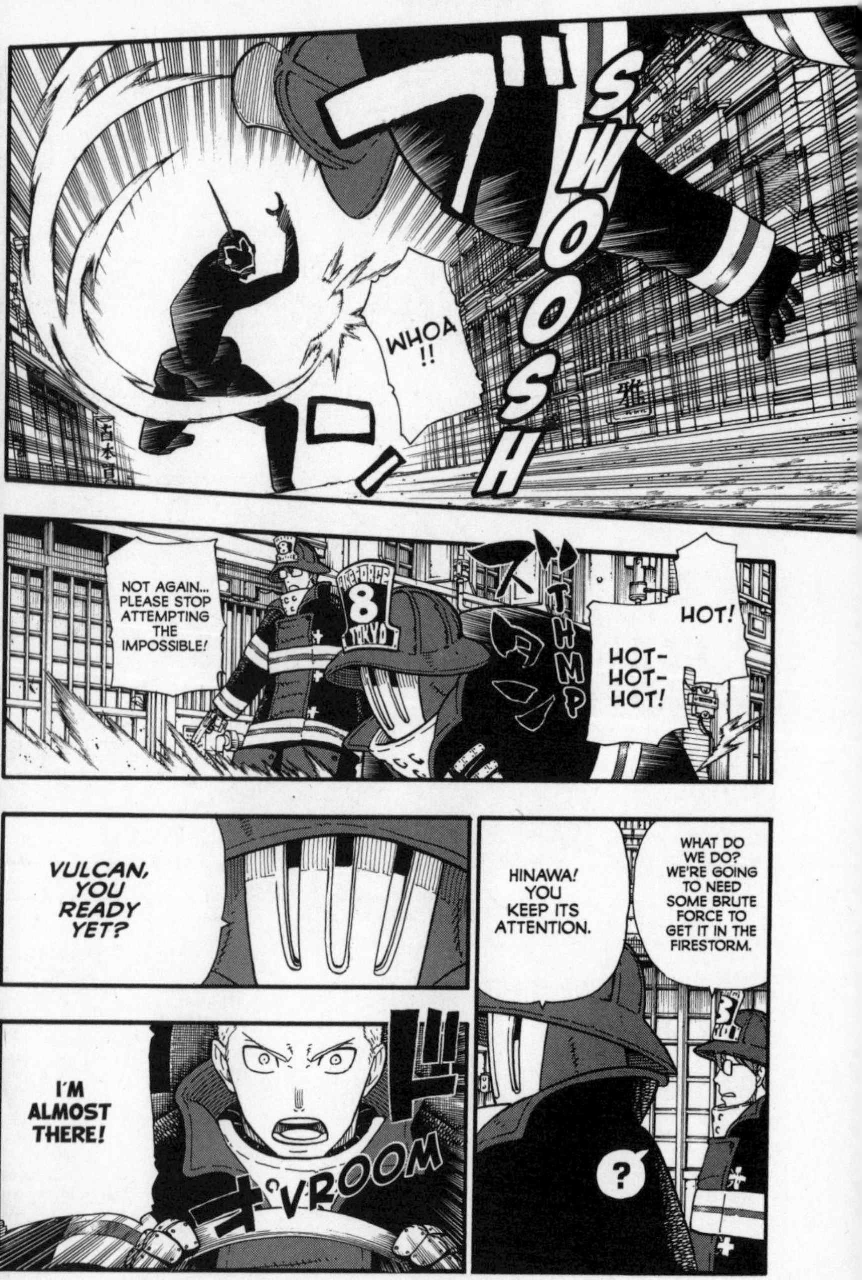
SWOOSH
WHOA!!
HOT!
HOT-HOT-HOT!
THMP
NOT AGAIN... PLEASE STOP ATTEMPTING THE IMPOSSIBLE!
WHAT DO WE DO? WE'RE GOING TO NEED SOME BRUTE FORCE TO GET IT IN THE FIRESTORM.
HINAWA! YOU KEEP ITS ATTENTION.
?
VULCAN, YOU READY YET?
I'M ALMOST THERE!
VROOM

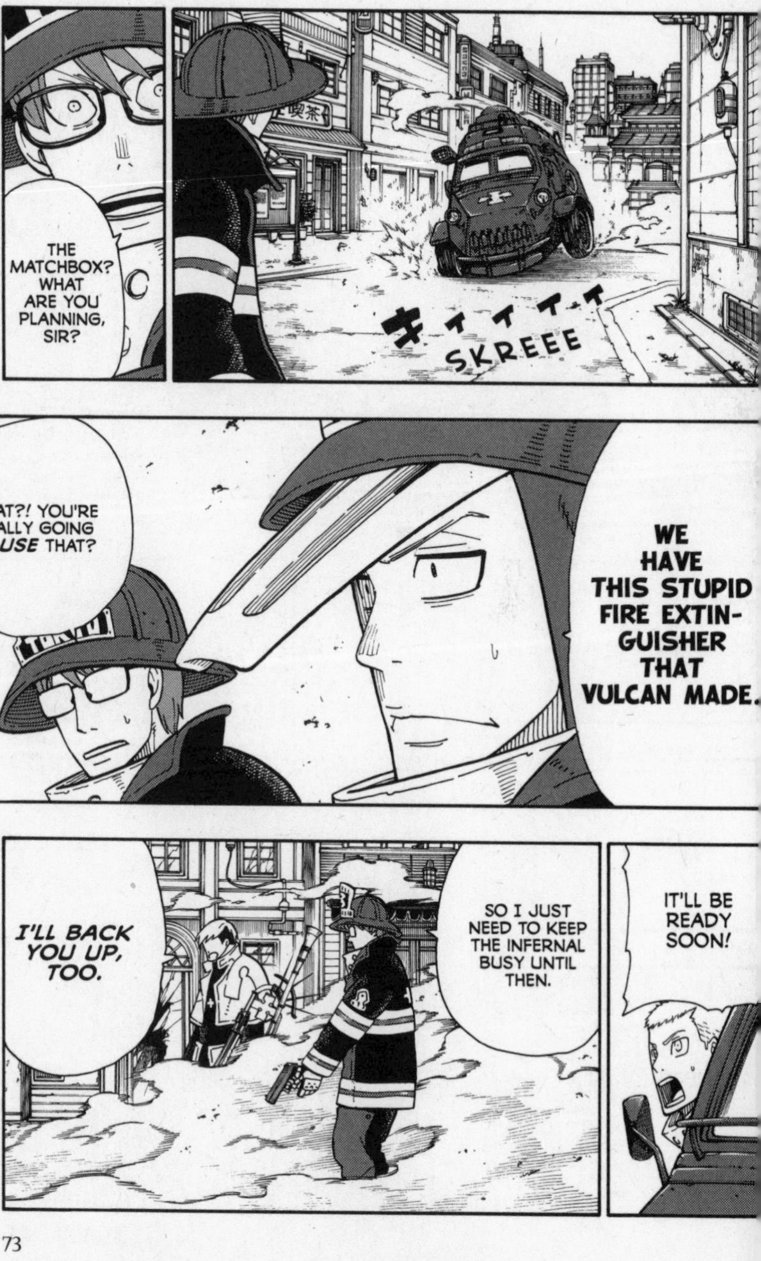
キィィィ
SKREEE
THE MATCHBOX? WHAT ARE YOU PLANNING, SIR?
WE HAVE THIS STUPID FIRE EXTIN-GUISHER THAT VULCAN MADE.
WHAT?! YOU'RE REALLY GOING TO *USE* THAT?
IT'LL BE READY SOON!
SO I JUST NEED TO KEEP THE INFERNAL BUSY UNTIL THEN.
I'LL BACK YOU UP, TOO.

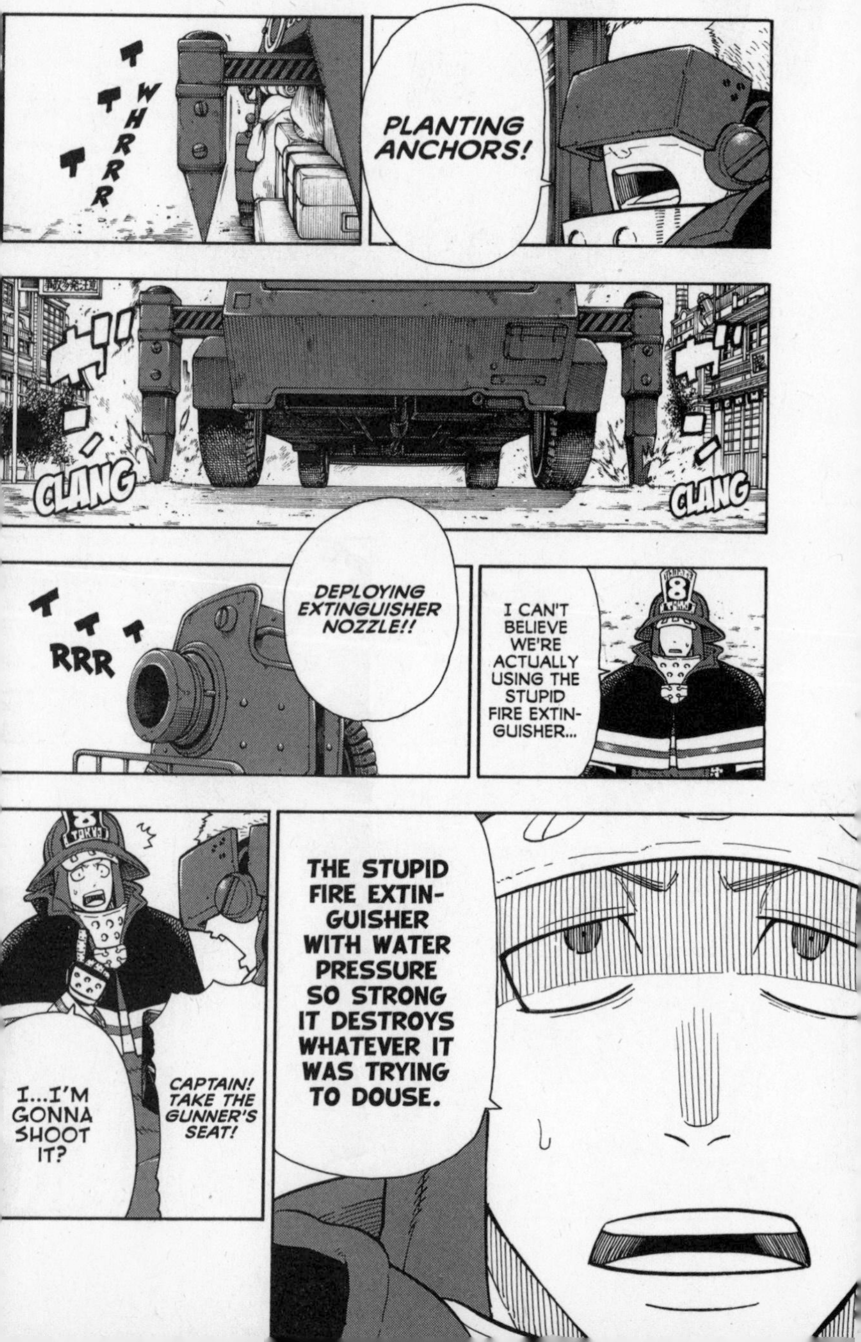
PLANTING ANCHORS!
T T T
WHRRR
CLANG
CLANG
I CAN'T BELIEVE WE'RE ACTUALLY USING THE STUPID FIRE EXTIN- GUISHER...
DEPLOYING EXTINGUISHER NOZZLE!!
T T T
RRR
THE STUPID FIRE EXTIN- GUISHER WITH WATER PRESSURE SO STRONG IT DESTROYS WHATEVER IT WAS TRYING TO DOUSE.
CAPTAIN! TAKE THE GUNNER'S SEAT!
I...I'M GONNA SHOOT IT?

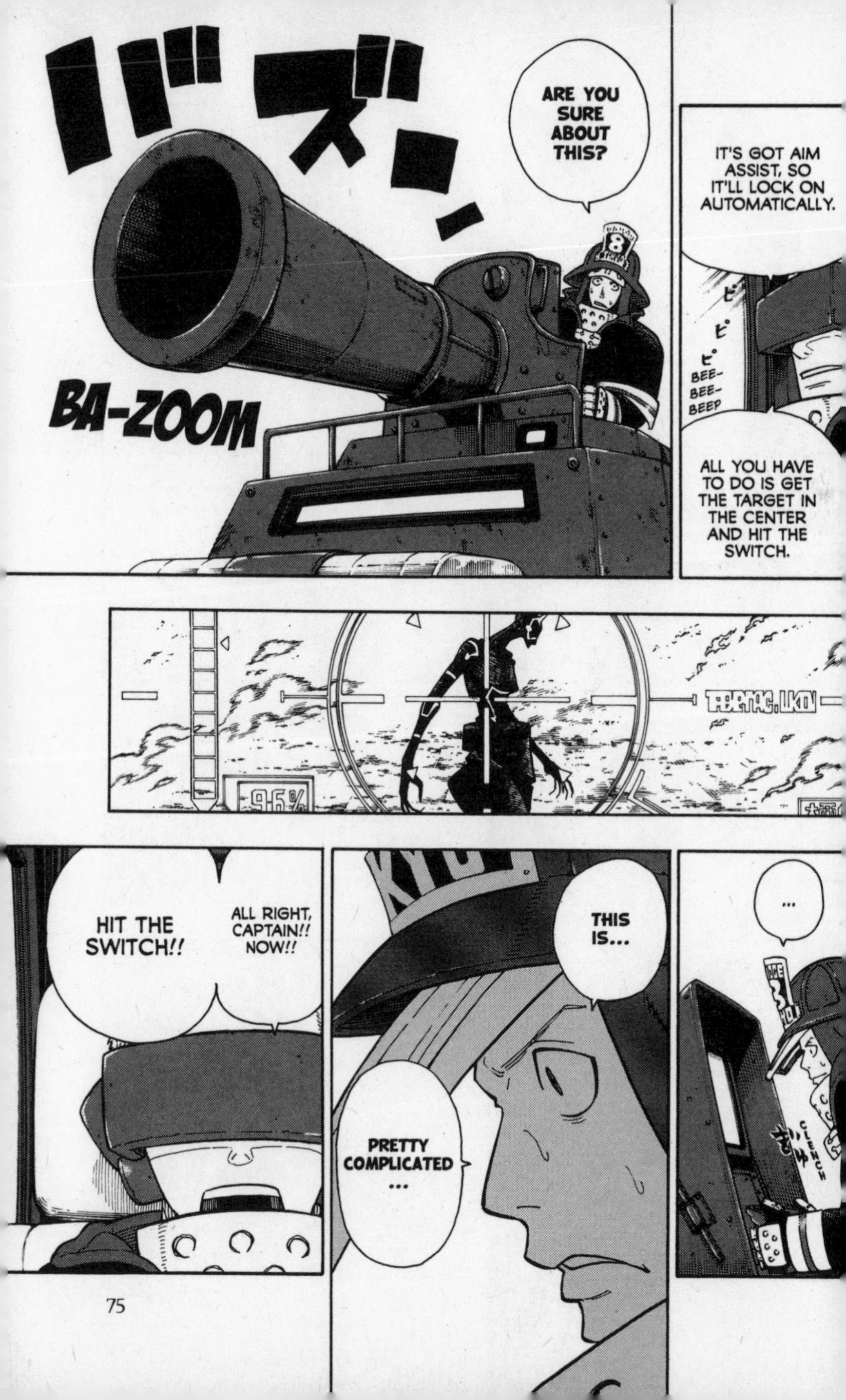
IT'S GOT AIM ASSIST, SO IT'LL LOCK ON AUTOMATICALLY.
BEE-BEE-BEEP
ALL YOU HAVE TO DO IS GET THE TARGET IN THE CENTER AND HIT THE SWITCH.
BA-ZOOM
ARE YOU SURE ABOUT THIS?
...
CLENCH
THIS IS...
PRETTY COMPLICATED ...
ALL RIGHT, CAPTAIN!! NOW!!
HIT THE SWITCH!!

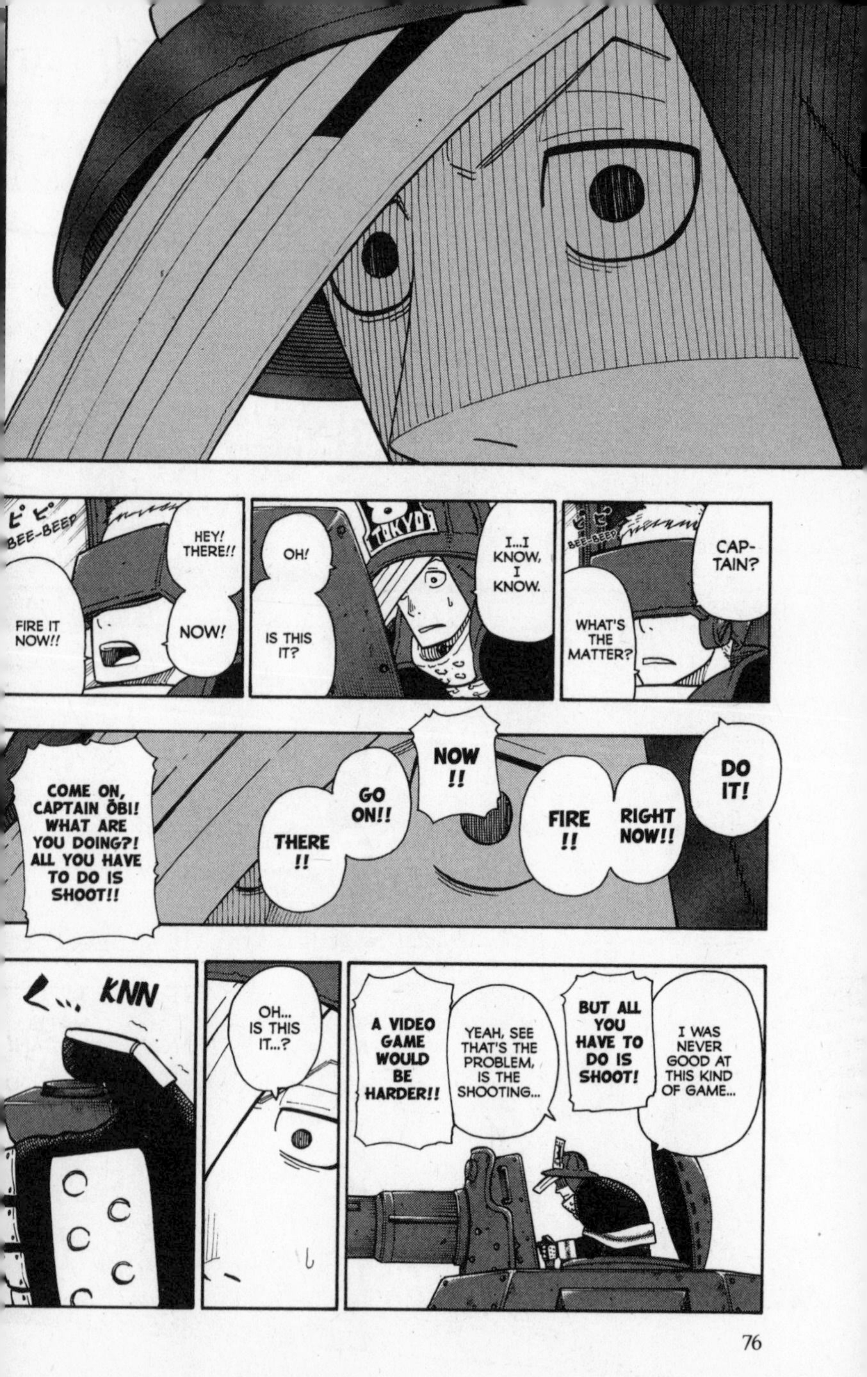
CAP-TAIN?
ピピ BEE-BEEP
WHAT'S THE MATTER?
I...I KNOW, I KNOW.
OH!
IS THIS IT?
HEY! THERE!!
ピピ BEE-BEEP
NOW!
FIRE IT NOW!!
DO IT!
RIGHT NOW!!
FIRE !!
NOW !!
GO ON!!
THERE !!
COME ON, CAPTAIN ŌBI! WHAT ARE YOU DOING?! ALL YOU HAVE TO DO IS SHOOT!!
I WAS NEVER GOOD AT THIS KIND OF GAME...
BUT ALL YOU HAVE TO DO IS SHOOT!
YEAH, SEE THAT'S THE PROBLEM, IS THE SHOOTING...
A VIDEO GAME WOULD BE HARDER!!
OH... IS THIS IT...?
く... KNN

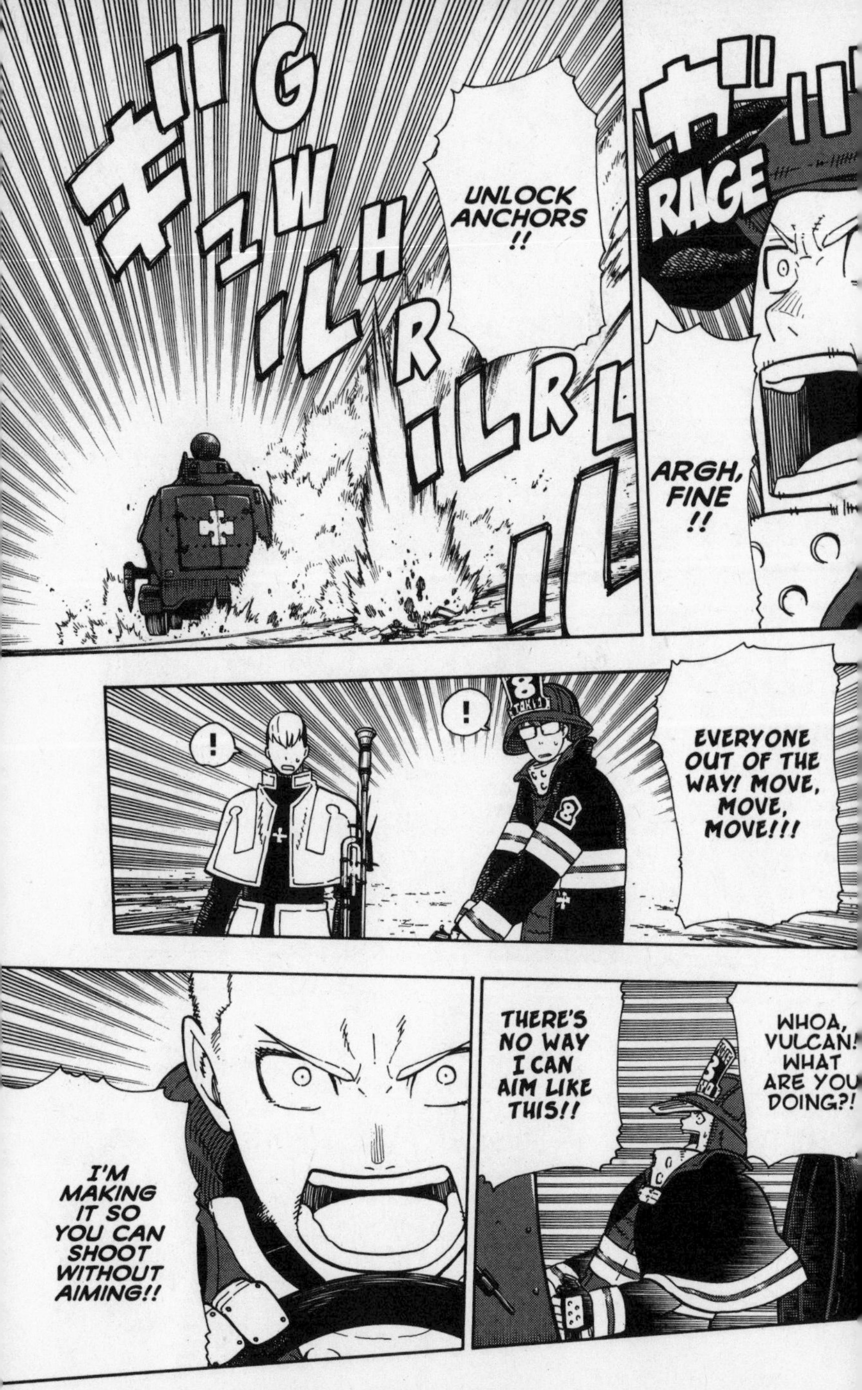
ガ"
RAGE
ARGH, FINE!!
UNLOCK ANCHORS!!
ギュ
GWHILRILRL
EVERYONE OUT OF THE WAY! MOVE, MOVE, MOVE!!!
!
!
WHOA, VULCAN! WHAT ARE YOU DOING?!
THERE'S NO WAY I CAN AIM LIKE THIS!!
I'M MAKING IT SO YOU CAN SHOOT WITHOUT AIMING!!

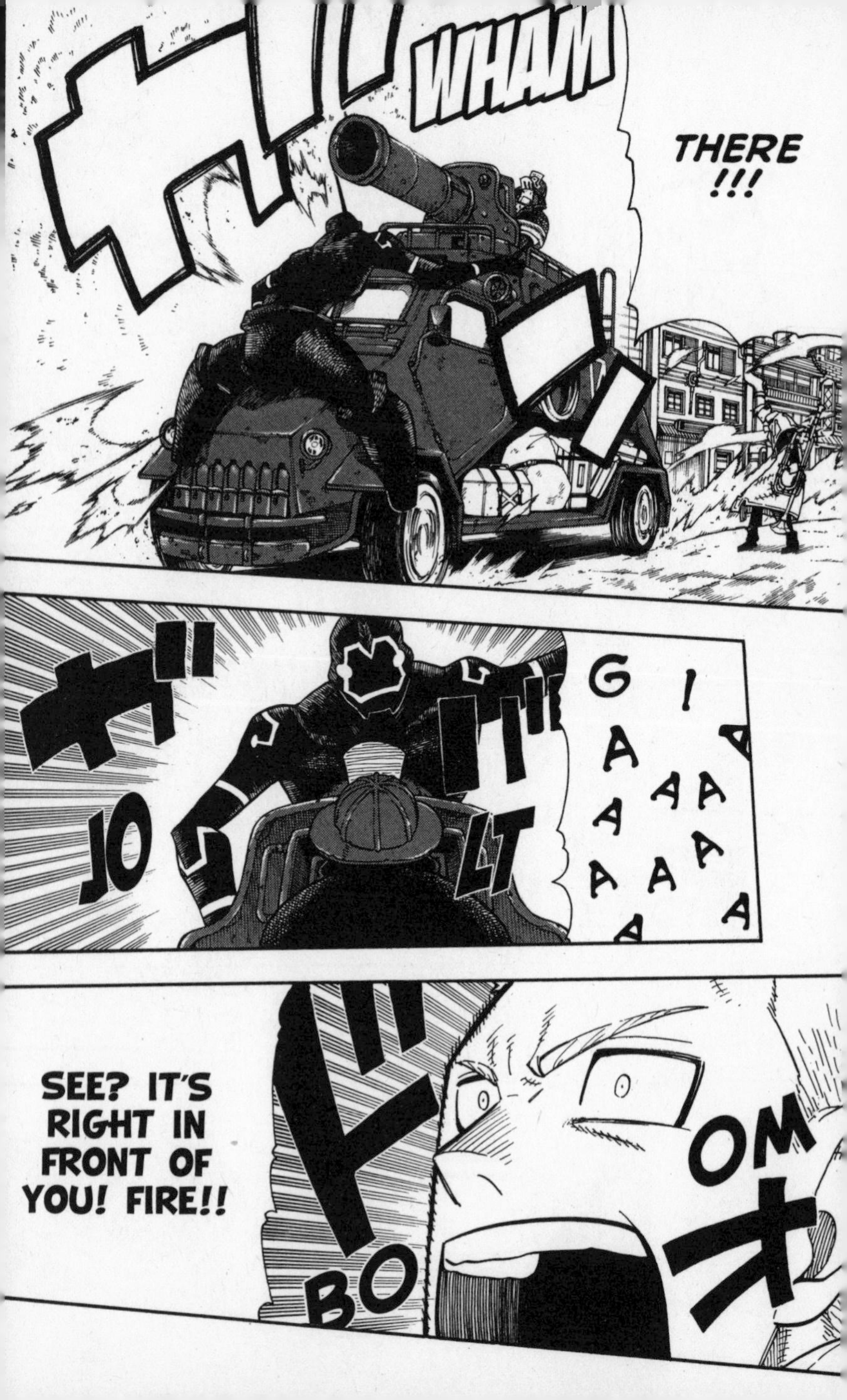
WHAM
THERE!!!
GIAAAAAAAAAAA
JOLT
BOOM
SEE? IT'S RIGHT IN FRONT OF YOU! FIRE!!

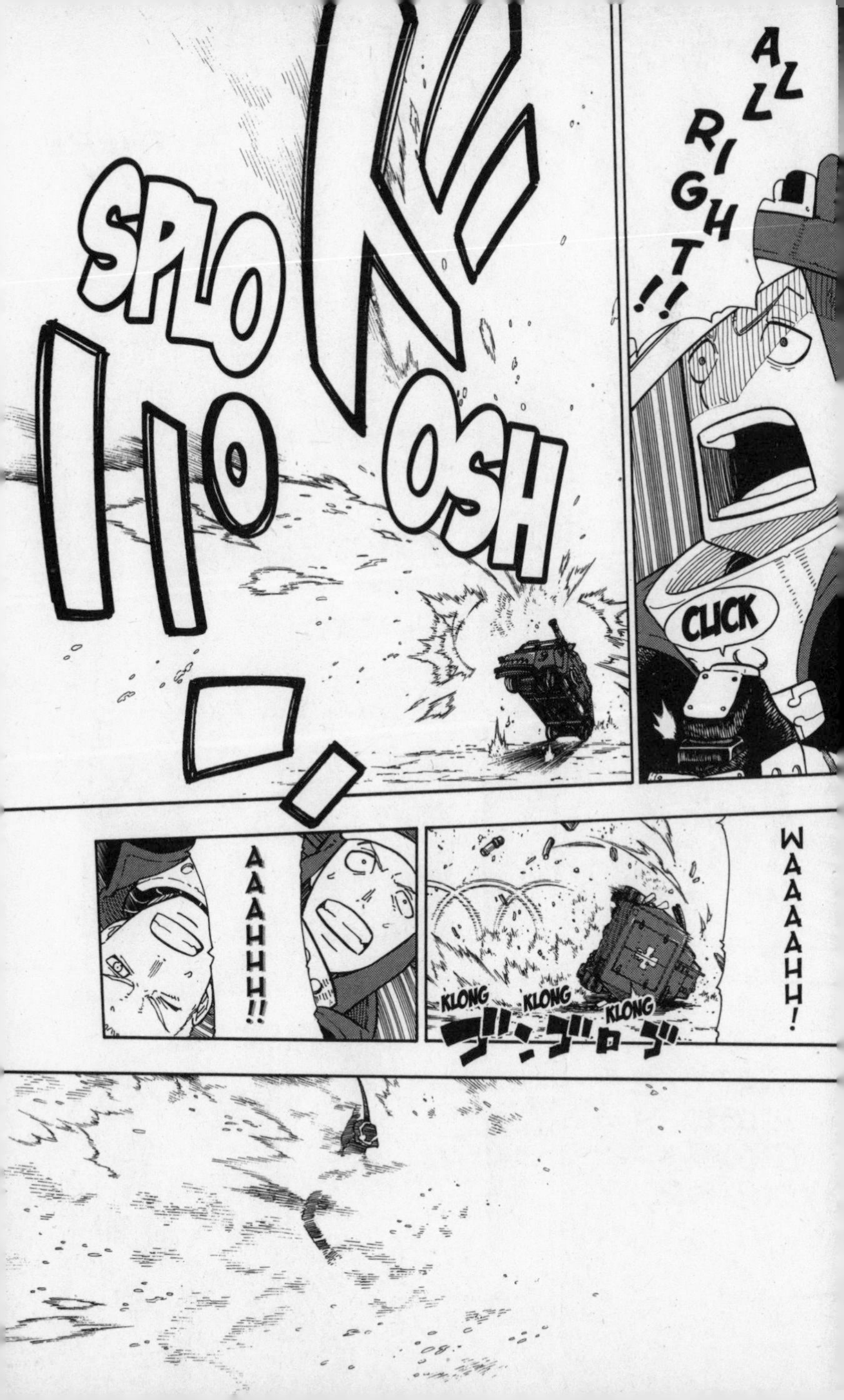

ALL RIGHT!!
CLICK
SPLOOSH!!
WAAAAAHH!
KLONG
KLONG
KLONG
AAAHHH!!

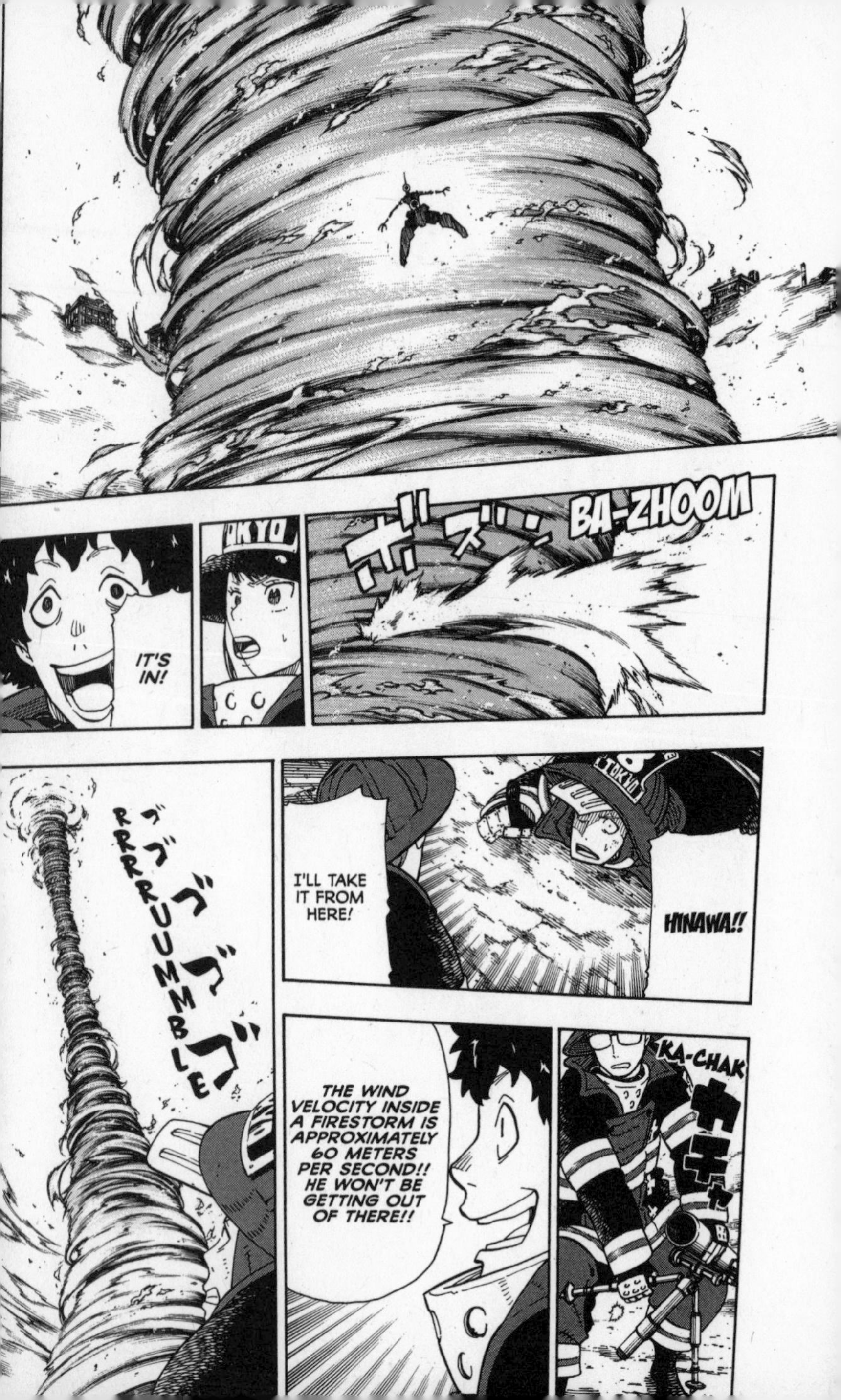
BA-ZHOOM
IT'S IN!
HINAWA!!
I'LL TAKE IT FROM HERE!
KA-CHAK
THE WIND VELOCITY INSIDE A FIRESTORM IS APPROXIMATELY 60 METERS PER SECOND!! HE WON'T BE GETTING OUT OF THERE!!
ゴゴゴゴ
RRRUMBLE

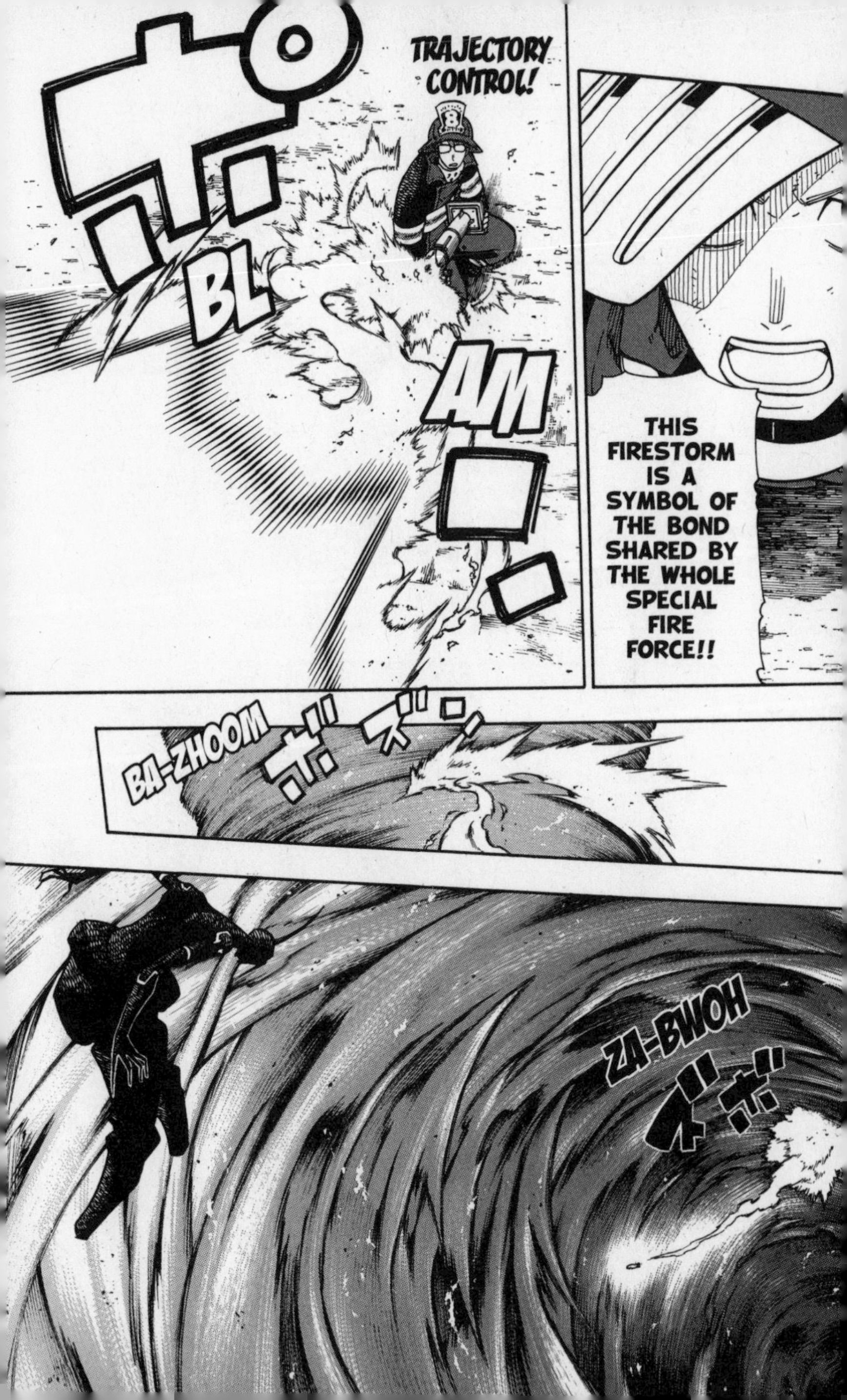
THIS FIRESTORM IS A SYMBOL OF THE BOND SHARED BY THE WHOLE SPECIAL FIRE FORCE!!
TRAJECTORY CONTROL!
BLAM
BA-ZHOOM
ZA-BWOH

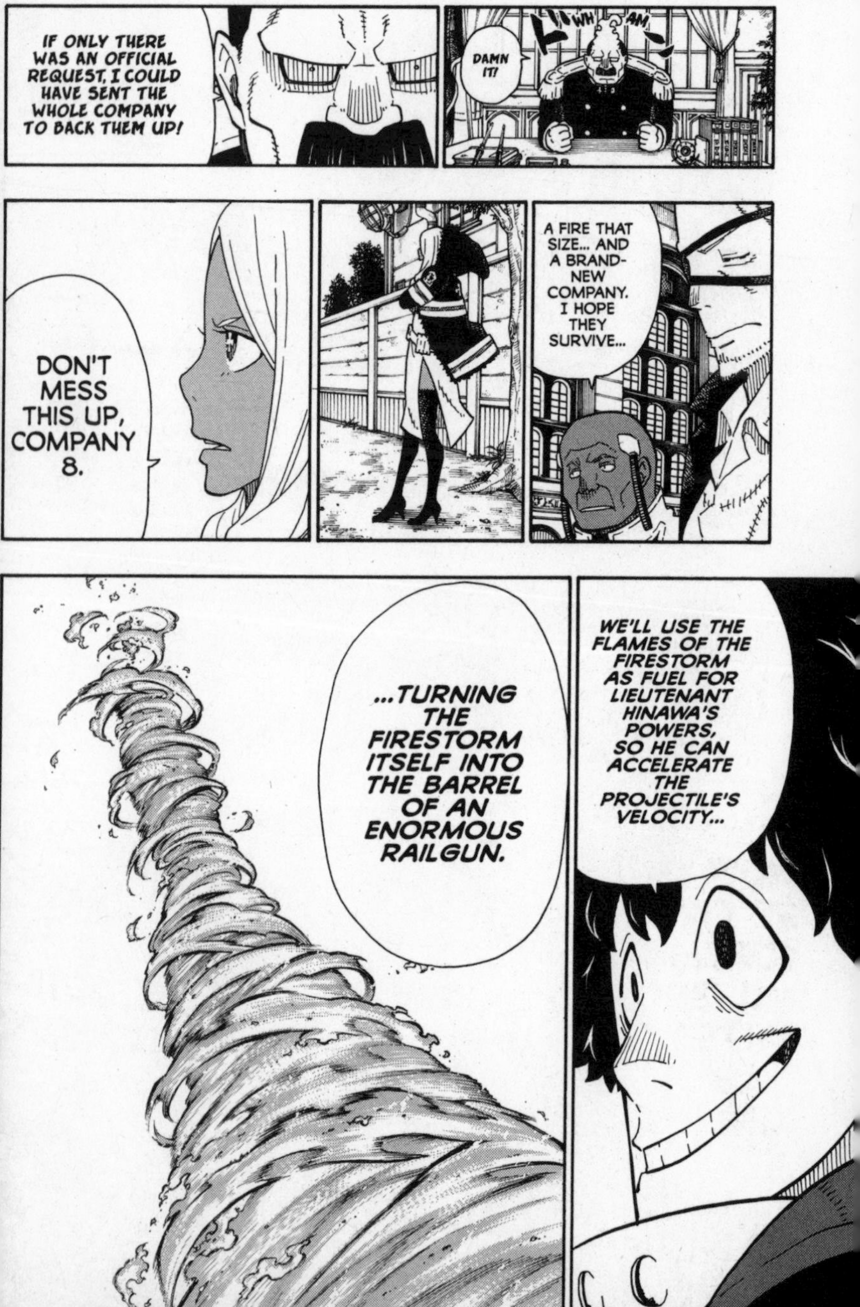
WHAM
DAMN IT!
IF ONLY THERE WAS AN OFFICIAL REQUEST, I COULD HAVE SENT THE WHOLE COMPANY TO BACK THEM UP!
A FIRE THAT SIZE... AND A BRAND-NEW COMPANY. I HOPE THEY SURVIVE...
DON'T MESS THIS UP, COMPANY 8.
WE'LL USE THE FLAMES OF THE FIRESTORM AS FUEL FOR LIEUTENANT HINAWA'S POWERS, SO HE CAN ACCELERATE THE PROJECTILE'S VELOCITY...
...TURNING THE FIRESTORM ITSELF INTO THE BARREL OF AN ENORMOUS RAILGUN.

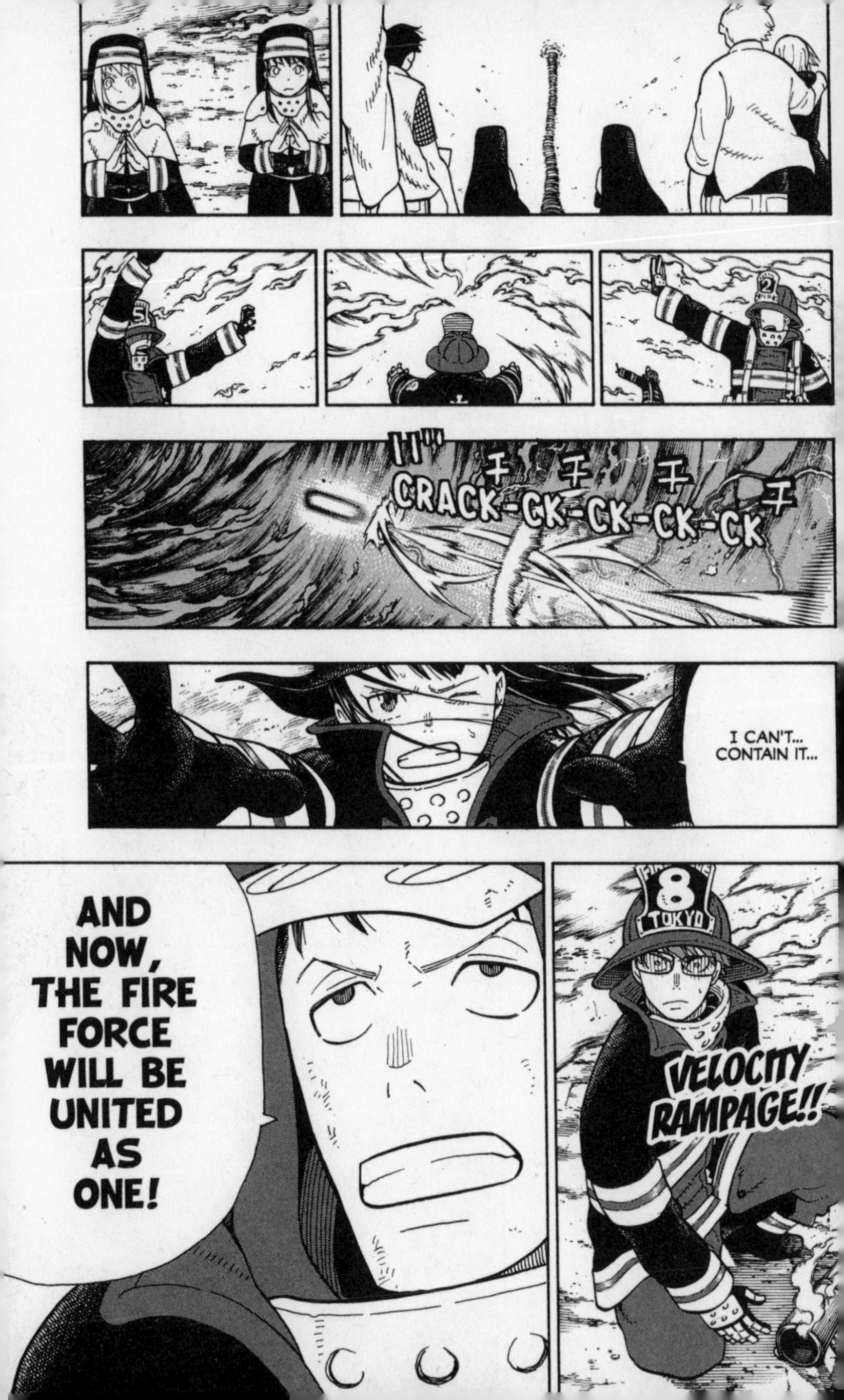
CRACK-CK-CK-CK-CK
I CAN'T... CONTAIN IT...
VELOCITY RAMPAGE!!
AND NOW, THE FIRE FORCE WILL BE UNITED AS ONE!

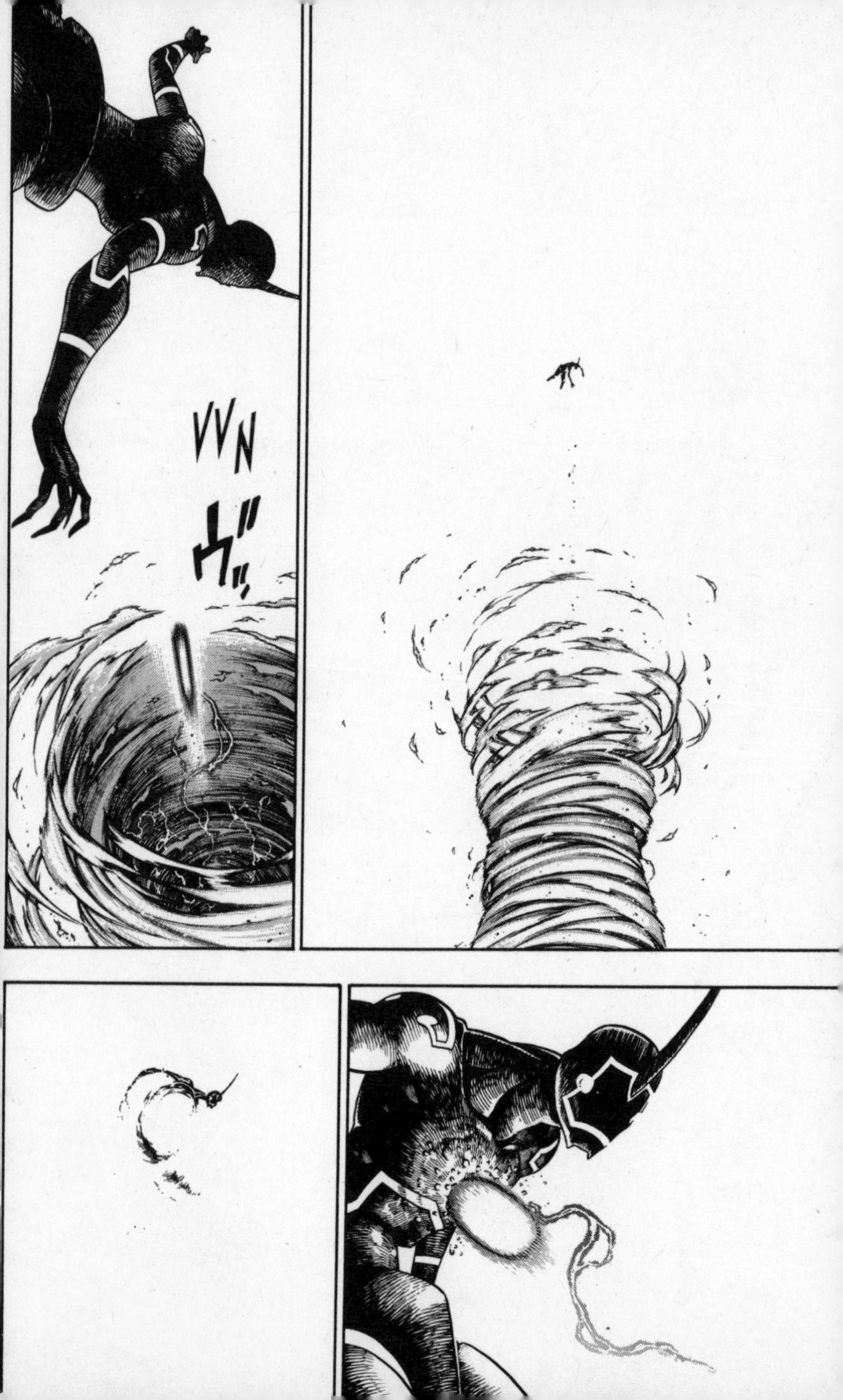
VVN
ヴ

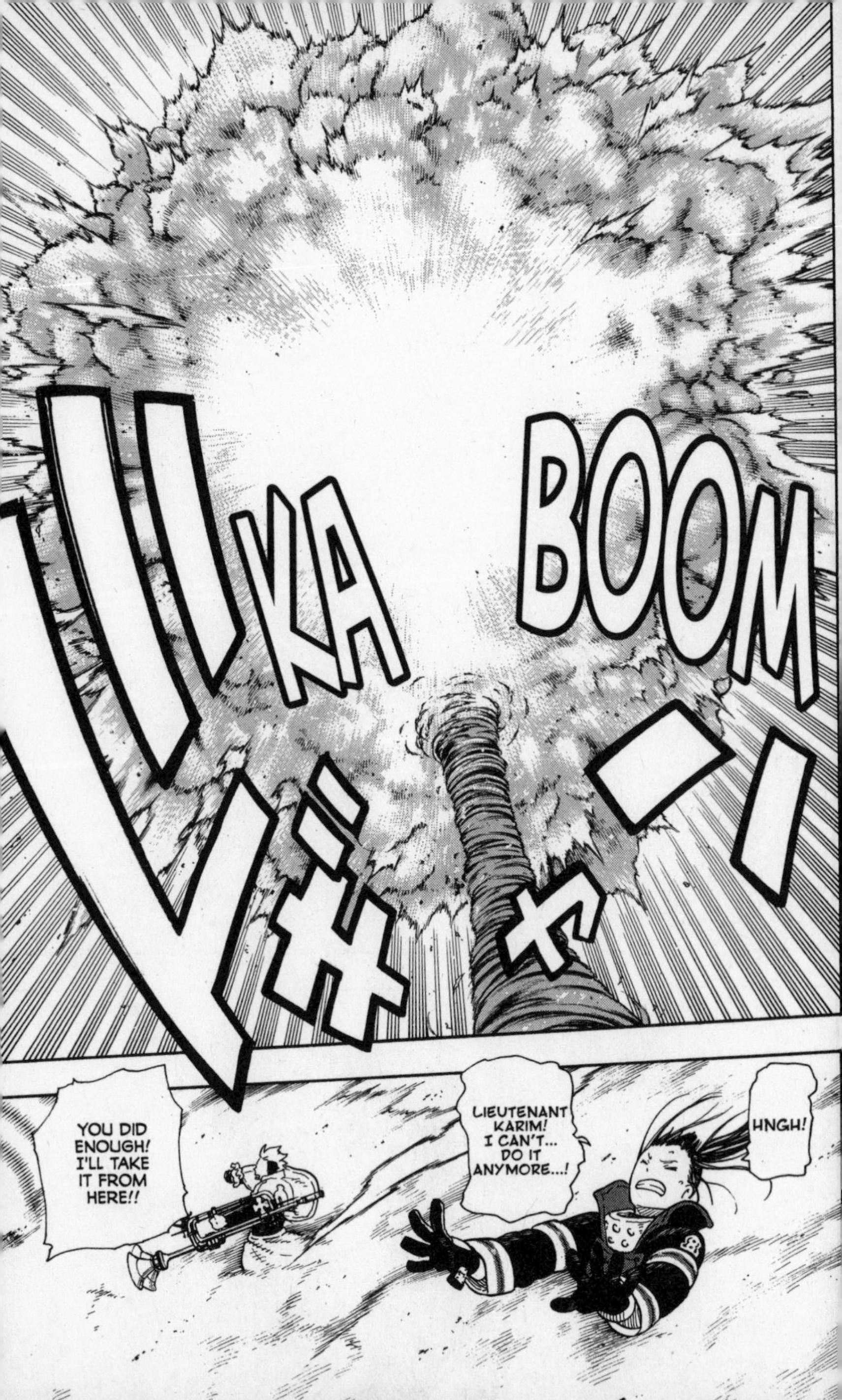
KA BOOM
HNGH!
LIEUTENANT KARIM! I CAN'T... DO IT ANYMORE...!
YOU DID ENOUGH! I'LL TAKE IT FROM HERE!!

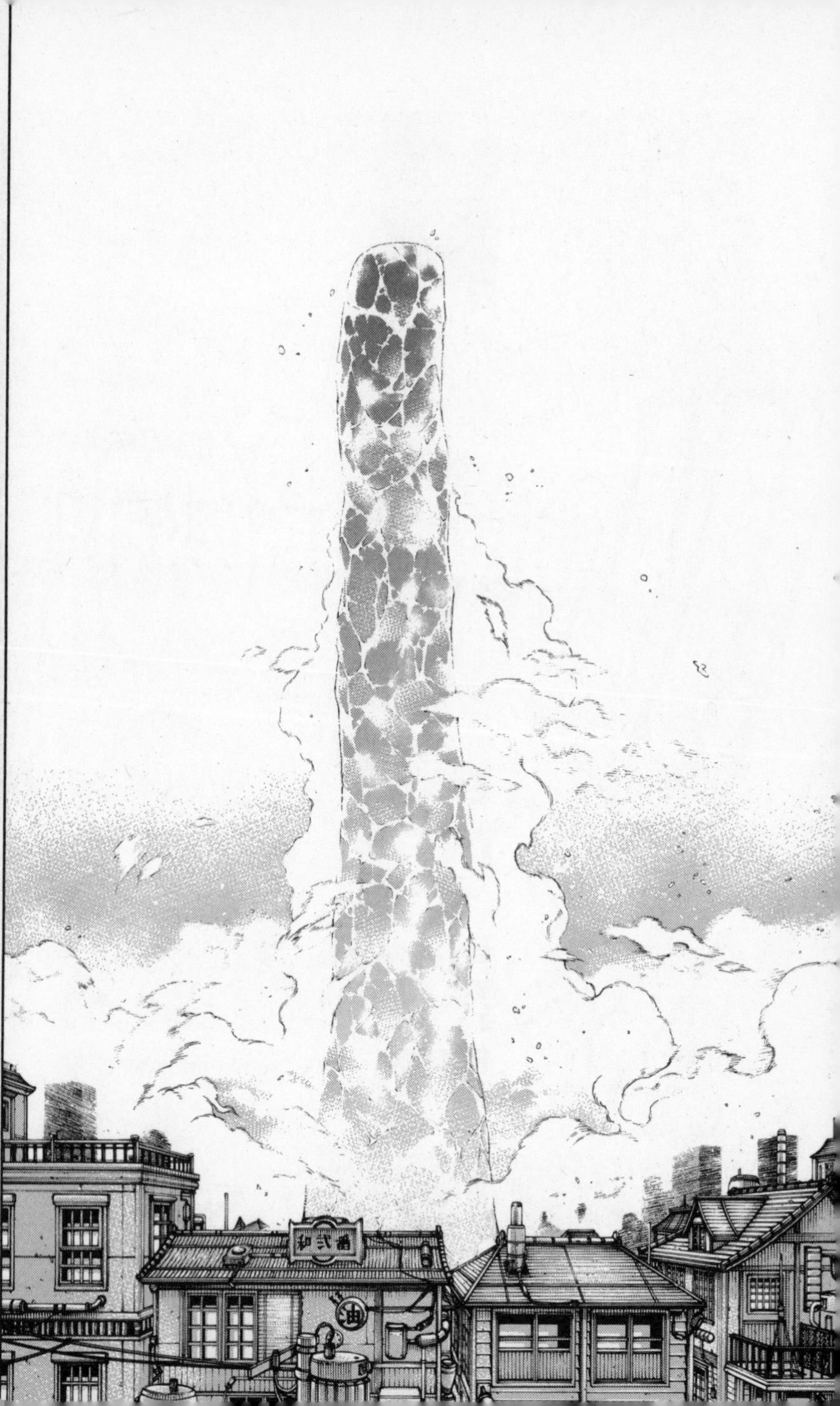
和弐番
油

CHAPTER CX: THE TIME TO CHOOSE

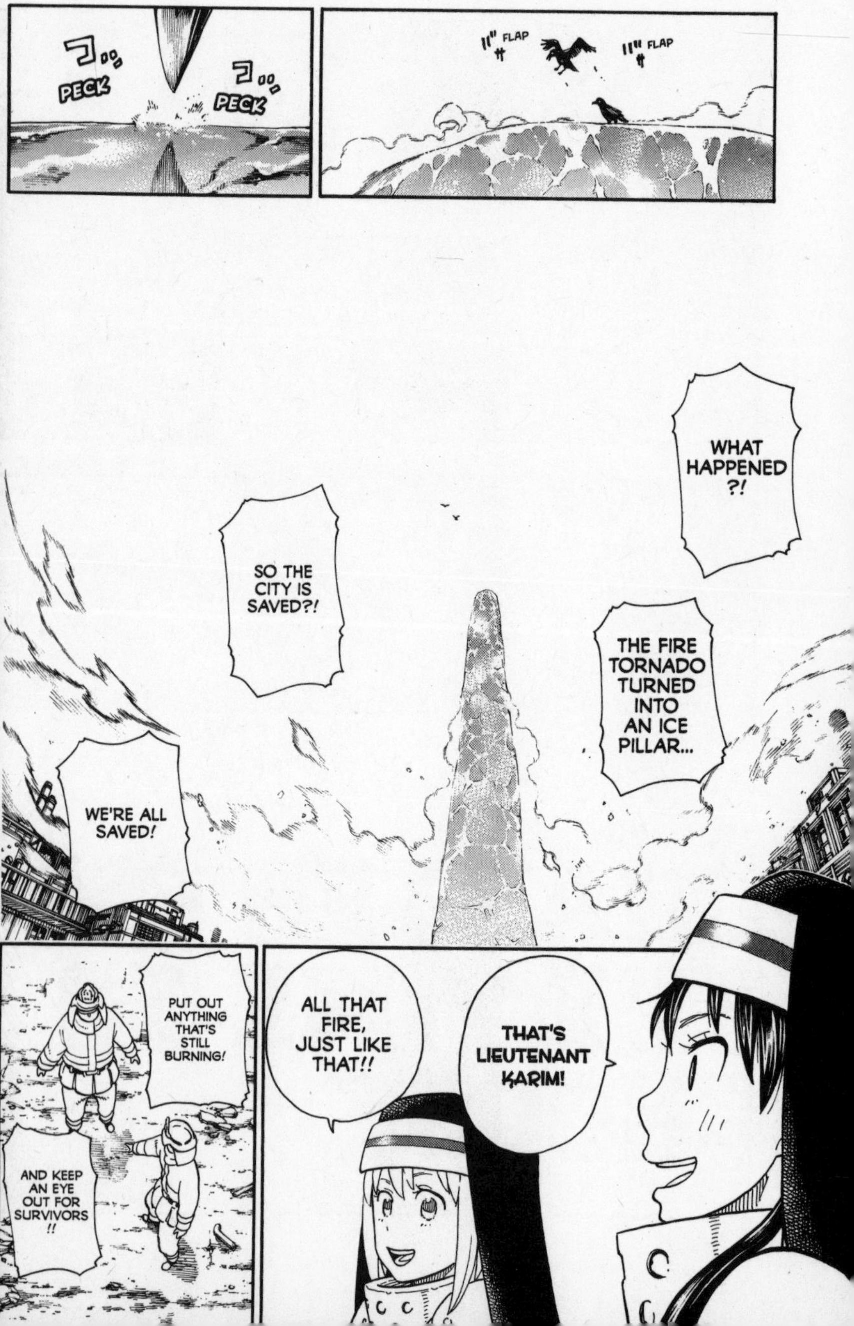
FLAP
FLAP
PECK
PECK
WHAT HAPPENED?!
THE FIRE TORNADO TURNED INTO AN ICE PILLAR...
SO THE CITY IS SAVED?!
WE'RE ALL SAVED!
THAT'S LIEUTENANT KARIM!
ALL THAT FIRE, JUST LIKE THAT!!
PUT OUT ANYTHING THAT'S STILL BURNING!
AND KEEP AN EYE OUT FOR SURVIVORS!!

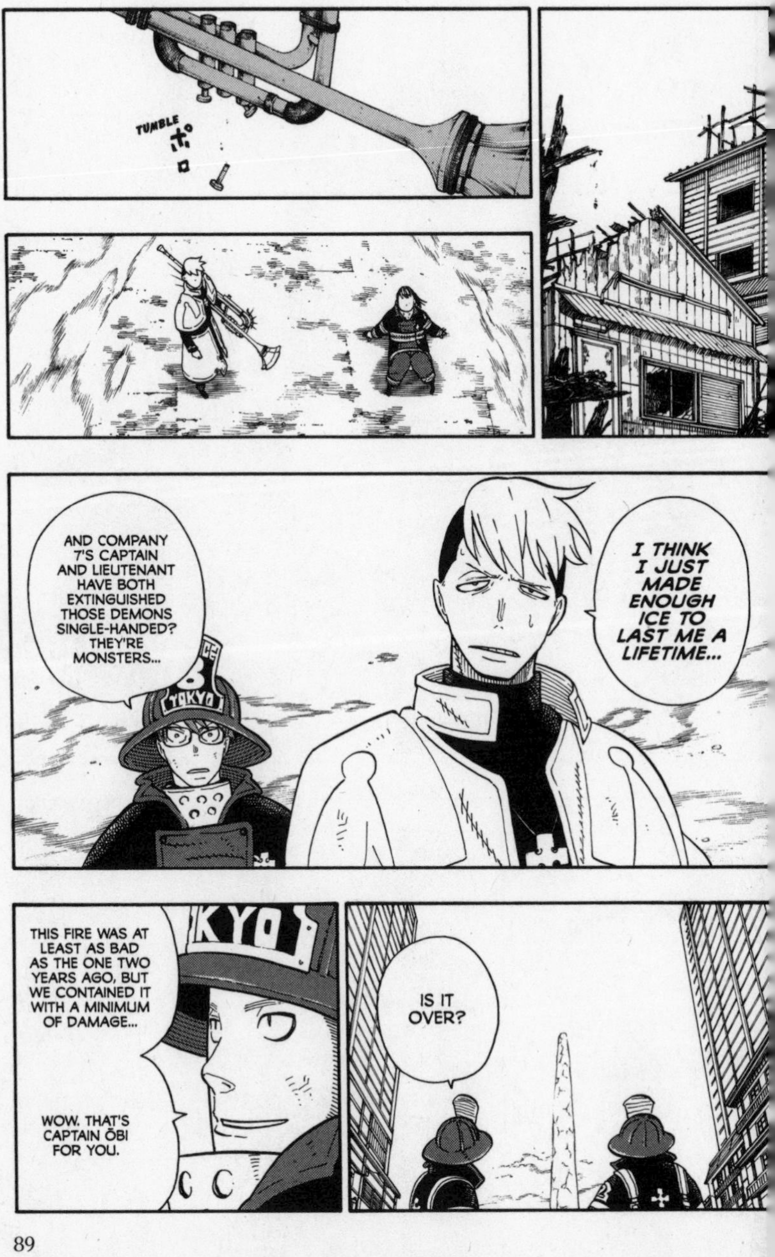
TUMBLE
I THINK I JUST MADE ENOUGH ICE TO LAST ME A LIFETIME...
AND COMPANY 7'S CAPTAIN AND LIEUTENANT HAVE BOTH EXTINGUISHED THOSE DEMONS SINGLE-HANDED? THEY'RE MONSTERS...
IS IT OVER?
THIS FIRE WAS AT LEAST AS BAD AS THE ONE TWO YEARS AGO, BUT WE CONTAINED IT WITH A MINIMUM OF DAMAGE...
WOW. THAT'S CAPTAIN ŌBI FOR YOU.

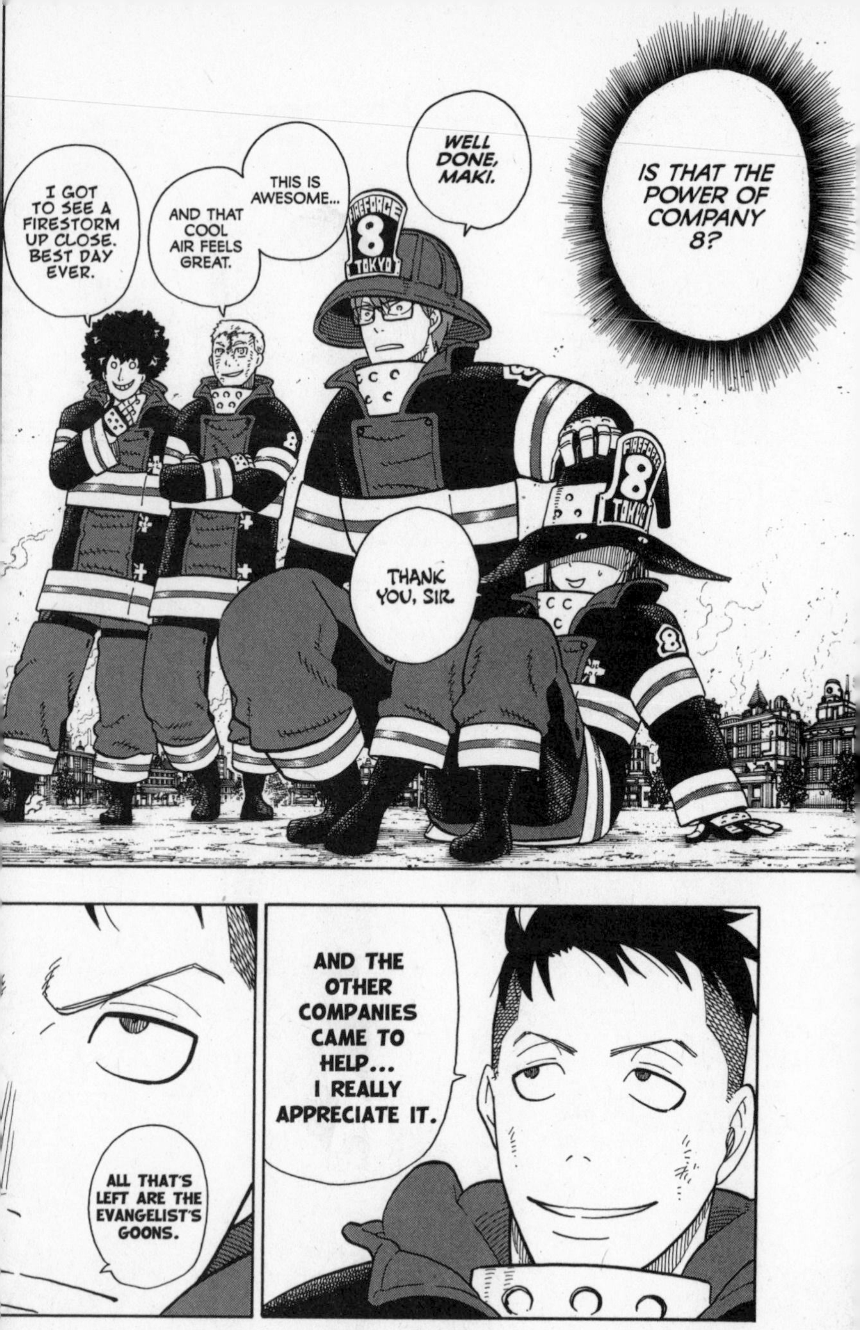
IS THAT THE POWER OF COMPANY 8?
WELL DONE, MAKI.
THIS IS AWESOME...
AND THAT COOL AIR FEELS GREAT.
I GOT TO SEE A FIRESTORM UP CLOSE. BEST DAY EVER.
THANK YOU, SIR.
AND THE OTHER COMPANIES CAME TO HELP... I REALLY APPRECIATE IT.
ALL THAT'S LEFT ARE THE EVANGELIST'S GOONS.

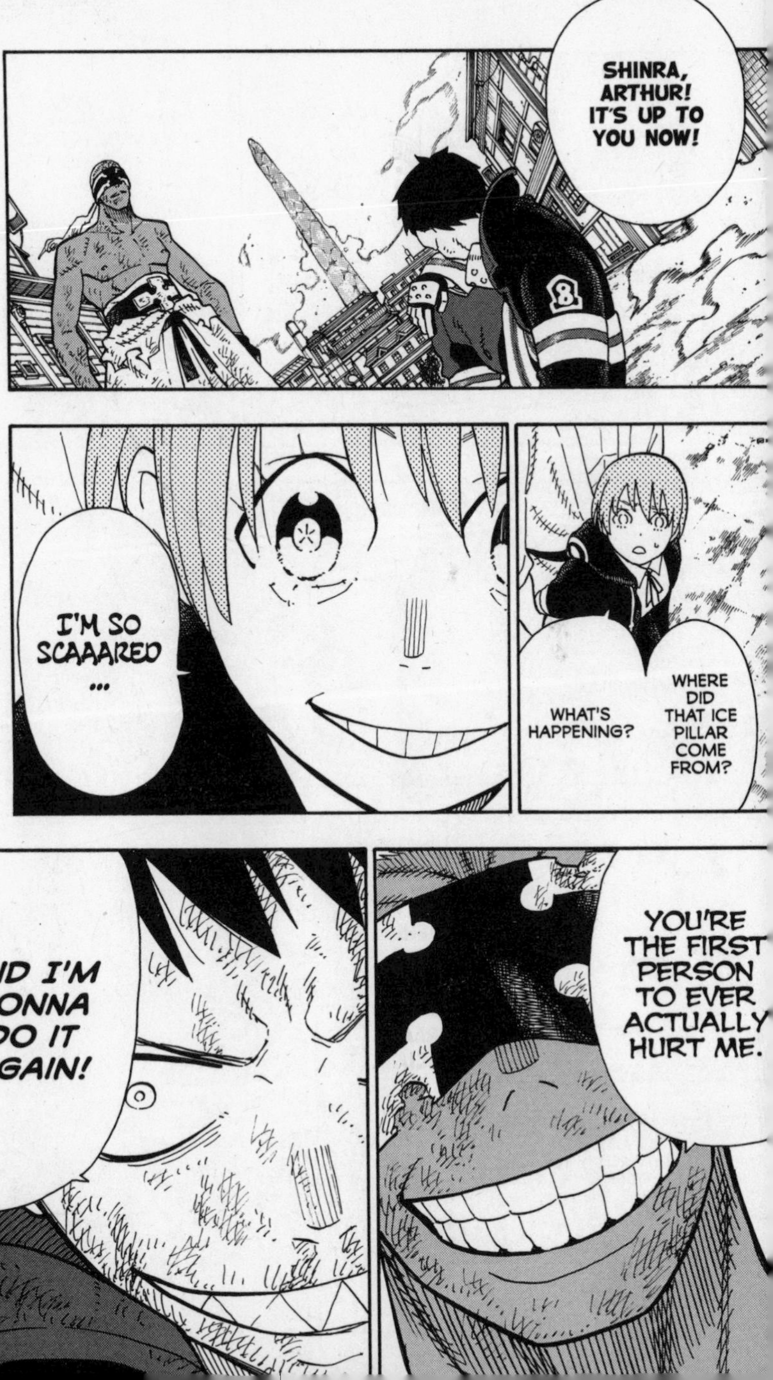
SHINRA, ARTHUR! IT'S UP TO YOU NOW!
WHERE DID THAT ICE PILLAR COME FROM?
WHAT'S HAPPENING?
I'M SO SCAAARED ...
YOU'RE THE FIRST PERSON TO EVER ACTUALLY HURT ME.
AND I'M GONNA DO IT AGAIN!

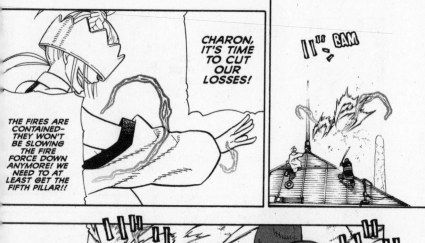

CHARON, IT'S TIME TO CUT OUR LOSSES!

THE FIRES ARE CONTAINED—THEY WON'T BE SLOWING THE FIRE FORCE DOWN ANYMORE! WE NEED TO AT LEAST GET THE FIFTH PILLAR!!

BAM

ADIEU, PLASMA BOY!

ZAP
ZAP
ZAP
ZAP

TMP

CRACKLE
CRACKLE
CRACKLE

STOP!!

SWISH

SHE USED MAGNETISM TO SLOW HER FALL?

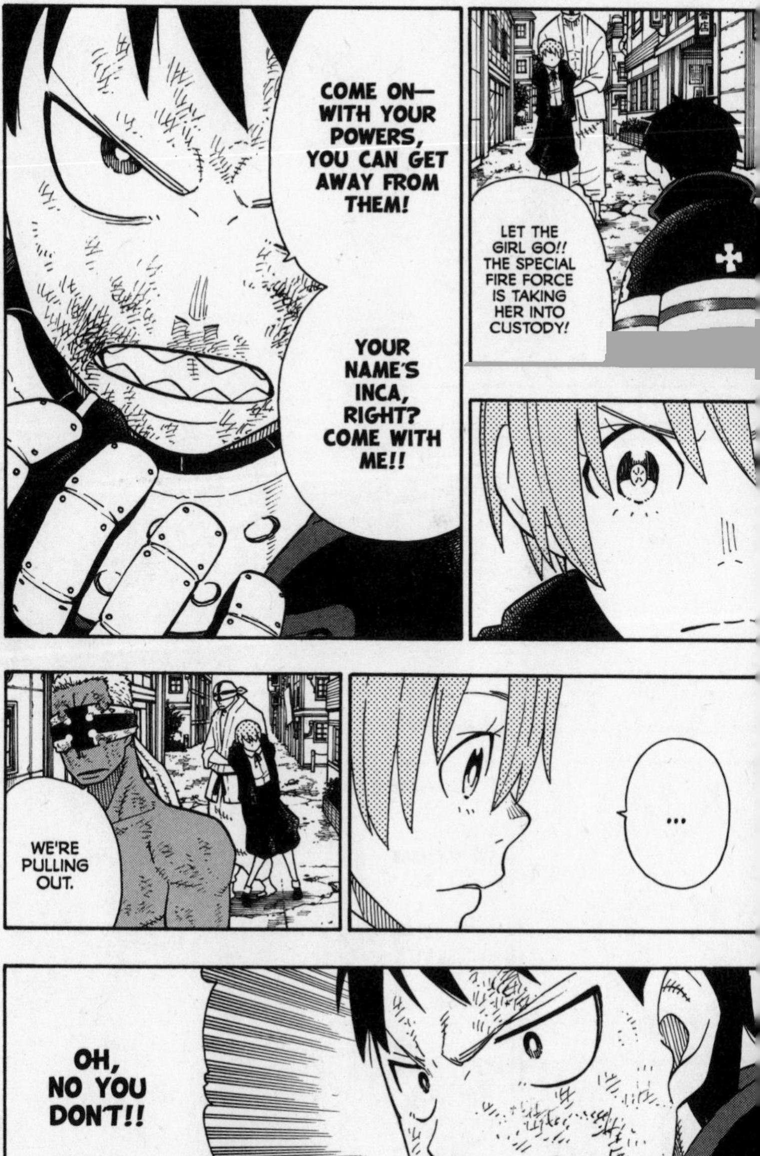
LET THE GIRL GO!! THE SPECIAL FIRE FORCE IS TAKING HER INTO CUSTODY!
COME ON— WITH YOUR POWERS, YOU CAN GET AWAY FROM THEM!
YOUR NAME'S INCA, RIGHT? COME WITH ME!!
...
WE'RE PULLING OUT.
OH, NO YOU DONT!!

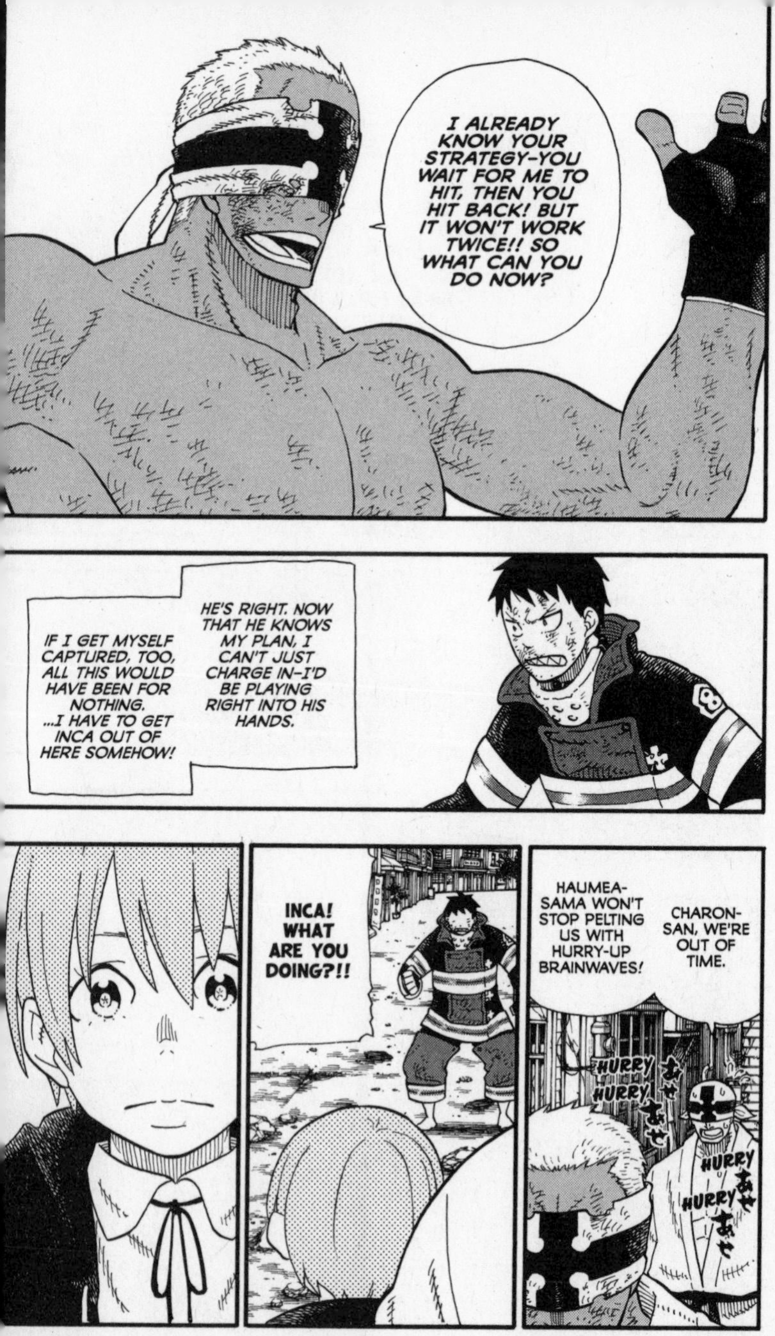
I ALREADY KNOW YOUR STRATEGY–YOU WAIT FOR ME TO HIT, THEN YOU HIT BACK! BUT IT WON'T WORK TWICE!! SO WHAT CAN YOU DO NOW?
HE'S RIGHT. NOW THAT HE KNOWS MY PLAN, I CAN'T JUST CHARGE IN–I'D BE PLAYING RIGHT INTO HIS HANDS.
IF I GET MYSELF CAPTURED, TOO, ALL THIS WOULD HAVE BEEN FOR NOTHING. ...I HAVE TO GET INCA OUT OF HERE SOMEHOW!
CHARON-SAN, WE'RE OUT OF TIME.
HAUMEA-SAMA WON'T STOP PELTING US WITH HURRY-UP BRAINWAVES!
HURRY HURRY
あせ あせ
HURRY HURRY
あせ あせ
INCA! WHAT ARE YOU DOING?!!

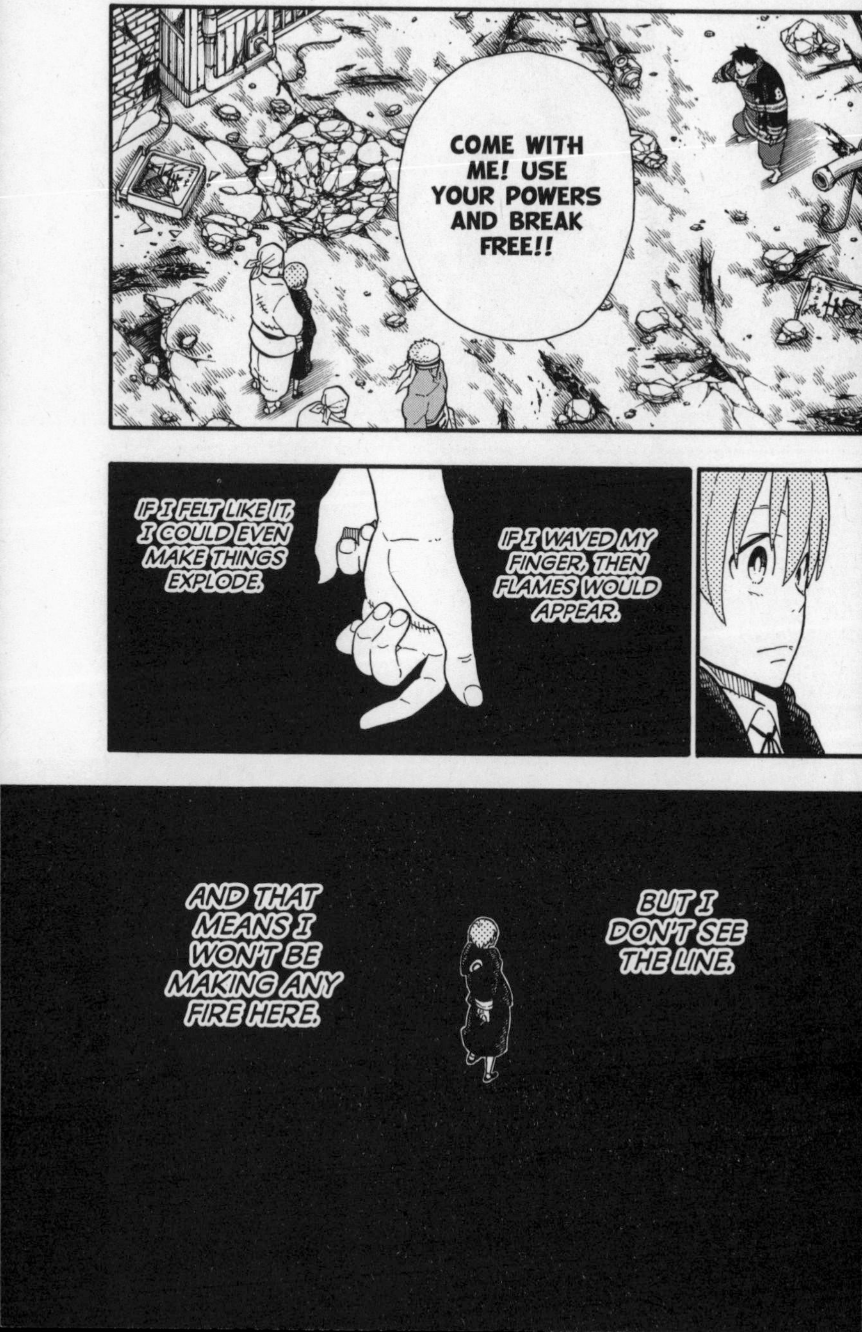
COME WITH ME! USE YOUR POWERS AND BREAK FREE!!
IF I WAVED MY FINGER, THEN FLAMES WOULD APPEAR.
IF I FELT LIKE IT, I COULD EVEN MAKE THINGS EXPLODE.
BUT I DON'T SEE THE LINE.
AND THAT MEANS I WON'T BE MAKING ANY FIRE HERE.

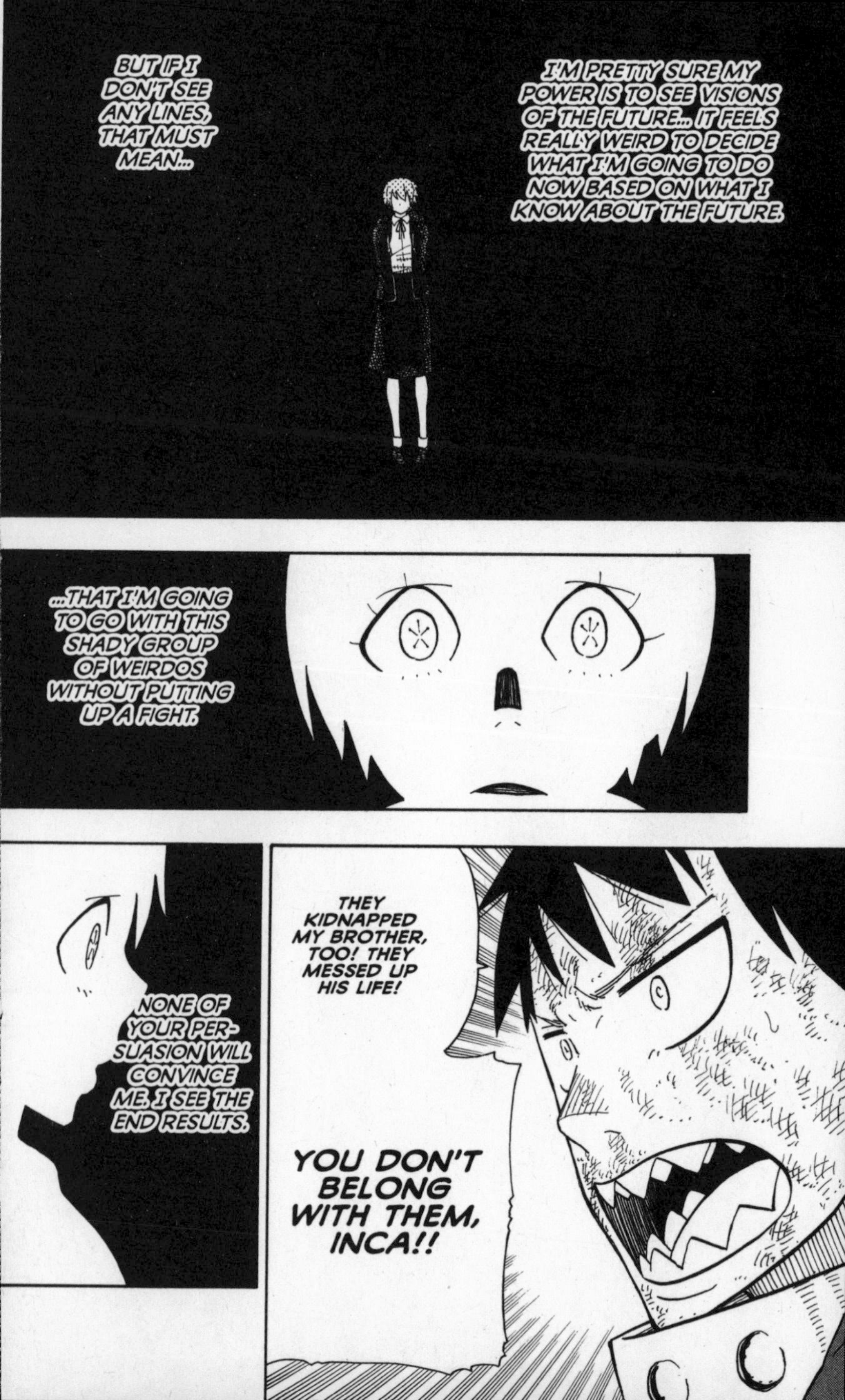
I'M PRETTY SURE MY POWER IS TO SEE VISIONS OF THE FUTURE... IT FEELS REALLY WEIRD TO DECIDE WHAT I'M GOING TO DO NOW BASED ON WHAT I KNOW ABOUT THE FUTURE.
BUT IF I DON'T SEE ANY LINES, THAT MUST MEAN...
...THAT I'M GOING TO GO WITH THIS SHADY GROUP OF WEIRDOS WITHOUT PUTTING UP A FIGHT.
THEY KIDNAPPED MY BROTHER, TOO! THEY MESSED UP HIS LIFE!
YOU DON'T BELONG WITH THEM, INCA!!
NONE OF YOUR PER-SUASION WILL CONVINCE ME. I SEE THE END RESULTS.

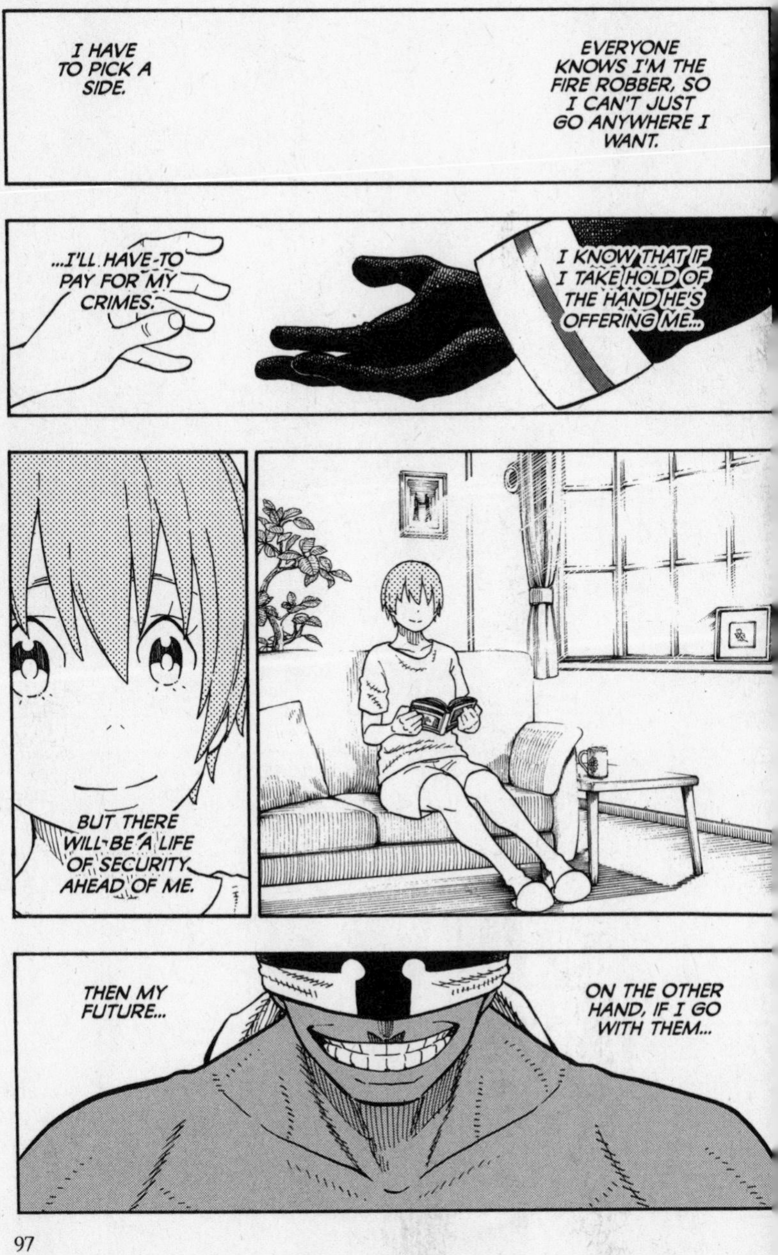
EVERYONE KNOWS I'M THE FIRE ROBBER, SO I CAN'T JUST GO ANYWHERE I WANT.
I HAVE TO PICK A SIDE.
I KNOW THAT IF I TAKE HOLD OF THE HAND HE'S OFFERING ME...
...I'LL HAVE TO PAY FOR MY CRIMES.
BUT THERE WILL BE A LIFE OF SECURITY AHEAD OF ME.
ON THE OTHER HAND, IF I GO WITH THEM...
THEN MY FUTURE...

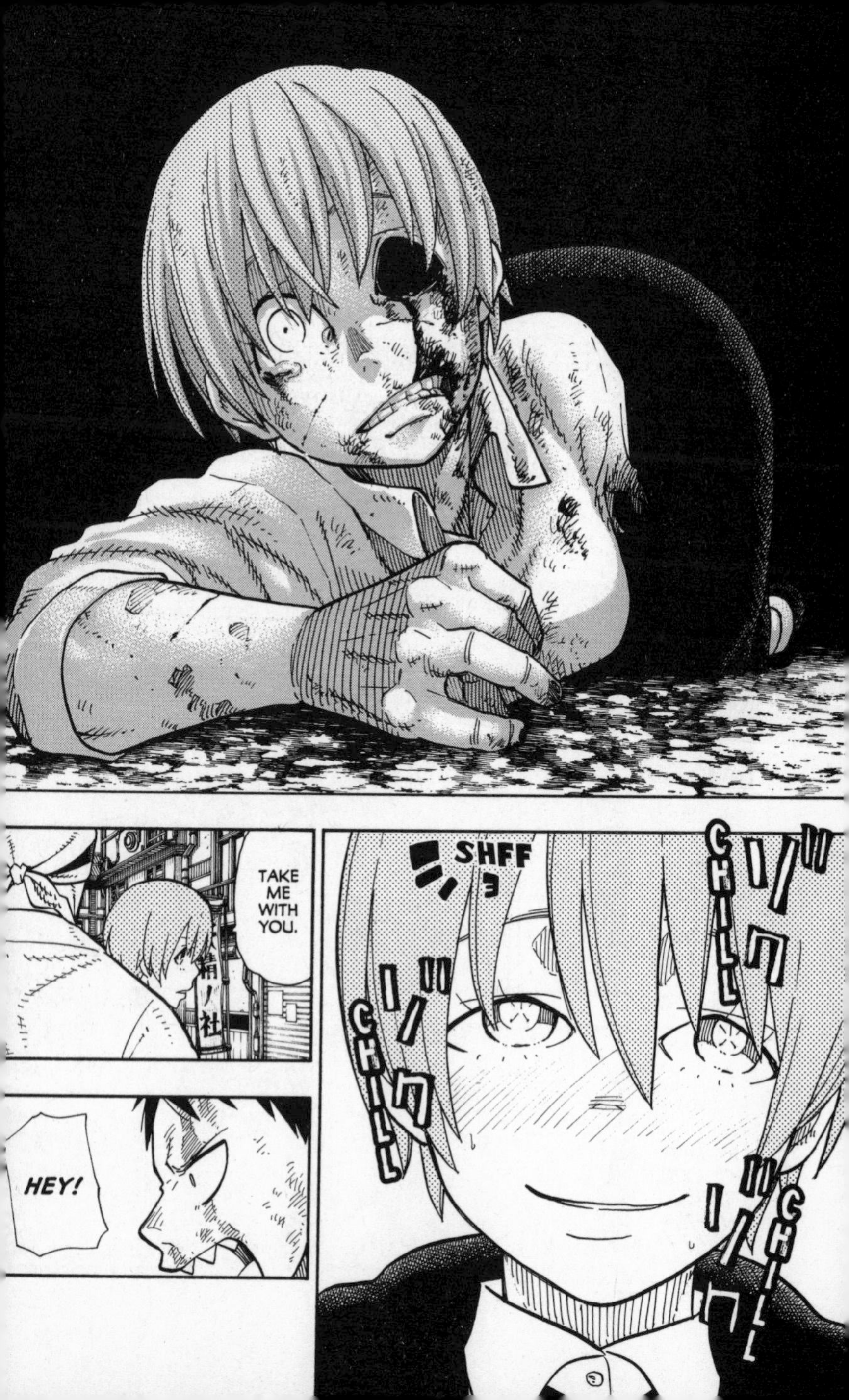
SHFF
CHILL
CHILL
CHILL
TAKE ME WITH YOU.
HEY!

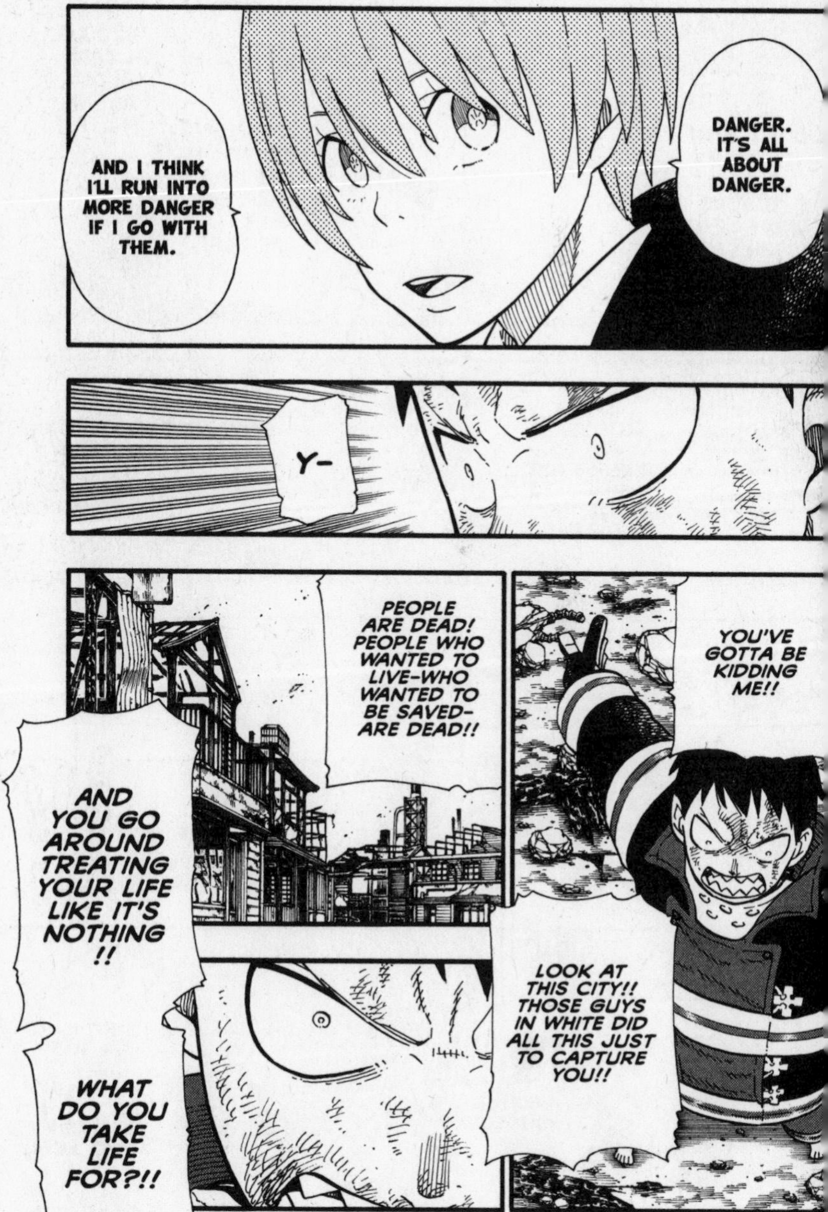
DANGER. IT'S ALL ABOUT DANGER.
AND I THINK I'LL RUN INTO MORE DANGER IF I GO WITH THEM.
Y-
YOU'VE GOTTA BE KIDDING ME!!
LOOK AT THIS CITY!! THOSE GUYS IN WHITE DID ALL THIS JUST TO CAPTURE YOU!!
PEOPLE ARE DEAD! PEOPLE WHO WANTED TO LIVE-WHO WANTED TO BE SAVED-ARE DEAD!!
AND YOU GO AROUND TREATING YOUR LIFE LIKE IT'S NOTHING!!
WHAT DO YOU TAKE LIFE FOR?!!

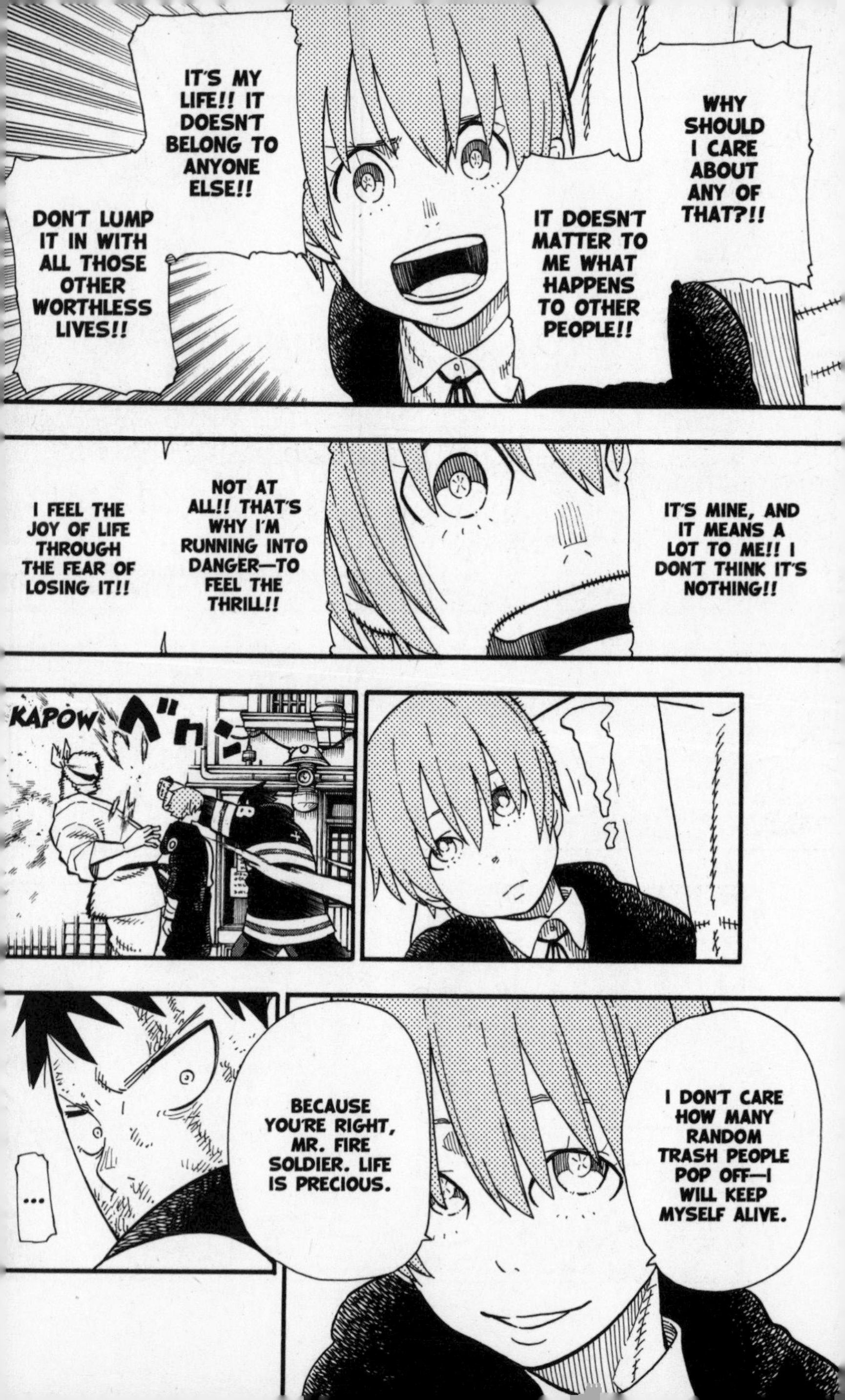
WHY SHOULD I CARE ABOUT ANY OF THAT?!!
IT DOESN'T MATTER TO ME WHAT HAPPENS TO OTHER PEOPLE!!
IT'S MY LIFE!! IT DOESN'T BELONG TO ANYONE ELSE!!
DON'T LUMP IT IN WITH ALL THOSE OTHER WORTHLESS LIVES!!
IT'S MINE, AND IT MEANS A LOT TO ME!! I DON'T THINK IT'S NOTHING!!
NOT AT ALL!! THAT'S WHY I'M RUNNING INTO DANGER—TO FEEL THE THRILL!!
I FEEL THE JOY OF LIFE THROUGH THE FEAR OF LOSING IT!!
KAPOW
I DON'T CARE HOW MANY RANDOM TRASH PEOPLE POP OFF—I WILL KEEP MYSELF ALIVE.
BECAUSE YOU'RE RIGHT, MR. FIRE SOLDIER. LIFE IS PRECIOUS.
...

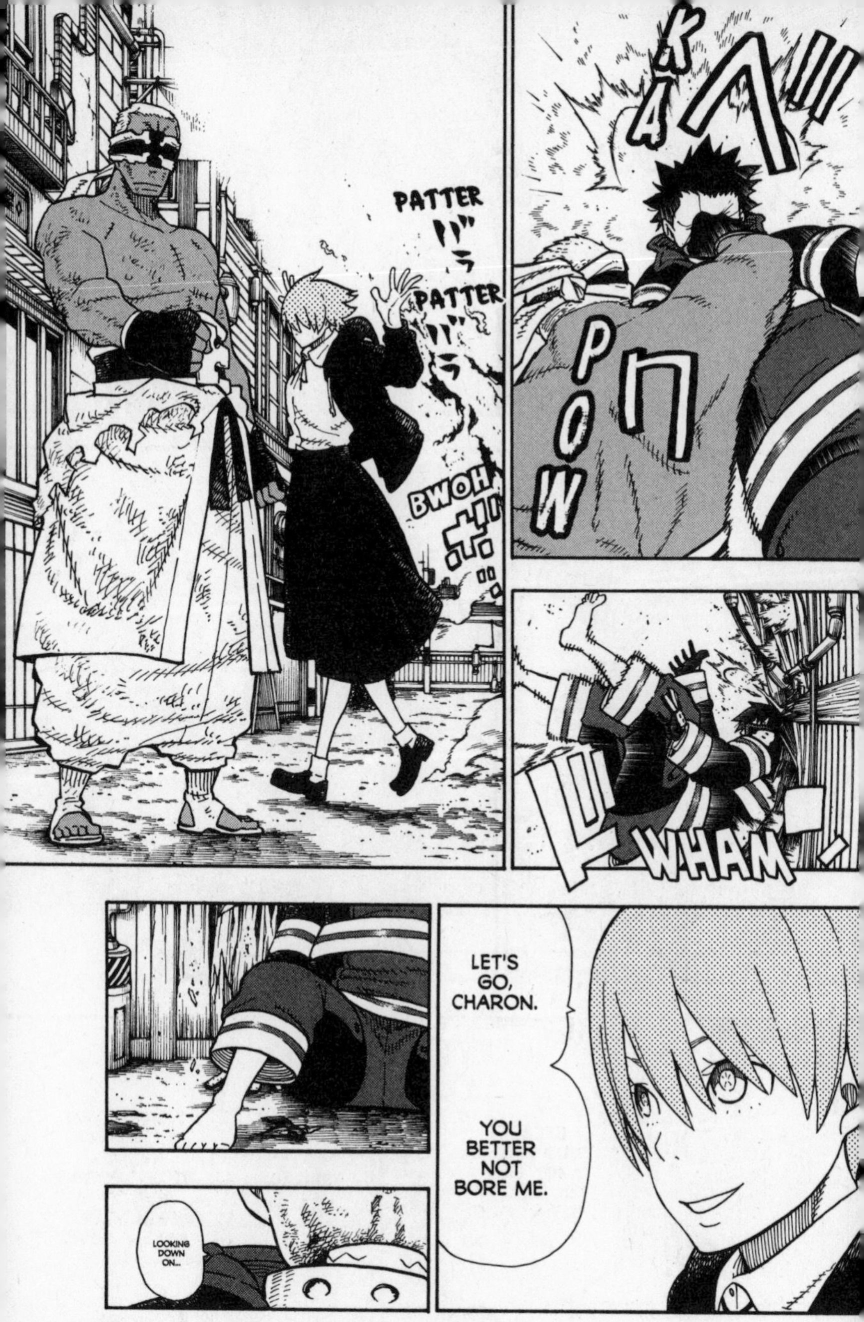
KA
POW
WHAM
PATTER
PATTER
BWOH
LET'S GO, CHARON.
YOU BETTER NOT BORE ME.
LOOKING DOWN ON...

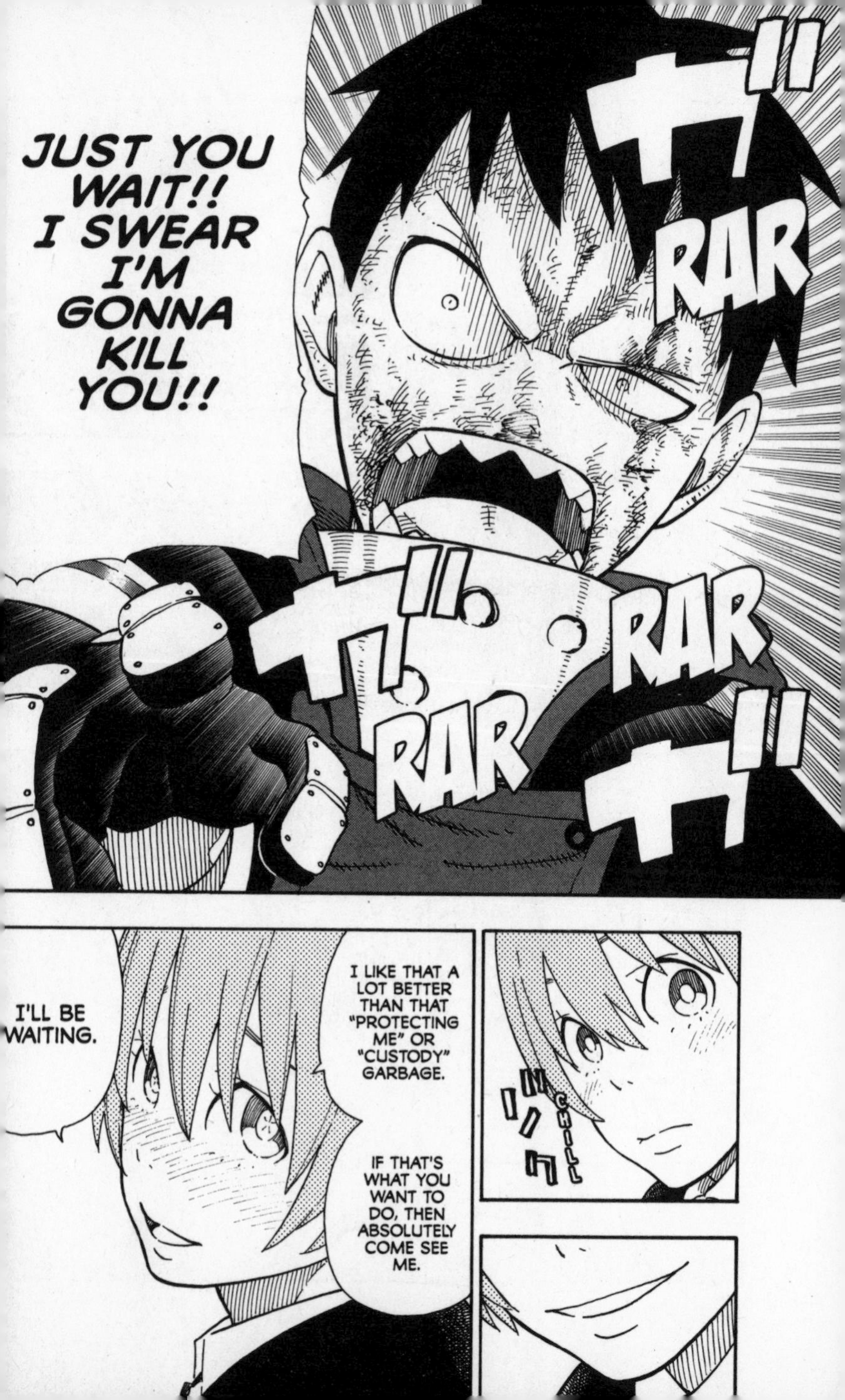
RAR
JUST YOU WAIT!! I SWEAR I'M GONNA KILL YOU!!
RAR
RAR
CHILL
I LIKE THAT A LOT BETTER THAN THAT "PROTECTING ME" OR "CUSTODY" GARBAGE.
IF THAT'S WHAT YOU WANT TO DO, THEN ABSOLUTELY COME SEE ME.
I'LL BE WAITING.

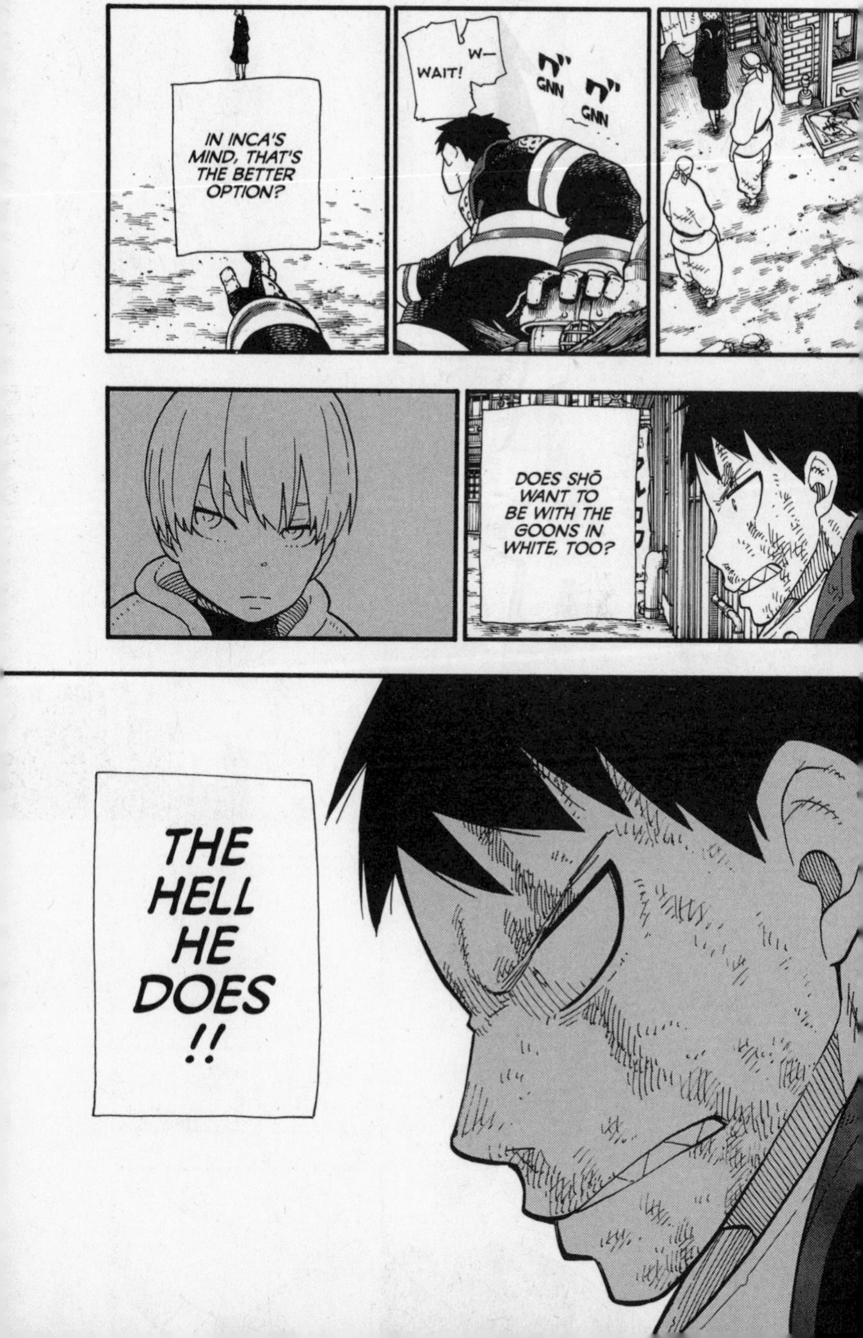
W—
WAIT!
GNN
GNN
IN INCA'S MIND, THAT'S THE BETTER OPTION?
DOES SHŌ WANT TO BE WITH THE GOONS IN WHITE, TOO?
THE HELL HE DOES !!

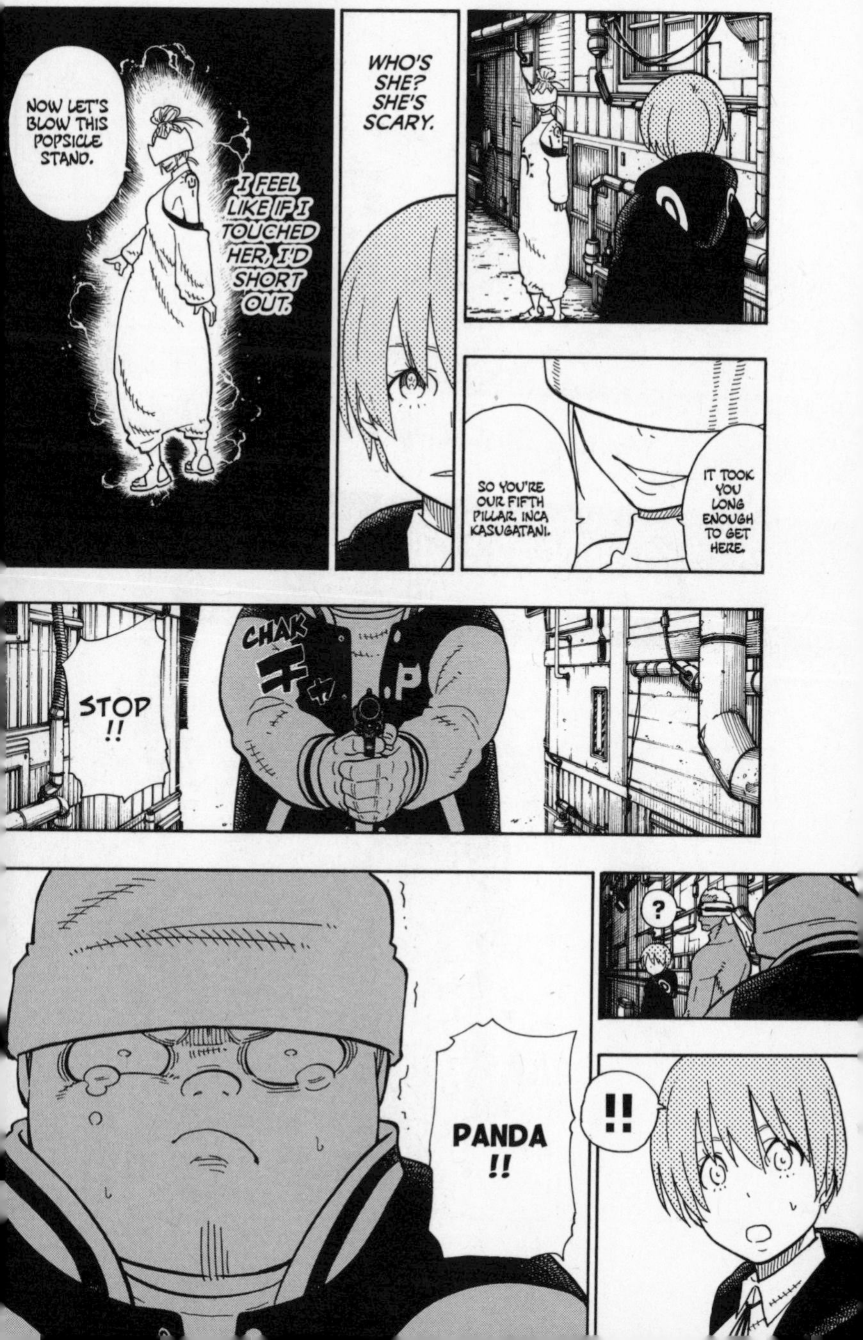
IT TOOK YOU LONG ENOUGH TO GET HERE.
SO YOU'RE OUR FIFTH PILLAR, INCA KASUGATANI.
WHO'S SHE? SHE'S SCARY.
NOW LET'S BLOW THIS POPSICLE STAND.
I FEEL LIKE IF I TOUCHED HER, I'D SHORT OUT.
CHAK
チャ
STOP !!
?
!!
PANDA !!

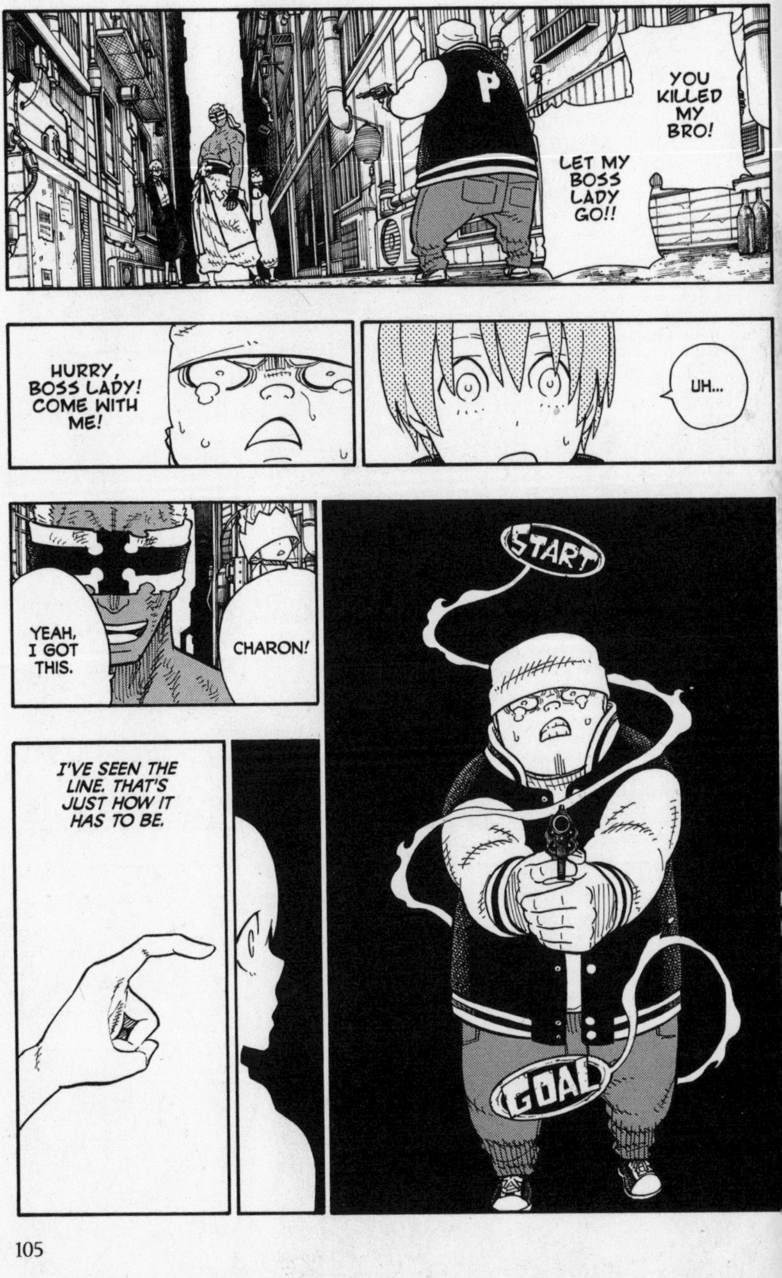
YOU KILLED MY BRO!
LET MY BOSS LADY GO!!
UH...
HURRY, BOSS LADY! COME WITH ME!
START
GOAL
CHARON!
YEAH, I GOT THIS.
I'VE SEEN THE LINE. THAT'S JUST HOW IT HAS TO BE.

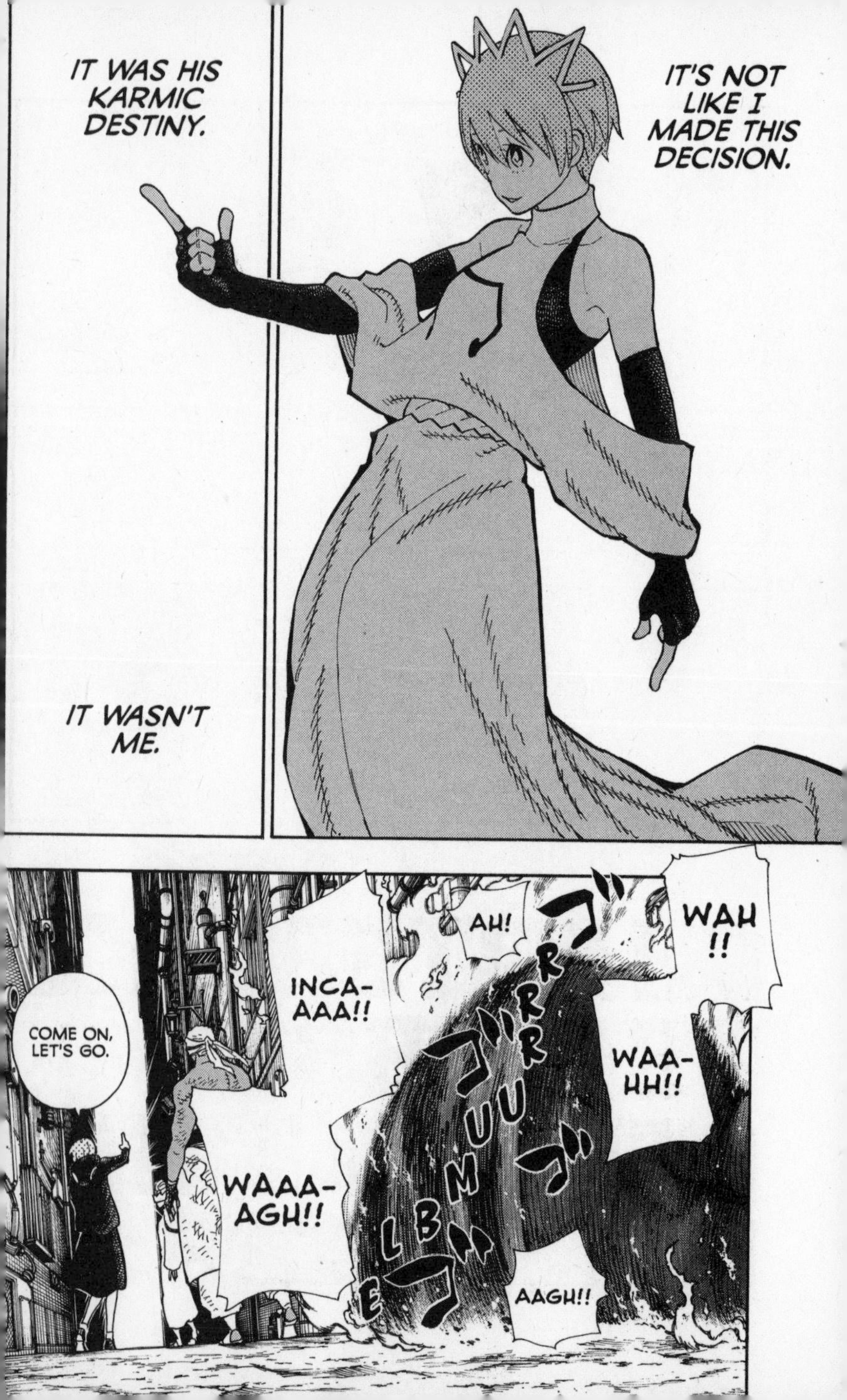
IT'S NOT LIKE I MADE THIS DECISION.
IT WAS HIS KARMIC DESTINY.
IT WASN'T ME.
WAH!!
AH!
WAA-HH!!
INCA-AAA!!
RRRUUMBLE
AAGH!!
WAAA-AGH!!
COME ON, LET'S GO.

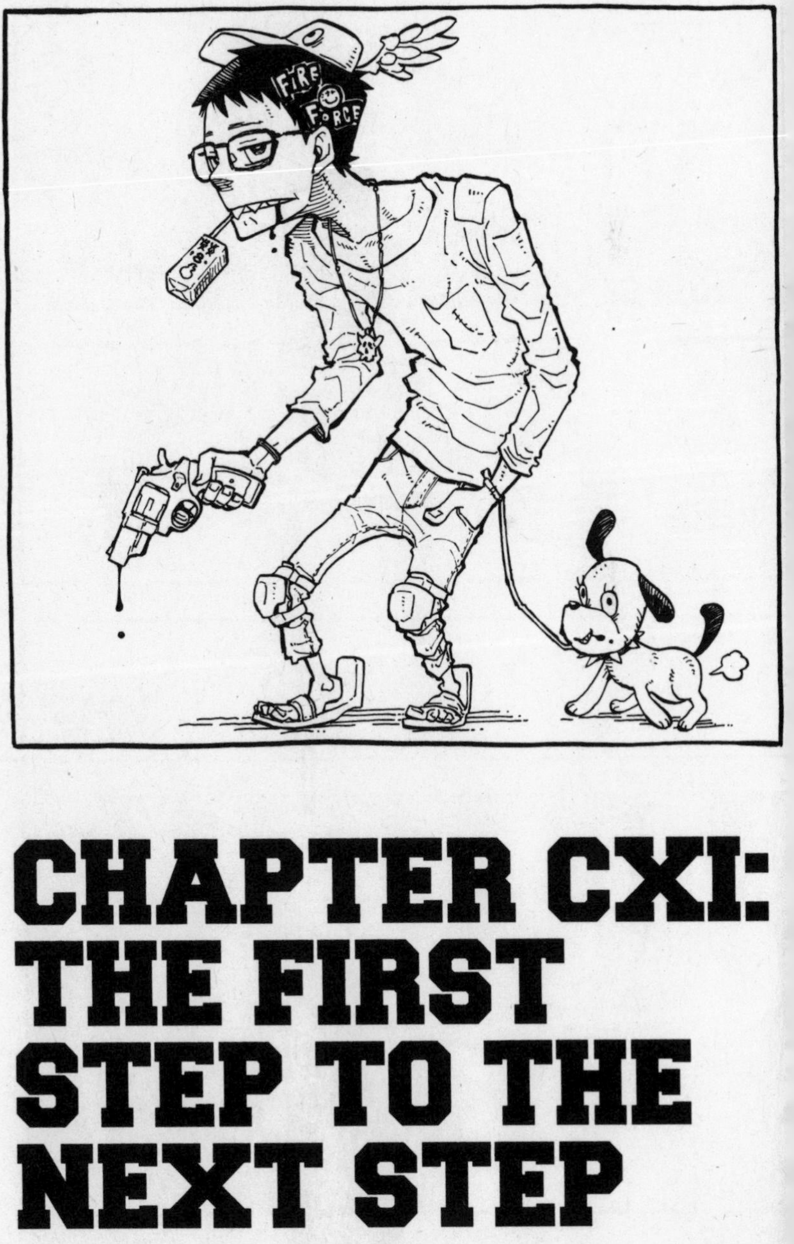
FIRE FORCE

CHAPTER CXI: THE FIRST STEP TO THE NEXT STEP

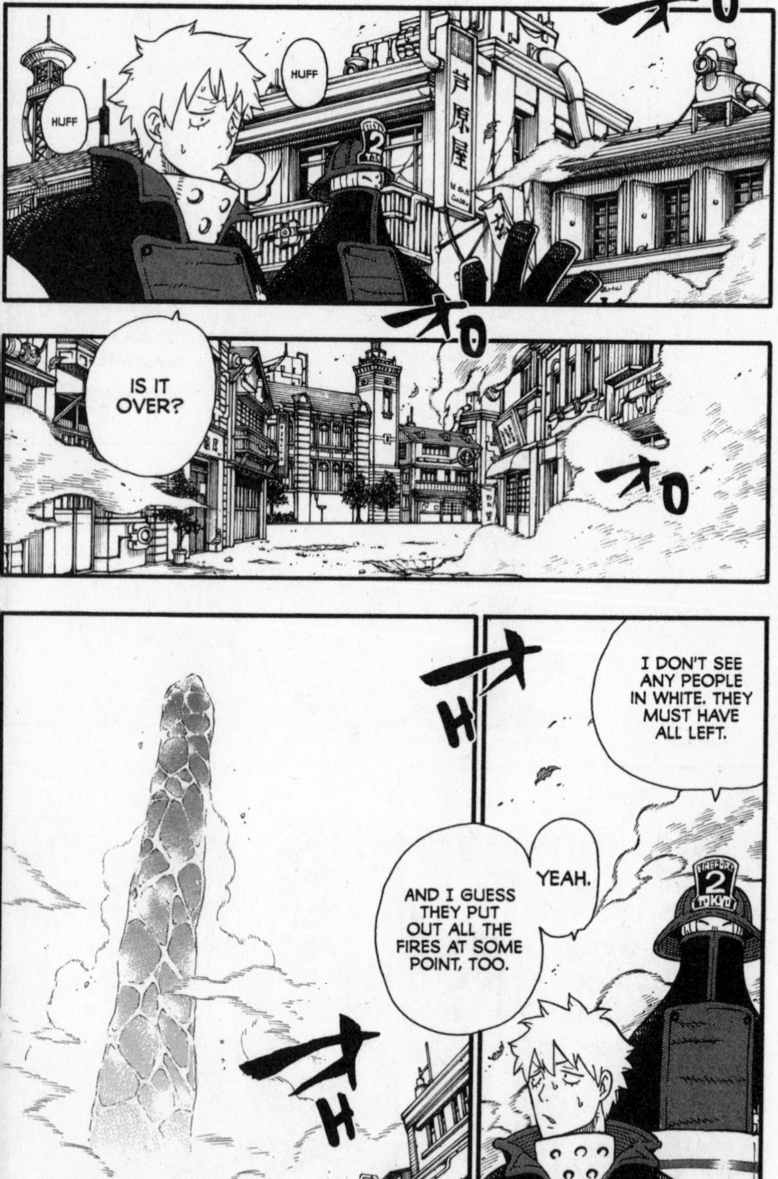
HUFF
HUFF
IS IT OVER?
I DON'T SEE ANY PEOPLE IN WHITE. THEY MUST HAVE ALL LEFT.
YEAH.
AND I GUESS THEY PUT OUT ALL THE FIRES AT SOME POINT, TOO.

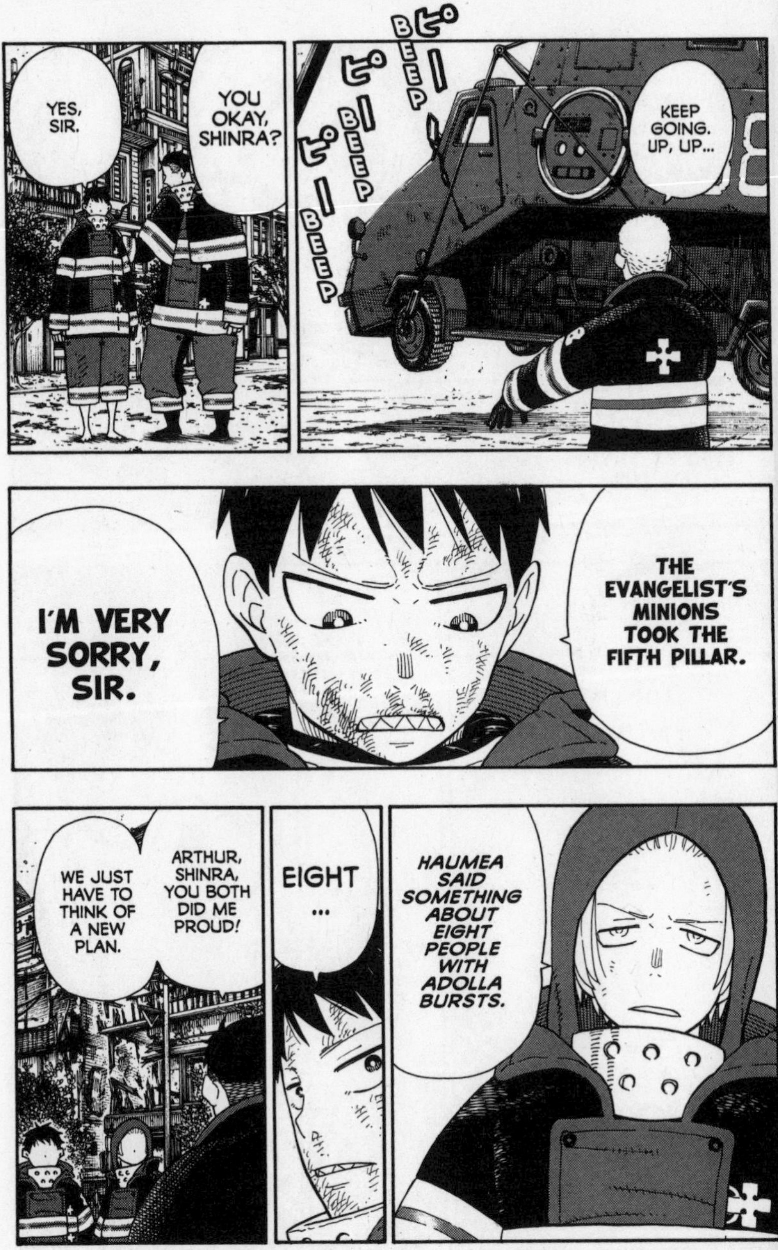
ピー BEEP
ピー BEEP
ピー BEEP
KEEP GOING. UP, UP...
YOU OKAY, SHINRA?
YES, SIR.
THE EVANGELIST'S MINIONS TOOK THE FIFTH PILLAR.
I'M VERY SORRY, SIR.
HAUMEA SAID SOMETHING ABOUT EIGHT PEOPLE WITH ADOLLA BURSTS.
EIGHT ...
ARTHUR, SHINRA, YOU BOTH DID ME PROUD!
WE JUST HAVE TO THINK OF A NEW PLAN.

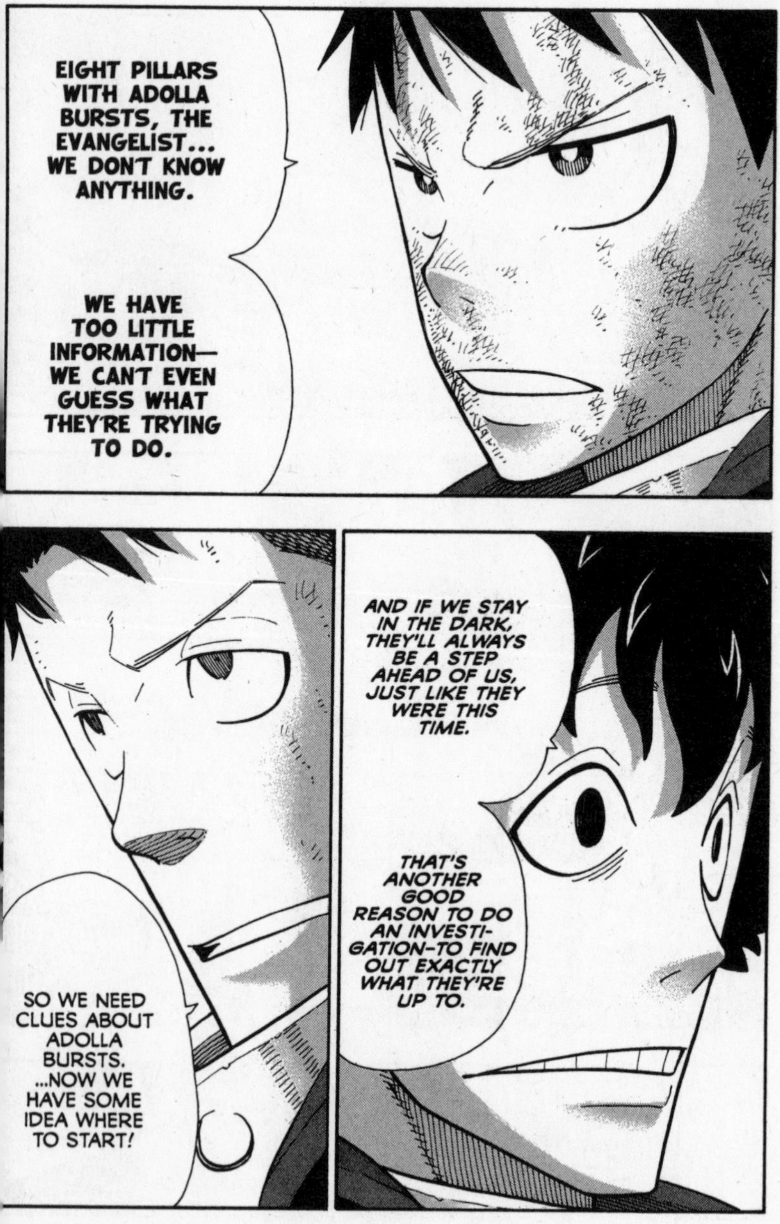
EIGHT PILLARS WITH ADOLLA BURSTS, THE EVANGELIST... WE DON'T KNOW ANYTHING.
WE HAVE TOO LITTLE INFORMATION— WE CAN'T EVEN GUESS WHAT THEY'RE TRYING TO DO.
AND IF WE STAY IN THE DARK, THEY'LL ALWAYS BE A STEP AHEAD OF US, JUST LIKE THEY WERE THIS TIME.
THAT'S ANOTHER GOOD REASON TO DO AN INVESTI-GATION—TO FIND OUT EXACTLY WHAT THEY'RE UP TO.
SO WE NEED CLUES ABOUT ADOLLA BURSTS. ...NOW WE HAVE SOME IDEA WHERE TO START!

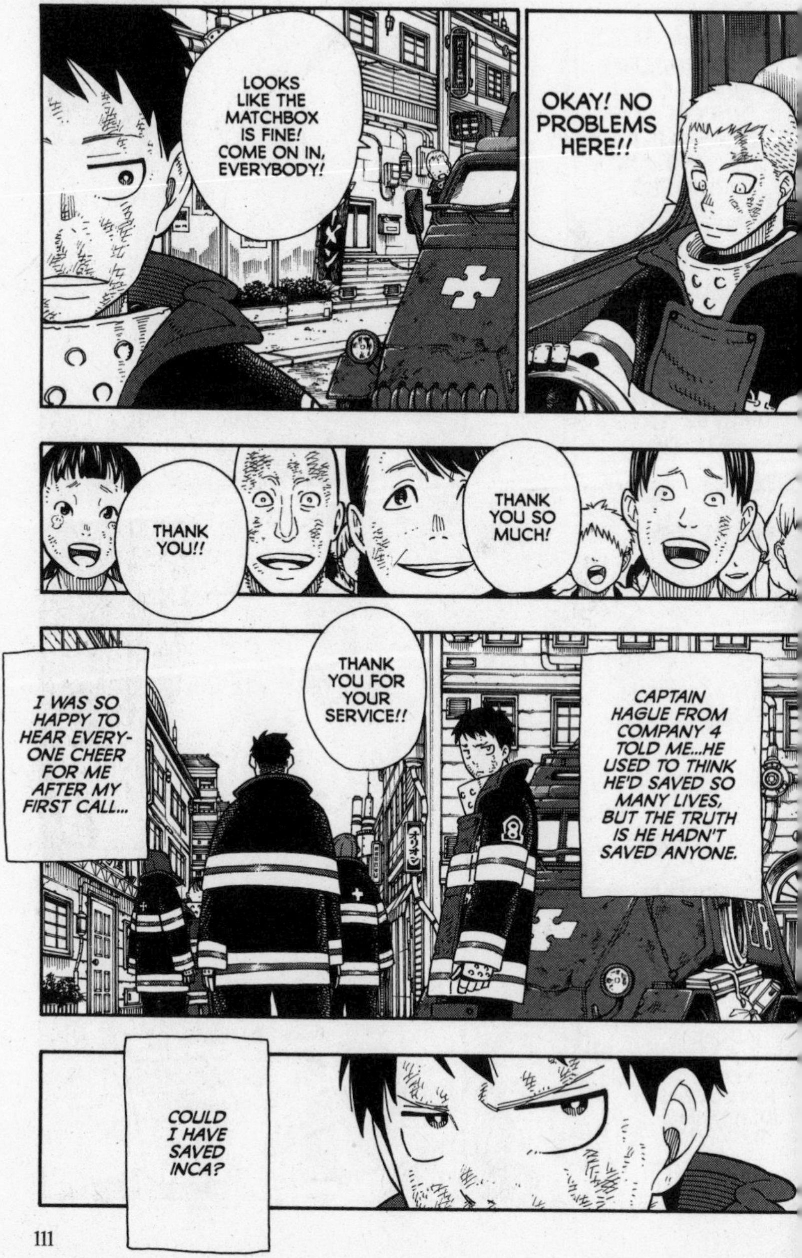
OKAY! NO PROBLEMS HERE!!
LOOKS LIKE THE MATCHBOX IS FINE! COME ON IN, EVERYBODY!
THANK YOU SO MUCH!
THANK YOU!!
CAPTAIN HAGUE FROM COMPANY 4 TOLD ME...HE USED TO THINK HE'D SAVED SO MANY LIVES, BUT THE TRUTH IS HE HADN'T SAVED ANYONE.
THANK YOU FOR YOUR SERVICE!!
I WAS SO HAPPY TO HEAR EVERY-ONE CHEER FOR ME AFTER MY FIRST CALL...
COULD I HAVE SAVED INCA?

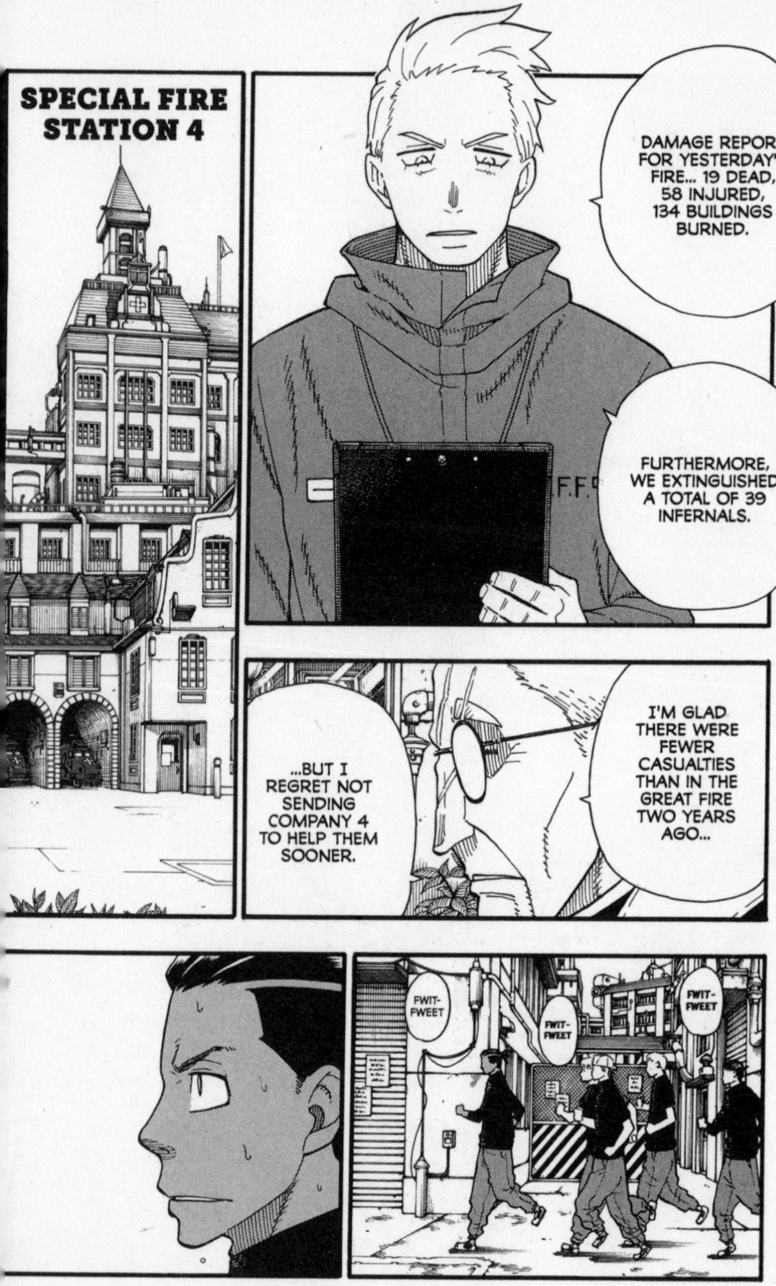
DAMAGE REPORT FOR YESTERDAY'S FIRE... 19 DEAD, 58 INJURED, 134 BUILDINGS BURNED.
FURTHERMORE, WE EXTINGUISHED A TOTAL OF 39 INFERNALS.
I'M GLAD THERE WERE FEWER CASUALTIES THAN IN THE GREAT FIRE TWO YEARS AGO...
...BUT I REGRET NOT SENDING COMPANY 4 TO HELP THEM SOONER.
SPECIAL FIRE STATION 4
FWIT-FWEET
FWIT-FWEET
FWIT-FWEET

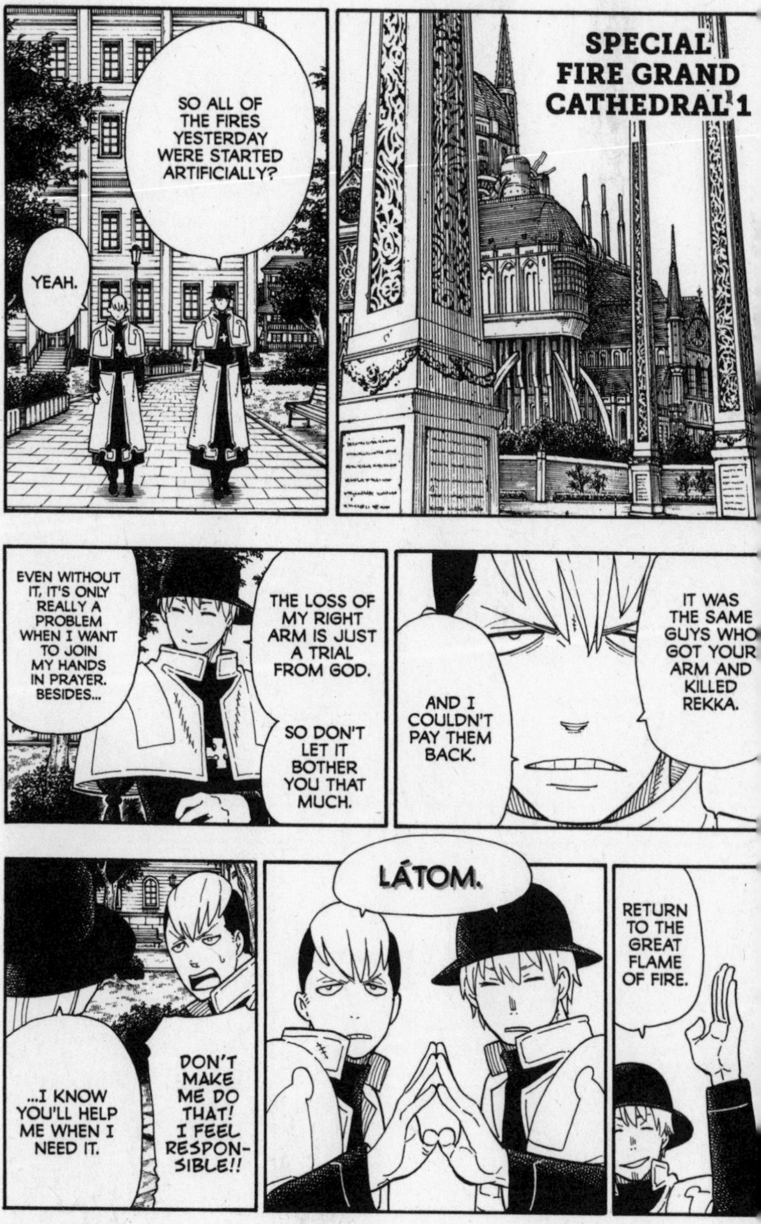
SPECIAL FIRE GRAND CATHEDRAL 1
SO ALL OF THE FIRES YESTERDAY WERE STARTED ARTIFICIALLY?
YEAH.
IT WAS THE SAME GUYS WHO GOT YOUR ARM AND KILLED REKKA.
AND I COULDN'T PAY THEM BACK.
THE LOSS OF MY RIGHT ARM IS JUST A TRIAL FROM GOD.
SO DON'T LET IT BOTHER YOU THAT MUCH.
EVEN WITHOUT IT, IT'S ONLY REALLY A PROBLEM WHEN I WANT TO JOIN MY HANDS IN PRAYER. BESIDES...
RETURN TO THE GREAT FLAME OF FIRE.
LÁTOM.
...I KNOW YOU'LL HELP ME WHEN I NEED IT.
DON'T MAKE ME DO THAT! I FEEL RESPONSIBLE!!

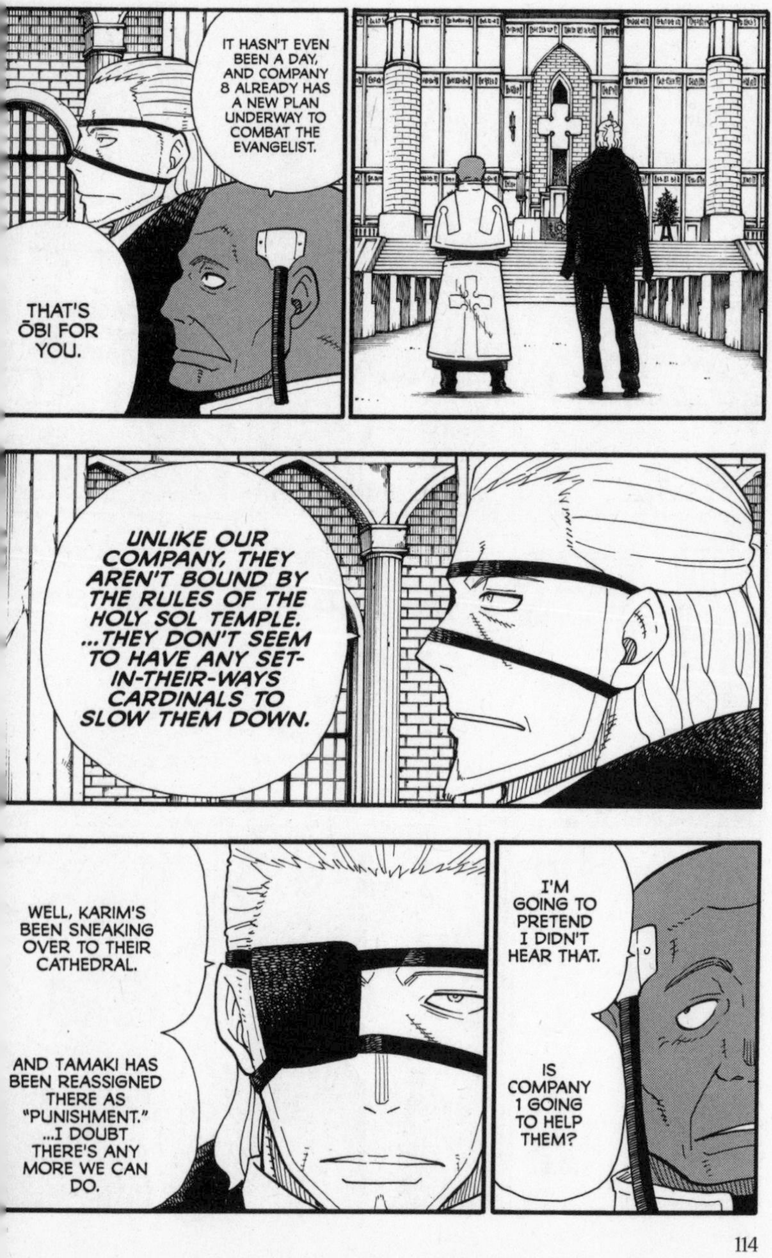
IT HASN'T EVEN BEEN A DAY, AND COMPANY 8 ALREADY HAS A NEW PLAN UNDERWAY TO COMBAT THE EVANGELIST.
THAT'S ŌBI FOR YOU.
UNLIKE OUR COMPANY, THEY AREN'T BOUND BY THE RULES OF THE HOLY SOL TEMPLE. ...THEY DON'T SEEM TO HAVE ANY SET-IN-THEIR-WAYS CARDINALS TO SLOW THEM DOWN.
I'M GOING TO PRETEND I DIDN'T HEAR THAT.
IS COMPANY 1 GOING TO HELP THEM?
WELL, KARIM'S BEEN SNEAKING OVER TO THEIR CATHEDRAL.
AND TAMAKI HAS BEEN REASSIGNED THERE AS "PUNISHMENT." ...I DOUBT THERE'S ANY MORE WE CAN DO.

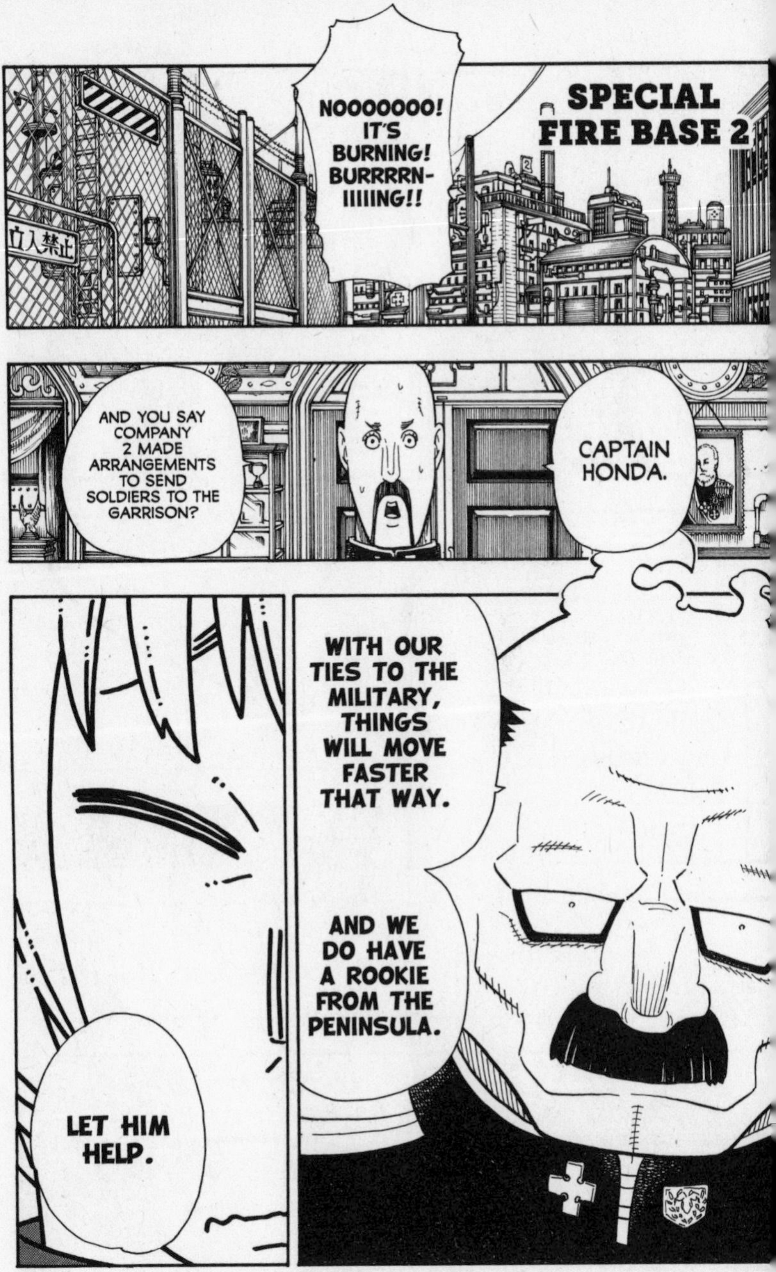
SPECIAL FIRE BASE 2
NOOOOOOO! IT'S BURNING! BURRRRN-IIIIING!!
立入禁止
CAPTAIN HONDA.
AND YOU SAY COMPANY 2 MADE ARRANGEMENTS TO SEND SOLDIERS TO THE GARRISON?
WITH OUR TIES TO THE MILITARY, THINGS WILL MOVE FASTER THAT WAY.
AND WE DO HAVE A ROOKIE FROM THE PENINSULA.
LET HIM HELP.

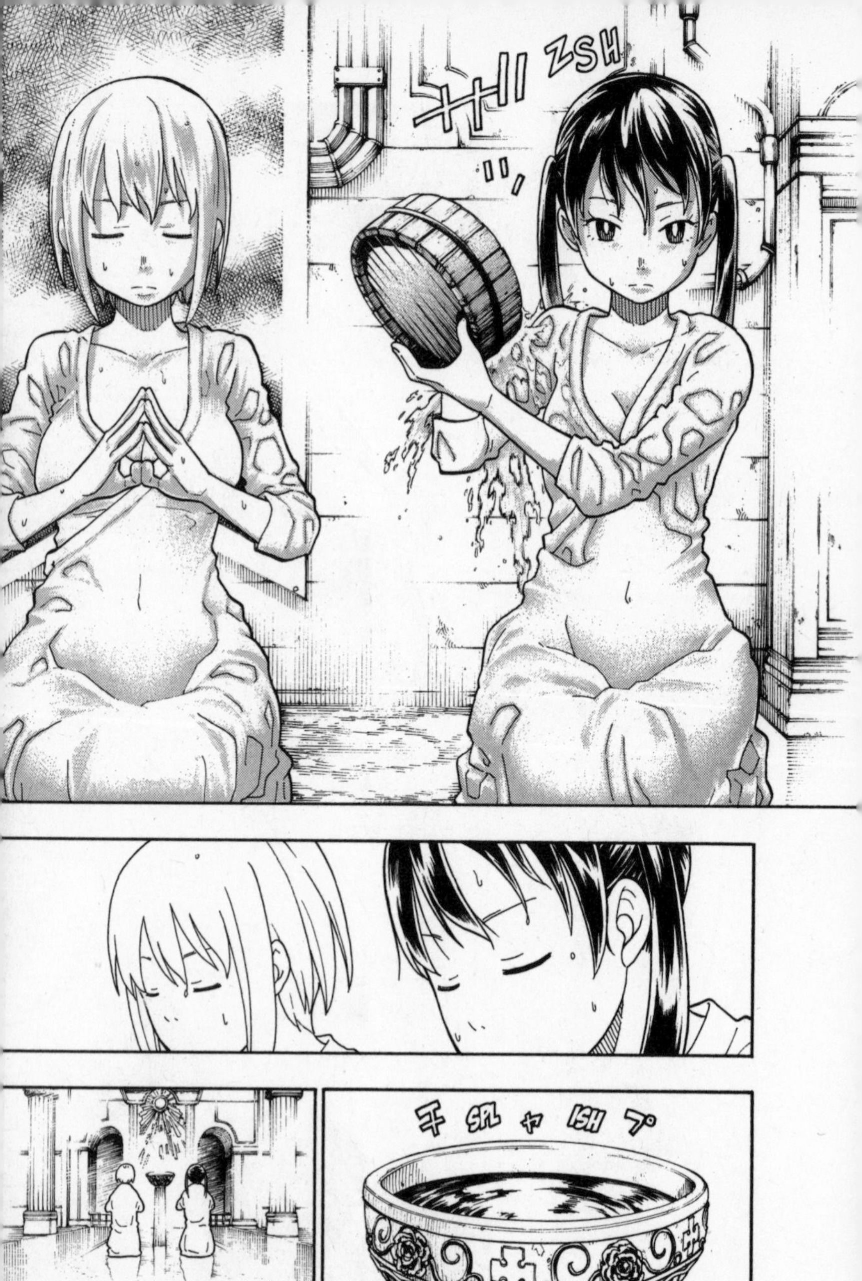
ZSH
SPL ISH

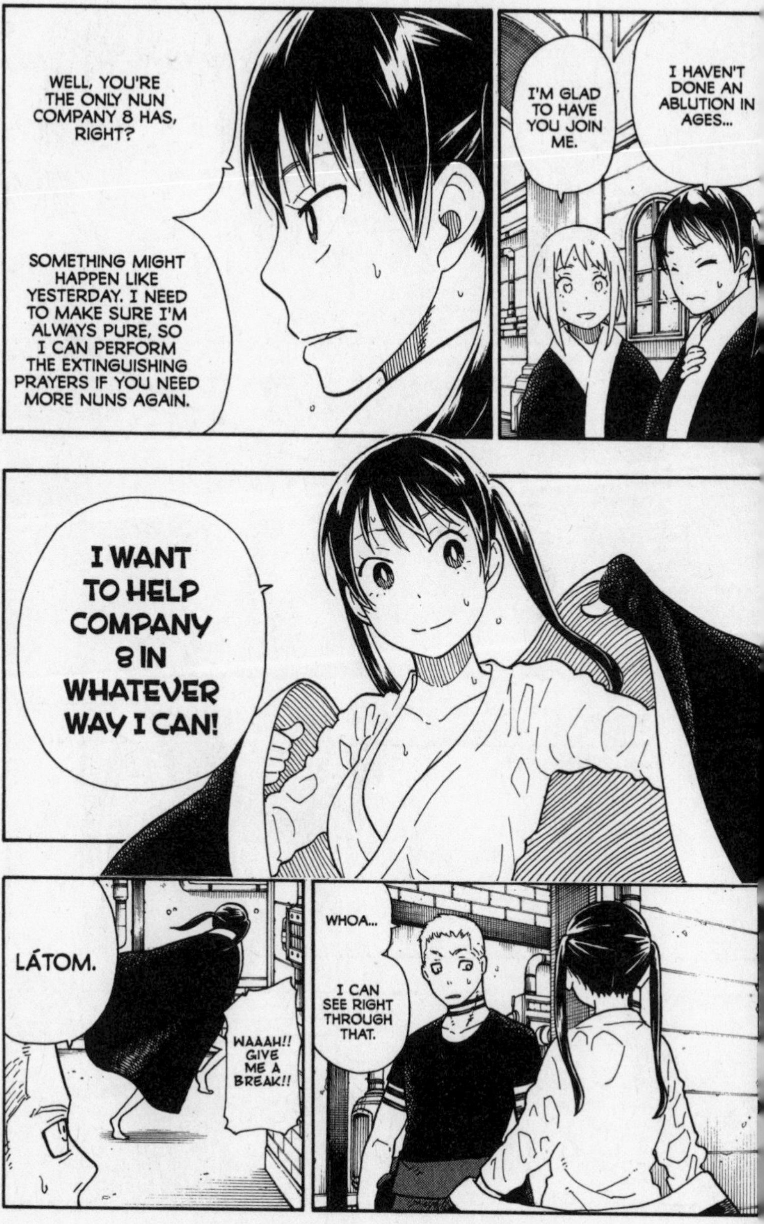
I HAVEN'T DONE AN ABLUTION IN AGES...
I'M GLAD TO HAVE YOU JOIN ME.
WELL, YOU'RE THE ONLY NUN COMPANY 8 HAS, RIGHT?
SOMETHING MIGHT HAPPEN LIKE YESTERDAY. I NEED TO MAKE SURE I'M ALWAYS PURE, SO I CAN PERFORM THE EXTINGUISHING PRAYERS IF YOU NEED MORE NUNS AGAIN.
I WANT TO HELP COMPANY 8 IN WHATEVER WAY I CAN!
WHOA...
I CAN SEE RIGHT THROUGH THAT.
WAAAH!! GIVE ME A BREAK!!
LÁTOM.

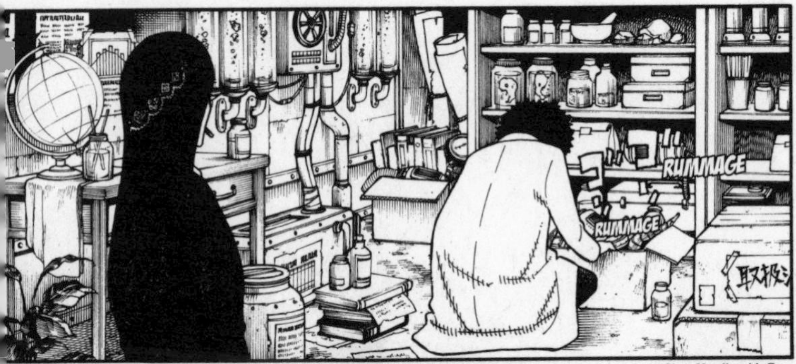
RUMMAGE
RUMMAGE
Sign: Handle with Care

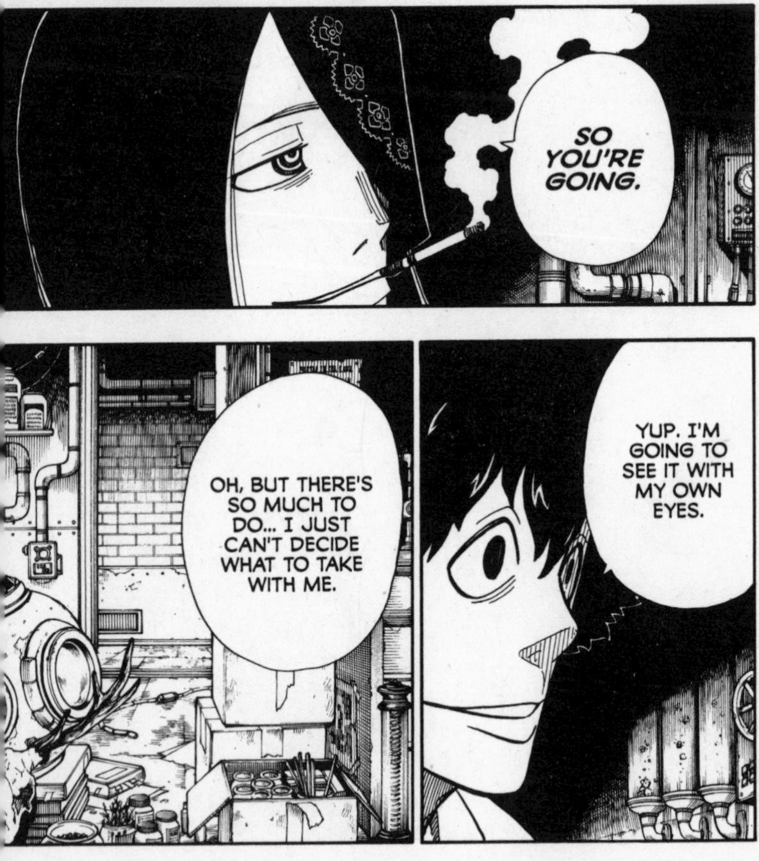
SO YOU'RE GOING.
YUP. I'M GOING TO SEE IT WITH MY OWN EYES.
OH, BUT THERE'S SO MUCH TO DO... I JUST CAN'T DECIDE WHAT TO TAKE WITH ME.

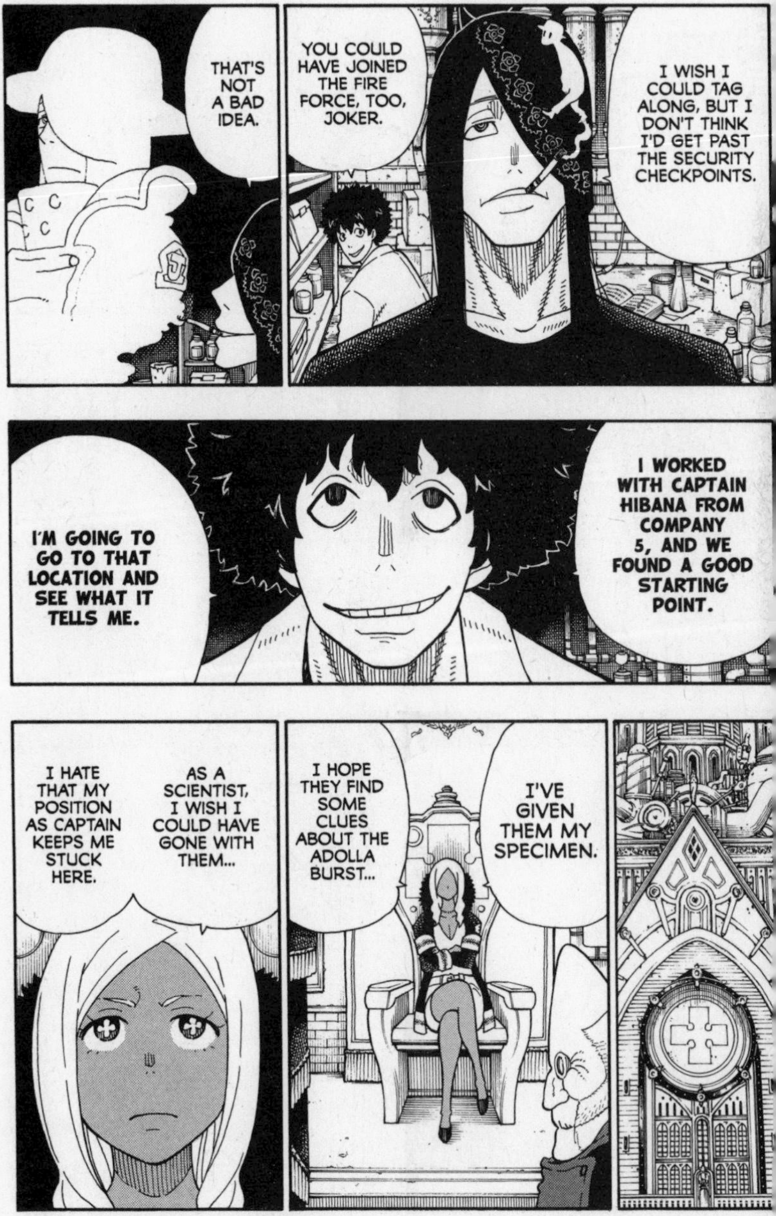
I WISH I COULD TAG ALONG, BUT I DON'T THINK I'D GET PAST THE SECURITY CHECKPOINTS.
YOU COULD HAVE JOINED THE FIRE FORCE, TOO, JOKER.
THAT'S NOT A BAD IDEA.
I WORKED WITH CAPTAIN HIBANA FROM COMPANY 5, AND WE FOUND A GOOD STARTING POINT.
I'M GOING TO GO TO THAT LOCATION AND SEE WHAT IT TELLS ME.
I'VE GIVEN THEM MY SPECIMEN.
I HOPE THEY FIND SOME CLUES ABOUT THE ADOLLA BURST...
AS A SCIENTIST, I WISH I COULD HAVE GONE WITH THEM...
I HATE THAT MY POSITION AS CAPTAIN KEEPS ME STUCK HERE.

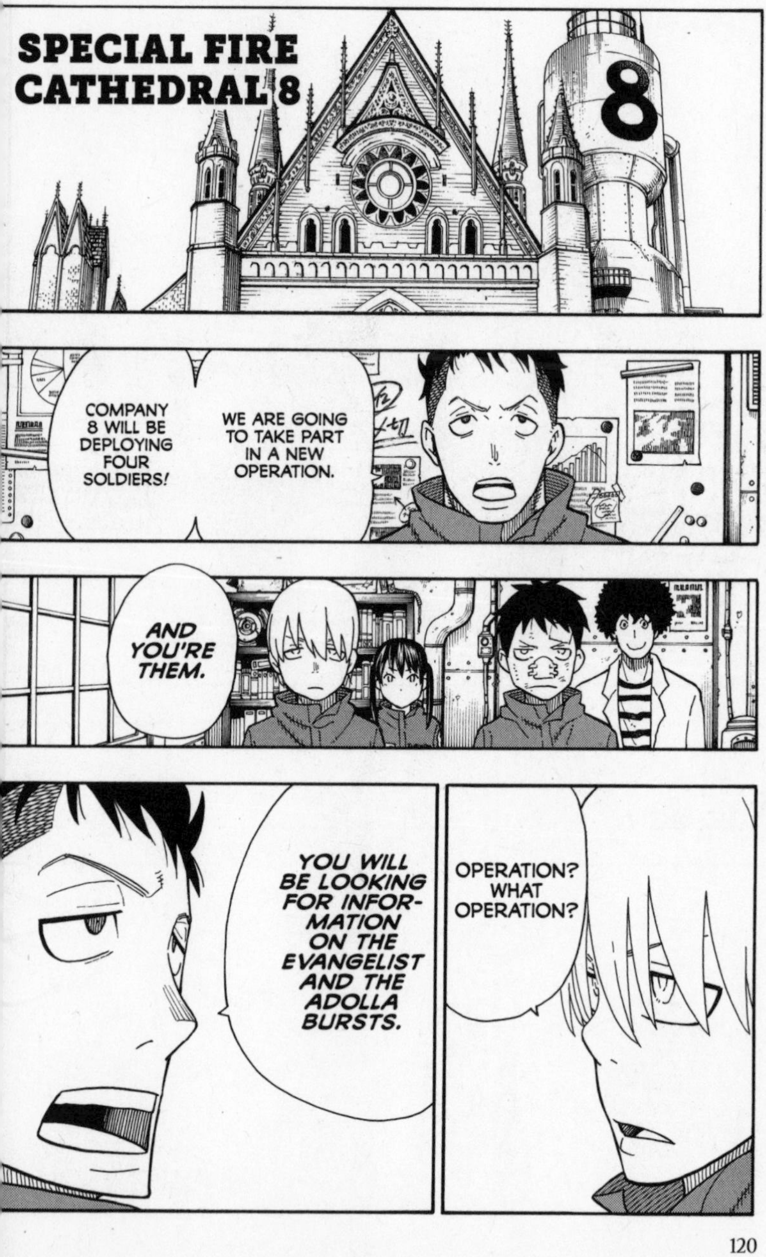
SPECIAL FIRE CATHEDRAL 8
8
WE ARE GOING TO TAKE PART IN A NEW OPERATION.
COMPANY 8 WILL BE DEPLOYING FOUR SOLDIERS!
AND YOU'RE THEM.
OPERATION? WHAT OPERATION?
YOU WILL BE LOOKING FOR INFORMATION ON THE EVANGELIST AND THE ADOLLA BURSTS.

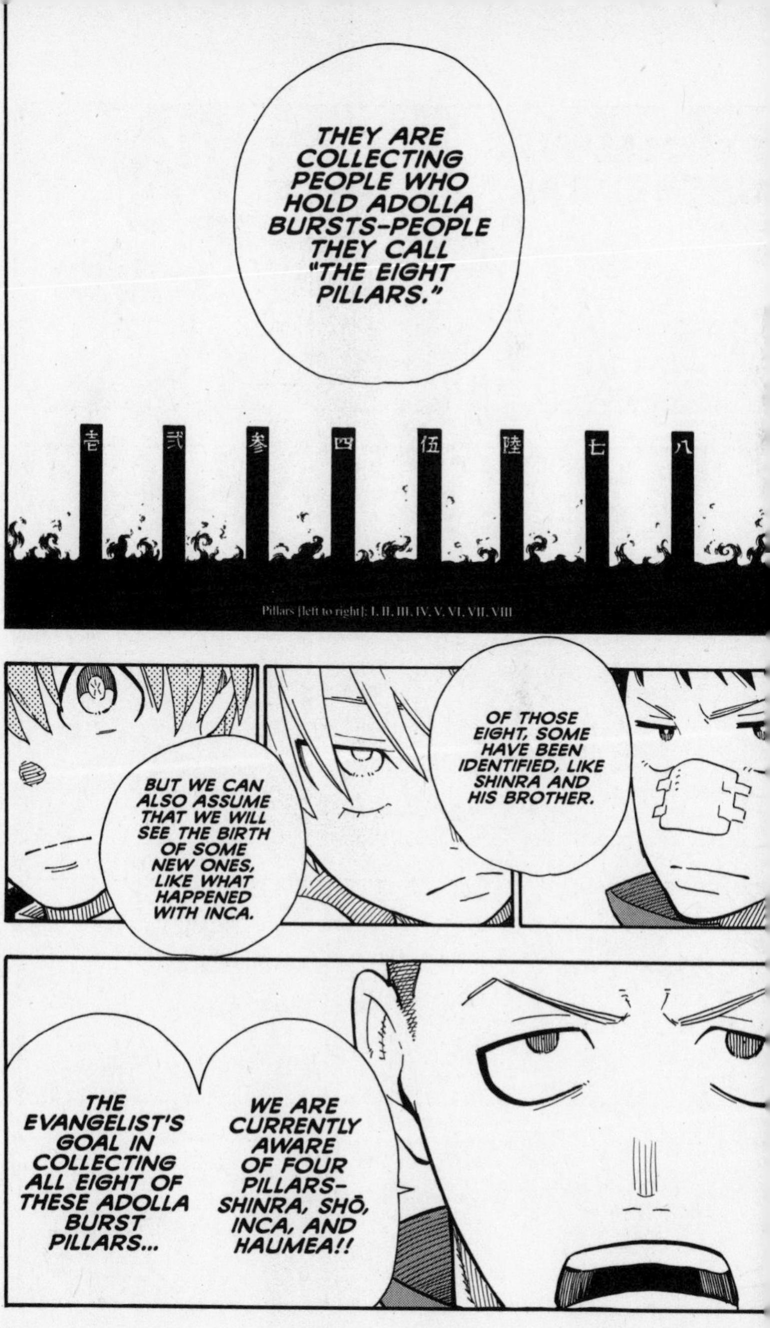
THEY ARE COLLECTING PEOPLE WHO HOLD ADOLLA BURSTS–PEOPLE THEY CALL "THE EIGHT PILLARS."
壱 弐 参 四 伍 陸 七 八
Pillars [left to right]: I, II, III, IV, V, VI, VII, VIII
OF THOSE EIGHT, SOME HAVE BEEN IDENTIFIED, LIKE SHINRA AND HIS BROTHER.
BUT WE CAN ALSO ASSUME THAT WE WILL SEE THE BIRTH OF SOME NEW ONES, LIKE WHAT HAPPENED WITH INCA.
WE ARE CURRENTLY AWARE OF FOUR PILLARS– SHINRA, SHŌ, INCA, AND HAUMEA!!
THE EVANGELIST'S GOAL IN COLLECTING ALL EIGHT OF THESE ADOLLA BURST PILLARS...

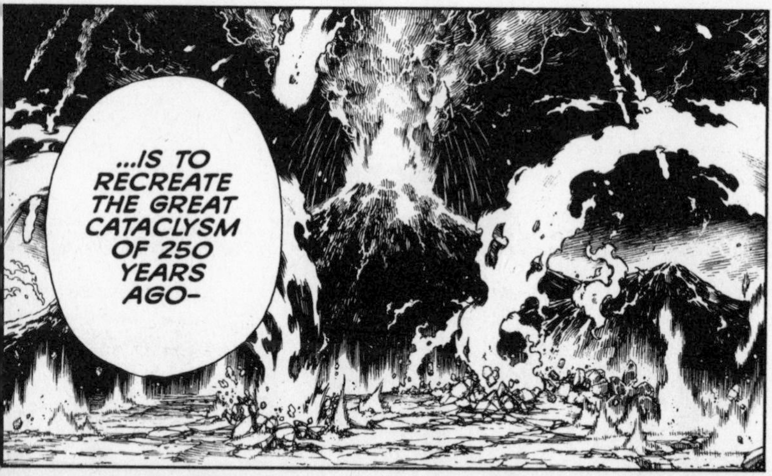
...IS TO RECREATE THE GREAT CATACLYSM OF 250 YEARS AGO-
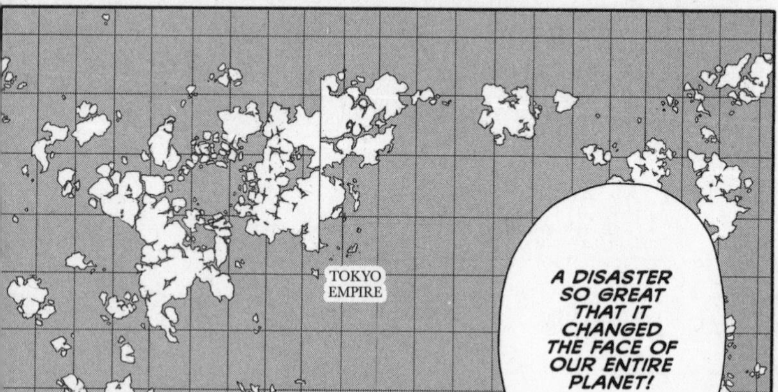
TOKYO EMPIRE
A DISASTER SO GREAT THAT IT CHANGED THE FACE OF OUR ENTIRE PLANET!
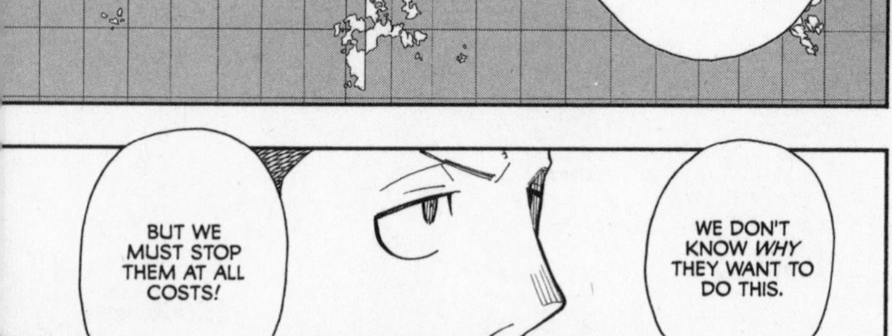
WE DON'T KNOW *WHY* THEY WANT TO DO THIS.
BUT WE MUST STOP THEM AT ALL COSTS!

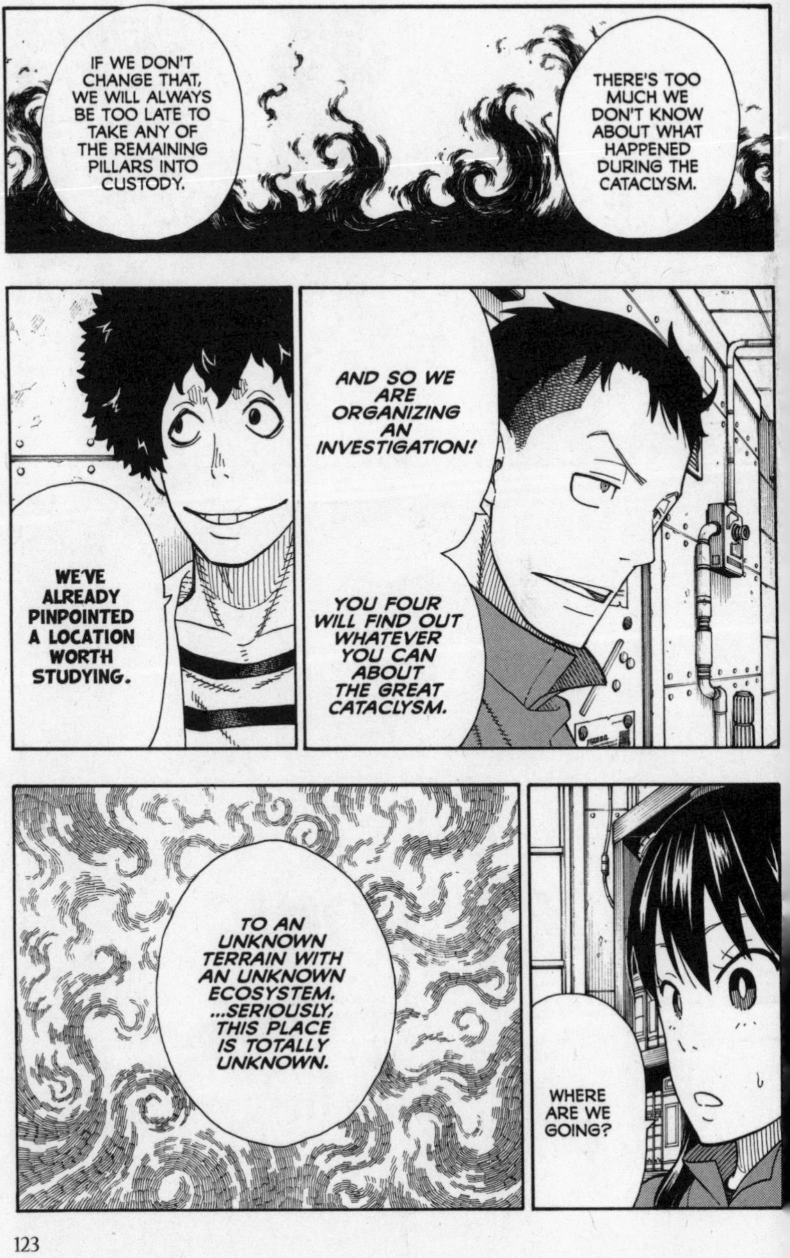
THERE'S TOO MUCH WE DON'T KNOW ABOUT WHAT HAPPENED DURING THE CATACLYSM.
IF WE DON'T CHANGE THAT, WE WILL ALWAYS BE TOO LATE TO TAKE ANY OF THE REMAINING PILLARS INTO CUSTODY.
AND SO WE ARE ORGANIZING AN INVESTIGATION!
YOU FOUR WILL FIND OUT WHATEVER YOU CAN ABOUT THE GREAT CATACLYSM.
WE'VE ALREADY PINPOINTED A LOCATION WORTH STUDYING.
WHERE ARE WE GOING?
TO AN UNKNOWN TERRAIN WITH AN UNKNOWN ECOSYSTEM. ...SERIOUSLY, THIS PLACE IS TOTALLY UNKNOWN.

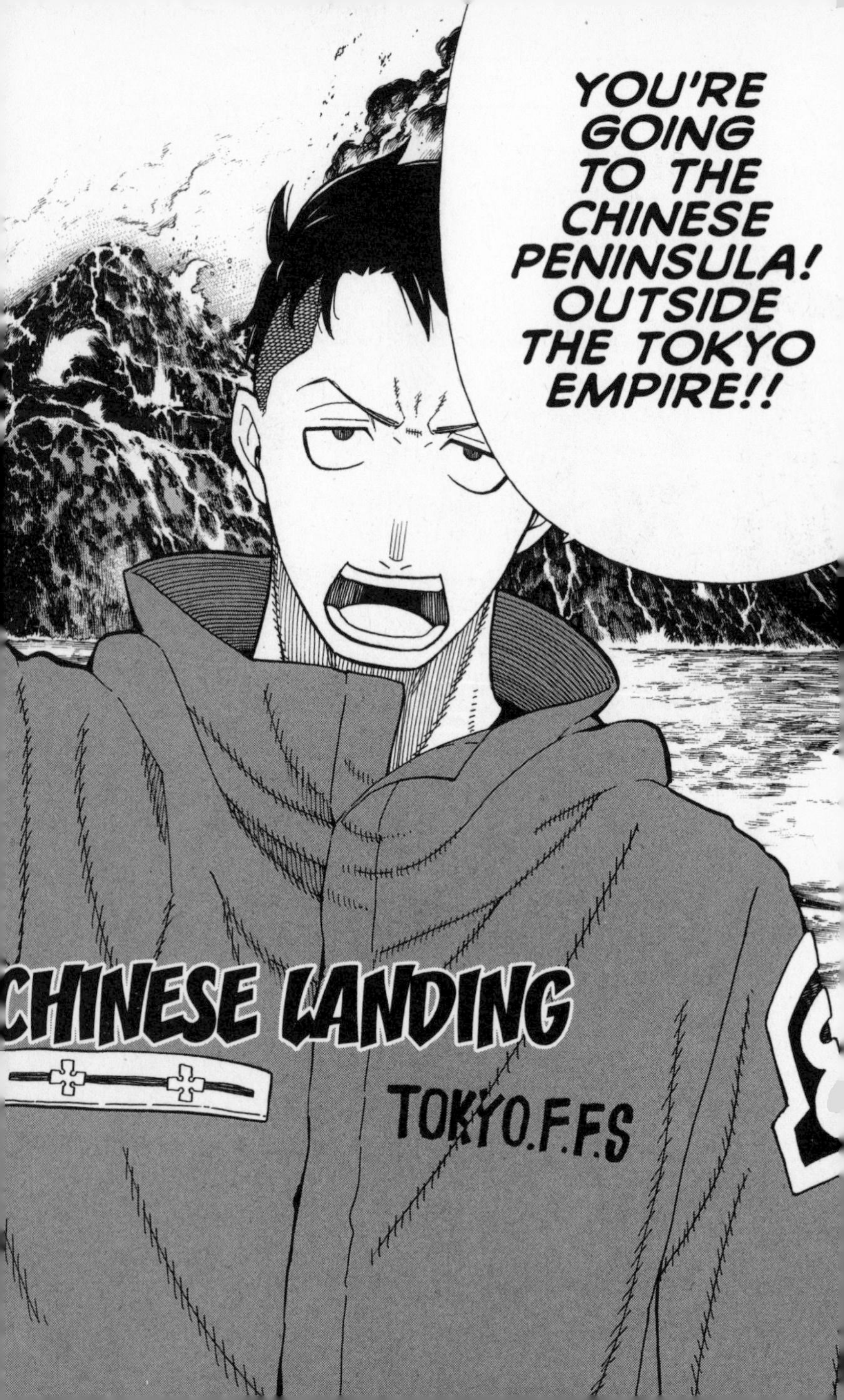
YOU'RE GOING TO THE CHINESE PENINSULA! OUTSIDE THE TOKYO EMPIRE!!
CHINESE LANDING
TOKYO.F.F.S

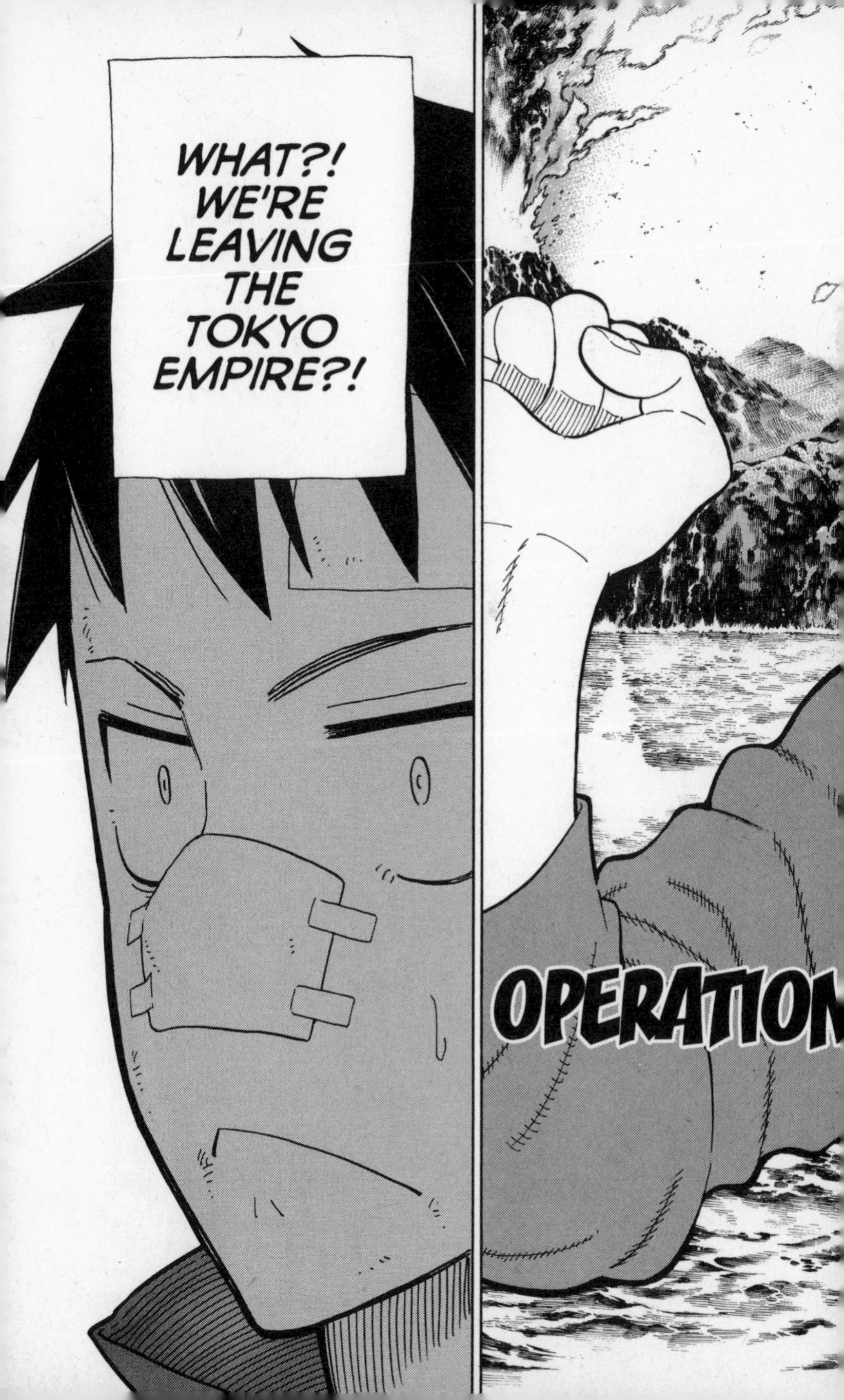
OPERATION
WHAT?! WE'RE LEAVING THE TOKYO EMPIRE?!

FIRE FORCE

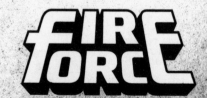

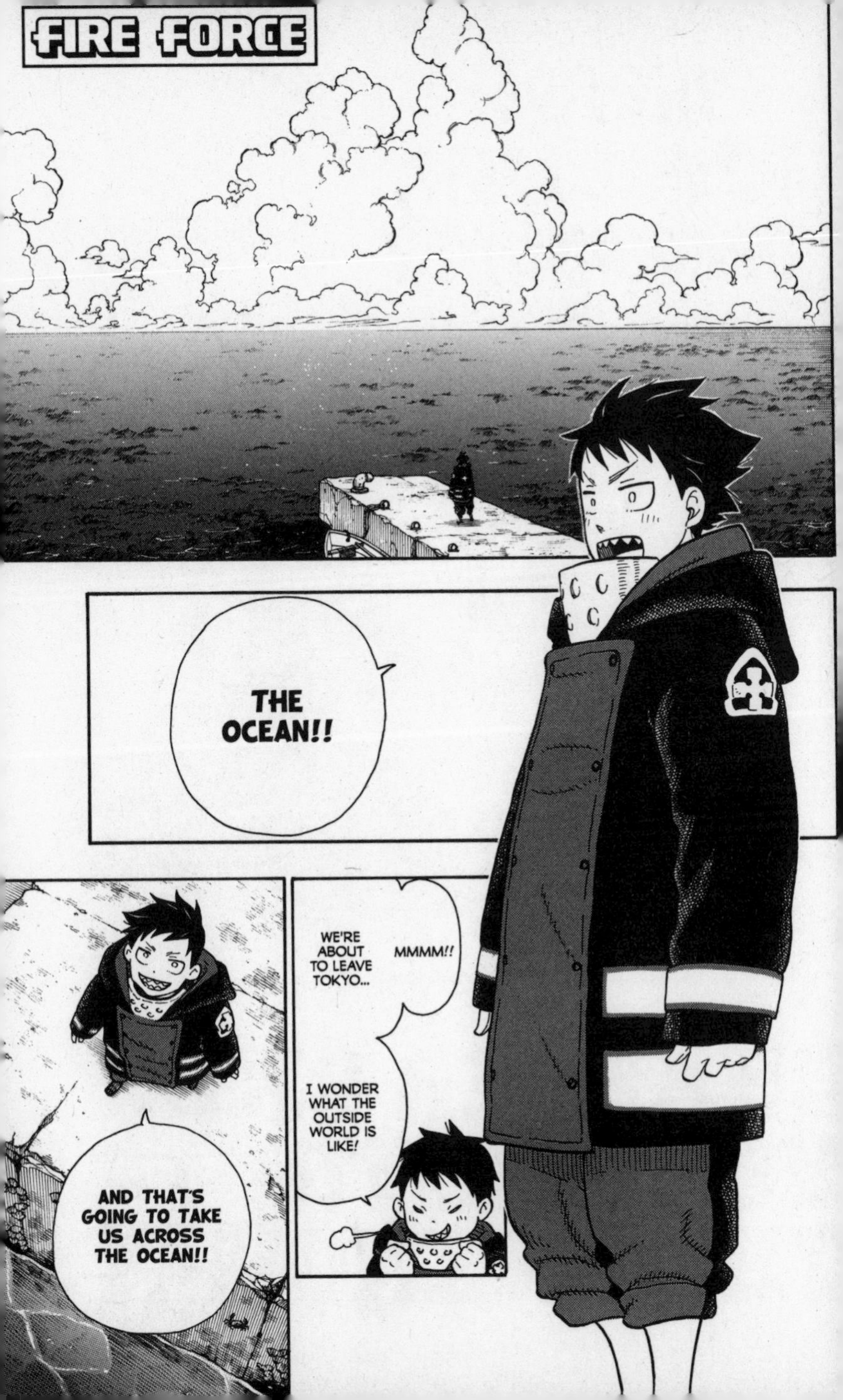
THE OCEAN!!
MMMM!!
WE'RE ABOUT TO LEAVE TOKYO...
I WONDER WHAT THE OUTSIDE WORLD IS LIKE!
AND THAT'S GOING TO TAKE US ACROSS THE OCEAN!!

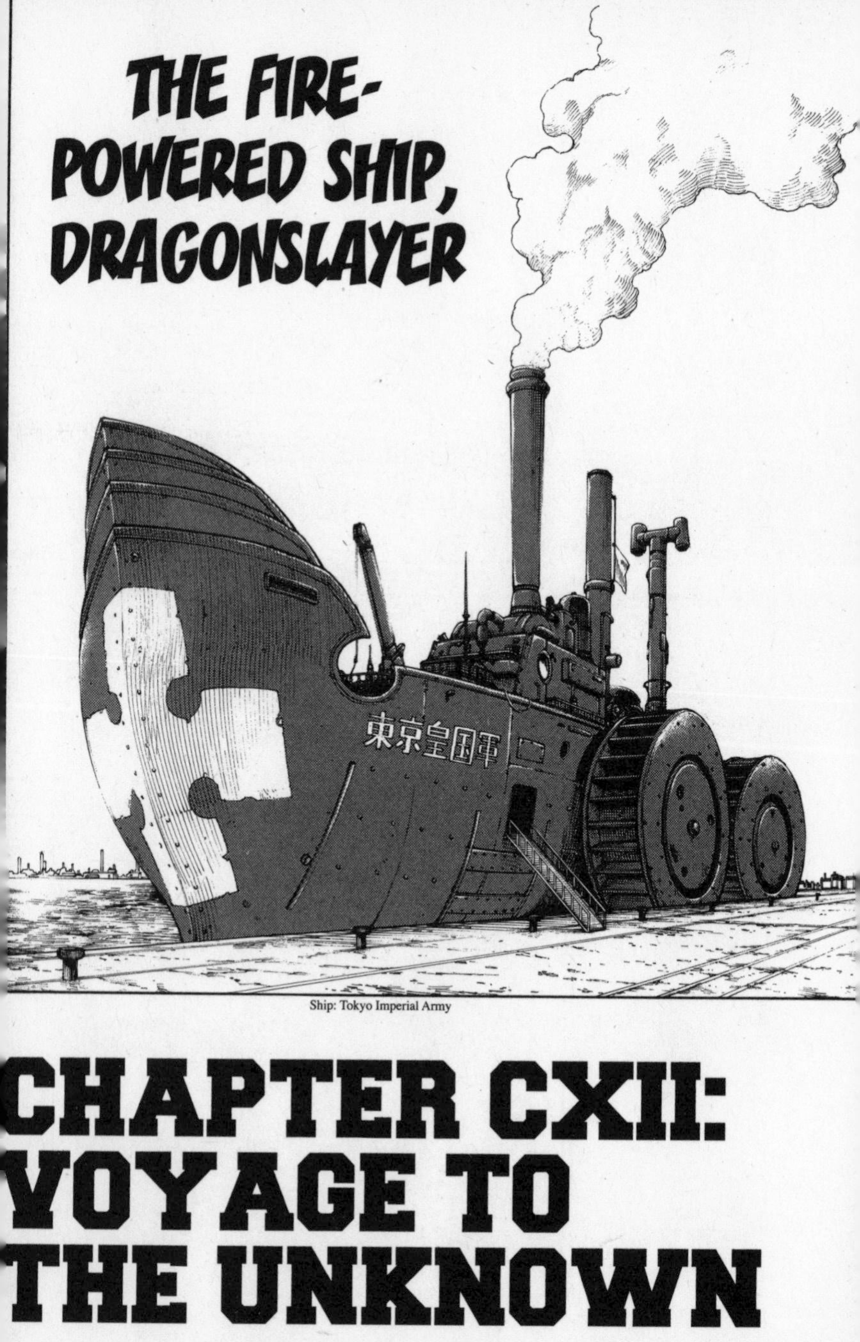
THE FIRE-POWERED SHIP, DRAGONSLAYER
東京皇国軍

Ship: Tokyo Imperial Army

CHAPTER CXII: VOYAGE TO THE UNKNOWN

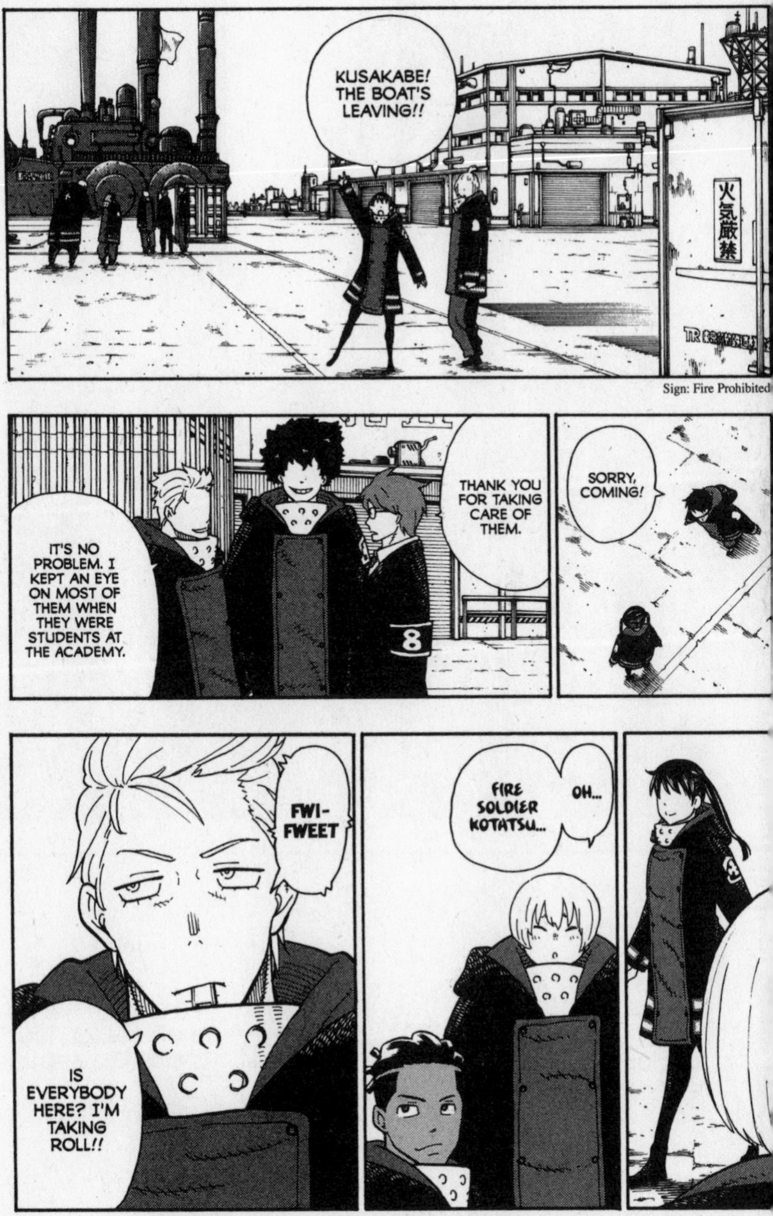
KUSAKABE! THE BOAT'S LEAVING!!
火気厳禁
SORRY, COMING!
THANK YOU FOR TAKING CARE OF THEM.
IT'S NO PROBLEM. I KEPT AN EYE ON MOST OF THEM WHEN THEY WERE STUDENTS AT THE ACADEMY.
OH...
FIRE SOLDIER KOTATSU...
FWI-FWEET
IS EVERYBODY HERE? I'M TAKING ROLL!!
Sign: Fire Prohibited

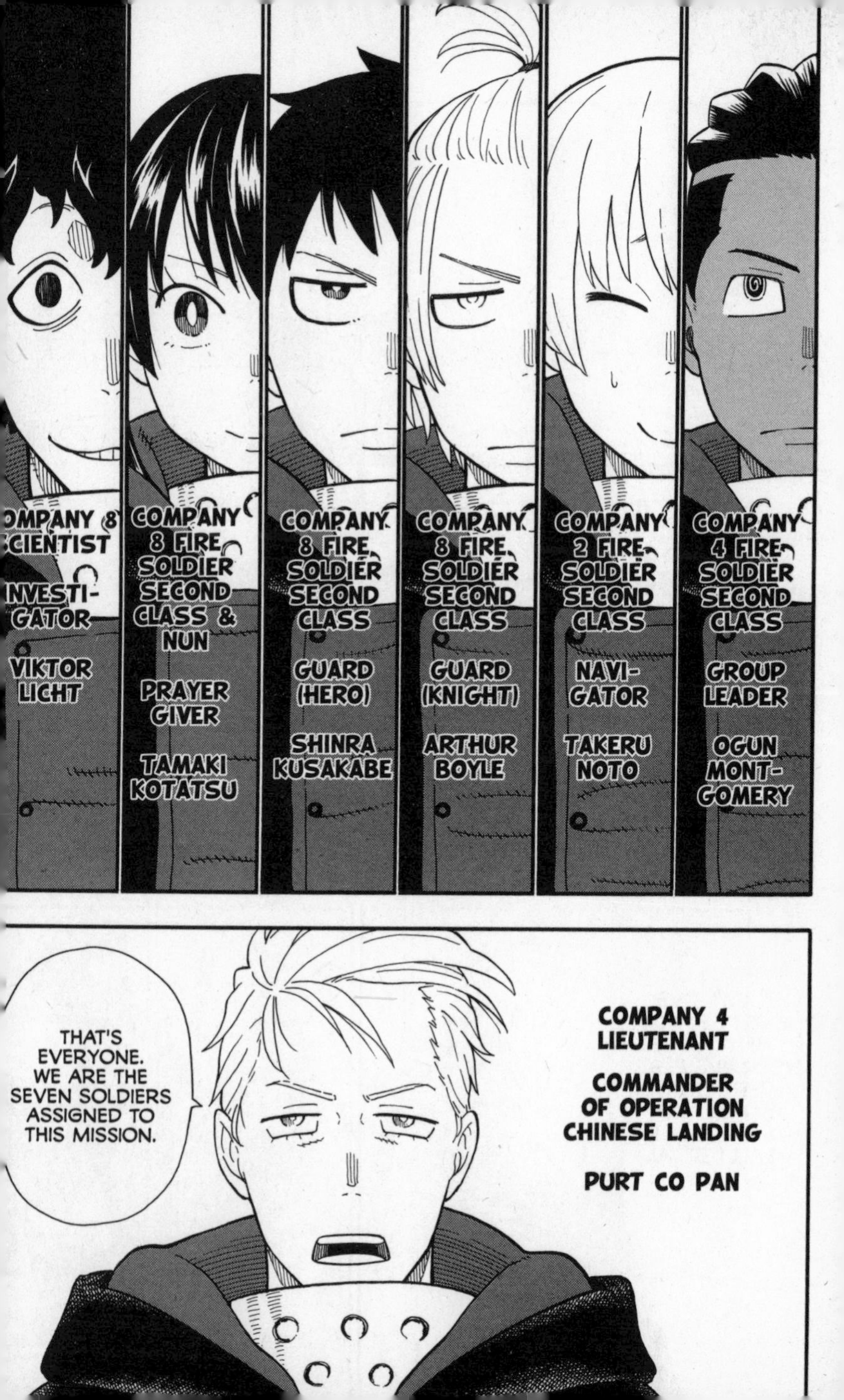
COMPANY 4 FIRE SOLDIER SECOND CLASS
GROUP LEADER
OGUN MONT-GOMERY
COMPANY 2 FIRE SOLDIER SECOND CLASS
NAVI-GATOR
TAKERU NOTO
COMPANY 8 FIRE SOLDIER SECOND CLASS
GUARD (KNIGHT)
ARTHUR BOYLE
COMPANY 8 FIRE SOLDIER SECOND CLASS
GUARD (HERO)
SHINRA KUSAKABE
COMPANY 8 FIRE SOLDIER SECOND CLASS & NUN
PRAYER GIVER
TAMAKI KOTATSU
OMPANY 8 CIENTIST
INVESTI-GATOR
VIKTOR LICHT
COMPANY 4 LIEUTENANT
COMMANDER OF OPERATION CHINESE LANDING
PURT CO PAN
THAT'S EVERYONE. WE ARE THE SEVEN SOLDIERS ASSIGNED TO THIS MISSION.

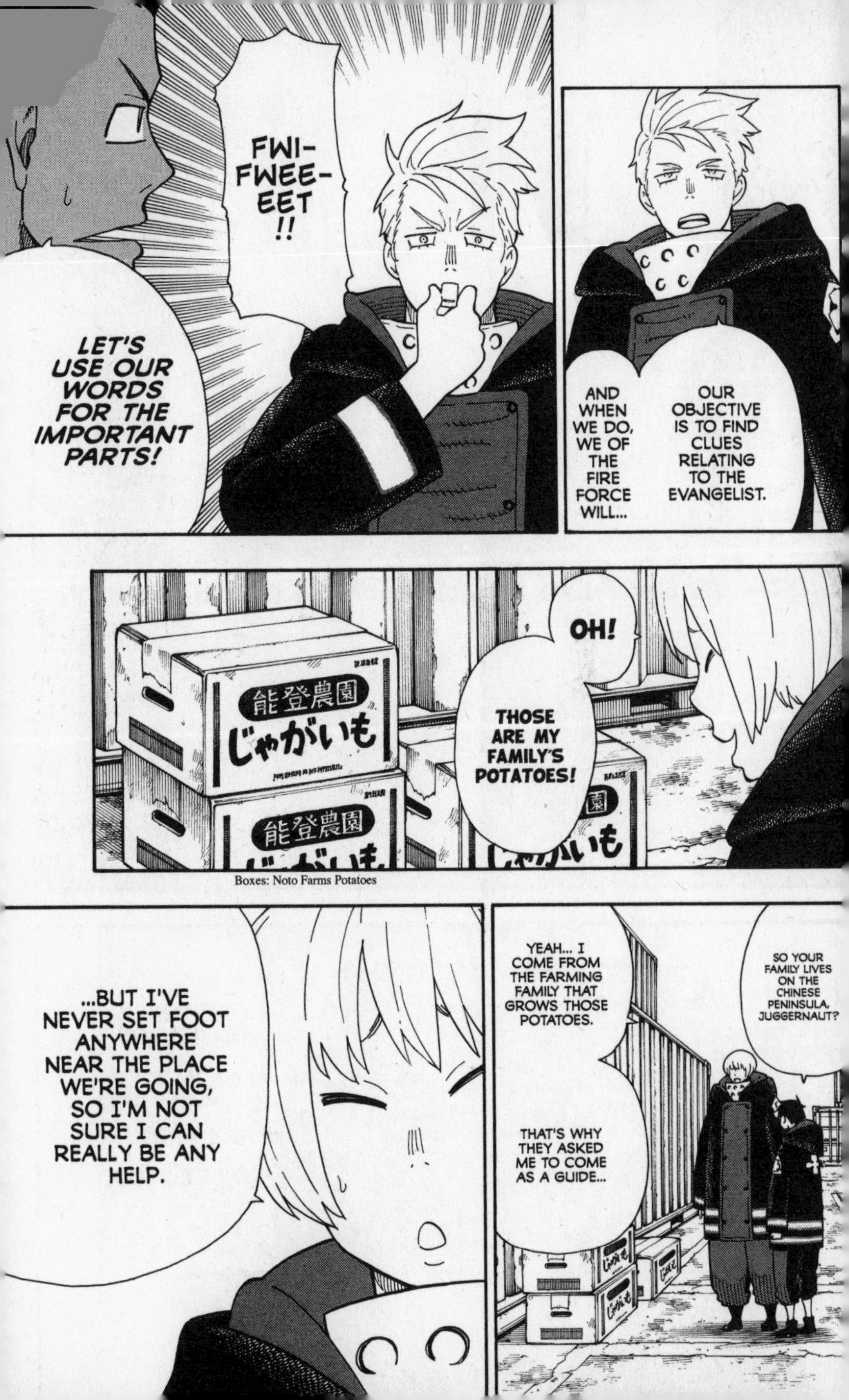
OUR OBJECTIVE IS TO FIND CLUES RELATING TO THE EVANGELIST.
AND WHEN WE DO, WE OF THE FIRE FORCE WILL...
FWI-FWEEE-EET !!
LET'S USE OUR WORDS FOR THE IMPORTANT PARTS!
OH!
THOSE ARE MY FAMILY'S POTATOES!
能登農園
じゃがいも
SO YOUR FAMILY LIVES ON THE CHINESE PENINSULA, JUGGERNAUT?
YEAH... I COME FROM THE FARMING FAMILY THAT GROWS THOSE POTATOES.
THAT'S WHY THEY ASKED ME TO COME AS A GUIDE...
...BUT I'VE NEVER SET FOOT ANYWHERE NEAR THE PLACE WE'RE GOING, SO I'M NOT SURE I CAN REALLY BE ANY HELP.
Boxes: Noto Farms Potatoes

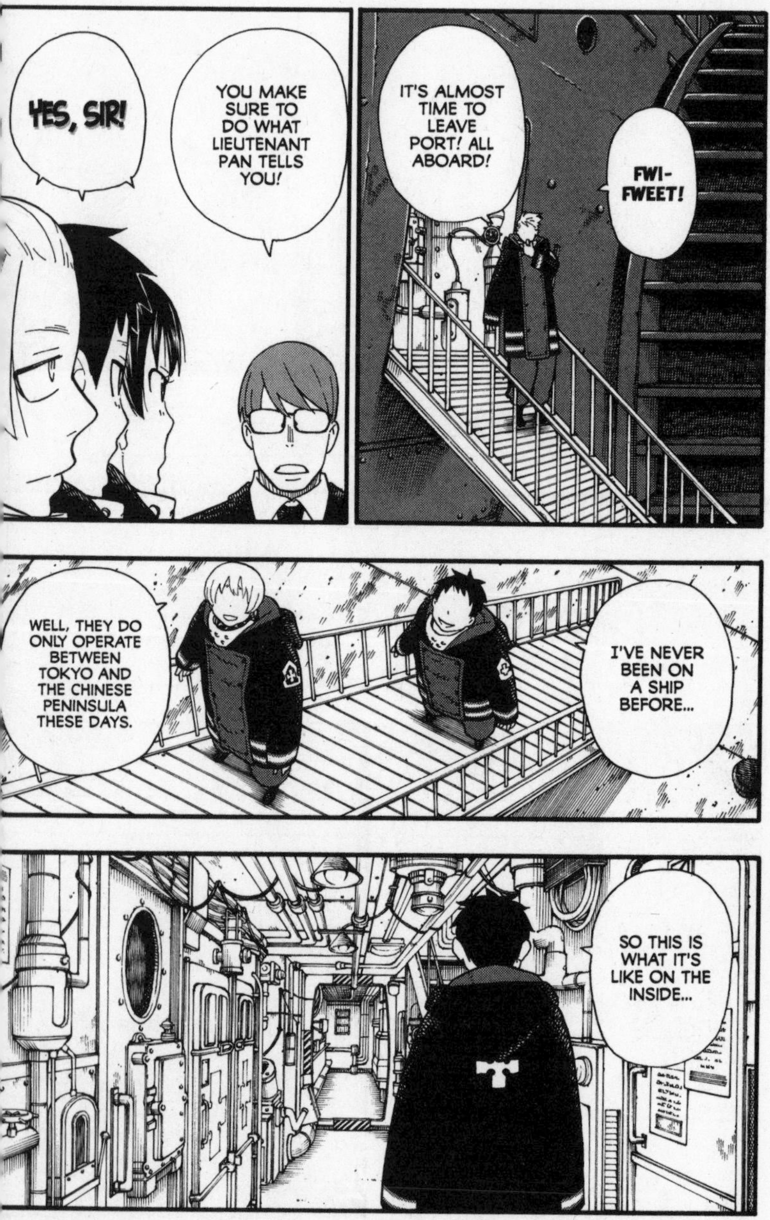
FWI-FWEET!
IT'S ALMOST TIME TO LEAVE PORT! ALL ABOARD!
YOU MAKE SURE TO DO WHAT LIEUTENANT PAN TELLS YOU!
YES, SIR!
I'VE NEVER BEEN ON A SHIP BEFORE...
WELL, THEY DO ONLY OPERATE BETWEEN TOKYO AND THE CHINESE PENINSULA THESE DAYS.
SO THIS IS WHAT IT'S LIKE ON THE INSIDE...

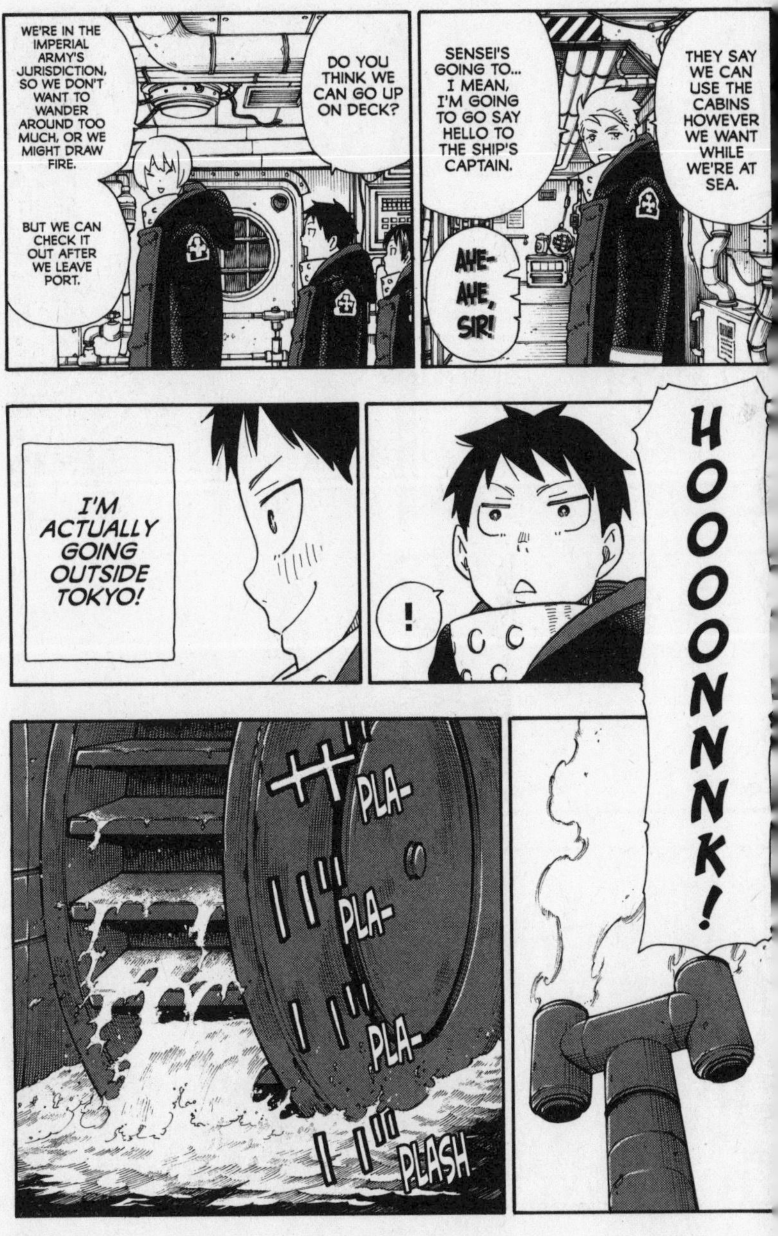
THEY SAY WE CAN USE THE CABINS HOWEVER WE WANT WHILE WE'RE AT SEA.
SENSEI'S GOING TO... I MEAN, I'M GOING TO GO SAY HELLO TO THE SHIP'S CAPTAIN.
AHE-AHE, SIR!
DO YOU THINK WE CAN GO UP ON DECK?
WE'RE IN THE IMPERIAL ARMY'S JURISDICTION, SO WE DON'T WANT TO WANDER AROUND TOO MUCH, OR WE MIGHT DRAW FIRE.
BUT WE CAN CHECK IT OUT AFTER WE LEAVE PORT.
HOOOONNNK!
!
I'M ACTUALLY GOING OUTSIDE TOKYO!
PLA-
PLA-
PLA-
PLASH

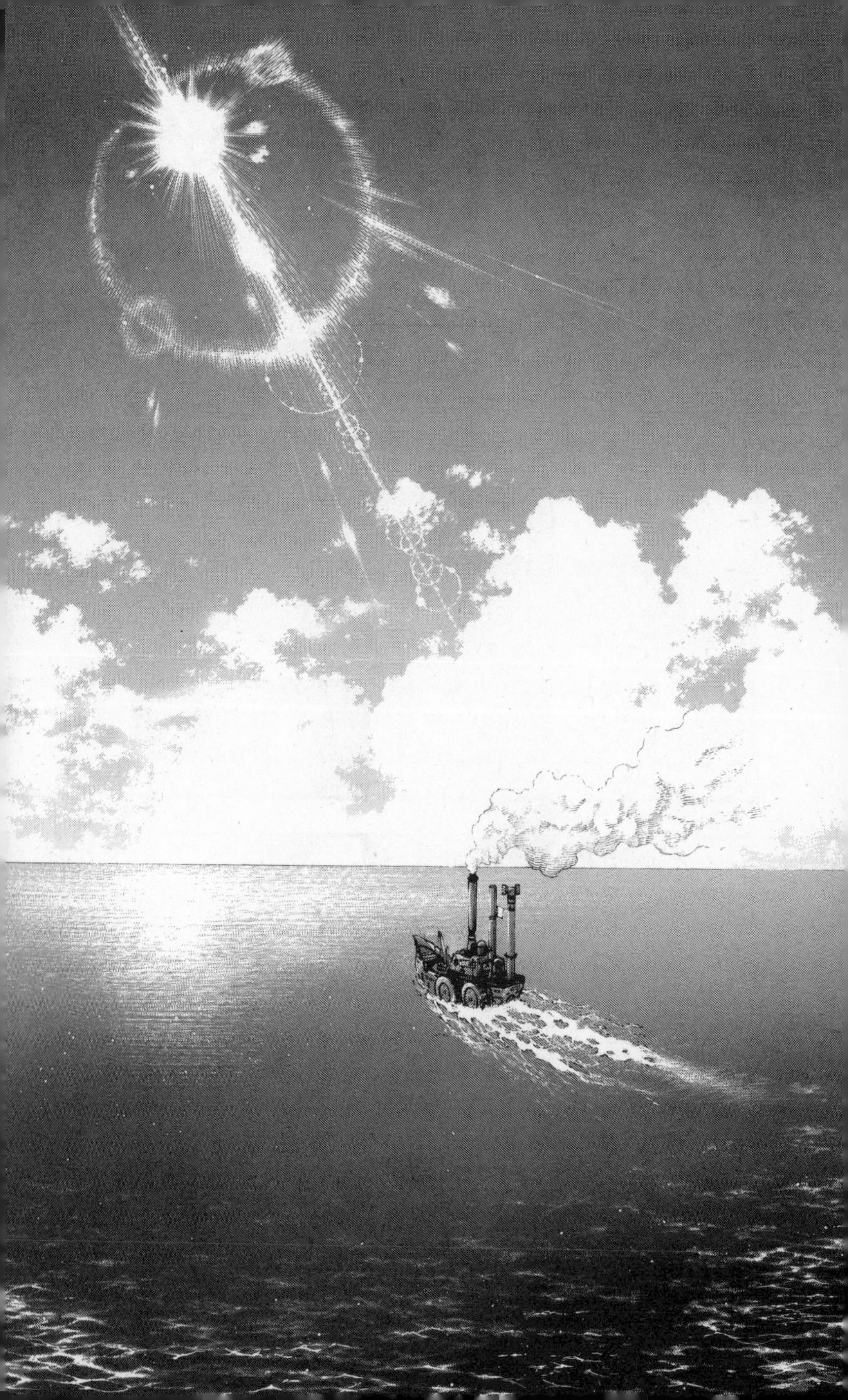

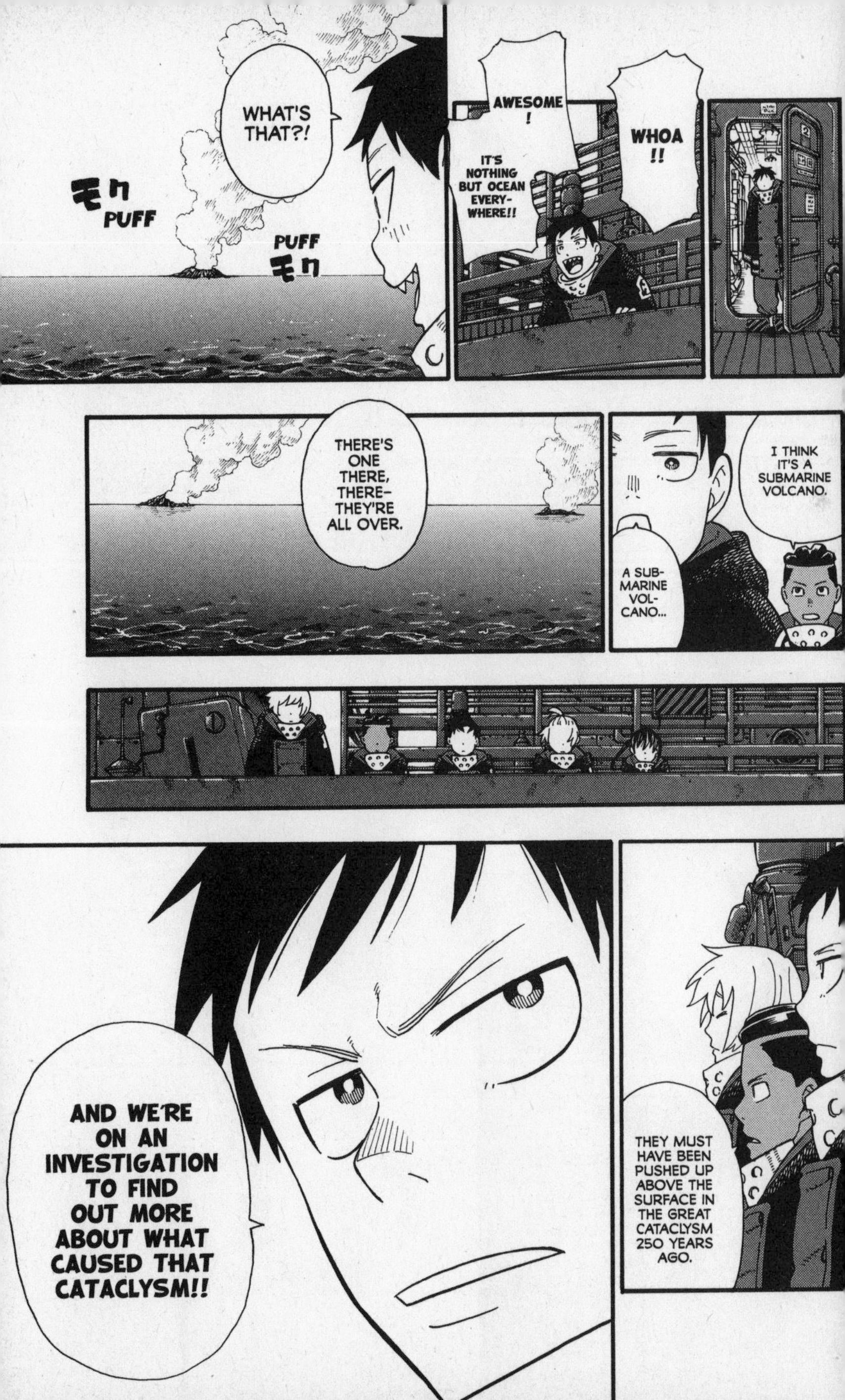
WHOA!!
AWESOME!
IT'S NOTHING BUT OCEAN EVERY-WHERE!!
WHAT'S THAT?!
モク PUFF
PUFF モク
I THINK IT'S A SUBMARINE VOLCANO.
A SUB-MARINE VOL-CANO...
THERE'S ONE THERE, THERE— THEY'RE ALL OVER.
THEY MUST HAVE BEEN PUSHED UP ABOVE THE SURFACE IN THE GREAT CATACLYSM 250 YEARS AGO.
AND WE'RE ON AN INVESTIGATION TO FIND OUT MORE ABOUT WHAT CAUSED THAT CATACLYSM!!

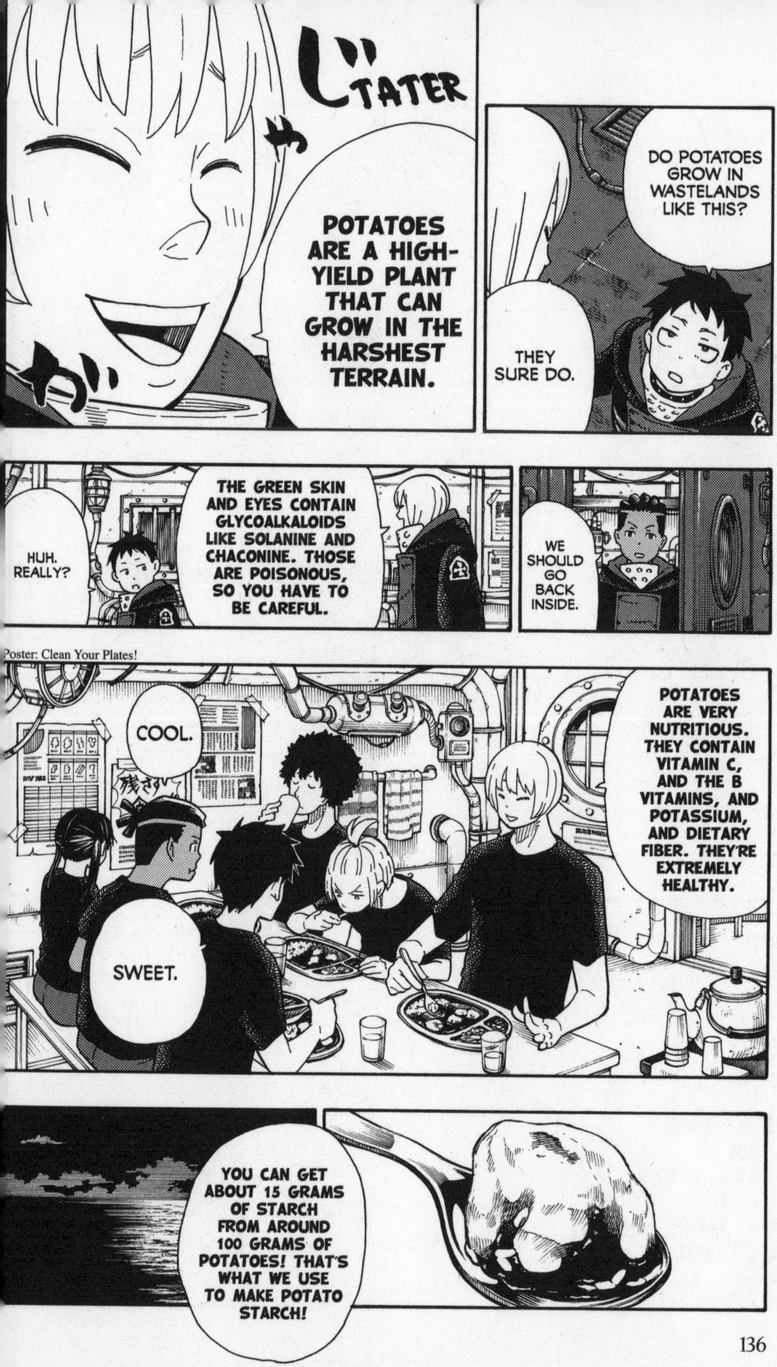
DO POTATOES GROW IN WASTELANDS LIKE THIS?
THEY SURE DO.
TATER
POTATOES ARE A HIGH-YIELD PLANT THAT CAN GROW IN THE HARSHEST TERRAIN.
WE SHOULD GO BACK INSIDE.
THE GREEN SKIN AND EYES CONTAIN GLYCOALKALOIDS LIKE SOLANINE AND CHACONINE. THOSE ARE POISONOUS, SO YOU HAVE TO BE CAREFUL.
HUH. REALLY?
Poster: Clean Your Plates!
POTATOES ARE VERY NUTRITIOUS. THEY CONTAIN VITAMIN C, AND THE B VITAMINS, AND POTASSIUM, AND DIETARY FIBER. THEY'RE EXTREMELY HEALTHY.
COOL.
SWEET.
YOU CAN GET ABOUT 15 GRAMS OF STARCH FROM AROUND 100 GRAMS OF POTATOES! THAT'S WHAT WE USE TO MAKE POTATO STARCH!

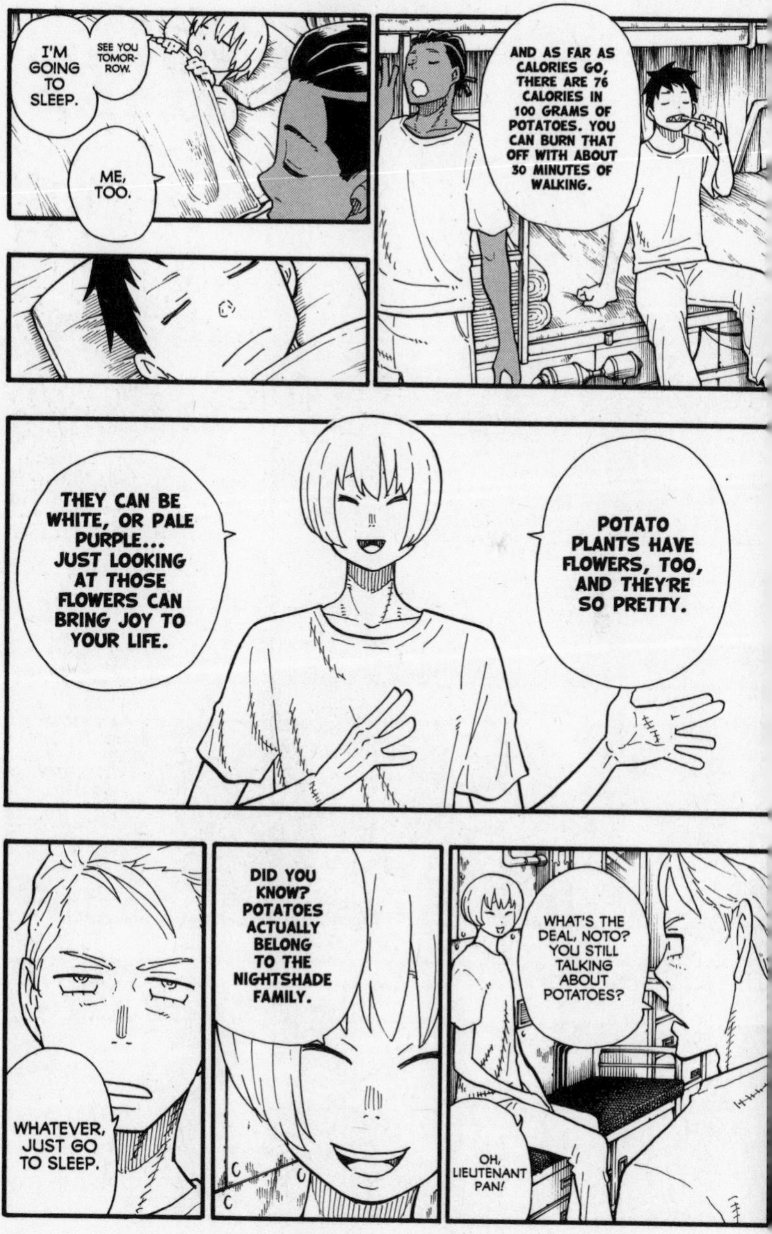
AND AS FAR AS CALORIES GO, THERE ARE 76 CALORIES IN 100 GRAMS OF POTATOES. YOU CAN BURN THAT OFF WITH ABOUT 30 MINUTES OF WALKING.
SEE YOU TOMOR-ROW.
I'M GOING TO SLEEP.
ME, TOO.
POTATO PLANTS HAVE FLOWERS, TOO, AND THEY'RE SO PRETTY.
THEY CAN BE WHITE, OR PALE PURPLE... JUST LOOKING AT THOSE FLOWERS CAN BRING JOY TO YOUR LIFE.
WHAT'S THE DEAL, NOTO? YOU STILL TALKING ABOUT POTATOES?
OH, LIEUTENANT PAN!
DID YOU KNOW? POTATOES ACTUALLY BELONG TO THE NIGHTSHADE FAMILY.
WHATEVER, JUST GO TO SLEEP.

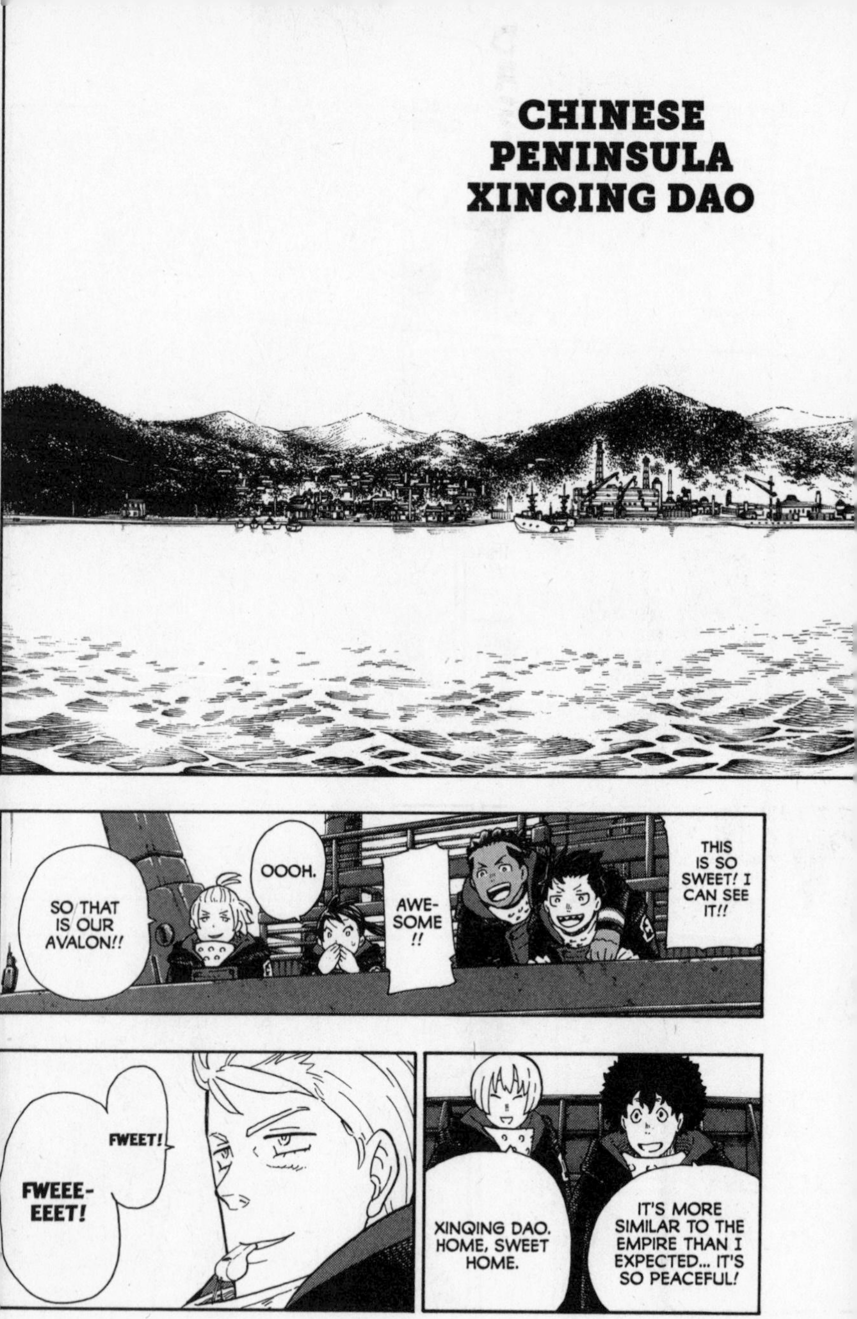
CHINESE PENINSULA XINQING DAO
THIS IS SO SWEET! I CAN SEE IT!!
AWE-SOME!!
OOOH.
SO THAT IS OUR AVALON!!
IT'S MORE SIMILAR TO THE EMPIRE THAN I EXPECTED... IT'S SO PEACEFUL!
XINQING DAO. HOME, SWEET HOME.
FWEET!
FWEEE-EEET!

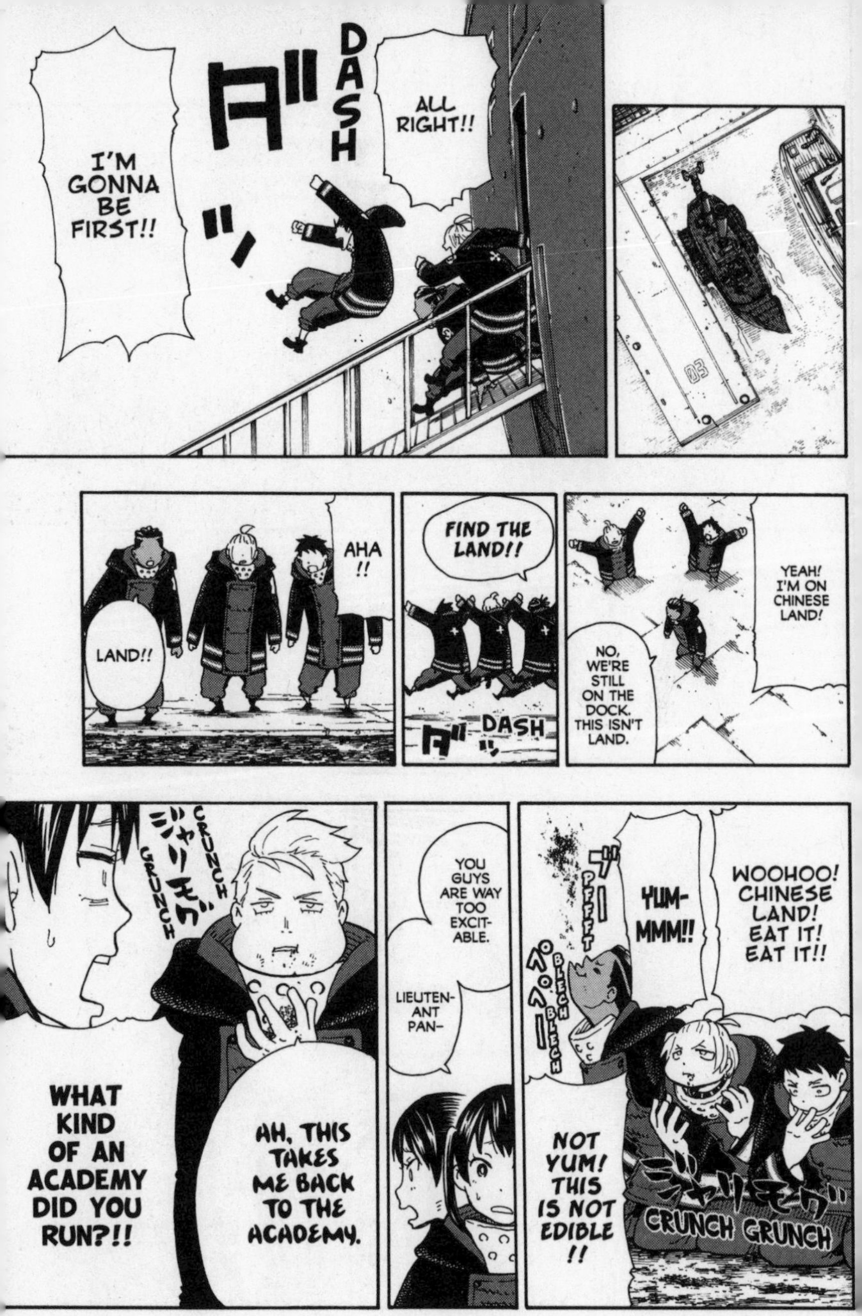
ALL RIGHT!!
DASH
I'M GONNA BE FIRST!!
YEAH! I'M ON CHINESE LAND!
NO, WE'RE STILL ON THE DOCK. THIS ISN'T LAND.
FIND THE LAND!!
DASH
AHA!!
LAND!!
WOOHOO! CHINESE LAND! EAT IT! EAT IT!!
YUM-MMM!!
PFFFT
BLECH BLECH
NOT YUM! THIS IS NOT EDIBLE!!
CRUNCH GRUNCH
YOU GUYS ARE WAY TOO EXCIT-ABLE.
LIEUTEN-ANT PAN-
CRUNCH GRUNCH
AH, THIS TAKES ME BACK TO THE ACADEMY.
WHAT KIND OF AN ACADEMY DID YOU RUN?!!

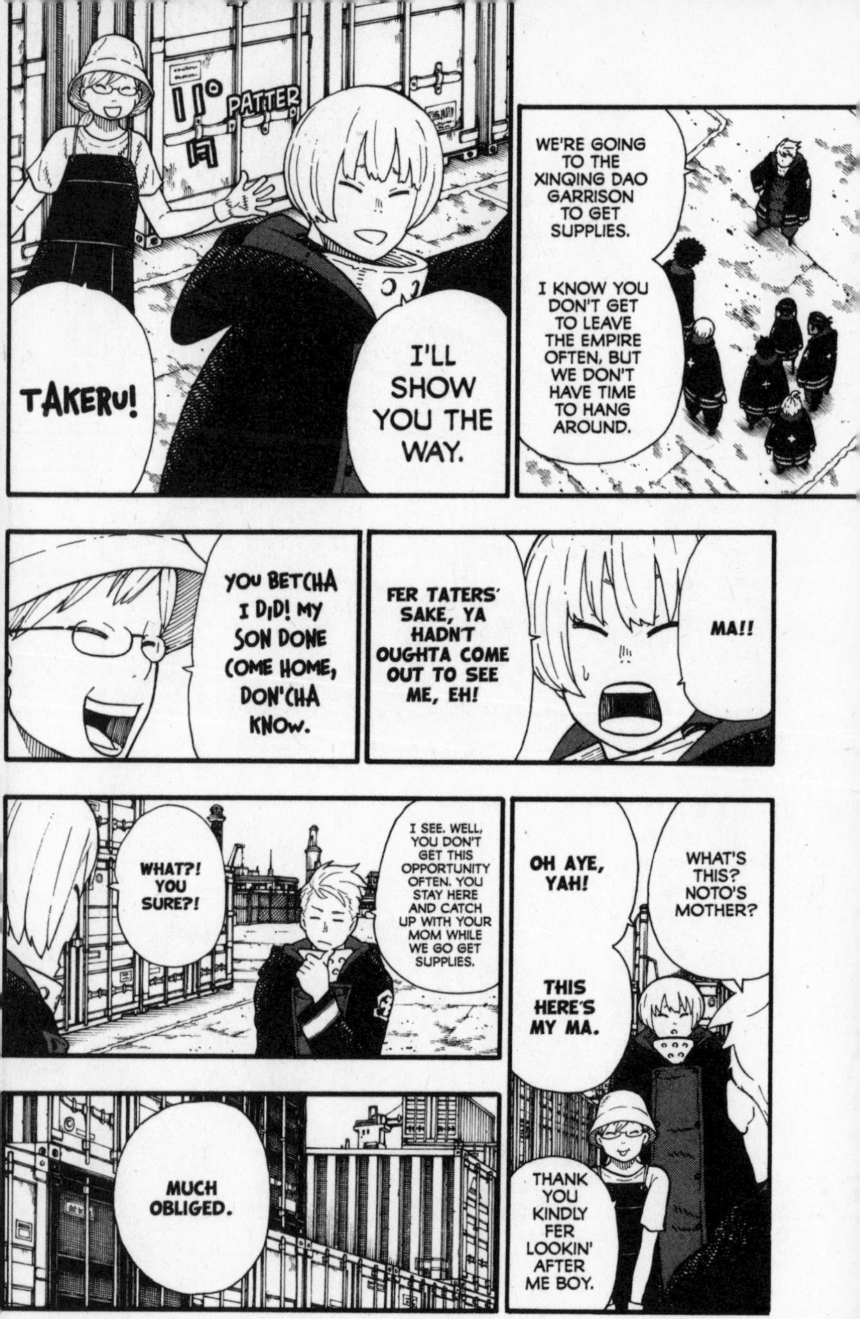
WE'RE GOING TO THE XINQING DAO GARRISON TO GET SUPPLIES.
I KNOW YOU DON'T GET TO LEAVE THE EMPIRE OFTEN, BUT WE DON'T HAVE TIME TO HANG AROUND.
PATTER
I'LL SHOW YOU THE WAY.
TAKERU!
MA!!
FER TATERS' SAKE, YA HADN'T OUGHTA COME OUT TO SEE ME, EH!
YOU BETCHA I DID! MY SON DONE COME HOME, DON'CHA KNOW.
WHAT'S THIS? NOTO'S MOTHER?
OH AYE, YAH!
THIS HERE'S MY MA.
THANK YOU KINDLY FER LOOKIN' AFTER ME BOY.
I SEE. WELL, YOU DON'T GET THIS OPPORTUNITY OFTEN. YOU STAY HERE AND CATCH UP WITH YOUR MOM WHILE WE GO GET SUPPLIES.
WHAT?! YOU SURE?!
MUCH OBLIGED.

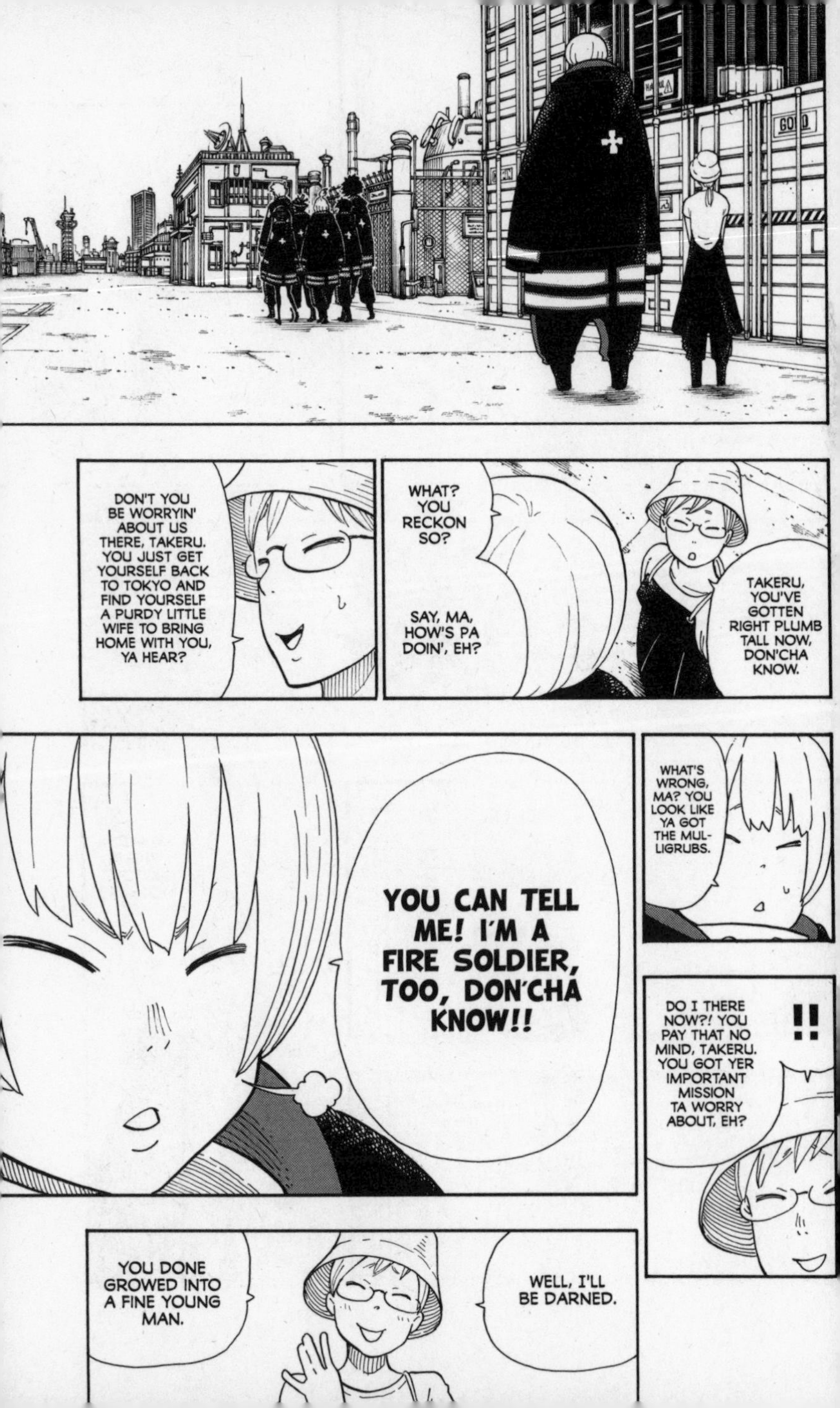
TAKERU, YOU'VE GOTTEN RIGHT PLUMB TALL NOW, DON'CHA KNOW.
WHAT? YOU RECKON SO?
SAY, MA, HOW'S PA DOIN', EH?
DON'T YOU BE WORRYIN' ABOUT US THERE, TAKERU. YOU JUST GET YOURSELF BACK TO TOKYO AND FIND YOURSELF A PURDY LITTLE WIFE TO BRING HOME WITH YOU, YA HEAR?
WHAT'S WRONG, MA? YOU LOOK LIKE YA GOT THE MUL-LIGRUBS.
!!
DO I THERE NOW?! YOU PAY THAT NO MIND, TAKERU. YOU GOT YER IMPORTANT MISSION TA WORRY ABOUT, EH?
YOU CAN TELL ME! I'M A FIRE SOLDIER, TOO, DON'CHA KNOW!!
WELL, I'LL BE DARNED.
YOU DONE GROWED INTO A FINE YOUNG MAN.

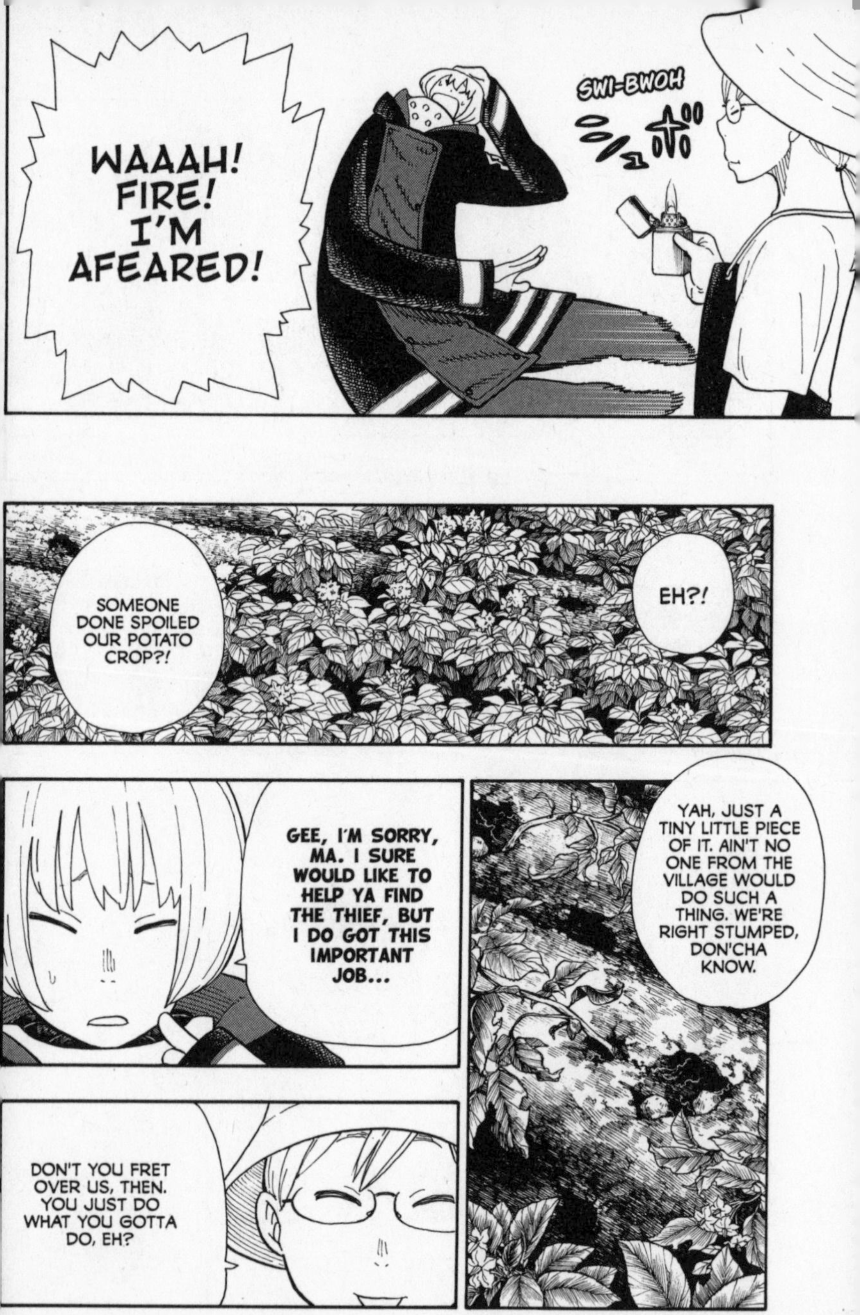
SWI-BWOH
WAAAH! FIRE! I'M AFEARED!
EH?!
SOMEONE DONE SPOILED OUR POTATO CROP?!
YAH, JUST A TINY LITTLE PIECE OF IT. AIN'T NO ONE FROM THE VILLAGE WOULD DO SUCH A THING. WE'RE RIGHT STUMPED, DON'CHA KNOW.
GEE, I'M SORRY, MA. I SURE WOULD LIKE TO HELP YA FIND THE THIEF, BUT I DO GOT THIS IMPORTANT JOB...
DON'T YOU FRET OVER US, THEN. YOU JUST DO WHAT YOU GOTTA DO, EH?

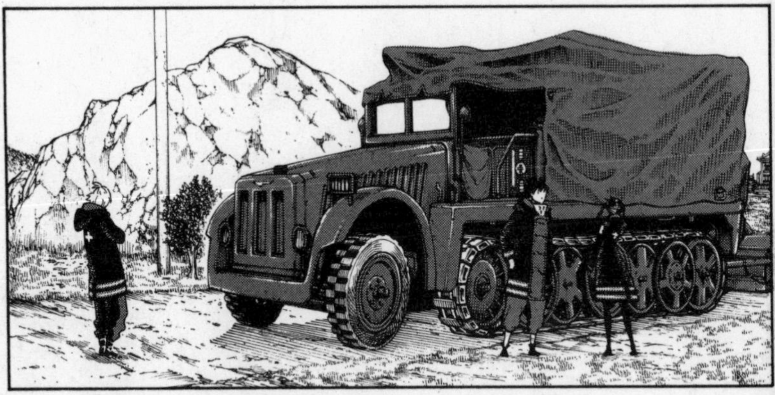

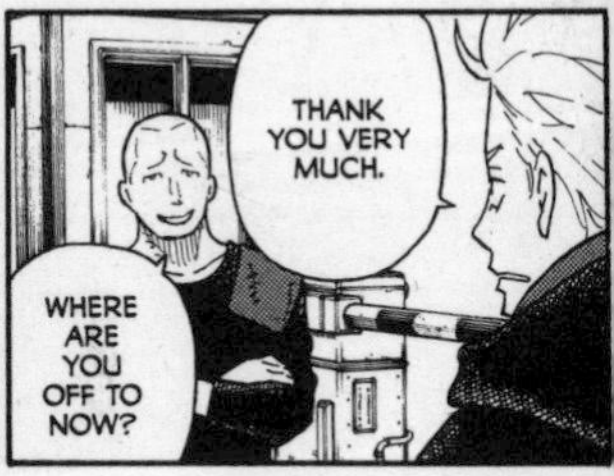
THANK YOU VERY MUCH.
WHERE ARE YOU OFF TO NOW?

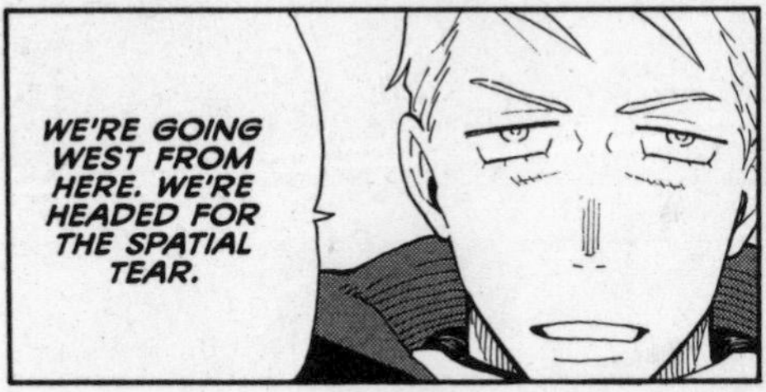
WE'RE GOING WEST FROM HERE. WE'RE HEADED FOR THE SPATIAL TEAR.

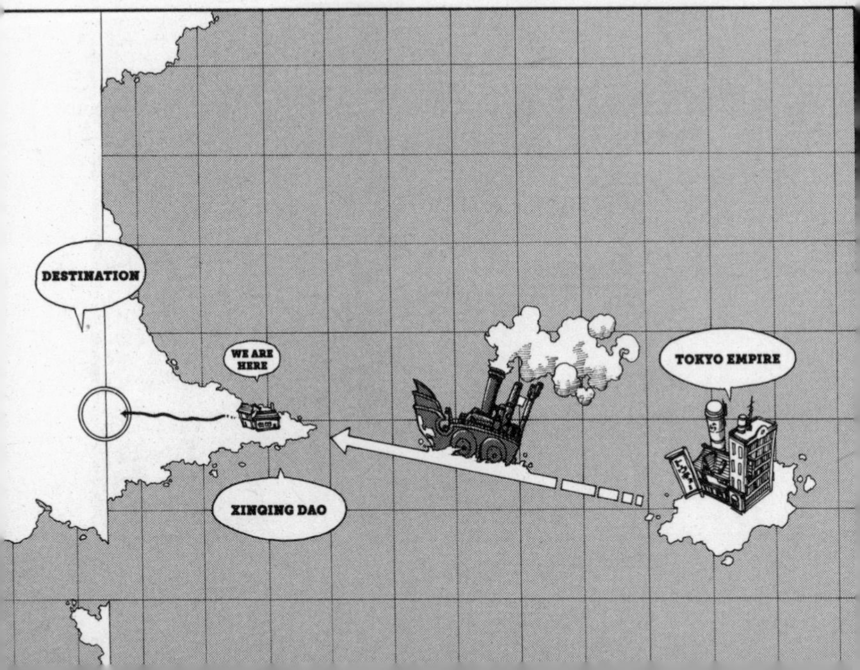
TOKYO EMPIRE
WE ARE HERE
DESTINATION
XINQING DAO

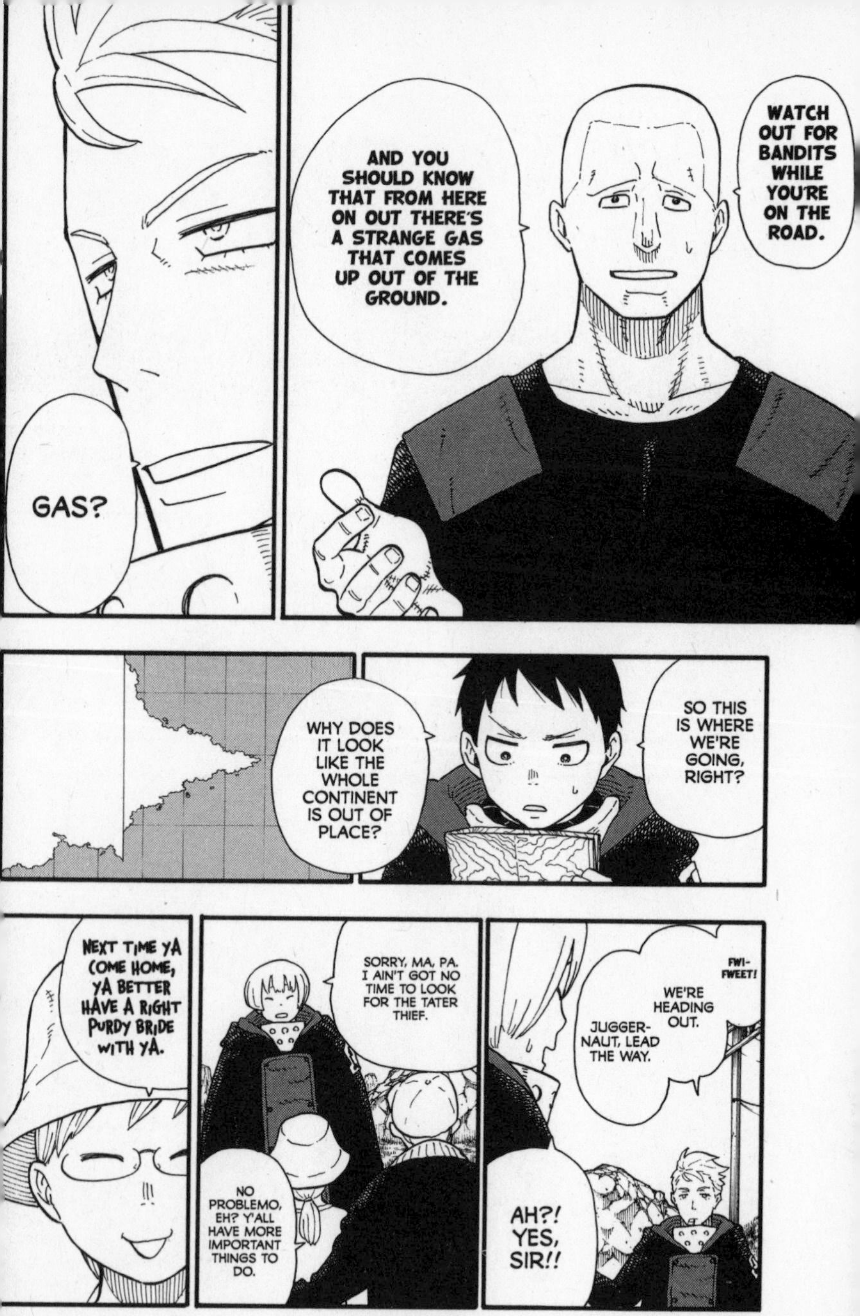
WATCH OUT FOR BANDITS WHILE YOU'RE ON THE ROAD.
AND YOU SHOULD KNOW THAT FROM HERE ON OUT THERE'S A STRANGE GAS THAT COMES UP OUT OF THE GROUND.
GAS?
SO THIS IS WHERE WE'RE GOING, RIGHT?
WHY DOES IT LOOK LIKE THE WHOLE CONTINENT IS OUT OF PLACE?
FWI-FWEET!
WE'RE HEADING OUT.
JUGGERNAUT, LEAD THE WAY.
AH?! YES, SIR!!
SORRY, MA, PA. I AIN'T GOT NO TIME TO LOOK FOR THE TATER THIEF.
NO PROBLEMO, EH? Y'ALL HAVE MORE IMPORTANT THINGS TO DO.
NEXT TIME YA COME HOME, YA BETTER HAVE A RIGHT PURDY BRIDE WITH YA.

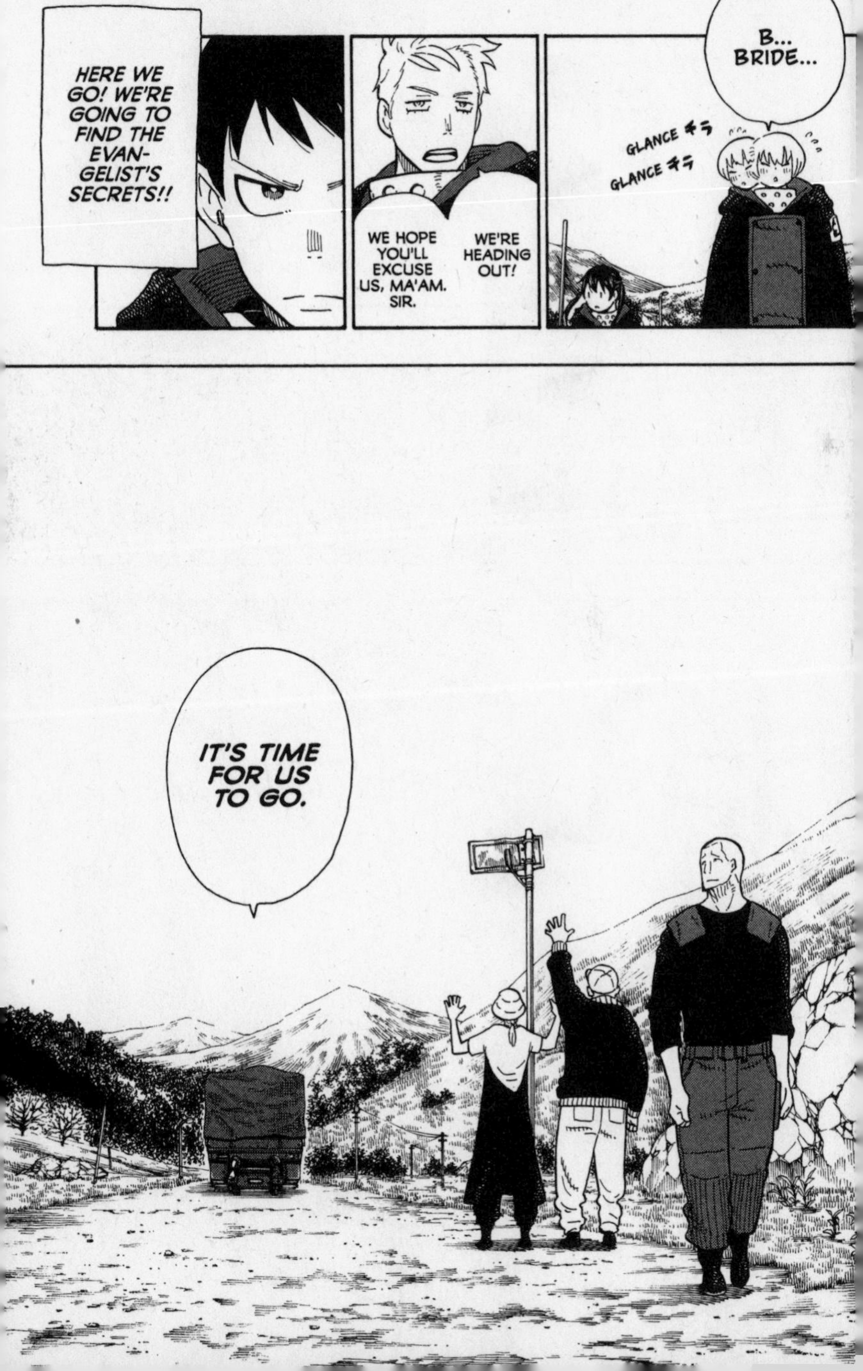
B... BRIDE...
GLANCE キラ
GLANCE キラ
WE'RE HEADING OUT!
WE HOPE YOU'LL EXCUSE US, MA'AM. SIR.
HERE WE GO! WE'RE GOING TO FIND THE EVAN-GELIST'S SECRETS!!
IT'S TIME FOR US TO GO.

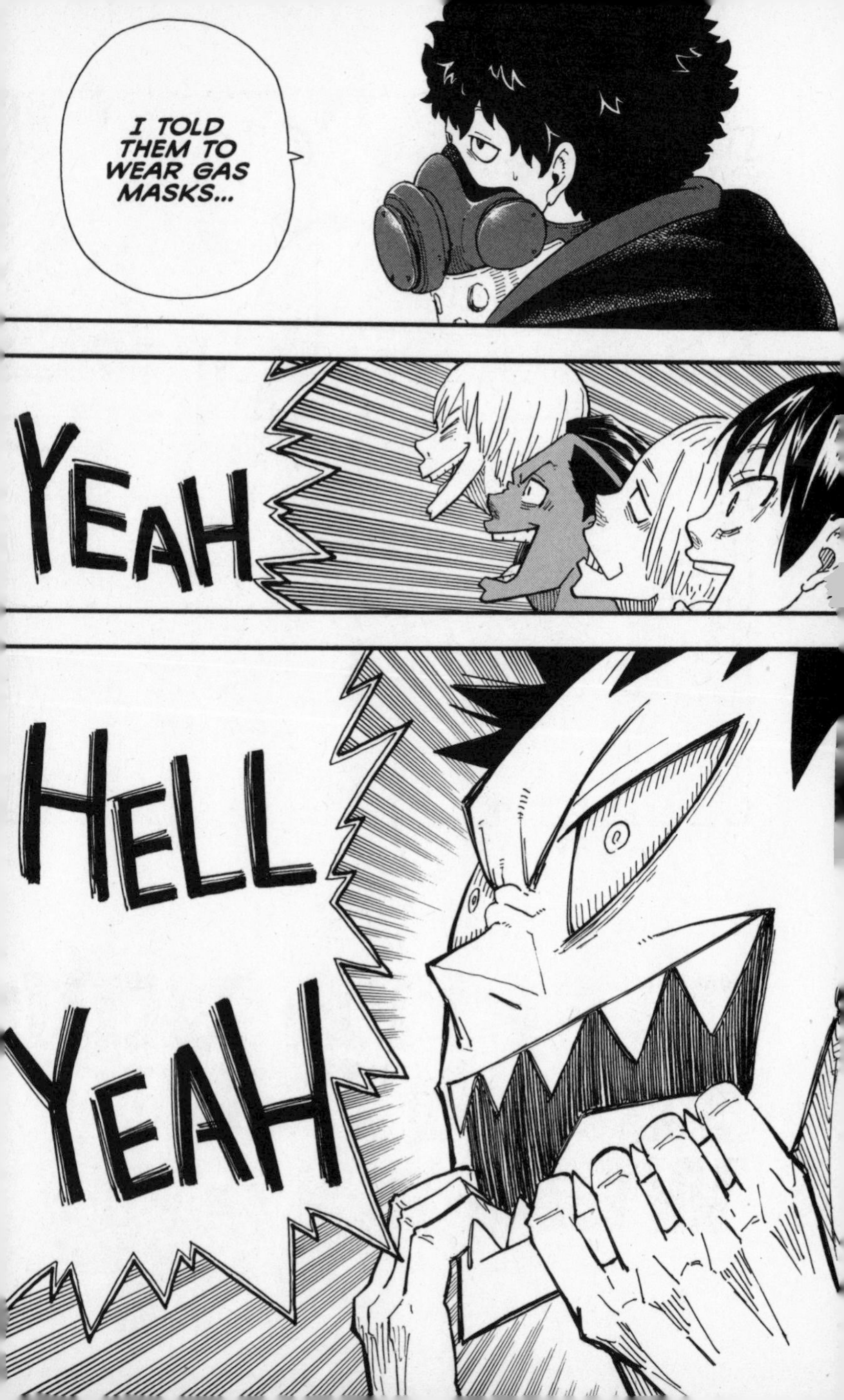
I TOLD THEM TO WEAR GAS MASKS...
YEAH
HELL YEAH

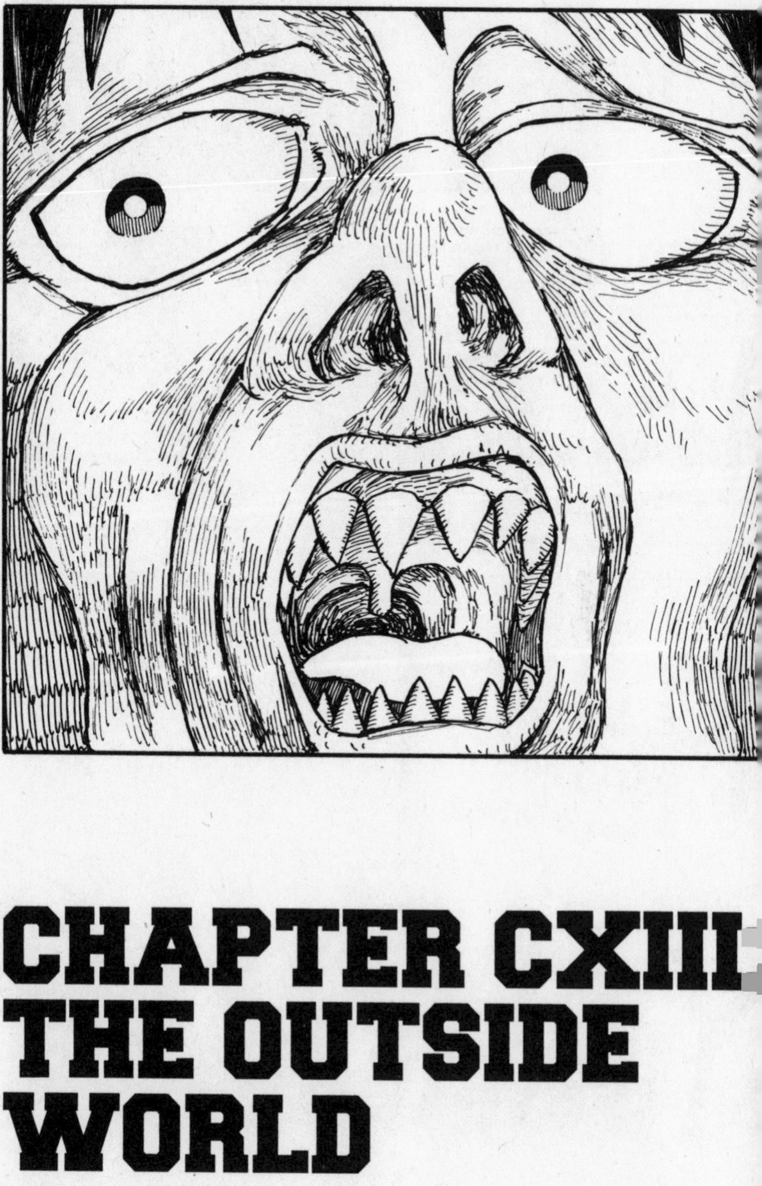

CHAPTER CXIII
THE OUTSIDE WORLD

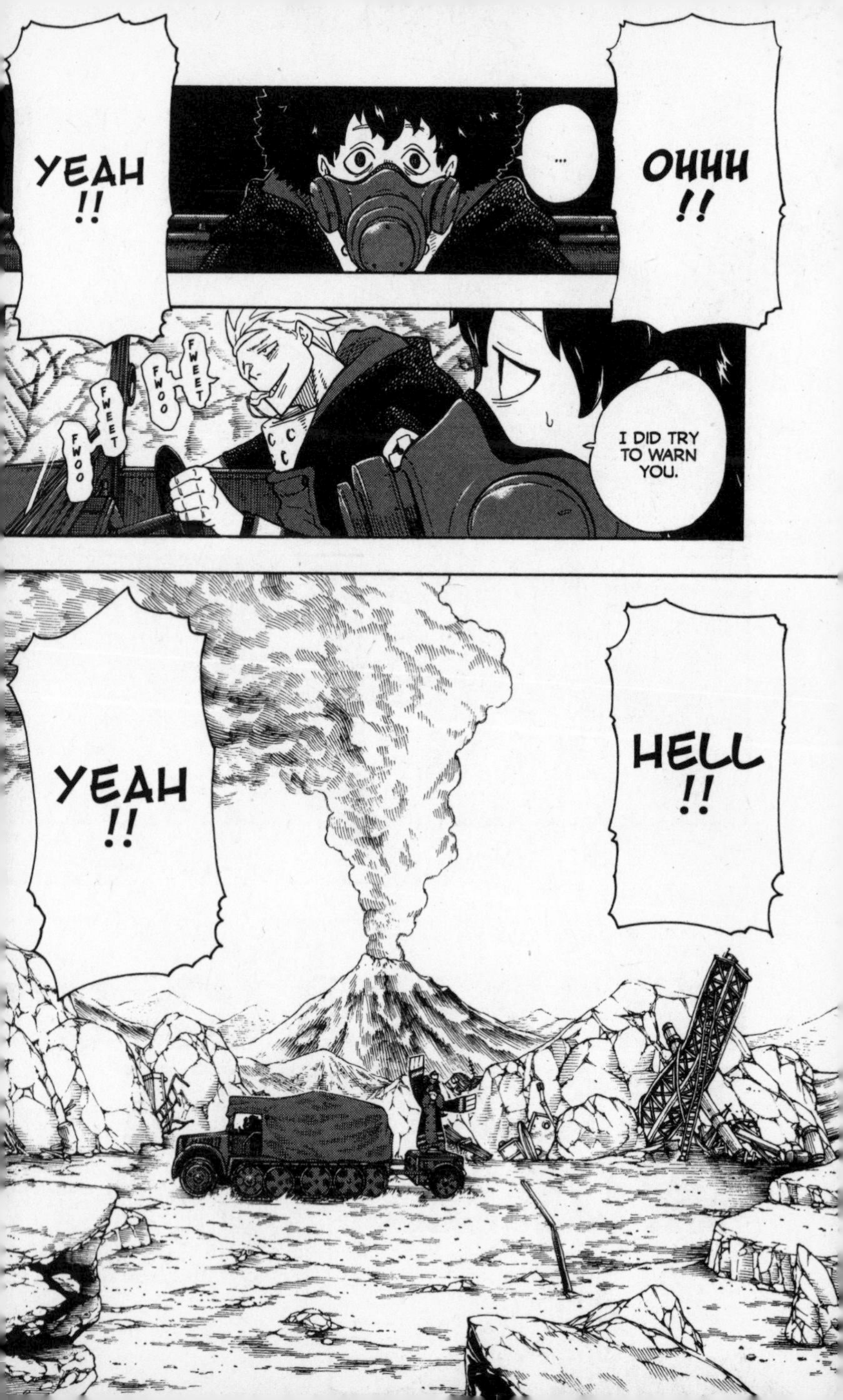
OHHH !!
...
YEAH !!
I DID TRY TO WARN YOU.
FWEET
FWOO
FWEET
FWOO
HELL !!
YEAH !!

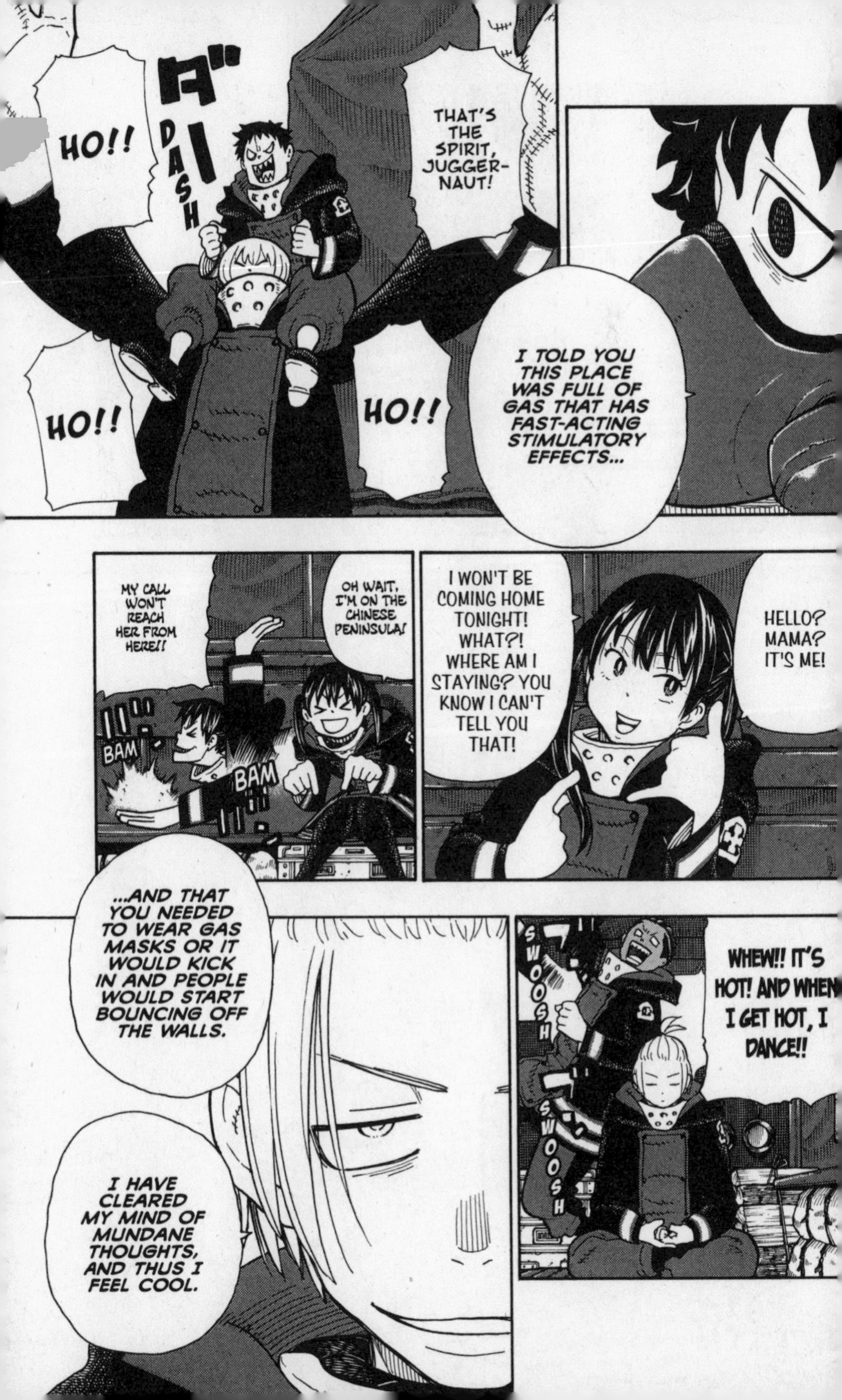
I TOLD YOU THIS PLACE WAS FULL OF GAS THAT HAS FAST-ACTING STIMULATORY EFFECTS...
THAT'S THE SPIRIT, JUGGERNAUT!
HO!!
DASH
HO!!
HO!!
HELLO? MAMA? IT'S ME!
I WON'T BE COMING HOME TONIGHT! WHAT?! WHERE AM I STAYING? YOU KNOW I CAN'T TELL YOU THAT!
OH WAIT, I'M ON THE CHINESE PENINSULA!
MY CALL WON'T REACH HER FROM HERE!!
BAM
BAM
WHEW!! IT'S HOT! AND WHEN I GET HOT, I DANCE!!
SWOOSH
SWOOSH
...AND THAT YOU NEEDED TO WEAR GAS MASKS OR IT WOULD KICK IN AND PEOPLE WOULD START BOUNCING OFF THE WALLS.
I HAVE CLEARED MY MIND OF MUNDANE THOUGHTS, AND THUS I FEEL COOL.

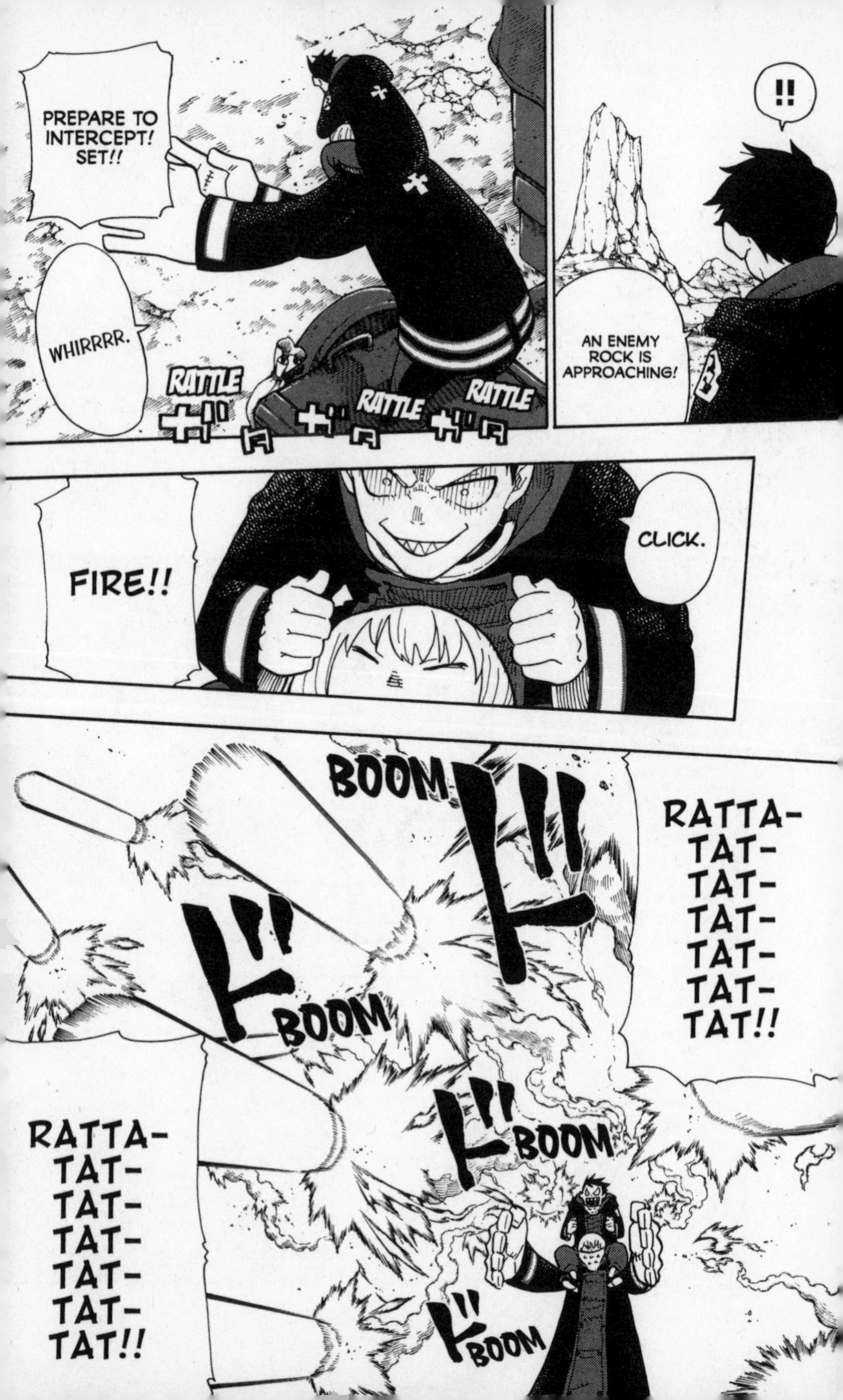
!!
AN ENEMY ROCK IS APPROACHING!
PREPARE TO INTERCEPT! SET!!
WHIRRRR.
RATTLE
RATTLE
RATTLE
CLICK.
FIRE!!
RATTA-TAT-TAT-TAT-TAT-TAT-TAT!!
BOOM
BOOM
BOOM
BOOM
RATTA-TAT-TAT-TAT-TAT-TAT-TAT!!

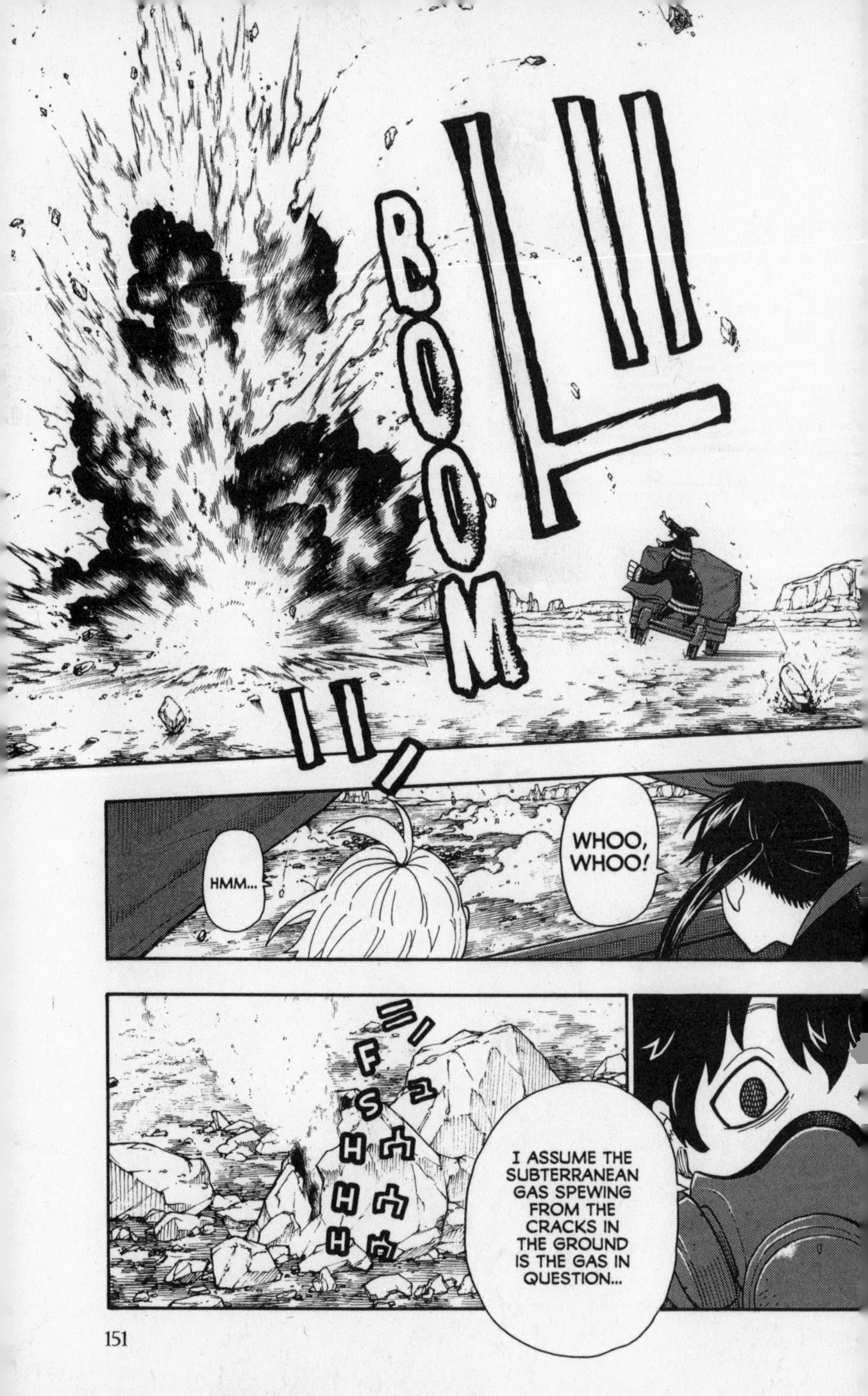
BOOM
WHOO, WHOO!
HMM...
I ASSUME THE SUBTERRANEAN GAS SPEWING FROM THE CRACKS IN THE GROUND IS THE GAS IN QUESTION...
FSHHH

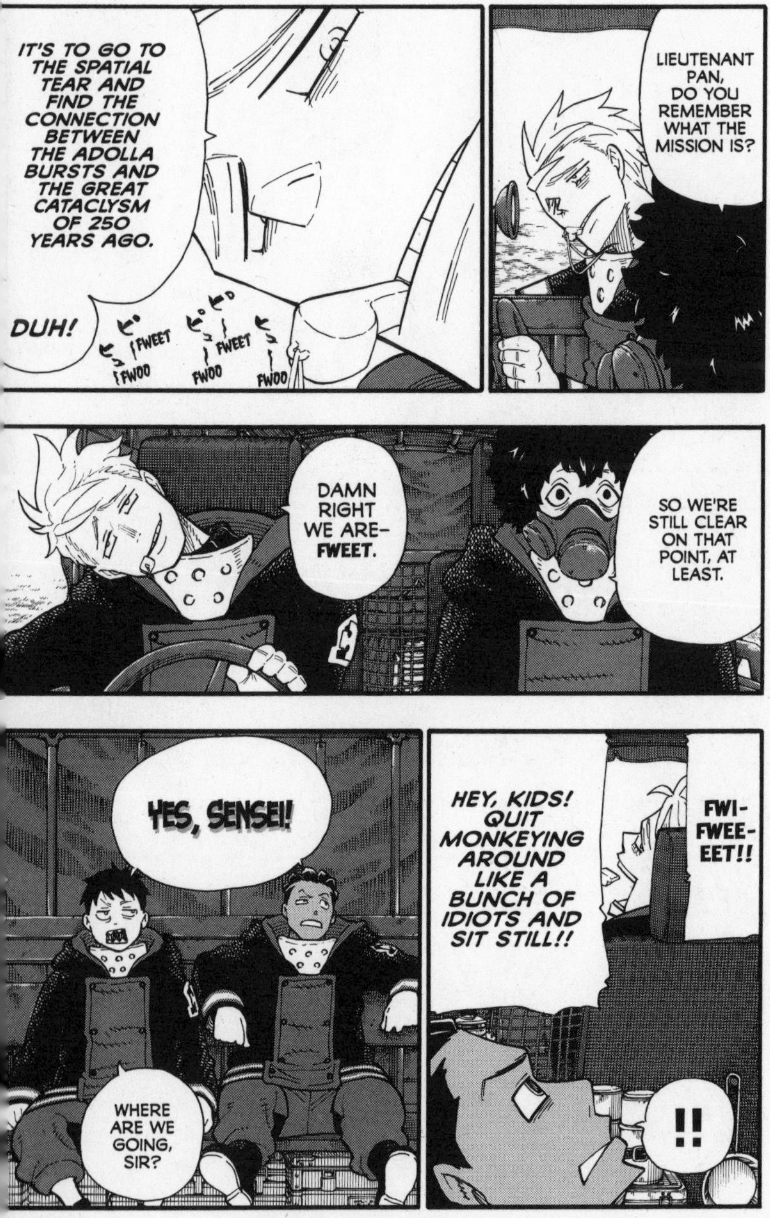
LIEUTENANT PAN, DO YOU REMEMBER WHAT THE MISSION IS?
IT'S TO GO TO THE SPATIAL TEAR AND FIND THE CONNECTION BETWEEN THE ADOLLA BURSTS AND THE GREAT CATACLYSM OF 250 YEARS AGO.
DUH!
FWEET
FWOO
FWEET
FWOO
FWOO
SO WE'RE STILL CLEAR ON THAT POINT, AT LEAST.
DAMN RIGHT WE ARE-FWEET.
HEY, KIDS! QUIT MONKEYING AROUND LIKE A BUNCH OF IDIOTS AND SIT STILL!!
FWI-FWEE-EET!!
!!
YES, SENSEI!
WHERE ARE WE GOING, SIR?

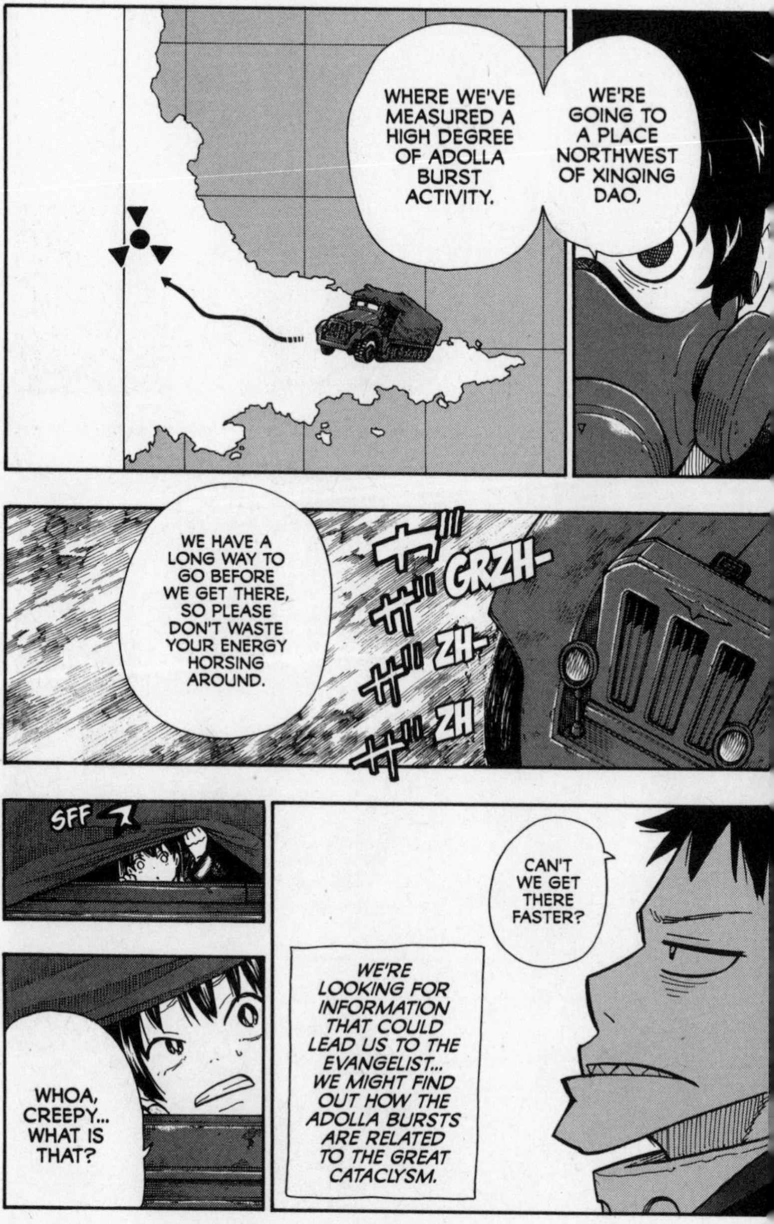
WE'RE GOING TO A PLACE NORTHWEST OF XINQING DAO,
WHERE WE'VE MEASURED A HIGH DEGREE OF ADOLLA BURST ACTIVITY.
GRZH-
ZH-
ZH
WE HAVE A LONG WAY TO GO BEFORE WE GET THERE, SO PLEASE DON'T WASTE YOUR ENERGY HORSING AROUND.
CAN'T WE GET THERE FASTER?
WE'RE LOOKING FOR INFORMATION THAT COULD LEAD US TO THE EVANGELIST... WE MIGHT FIND OUT HOW THE ADOLLA BURSTS ARE RELATED TO THE GREAT CATACLYSM.
SFF
WHOA, CREEPY... WHAT IS THAT?

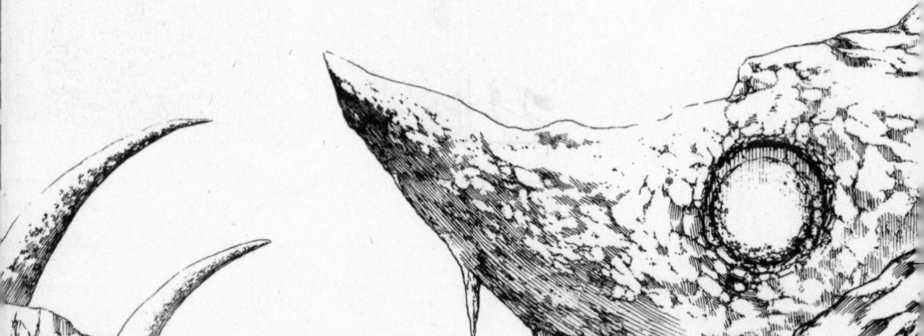

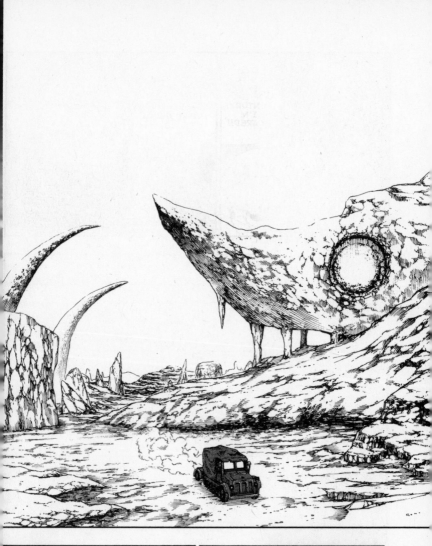

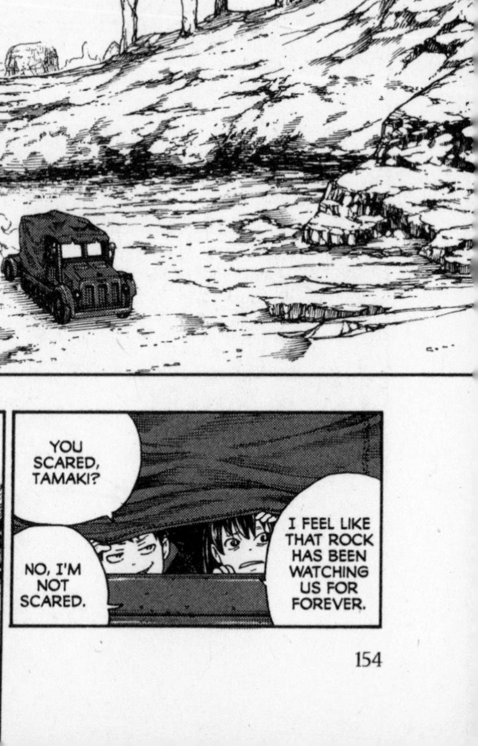
YOU SCARED, TAMAKI?
I FEEL LIKE THAT ROCK HAS BEEN WATCHING US FOR FOREVER.
NO, I'M NOT SCARED.

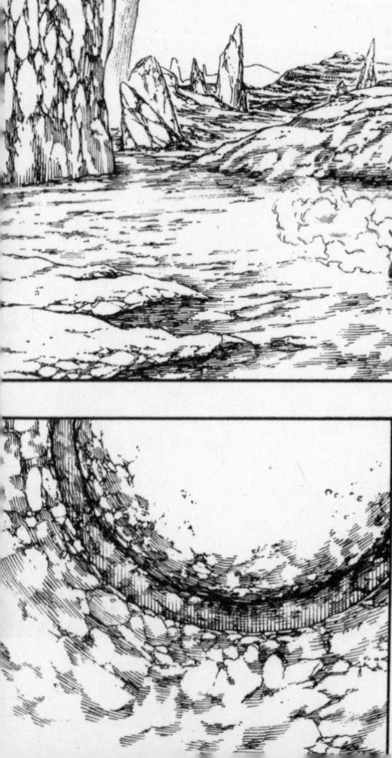

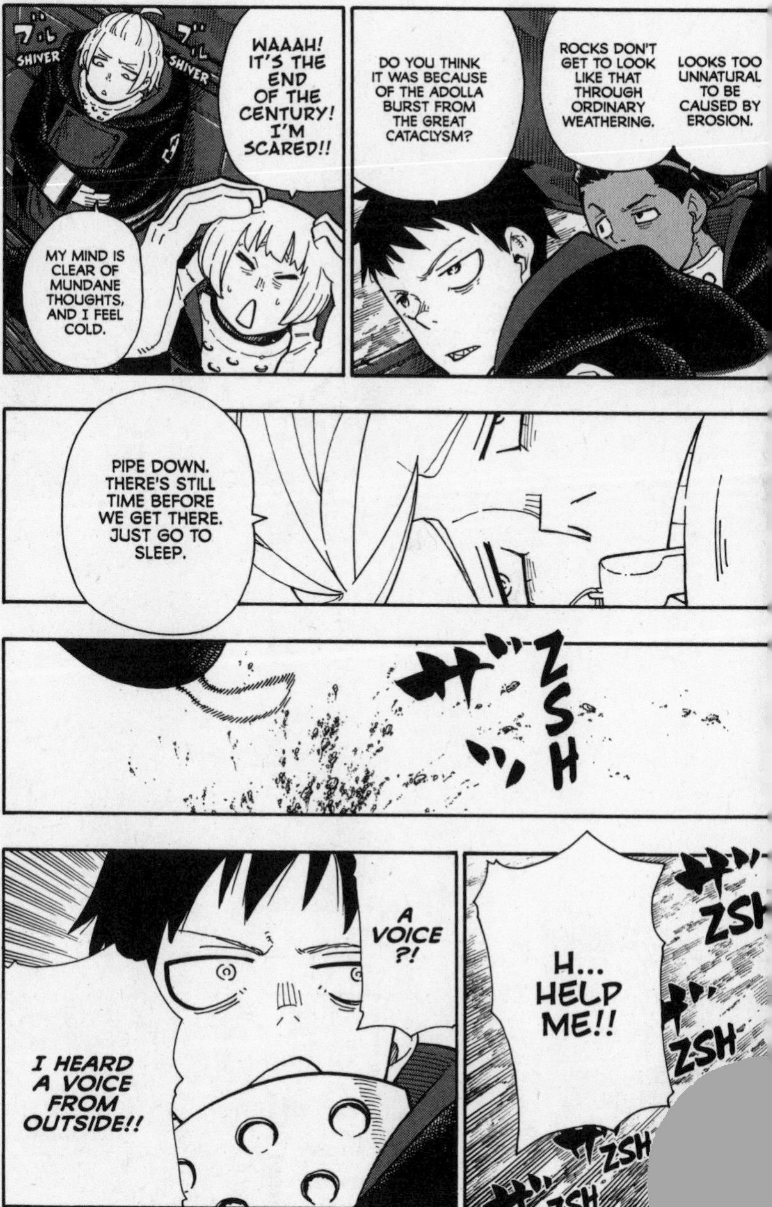
LOOKS TOO UNNATURAL TO BE CAUSED BY EROSION.
ROCKS DON'T GET TO LOOK LIKE THAT THROUGH ORDINARY WEATHERING.
DO YOU THINK IT WAS BECAUSE OF THE ADOLLA BURST FROM THE GREAT CATACLYSM?
WAAAH! IT'S THE END OF THE CENTURY! I'M SCARED!!
SHIVER
SHIVER
MY MIND IS CLEAR OF MUNDANE THOUGHTS, AND I FEEL COLD.
PIPE DOWN. THERE'S STILL TIME BEFORE WE GET THERE. JUST GO TO SLEEP.
ZSH
ZSH
ZSH
H... HELP ME!!
ZSH
ZSH
A VOICE ?!
I HEARD A VOICE FROM OUTSIDE!!

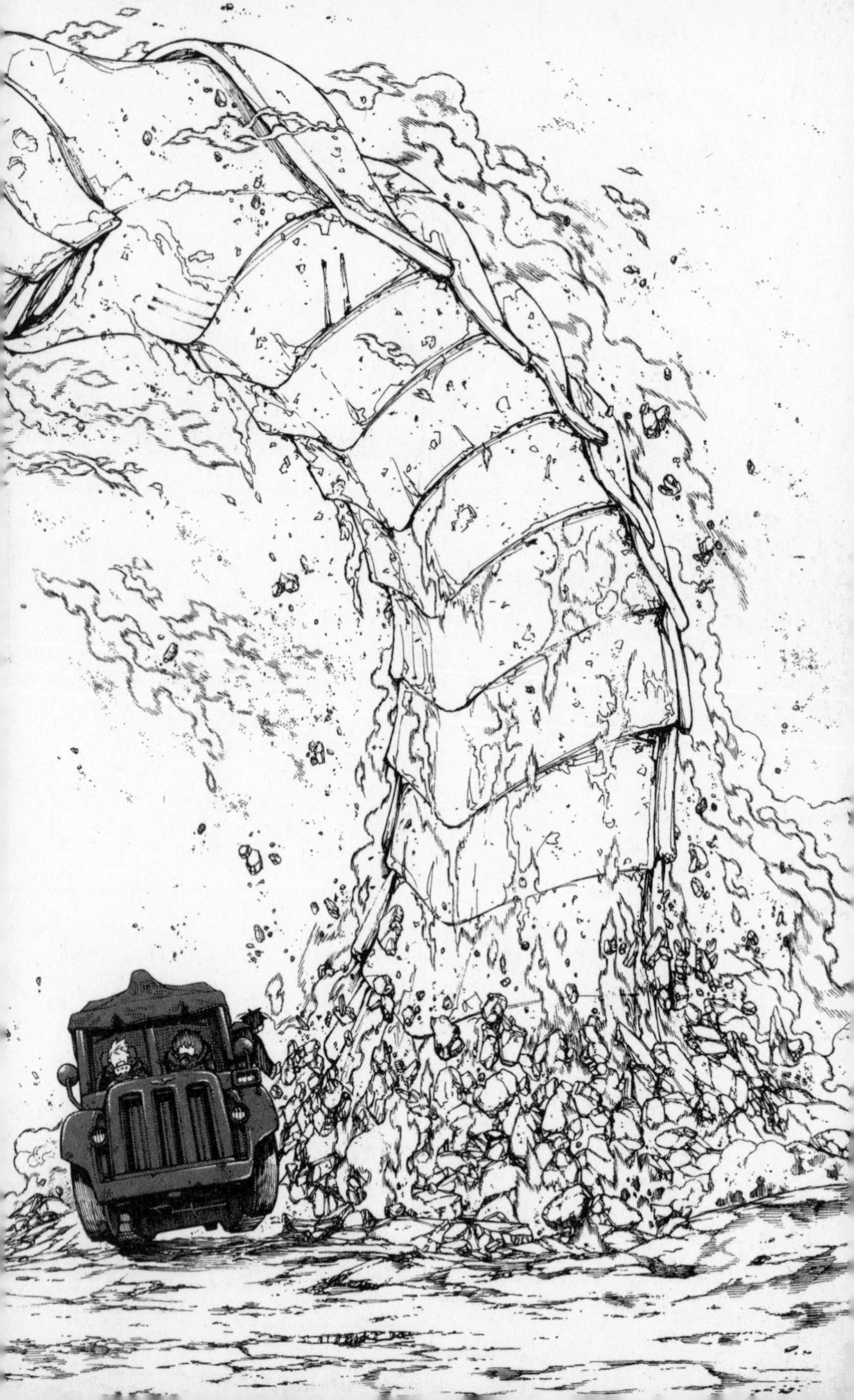

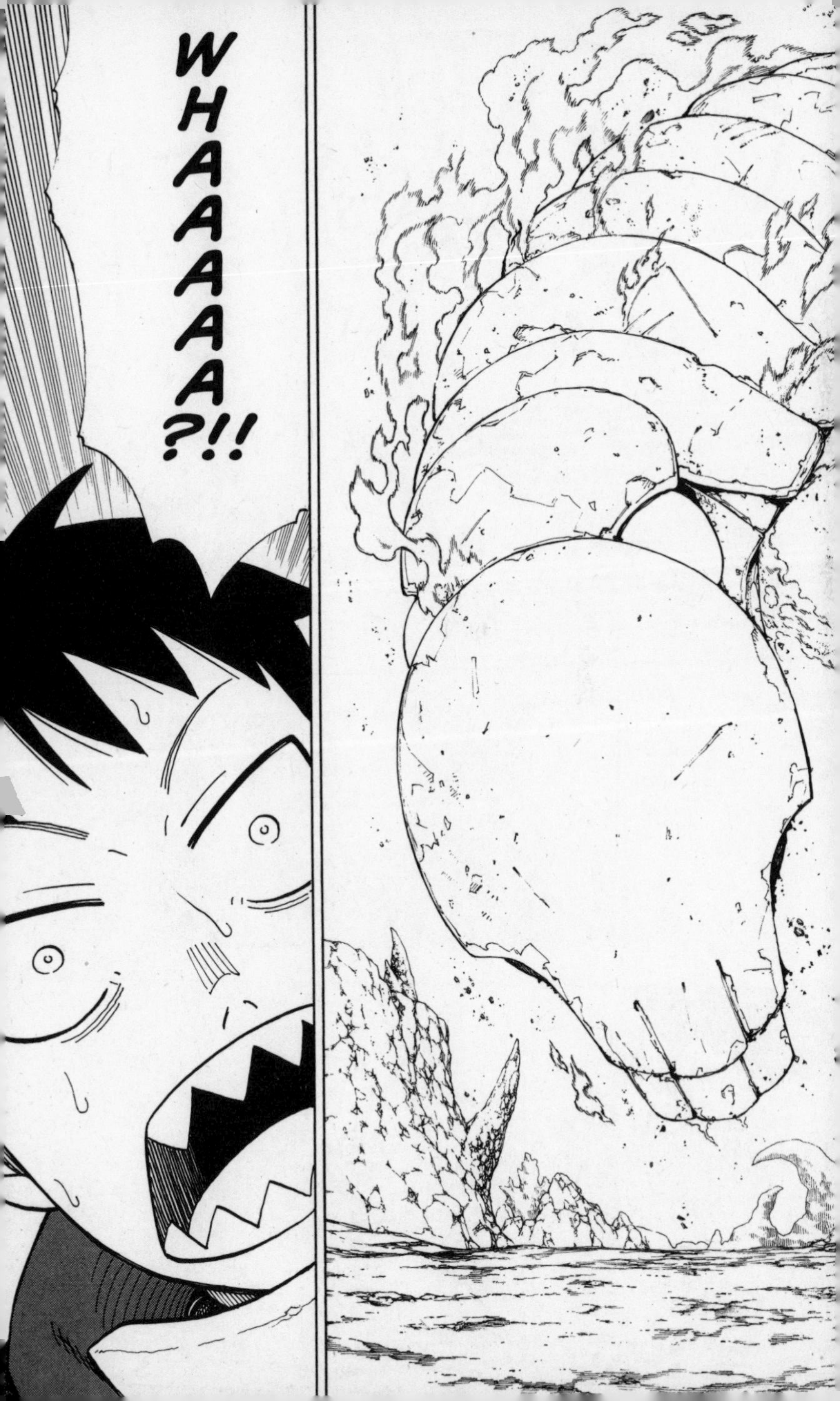
WHAAAAA?!!

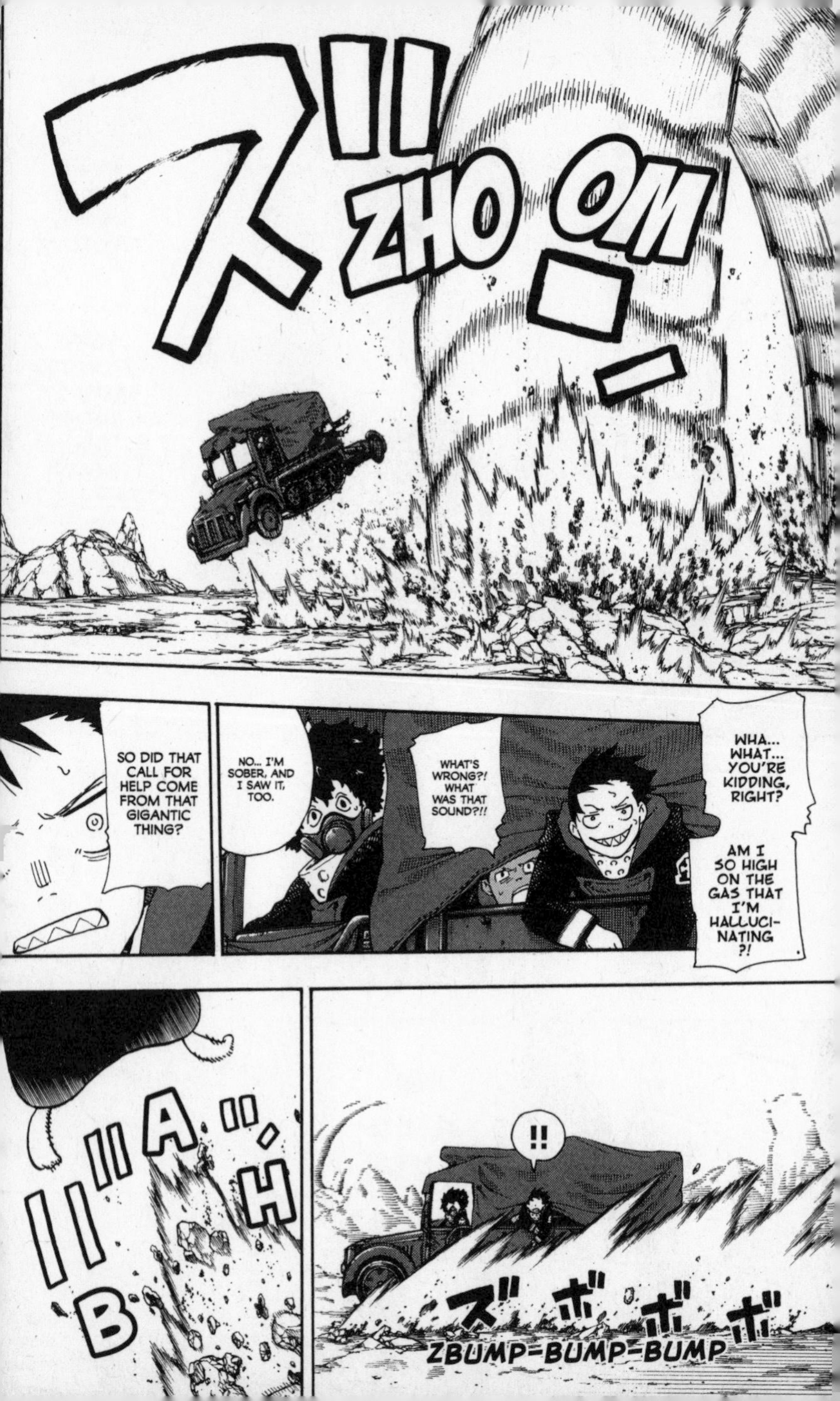
ZHOOM
WHA... WHAT... YOU'RE KIDDING, RIGHT?
AM I SO HIGH ON THE GAS THAT I'M HALLUCINATING?!
WHAT'S WRONG?! WHAT WAS THAT SOUND?!!
NO... I'M SOBER, AND I SAW IT, TOO.
SO DID THAT CALL FOR HELP COME FROM THAT GIGANTIC THING?
!!
ズボボボ
ZBUMP-BUMP-BUMP
BAH

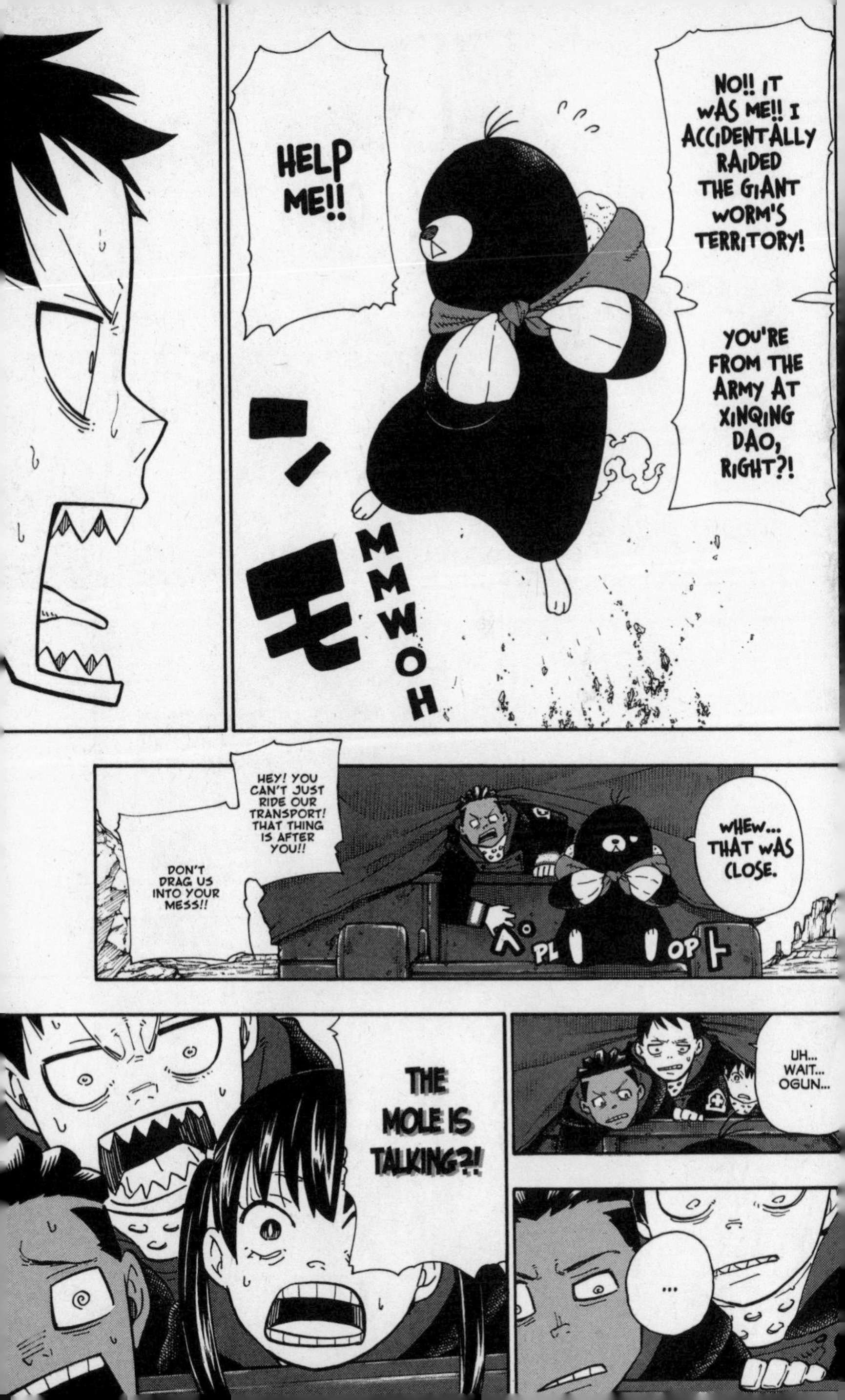
NO!! IT WAS ME!! I ACCIDENTALLY RAIDED THE GIANT WORM'S TERRITORY!
HELP ME!!
YOU'RE FROM THE ARMY AT XINQING DAO, RIGHT?!
MMWOH
WHEW... THAT WAS CLOSE.
HEY! YOU CAN'T JUST RIDE OUR TRANSPORT! THAT THING IS AFTER YOU!!
DON'T DRAG US INTO YOUR MESS!!
PLOP
UH... WAIT... OGUN...
...
THE MOLE IS TALKING?!

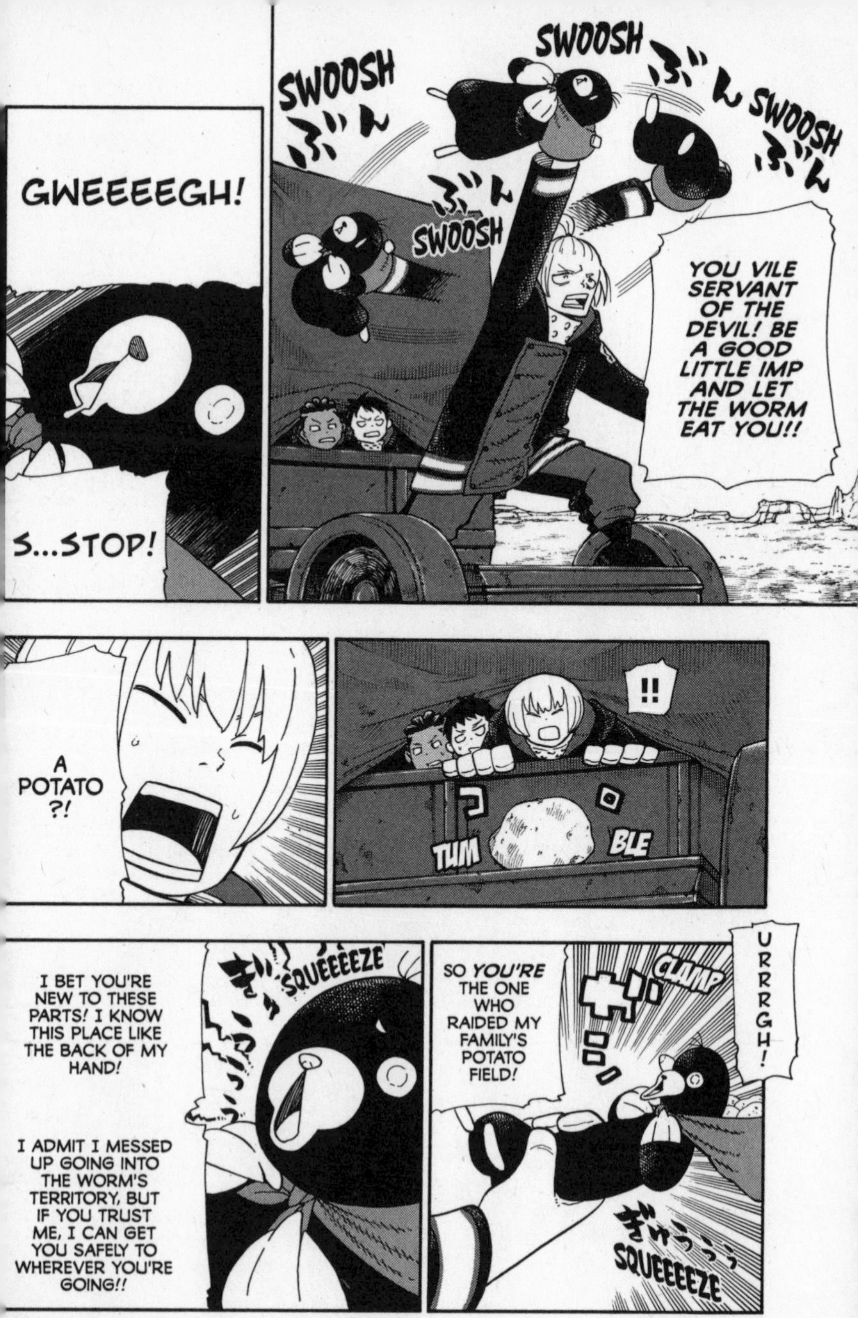
SWOOSH
ぶん
SWOOSH
ぶん
SWOOSH
ぶん
SWOOSH
ぶん
SWOOSH
YOU VILE SERVANT OF THE DEVIL! BE A GOOD LITTLE IMP AND LET THE WORM EAT YOU!!
GWEEEEGH!
S...STOP!
!!
TUM BLE
A POTATO ?!
URRRGH!
CLAMP
SO YOU'RE THE ONE WHO RAIDED MY FAMILY'S POTATO FIELD!
SQUEEEEZE
SQUEEEEZE
I BET YOU'RE NEW TO THESE PARTS! I KNOW THIS PLACE LIKE THE BACK OF MY HAND!
I ADMIT I MESSED UP GOING INTO THE WORM'S TERRITORY, BUT IF YOU TRUST ME, I CAN GET YOU SAFELY TO WHEREVER YOU'RE GOING!!

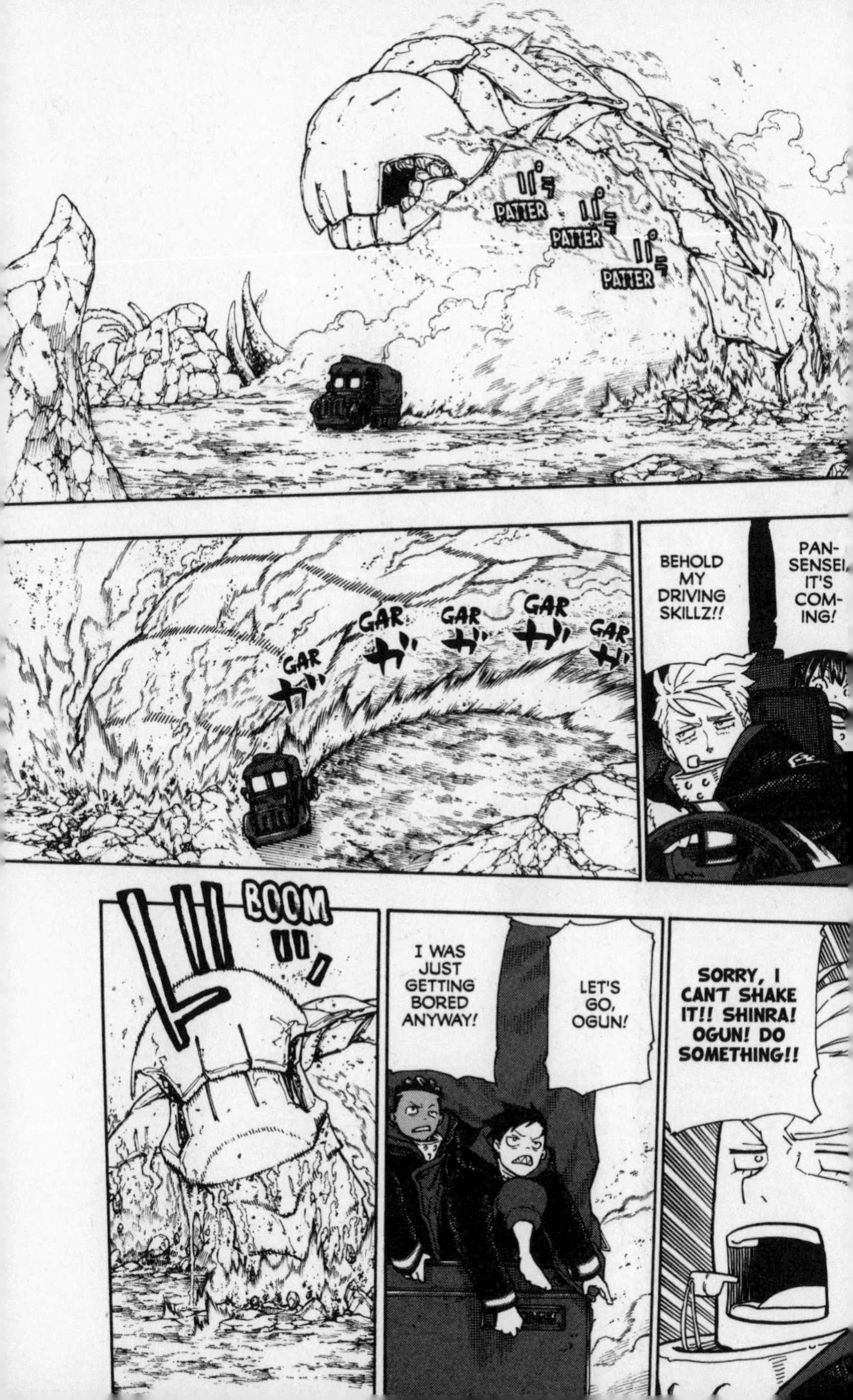

PATTER
PATTER
PATTER
PAN-SENSEI, IT'S COMING!
BEHOLD MY DRIVING SKILLZ!!
GAR
GAR
GAR
GAR
GAR
SORRY, I CAN'T SHAKE IT!! SHINRA! OGUN! DO SOMETHING!!
LET'S GO, OGUN!
I WAS JUST GETTING BORED ANYWAY!
BOOM

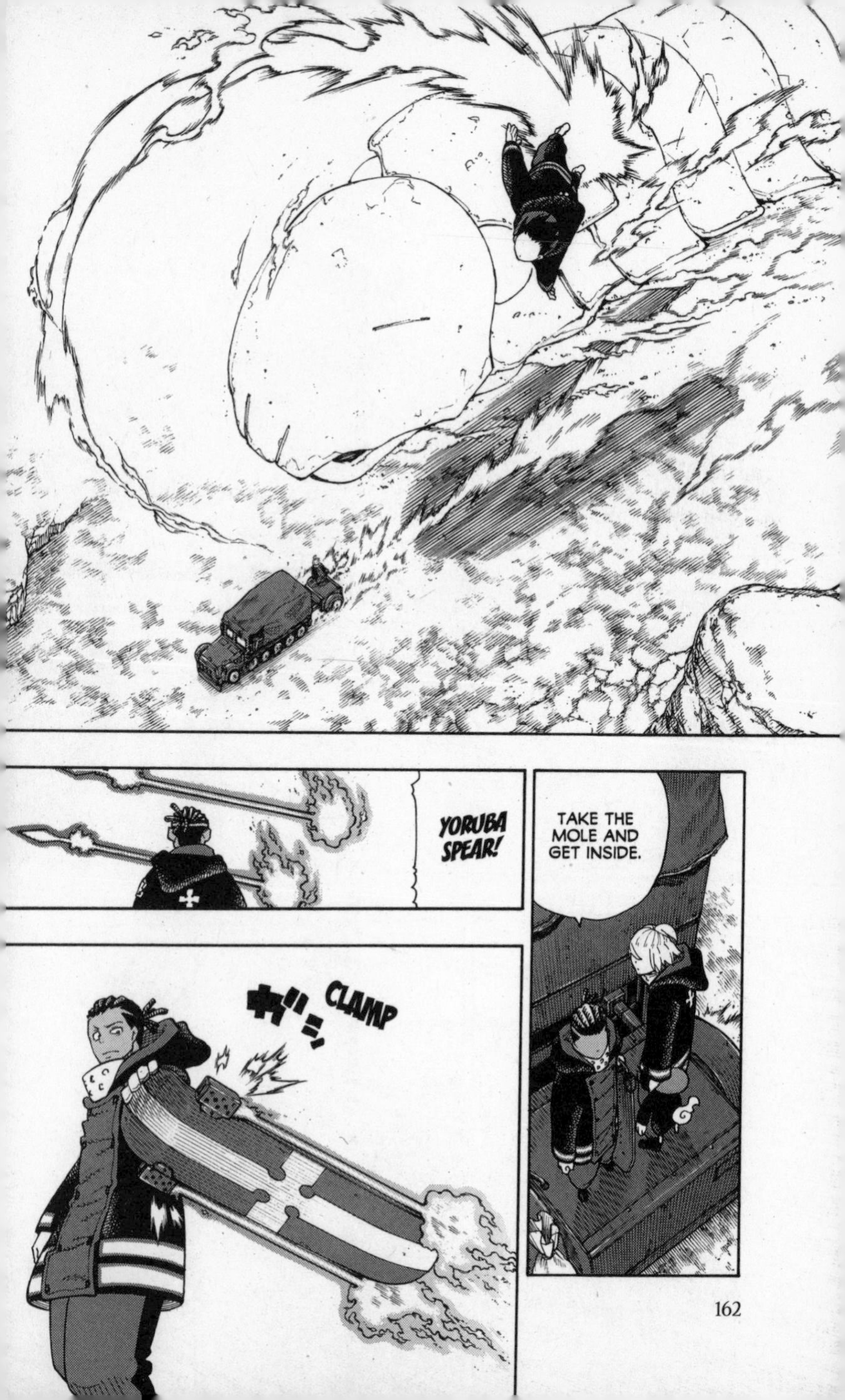
TAKE THE MOLE AND GET INSIDE.
YORUBA SPEAR!
CLAMP

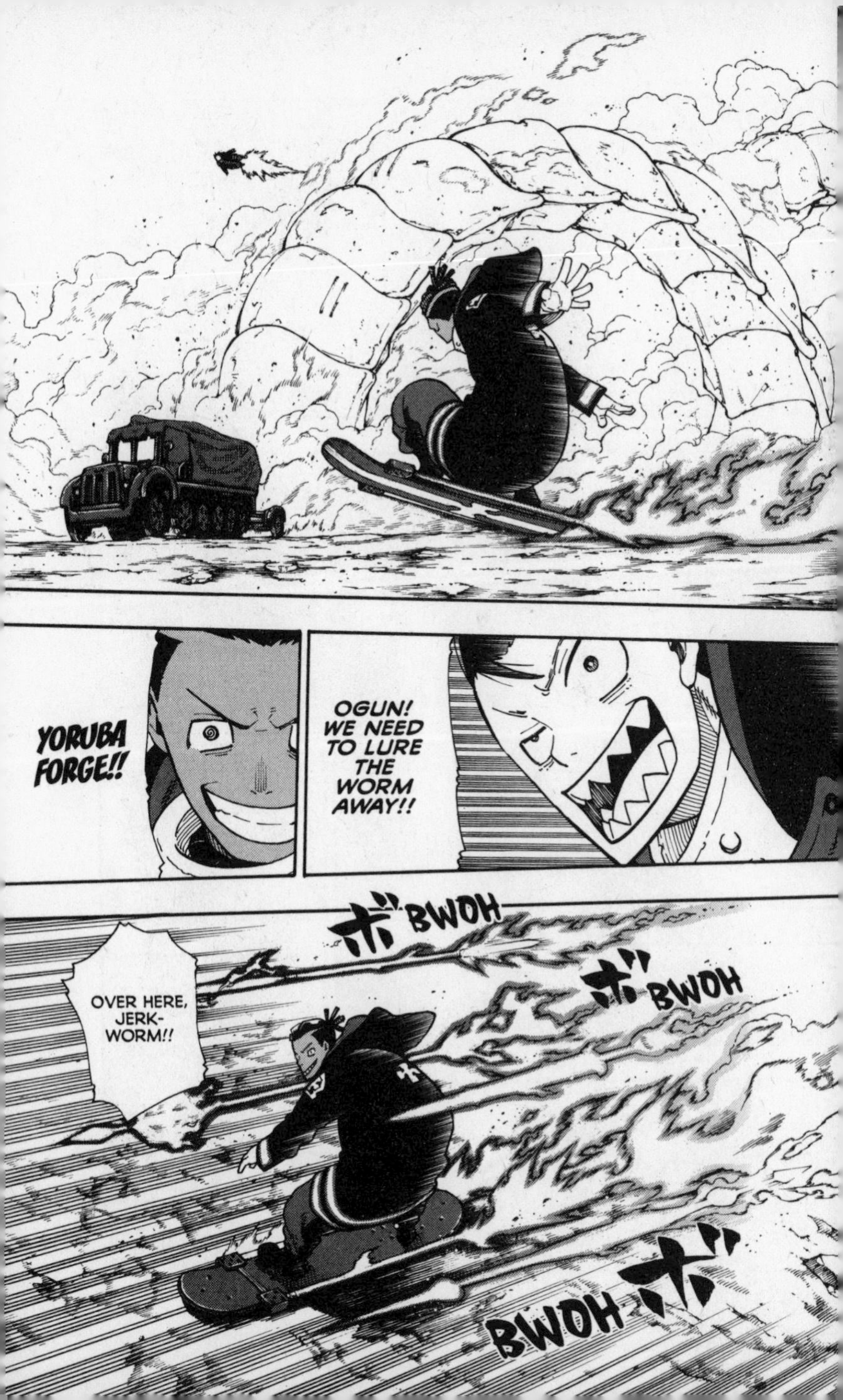
OGUN! WE NEED TO LURE THE WORM AWAY!!
YORUBA FORGE!!
ボ BWOH
ボ BWOH
OVER HERE, JERK-WORM!!
ボ BWOH

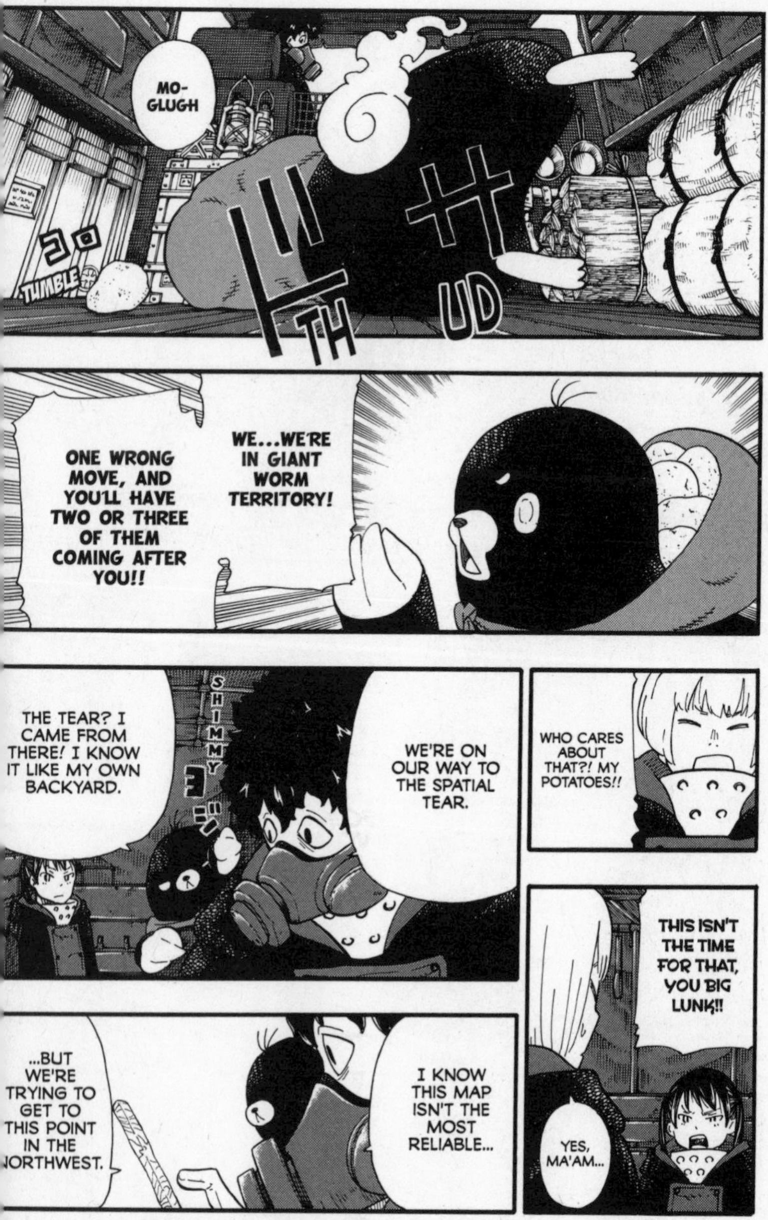
MO-GLUGH
TH UD
TUMBLE
WE...WE'RE IN GIANT WORM TERRITORY!
ONE WRONG MOVE, AND YOU'LL HAVE TWO OR THREE OF THEM COMING AFTER YOU!!
WHO CARES ABOUT THAT?! MY POTATOES!!
WE'RE ON OUR WAY TO THE SPATIAL TEAR.
SHIMMY
THE TEAR? I CAME FROM THERE! I KNOW IT LIKE MY OWN BACKYARD.
THIS ISN'T THE TIME FOR THAT, YOU BIG LUNK!!
YES, MA'AM...
I KNOW THIS MAP ISN'T THE MOST RELIABLE...
...BUT WE'RE TRYING TO GET TO THIS POINT IN THE NORTHWEST.

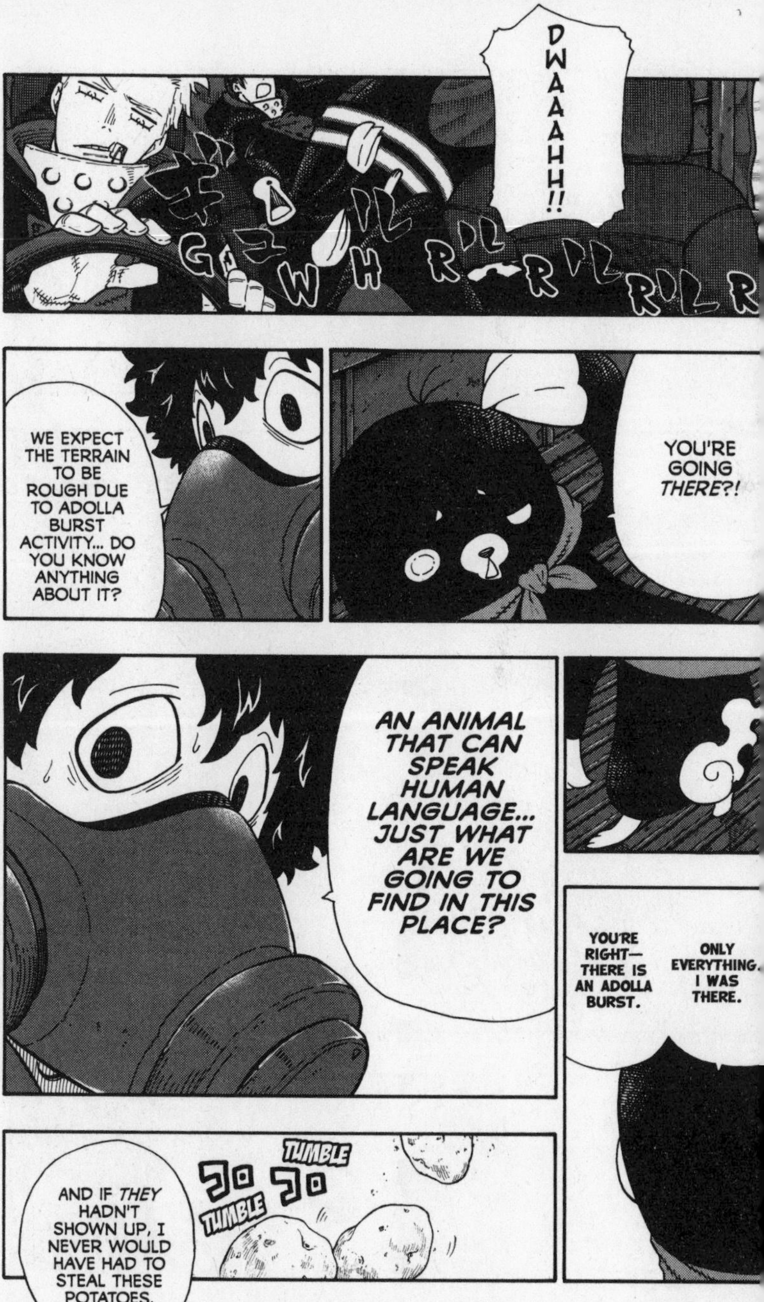
DWAAAAHH!!
YOU'RE GOING *THERE?!*
WE EXPECT THE TERRAIN TO BE ROUGH DUE TO ADOLLA BURST ACTIVITY... DO YOU KNOW ANYTHING ABOUT IT?
ONLY EVERYTHING. I WAS THERE.
YOU'RE RIGHT—THERE IS AN ADOLLA BURST.
AN ANIMAL THAT CAN SPEAK HUMAN LANGUAGE... JUST WHAT ARE WE GOING TO FIND IN THIS PLACE?
TUMBLE
TUMBLE
AND IF *THEY* HADN'T SHOWN UP, I NEVER WOULD HAVE HAD TO STEAL THESE POTATOES.

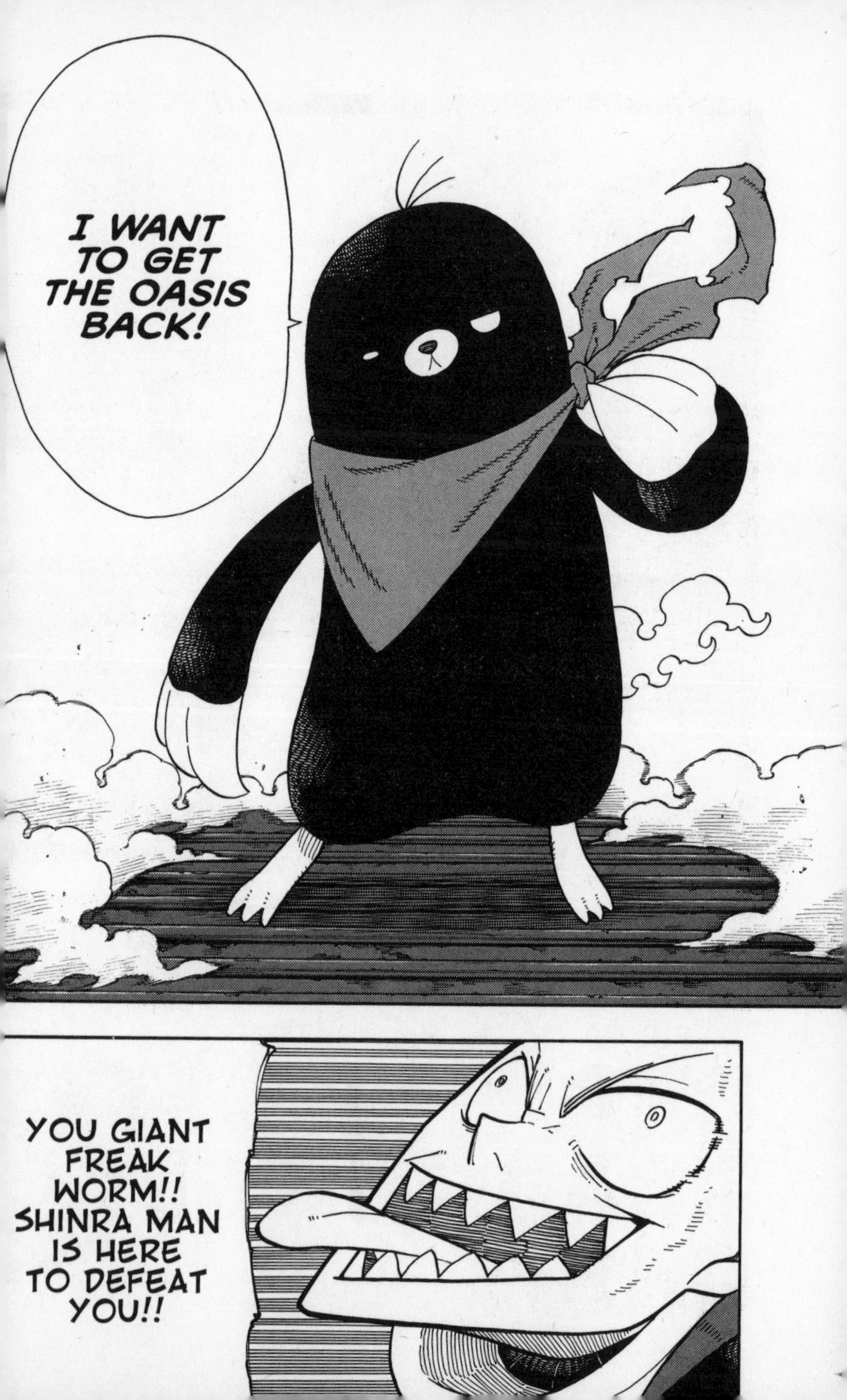
I WANT TO GET THE OASIS BACK!
YOU GIANT FREAK WORM!! SHINRA MAN IS HERE TO DEFEAT YOU!!

Enn Enn no Shouboutai is what *Fire Force* is called in Japane

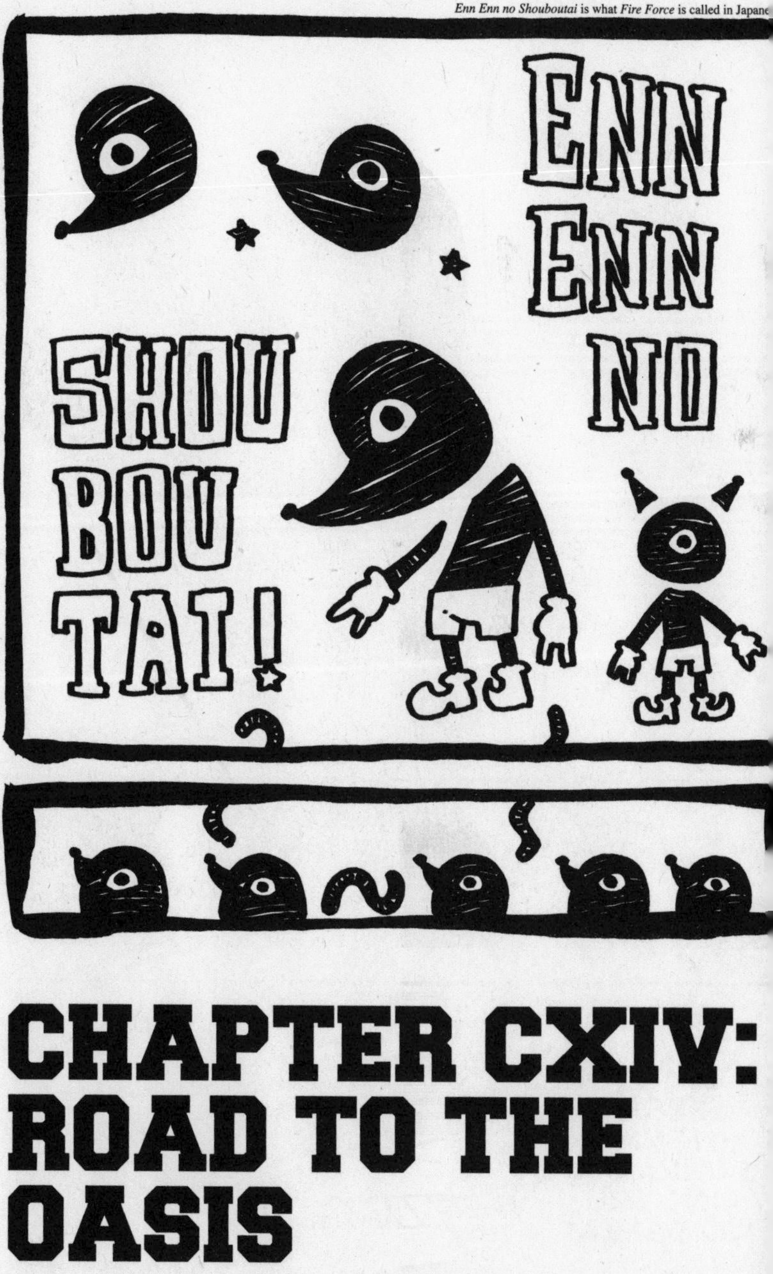
ENN
ENN
NO
SHOU
BOU
TAI!

CHAPTER CXIV: ROAD TO THE OASIS

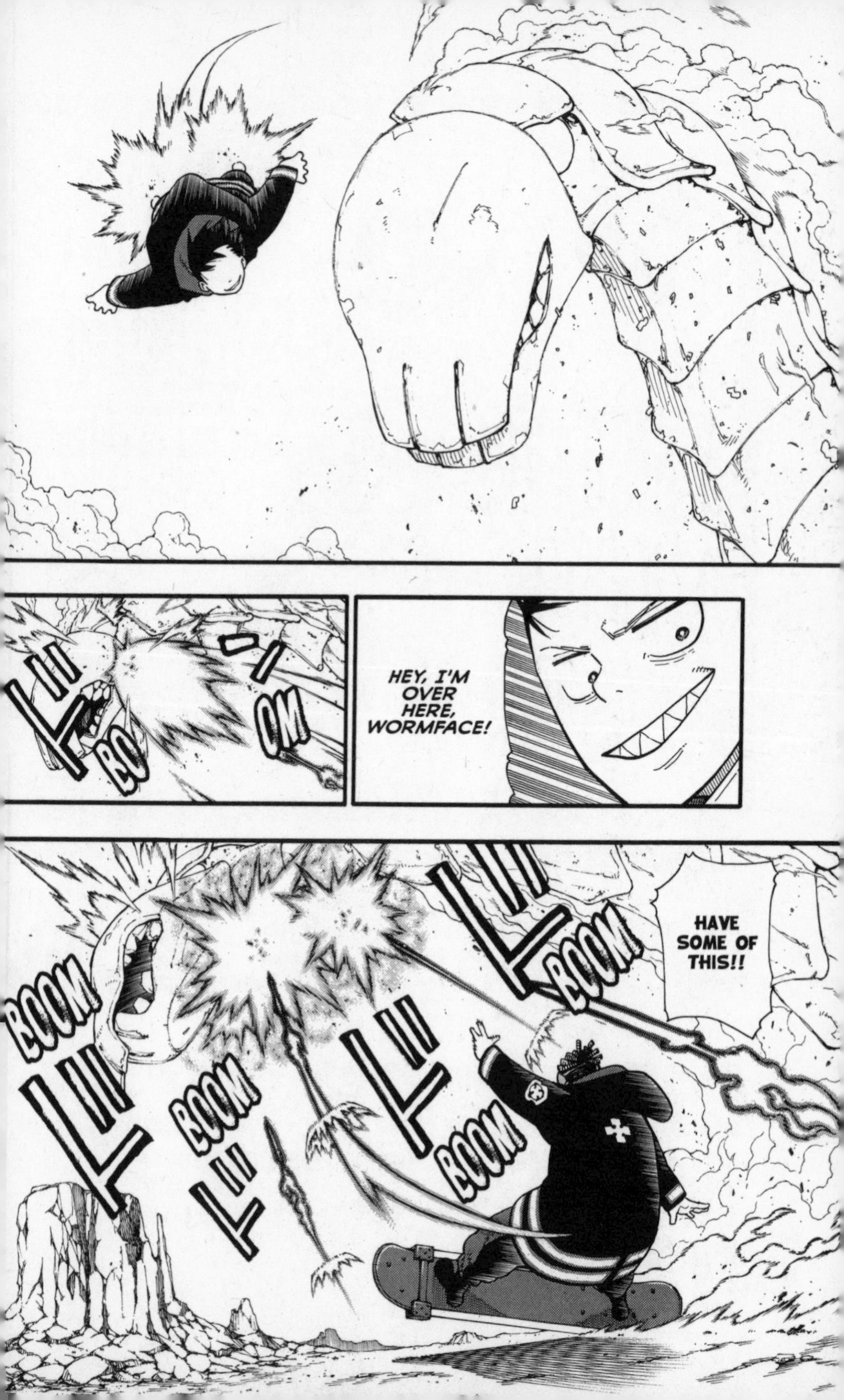
HEY, I'M OVER HERE, WORMFACE!
BOOM
HAVE SOME OF THIS!!
BOOM
BOOM
BOOM
BOOM

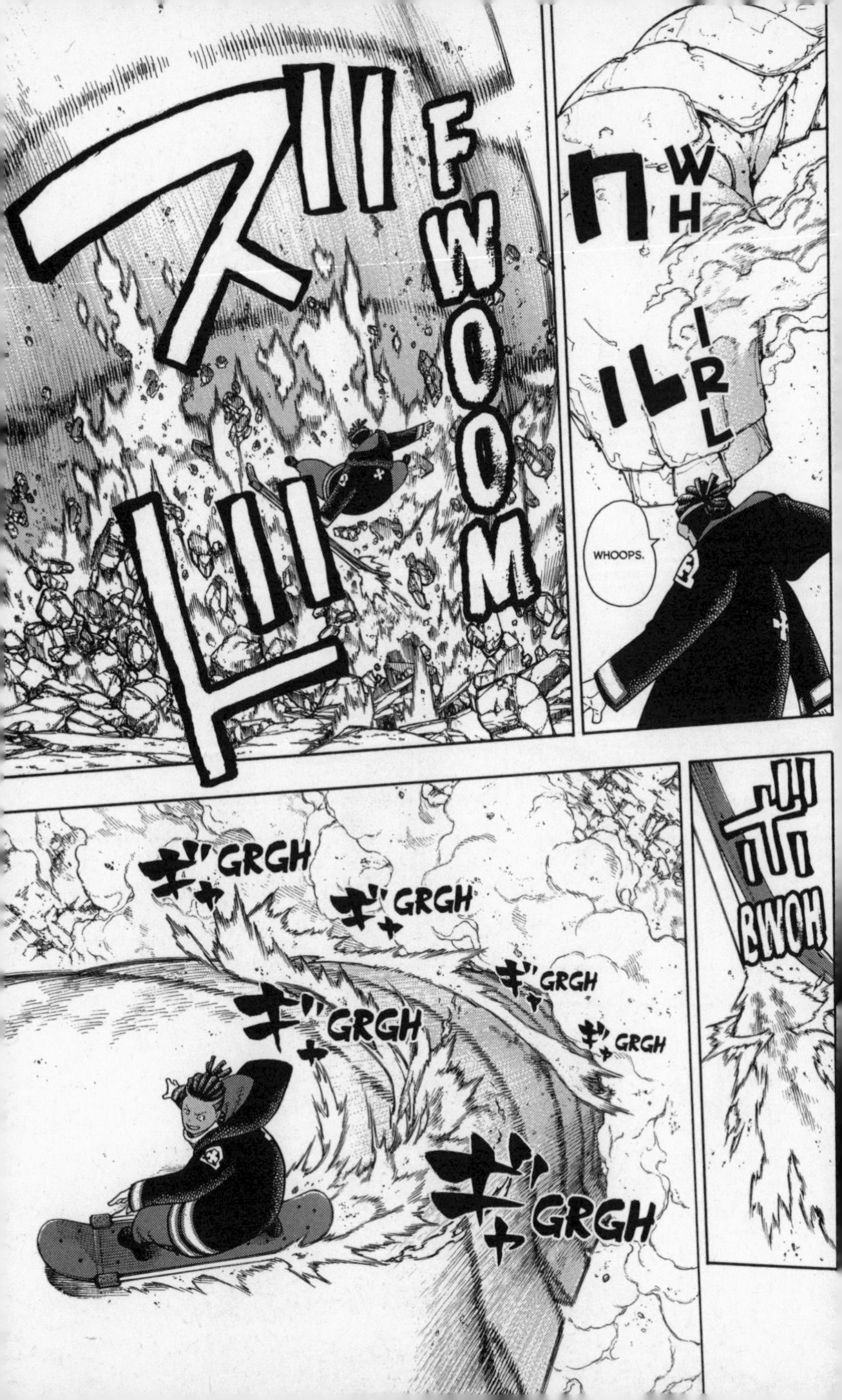
WHIRL
WHOOPS.
FWOOM
BWOH
GRGH
GRGH
GRGH
GRGH
GRGH
GRGH

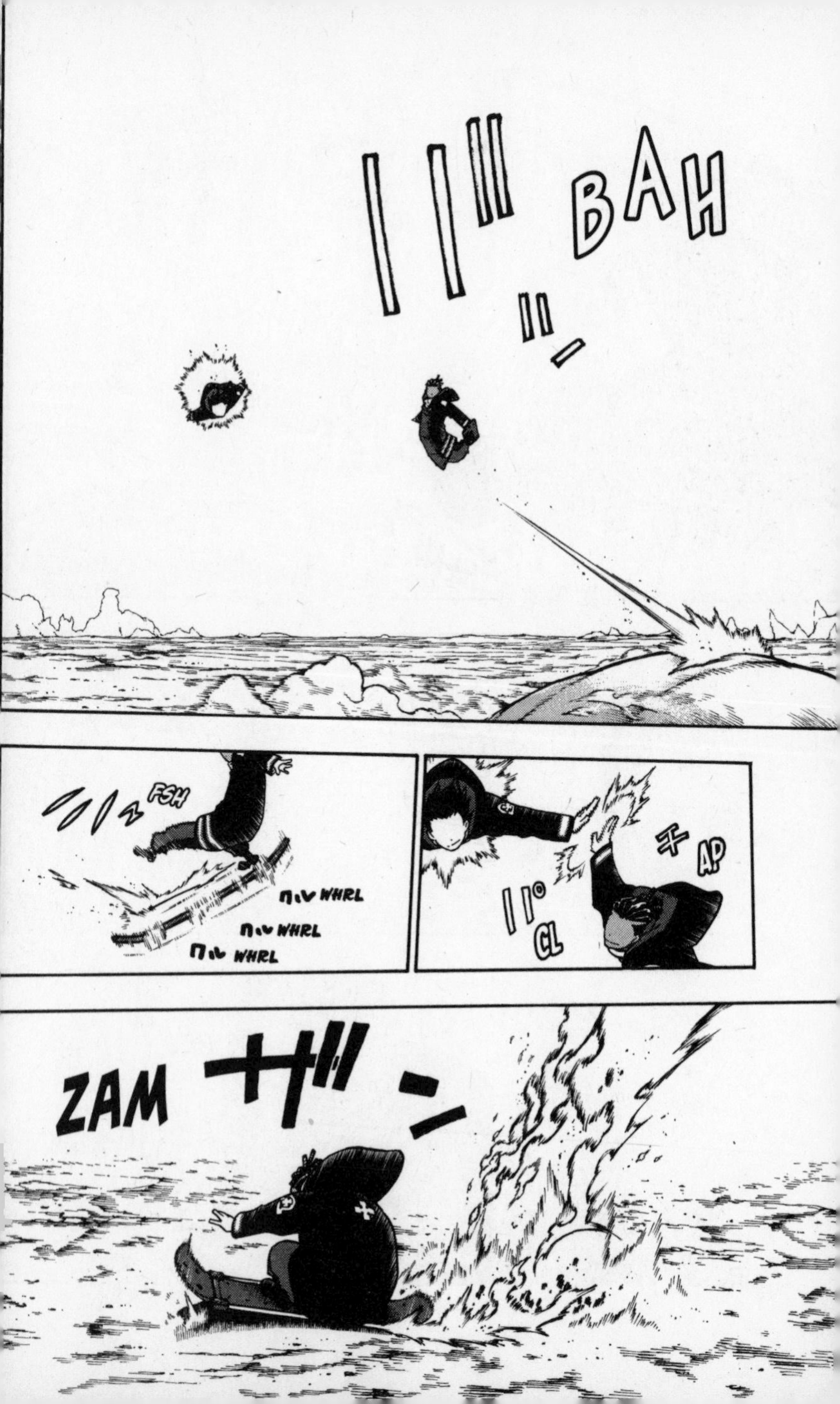
BAH
AP
CL
FSH
WHRL
WHRL
WHRL
ZAM

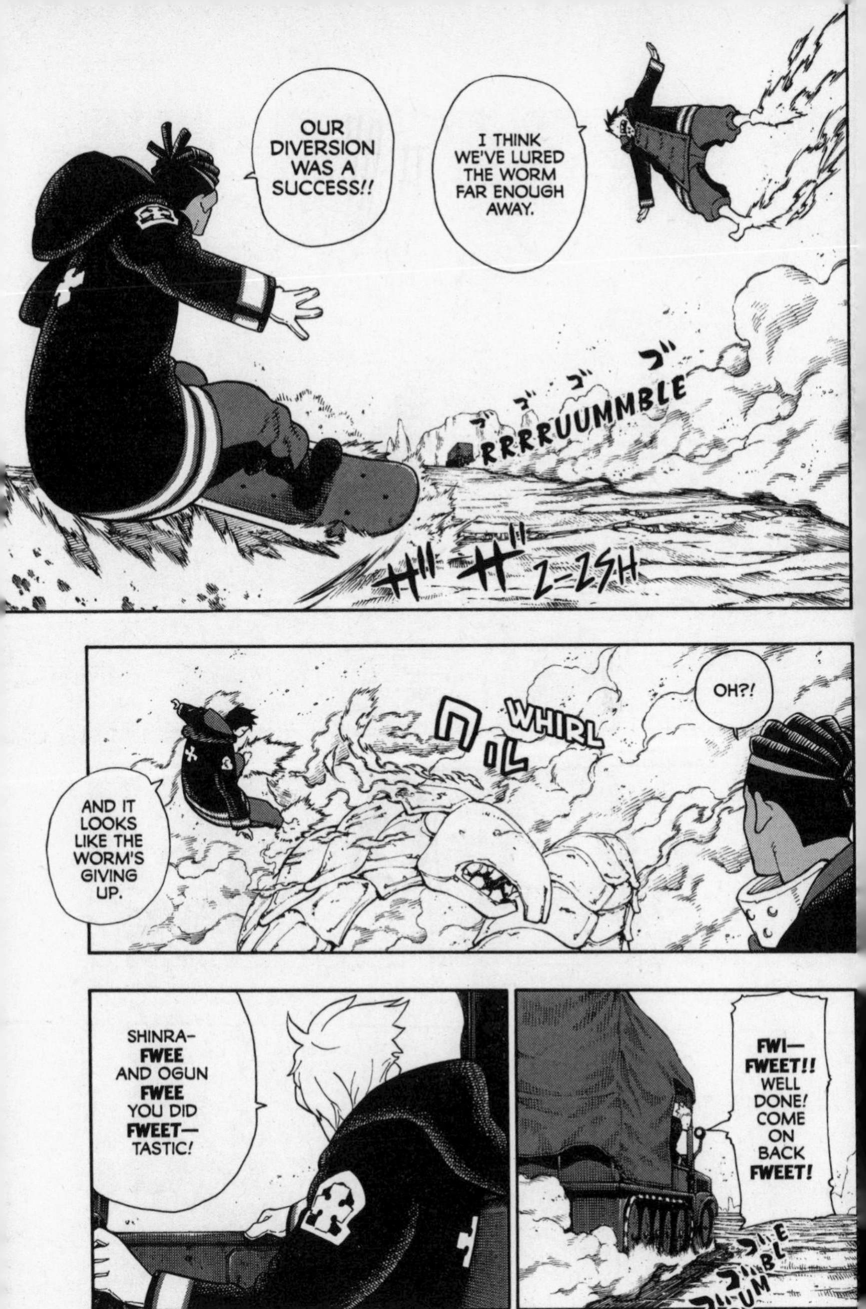
I THINK WE'VE LURED THE WORM FAR ENOUGH AWAY.
OUR DIVERSION WAS A SUCCESS!!
RRRRUUMMBLE
Z-ZSH
OH?!
WHIRL
AND IT LOOKS LIKE THE WORM'S GIVING UP.
FWI— FWEET!! WELL DONE! COME ON BACK FWEET!
RRRUMBLE
SHINRA- FWEE AND OGUN FWEE YOU DID FWEET— TASTIC!

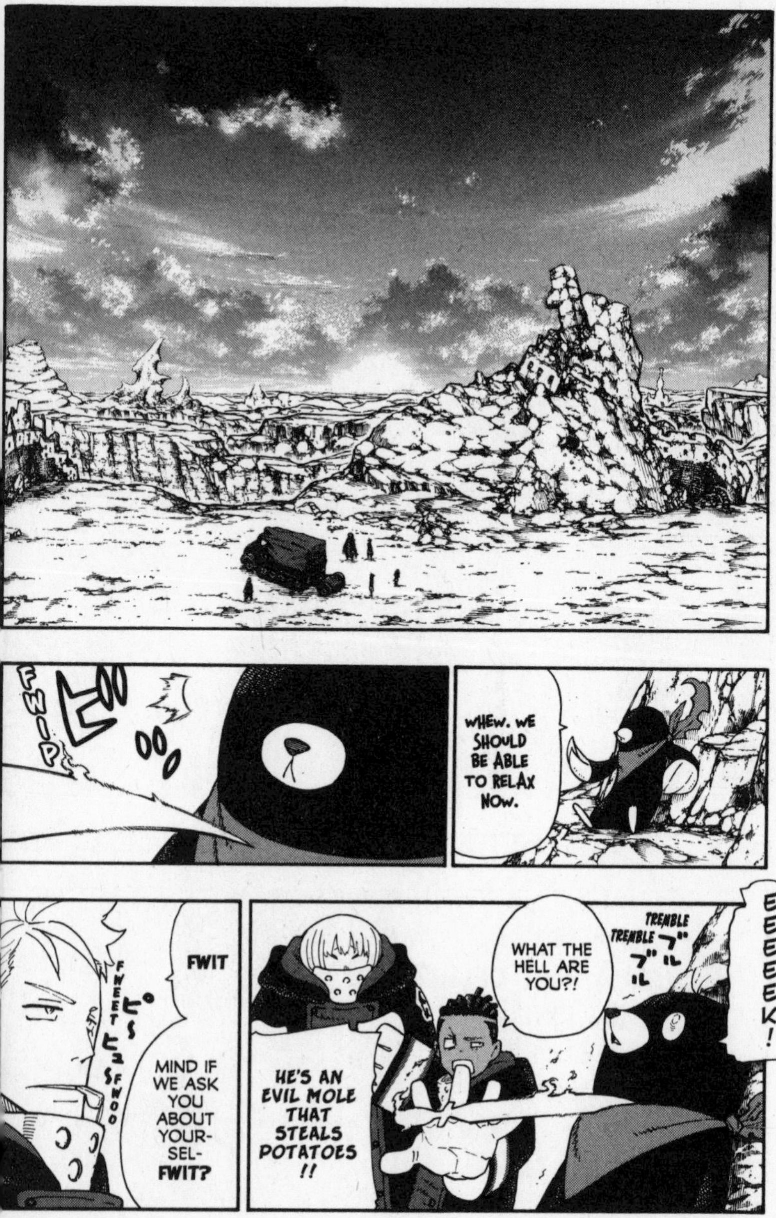

WHEW. WE SHOULD BE ABLE TO RELAX NOW.
FWIP
EEEEEK!
TREMBLE TREMBLE
WHAT THE HELL ARE YOU?!
HE'S AN EVIL MOLE THAT STEALS POTATOES!!
FWIT
FWEET
FWOO
MIND IF WE ASK YOU ABOUT YOURSEL-FWIT?

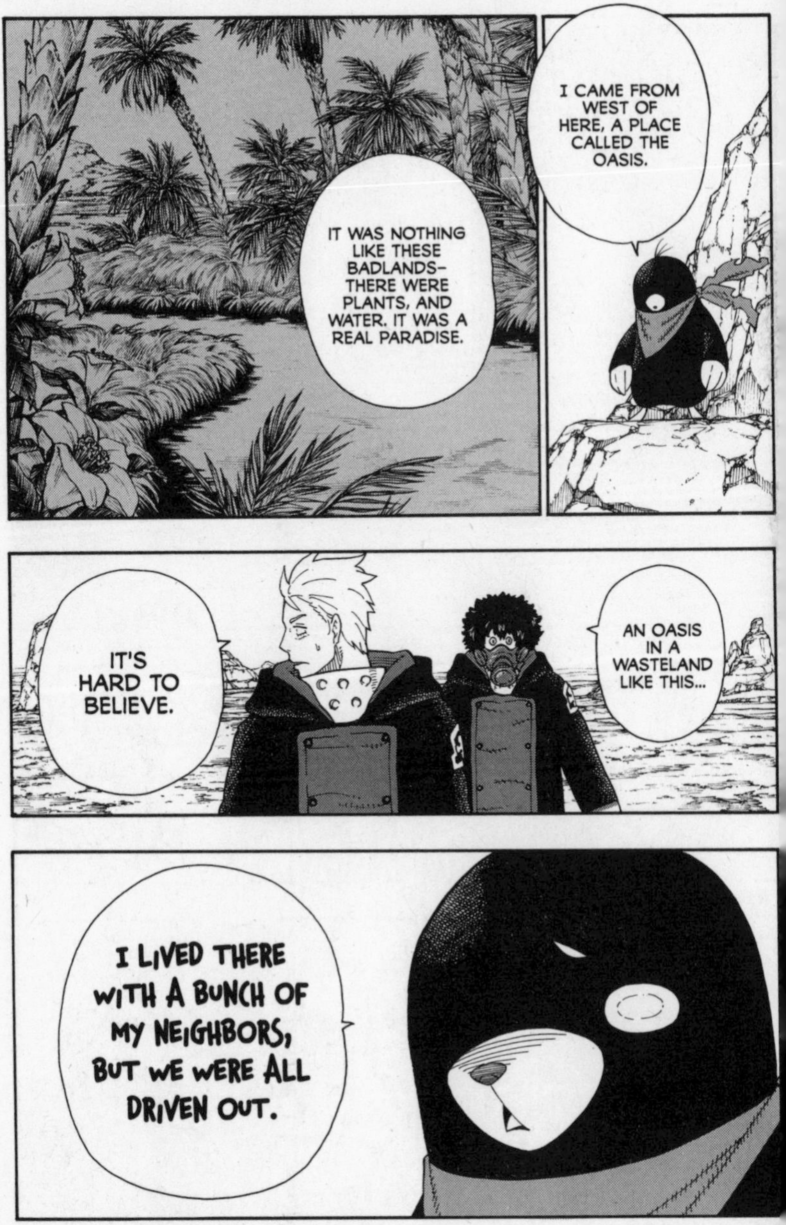
I CAME FROM WEST OF HERE, A PLACE CALLED THE OASIS.
IT WAS NOTHING LIKE THESE BADLANDS– THERE WERE PLANTS, AND WATER. IT WAS A REAL PARADISE.
AN OASIS IN A WASTELAND LIKE THIS...
IT'S HARD TO BELIEVE.
I LIVED THERE WITH A BUNCH OF MY NEIGHBORS, BUT WE WERE ALL DRIVEN OUT.

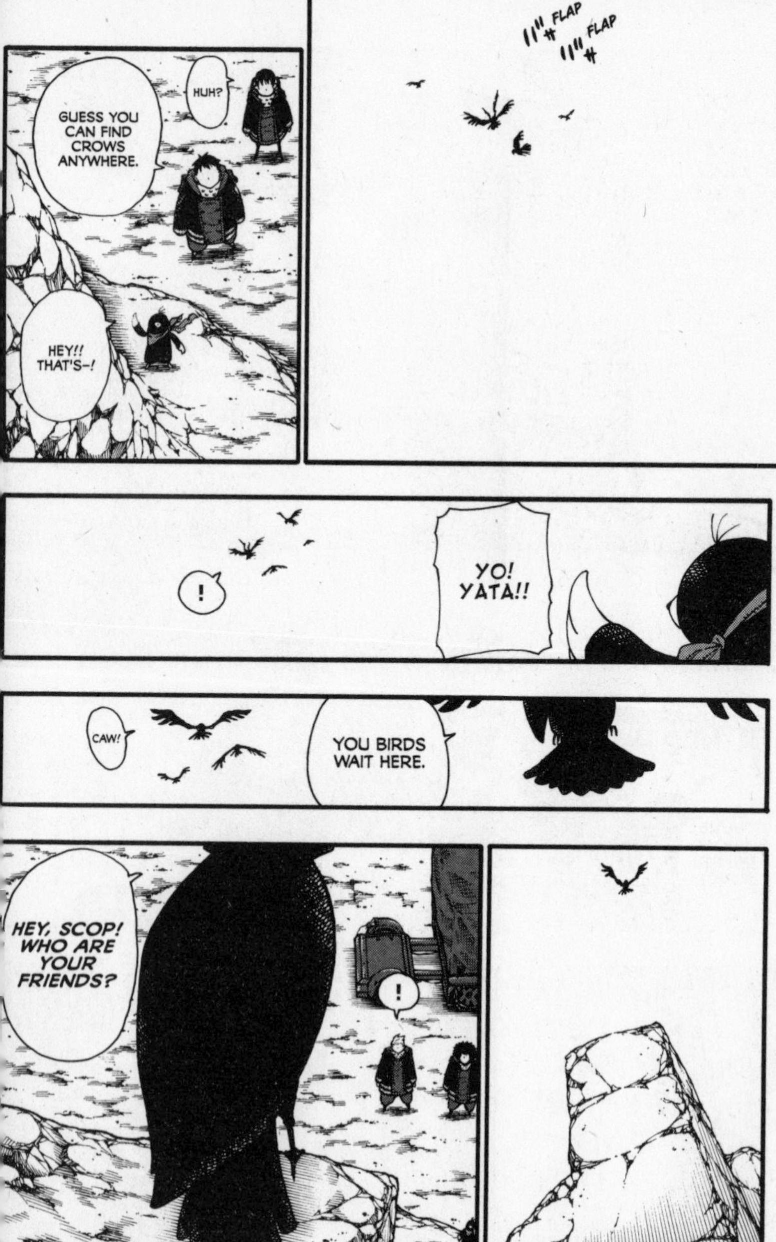
FLAP
FLAP
HUH?
GUESS YOU CAN FIND CROWS ANYWHERE.
HEY!! THAT'S–!
YO! YATA!!
!
YOU BIRDS WAIT HERE.
CAW!
HEY, SCOP! WHO ARE YOUR FRIENDS?
!

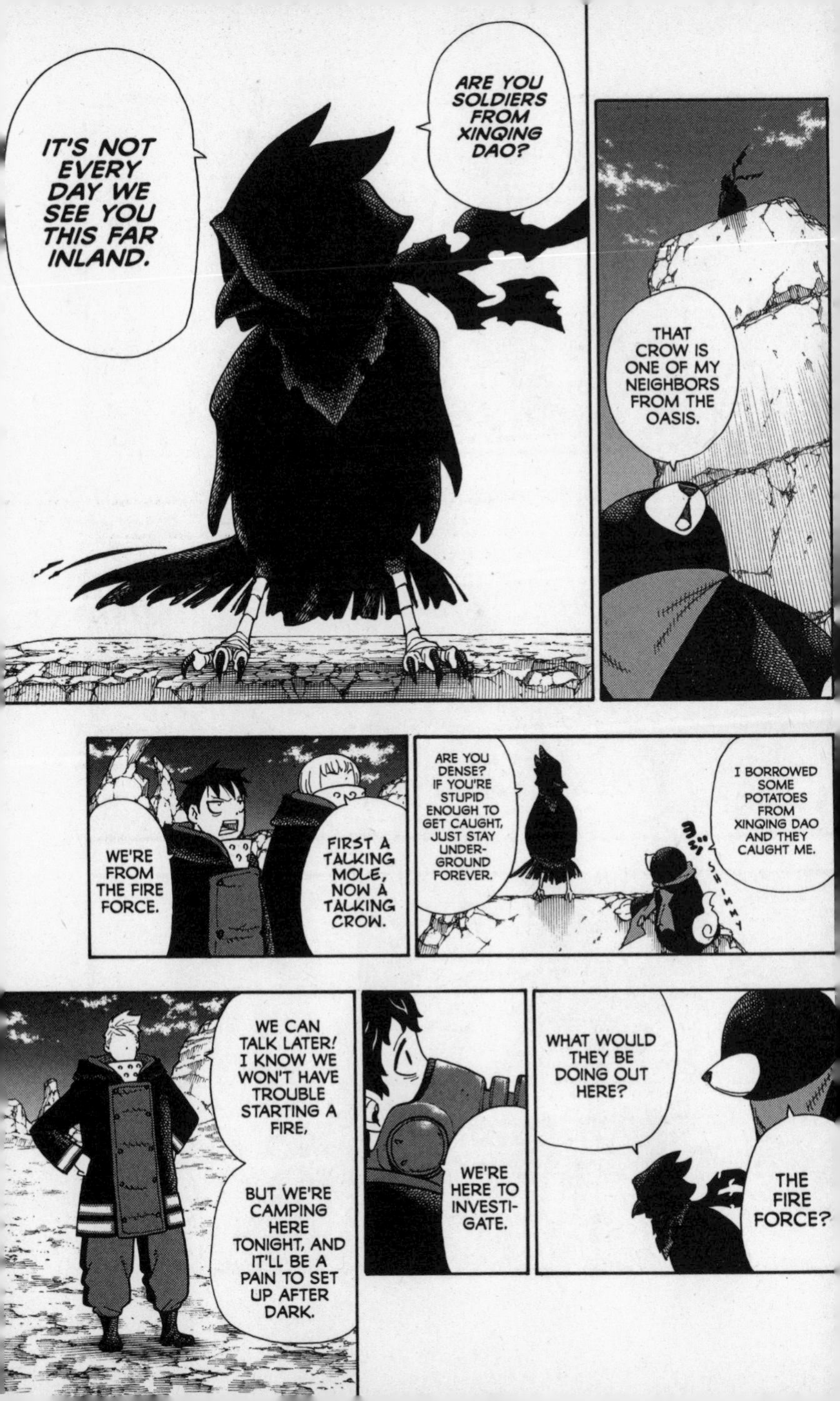
THAT CROW IS ONE OF MY NEIGHBORS FROM THE OASIS.
ARE YOU SOLDIERS FROM XINQING DAO?
IT'S NOT EVERY DAY WE SEE YOU THIS FAR INLAND.
I BORROWED SOME POTATOES FROM XINQING DAO AND THEY CAUGHT ME.
SHIMMY
ARE YOU DENSE? IF YOU'RE STUPID ENOUGH TO GET CAUGHT, JUST STAY UNDERGROUND FOREVER.
FIRST A TALKING MOLE, NOW A TALKING CROW.
WE'RE FROM THE FIRE FORCE.
THE FIRE FORCE?
WHAT WOULD THEY BE DOING OUT HERE?
WE'RE HERE TO INVESTIGATE.
WE CAN TALK LATER! I KNOW WE WON'T HAVE TROUBLE STARTING A FIRE,
BUT WE'RE CAMPING HERE TONIGHT, AND IT'LL BE A PAIN TO SET UP AFTER DARK.

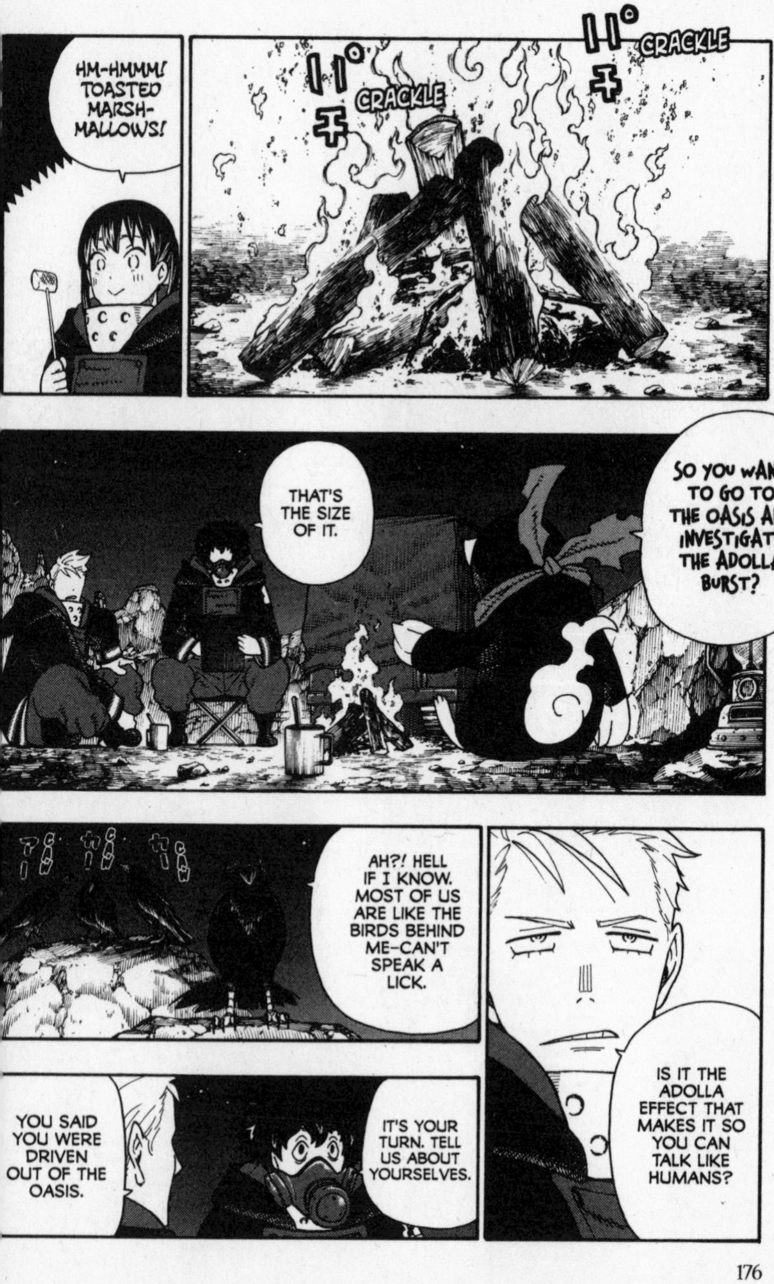
CRACKLE
CRACKLE
HM-HMMM! TOASTED MARSH-MALLOWS!
SO YOU WANT TO GO TO THE OASIS AND INVESTIGATE THE ADOLLA BURST?
THAT'S THE SIZE OF IT.
IS IT THE ADOLLA EFFECT THAT MAKES IT SO YOU CAN TALK LIKE HUMANS?
AH?! HELL IF I KNOW. MOST OF US ARE LIKE THE BIRDS BEHIND ME—CAN'T SPEAK A LICK.
IT'S YOUR TURN. TELL US ABOUT YOURSELVES.
YOU SAID YOU WERE DRIVEN OUT OF THE OASIS.

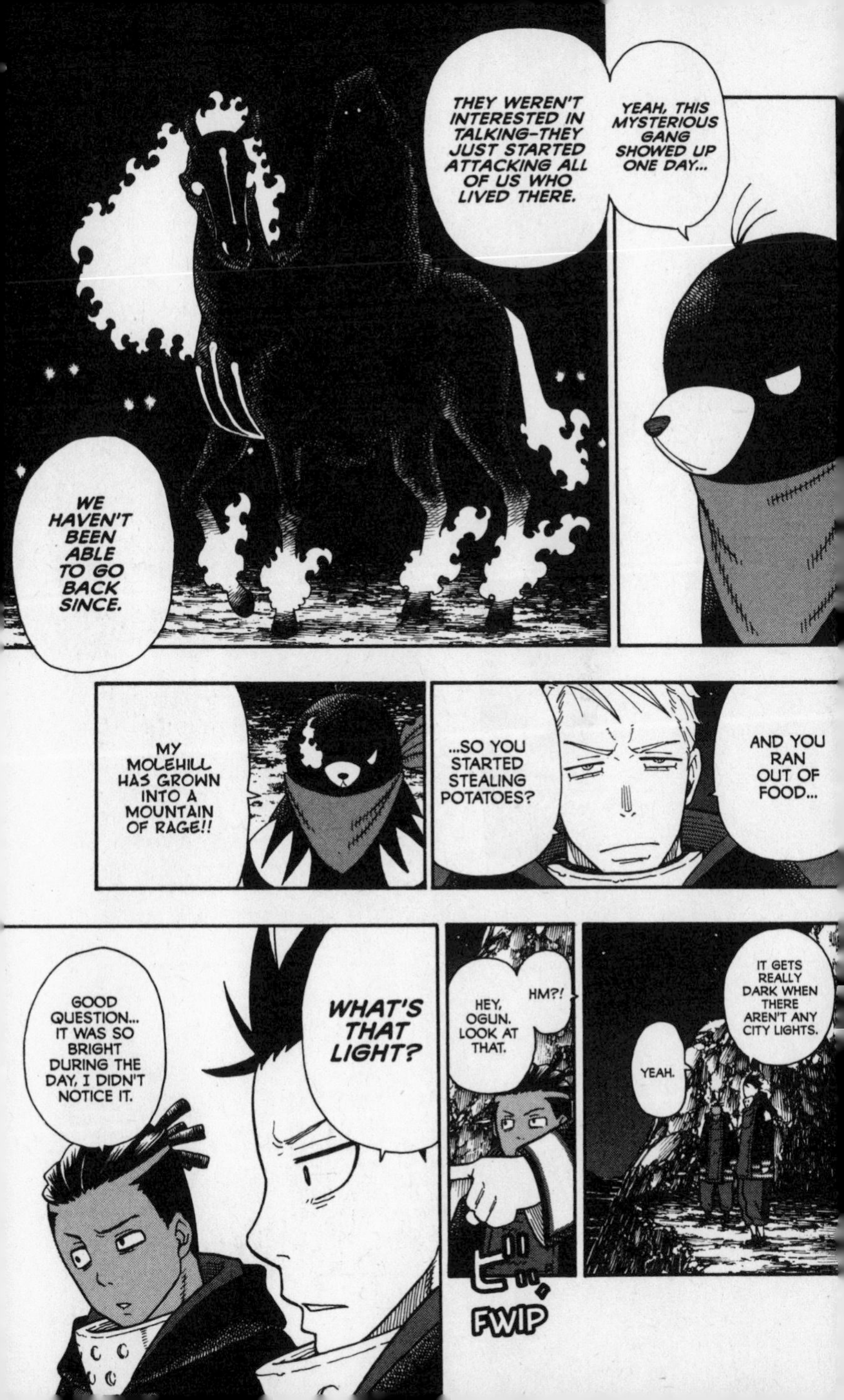
YEAH, THIS MYSTERIOUS GANG SHOWED UP ONE DAY...
THEY WEREN'T INTERESTED IN TALKING—THEY JUST STARTED ATTACKING ALL OF US WHO LIVED THERE.
WE HAVEN'T BEEN ABLE TO GO BACK SINCE.
AND YOU RAN OUT OF FOOD...
...SO YOU STARTED STEALING POTATOES?
MY MOLEHILL HAS GROWN INTO A MOUNTAIN OF RAGE!!
IT GETS REALLY DARK WHEN THERE AREN'T ANY CITY LIGHTS.
YEAH.
HM?!
HEY, OGUN. LOOK AT THAT.
FWIP
WHAT'S THAT LIGHT?
GOOD QUESTION... IT WAS SO BRIGHT DURING THE DAY, I DIDN'T NOTICE IT.

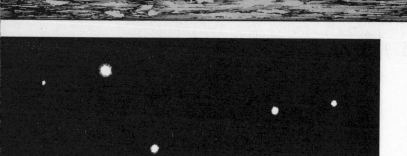

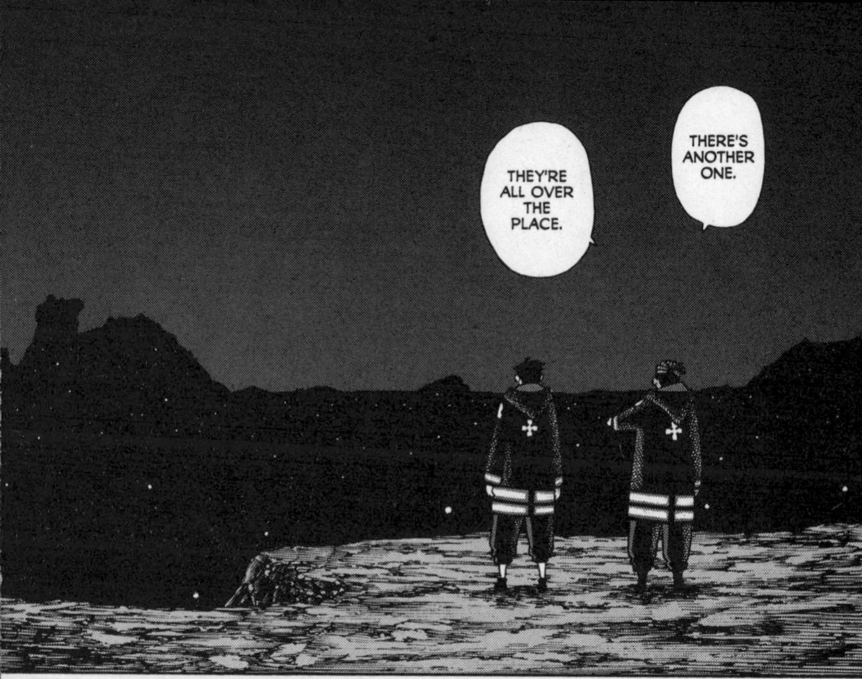
THERE'S ANOTHER ONE.
THEY'RE ALL OVER THE PLACE.

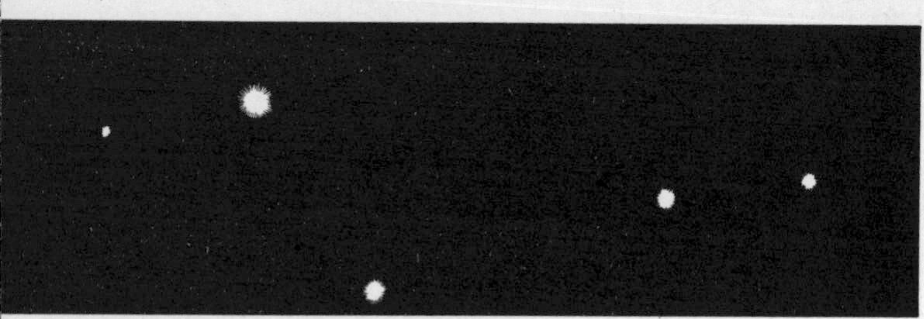

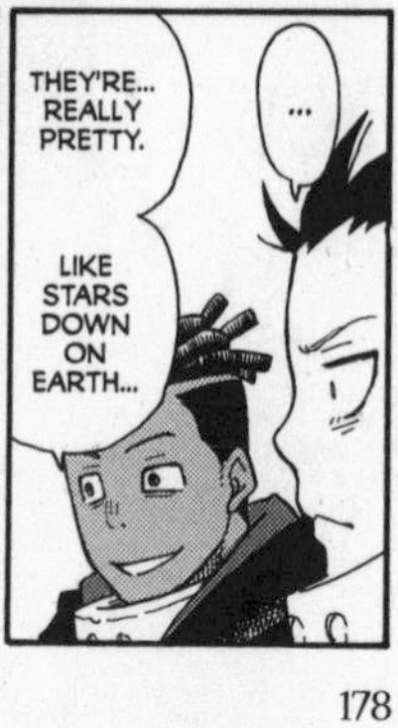
...
THEY'RE... REALLY PRETTY.
LIKE STARS DOWN ON EARTH...

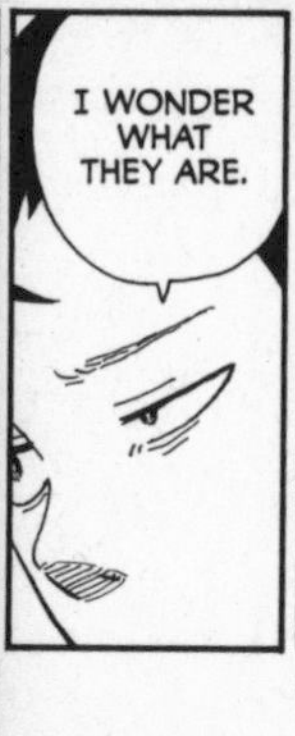
I WONDER WHAT THEY ARE.

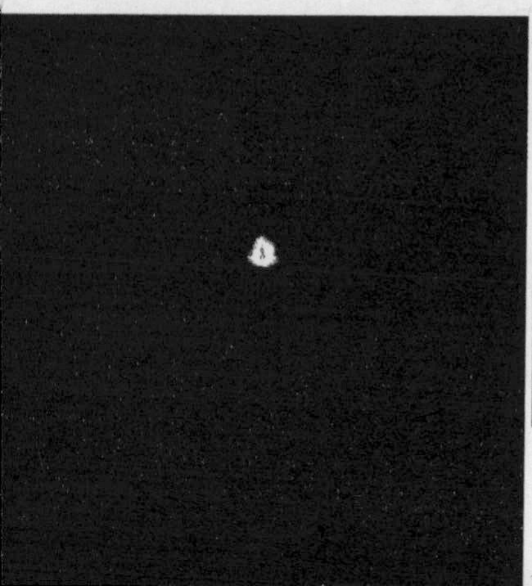

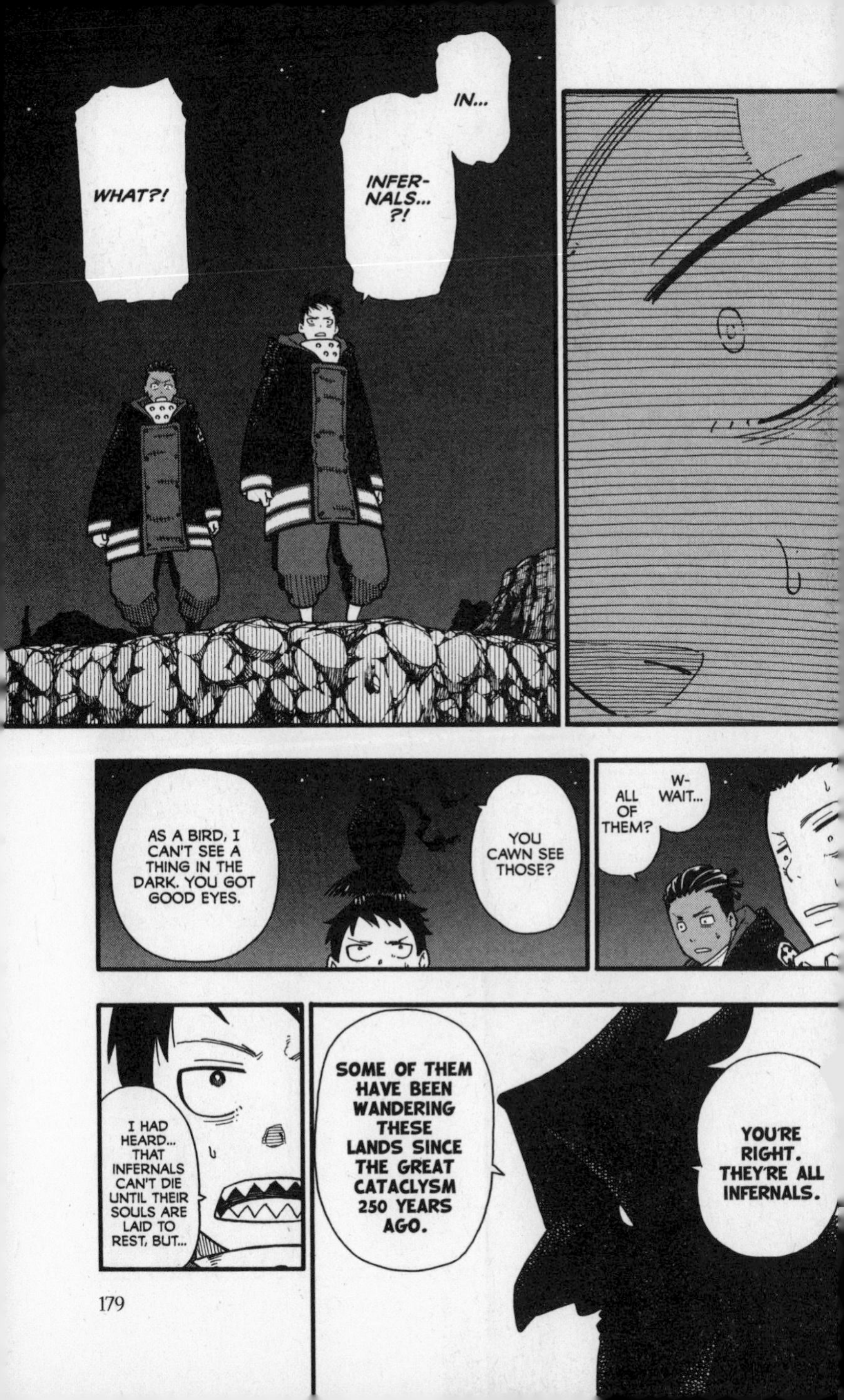
IN... INFER-NALS...?!
WHAT?!
W-WAIT...
ALL OF THEM?
YOU CAWN SEE THOSE?
AS A BIRD, I CAN'T SEE A THING IN THE DARK. YOU GOT GOOD EYES.
YOU'RE RIGHT. THEY'RE ALL INFERNALS.
SOME OF THEM HAVE BEEN WANDERING THESE LANDS SINCE THE GREAT CATACLYSM 250 YEARS AGO.
I HAD HEARD... THAT INFERNALS CAN'T DIE UNTIL THEIR SOULS ARE LAID TO REST, BUT...

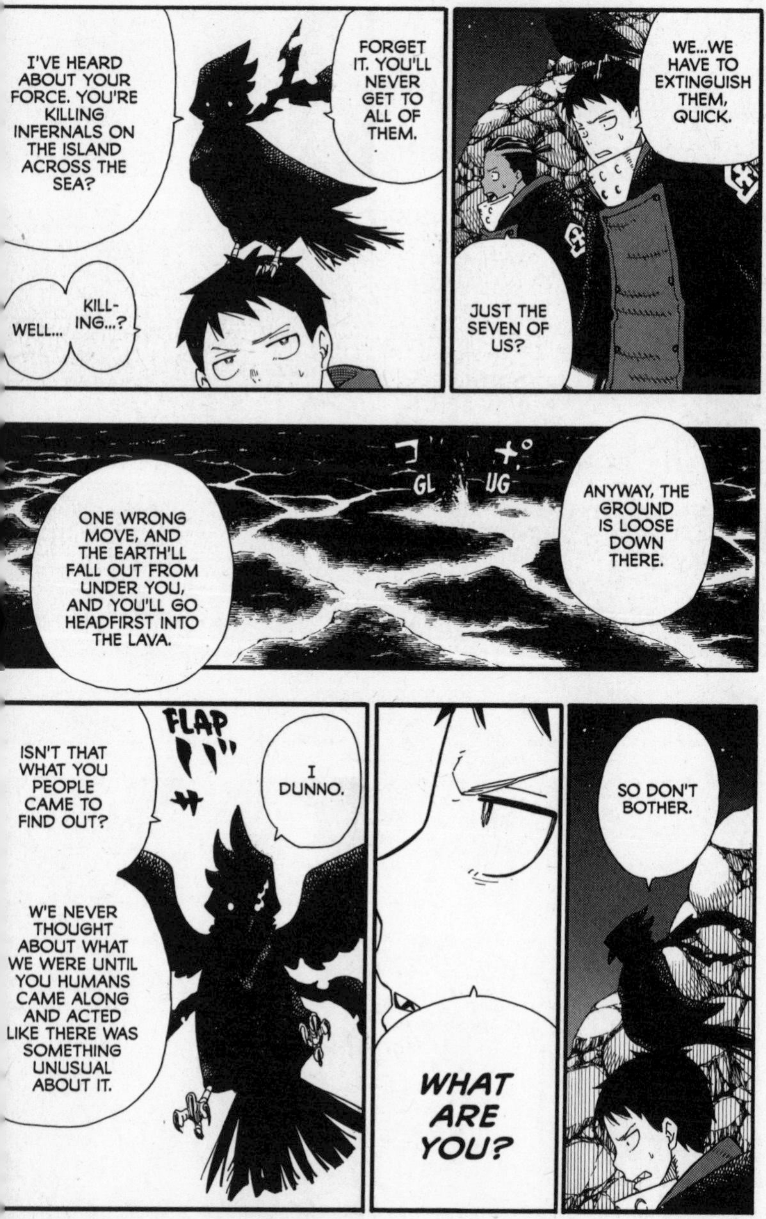

WE...WE HAVE TO EXTINGUISH THEM, QUICK.
JUST THE SEVEN OF US?
FORGET IT. YOU'LL NEVER GET TO ALL OF THEM.
I'VE HEARD ABOUT YOUR FORCE. YOU'RE KILLING INFERNALS ON THE ISLAND ACROSS THE SEA?
KILL-ING...?
WELL...
ANYWAY, THE GROUND IS LOOSE DOWN THERE.
GL UG
ONE WRONG MOVE, AND THE EARTH'LL FALL OUT FROM UNDER YOU, AND YOU'LL GO HEADFIRST INTO THE LAVA.
SO DON'T BOTHER.
WHAT ARE YOU?
I DUNNO.
FLAP
ISN'T THAT WHAT YOU PEOPLE CAME TO FIND OUT?
W'E NEVER THOUGHT ABOUT WHAT WE WERE UNTIL YOU HUMANS CAME ALONG AND ACTED LIKE THERE WAS SOMETHING UNUSUAL ABOUT IT.

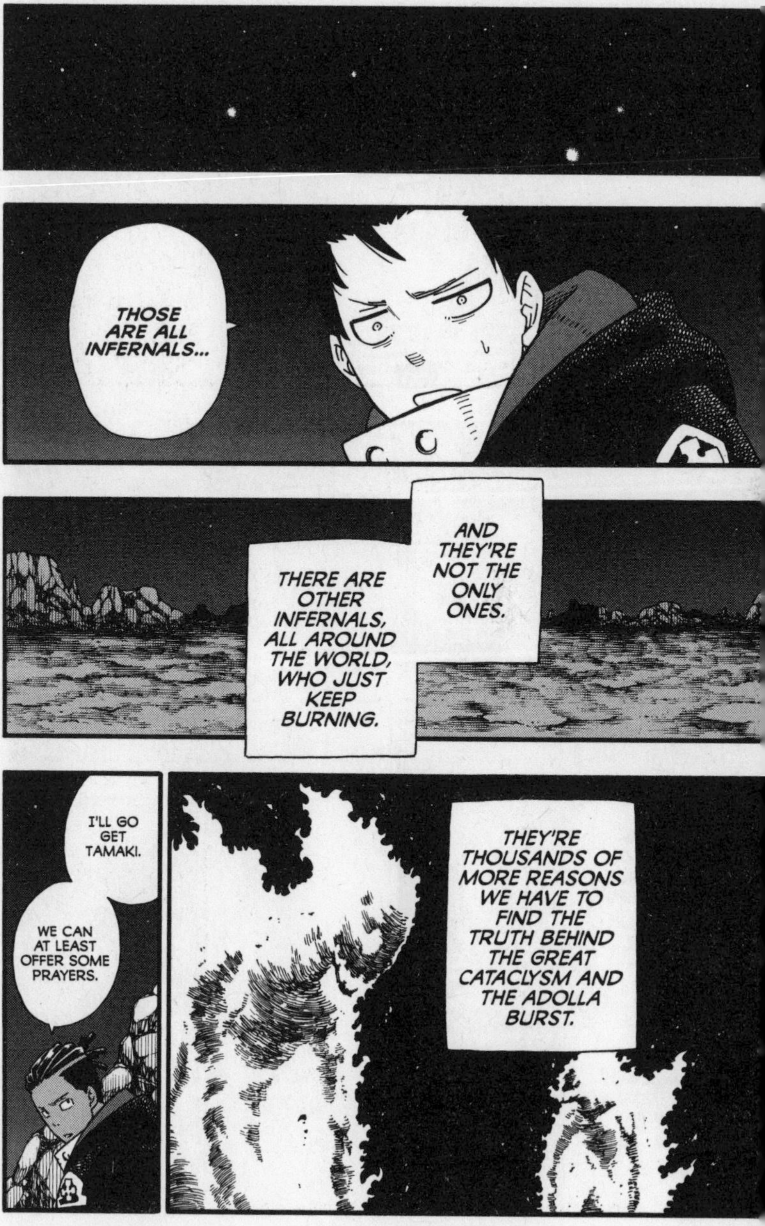
THOSE ARE ALL INFERNALS...
AND THEY'RE NOT THE ONLY ONES.
THERE ARE OTHER INFERNALS, ALL AROUND THE WORLD, WHO JUST KEEP BURNING.
THEY'RE THOUSANDS OF MORE REASONS WE HAVE TO FIND THE TRUTH BEHIND THE GREAT CATACLYSM AND THE ADOLLA BURST.
I'LL GO GET TAMAKI.
WE CAN AT LEAST OFFER SOME PRAYERS.

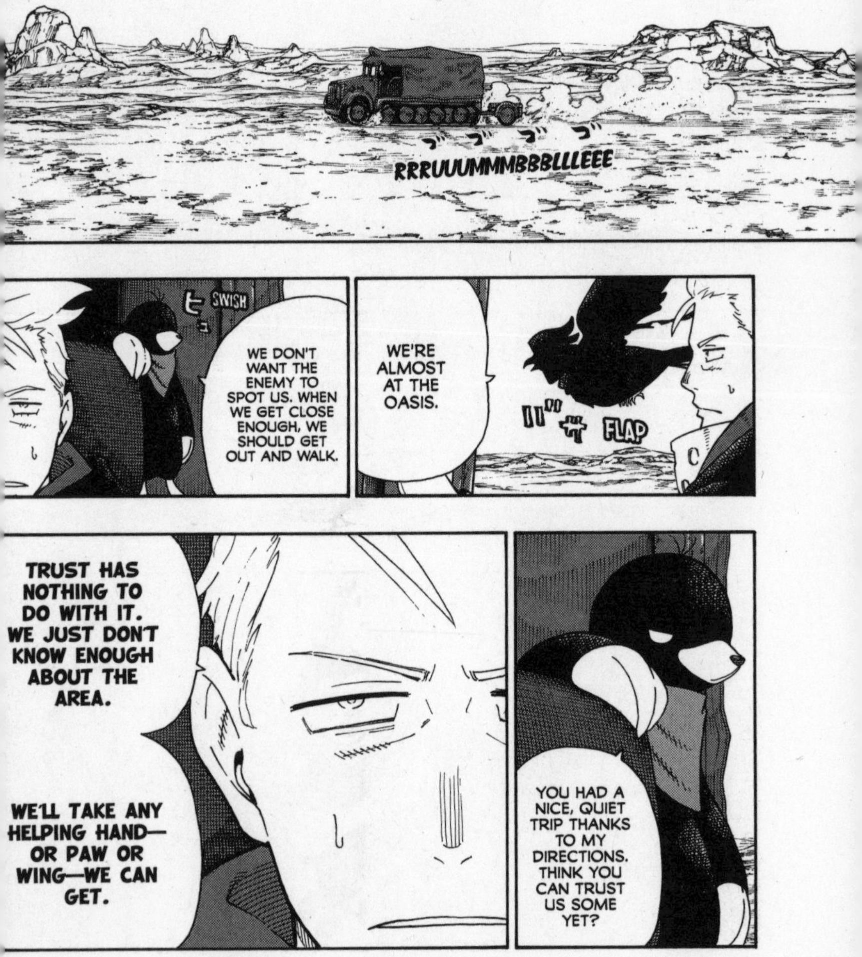
RRRUUUMMMBBBLLLEEE
FLAP
WE'RE ALMOST AT THE OASIS.
SWISH
WE DON'T WANT THE ENEMY TO SPOT US. WHEN WE GET CLOSE ENOUGH, WE SHOULD GET OUT AND WALK.
YOU HAD A NICE, QUIET TRIP THANKS TO MY DIRECTIONS. THINK YOU CAN TRUST US SOME YET?
TRUST HAS NOTHING TO DO WITH IT. WE JUST DON'T KNOW ENOUGH ABOUT THE AREA.
WE'LL TAKE ANY HELPING HAND— OR PAW OR WING—WE CAN GET.

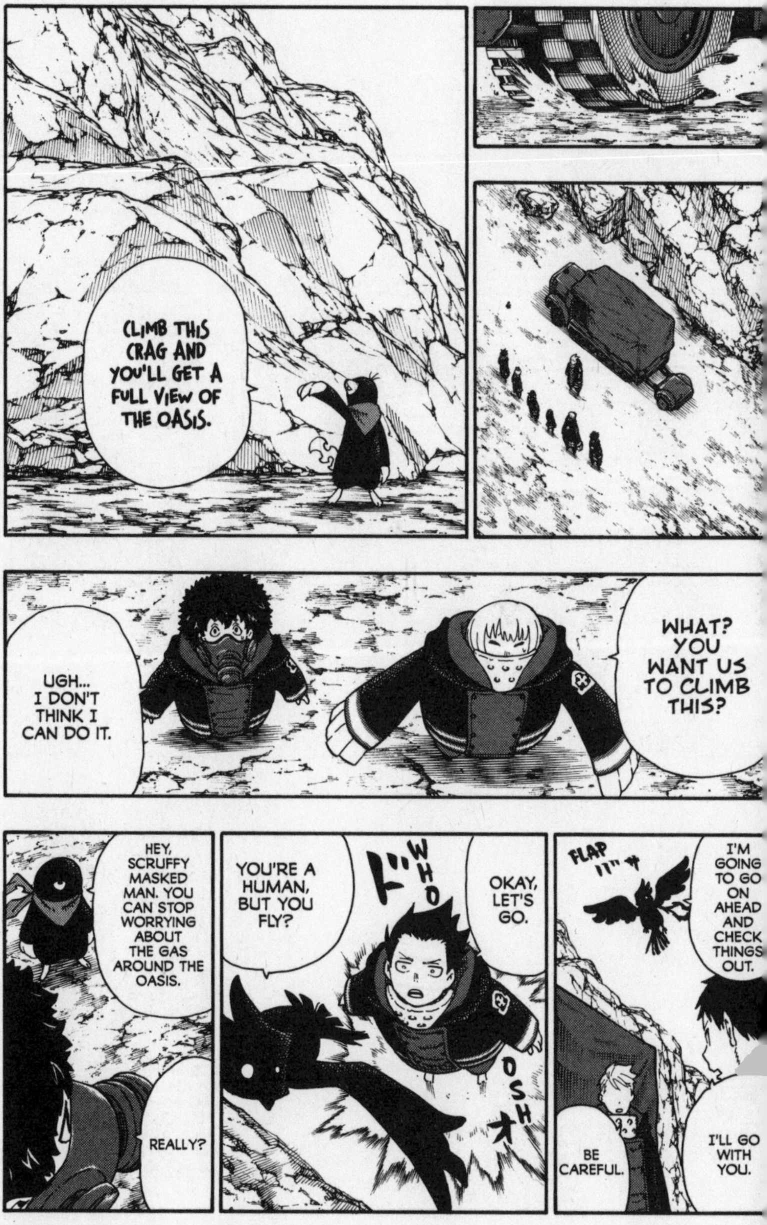
CLIMB THIS CRAG AND YOU'LL GET A FULL VIEW OF THE OASIS.
WHAT? YOU WANT US TO CLIMB THIS?
UGH... I DON'T THINK I CAN DO IT.
FLAP
I'M GOING TO GO ON AHEAD AND CHECK THINGS OUT.
I'LL GO WITH YOU.
BE CAREFUL.
WHOOSH
OKAY, LET'S GO.
YOU'RE A HUMAN, BUT YOU FLY?
HEY, SCRUFFY MASKED MAN. YOU CAN STOP WORRYING ABOUT THE GAS AROUND THE OASIS.
REALLY?

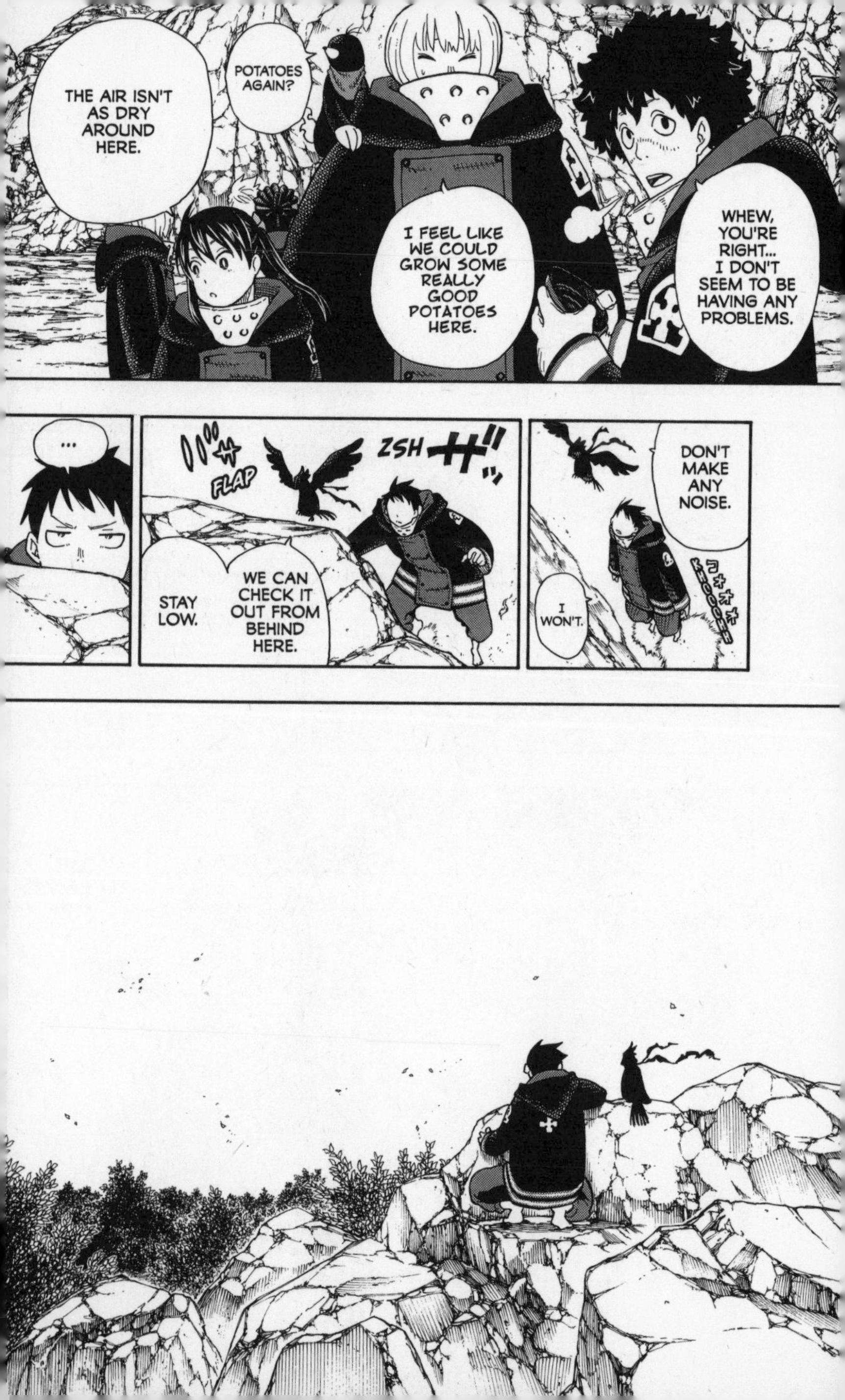
WHEW, YOU'RE RIGHT... I DON'T SEEM TO BE HAVING ANY PROBLEMS.
I FEEL LIKE WE COULD GROW SOME REALLY GOOD POTATOES HERE.
POTATOES AGAIN?
THE AIR ISN'T AS DRY AROUND HERE.
DON'T MAKE ANY NOISE.
KHOOOHH
I WON'T.
ZSH
FLAP
WE CAN CHECK IT OUT FROM BEHIND HERE.
STAY LOW.
...

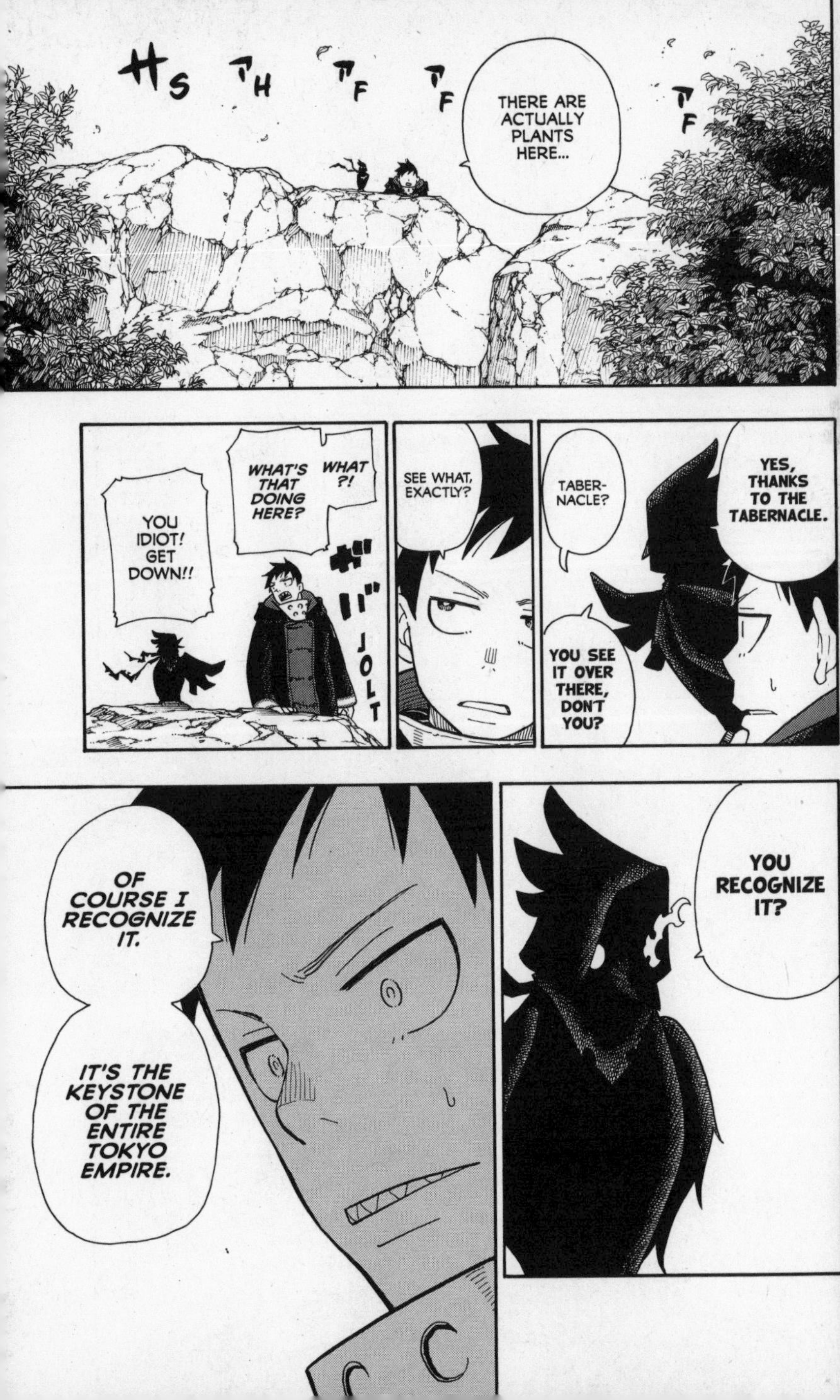
HS
TH
TF
TF
TF
THERE ARE ACTUALLY PLANTS HERE...
YES, THANKS TO THE TABERNACLE.
TABER-NACLE?
YOU SEE IT OVER THERE, DON'T YOU?
SEE WHAT, EXACTLY?
WHAT ?!
WHAT'S THAT DOING HERE?
JOLT
YOU IDIOT! GET DOWN!!
YOU RECOGNIZE IT?
OF COURSE I RECOGNIZE IT.
IT'S THE KEYSTONE OF THE ENTIRE TOKYO EMPIRE.

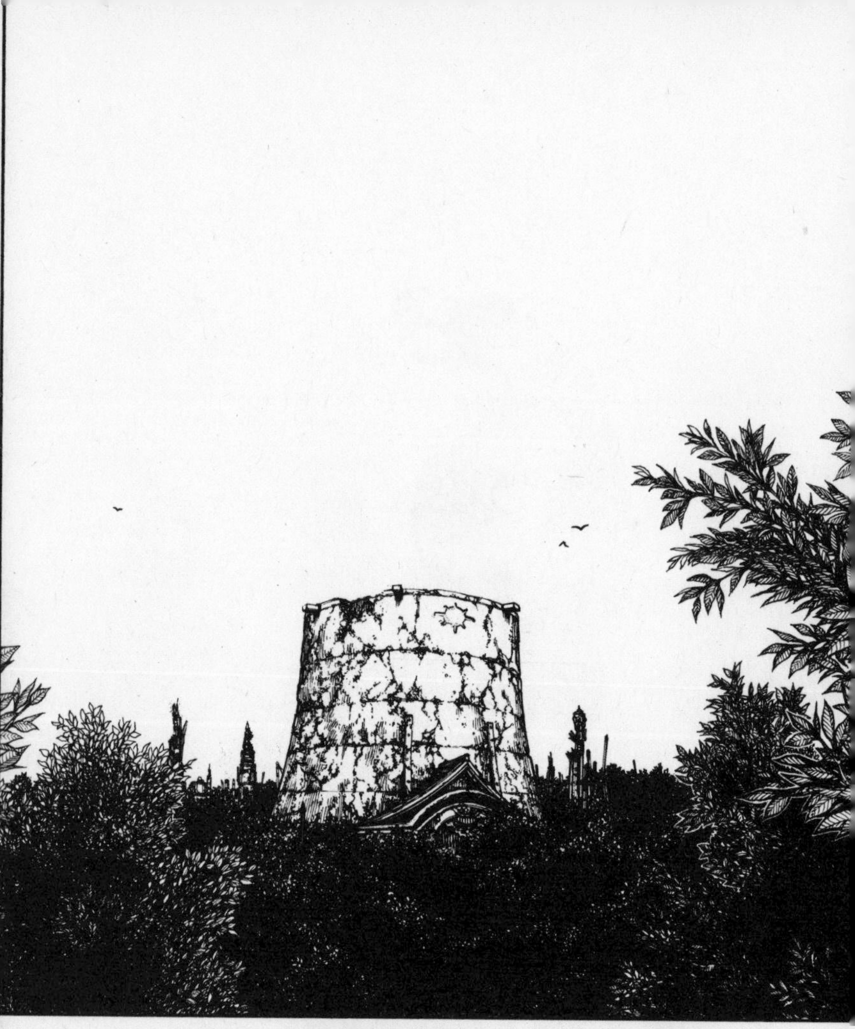
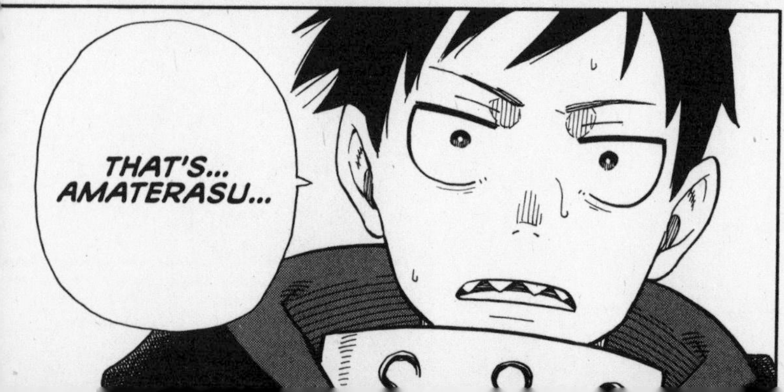
THAT'S... AMATERASU...

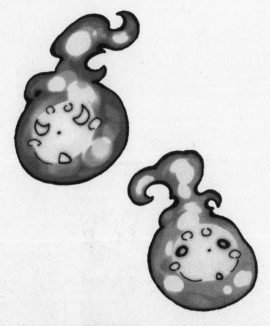

TO BE CONTINUED IN VOLUME 14!!

Translation Notes:

Heave ho, page 71

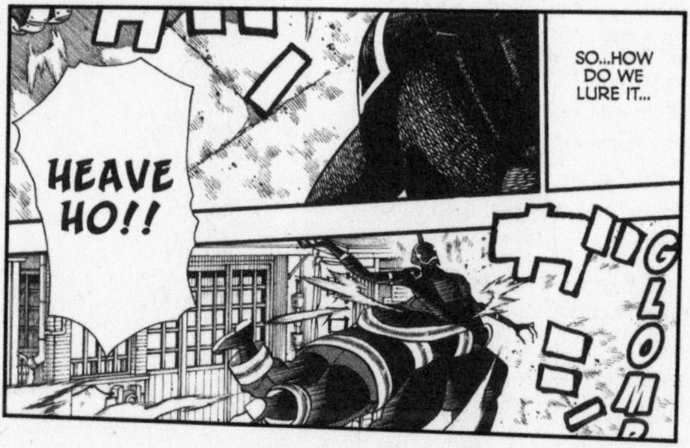
SO...HOW DO WE LURE IT...
HEAVE HO!!

In the original text, as Captain Ōbi attempts to give this Infernal the old heave-ho, he shouts *"dosukoi!"* This is a phrase derived from *dokkoi*, an interjection used when doing heavy labor (something like an "oof!"), or when stopping someone from doing something. It is most commonly associated with sumo wrestling, thus creating the perhaps comical image of the Captain attempting to wrestle a demon out of a sumo ring.

Purt Co Pan, page 130

Readers no doubt recognize Lieutenant Pan from Shinra's visit to Company 4. Mythology enthusiasts may recognize the name Pan as being shared with that of the Greek shepherd god, who is also a patron of rustic music and is well known for his unique flute called a panpipe. When written in Japanese, the Lieutenant's full name sounds remarkably similar to that of iconic musician from Nirvana, Kurt Cobain.

Fer taters' sake, page 140

The Noto family uses what appears to be a new dialect that has come about after the Great Cataclysm, and incorporates elements from several different rural dialects all over Japan, as well as some that don't seem to exist in any now-extant Japanese dialect. The translators have attempted to recreate the effect by using elements of the American Appalachian dialect combined with some more Northern dialects and maybe a touch of Irish.

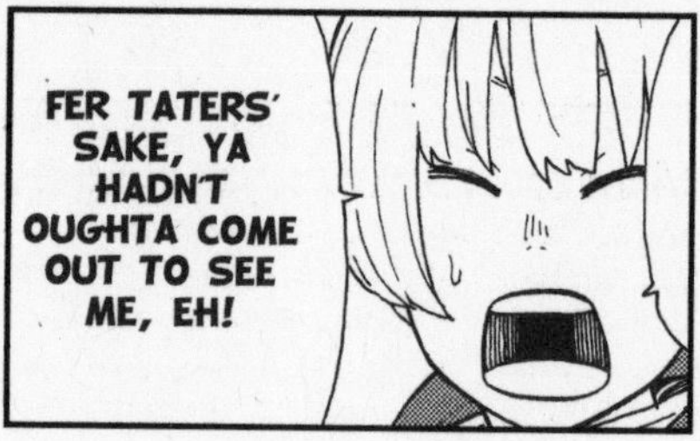
FER TATERS' SAKE, YA HADN'T OUGHTA COME OUT TO SEE ME, EH!

The end of the century, page 155

Juggernaut's reaction to the strange rock formations remains unclear. Perhaps he is overreacting because he's still being affected by the gas in the air, or perhaps something deep in his brain is reminded of the demonic forms of the members of heavy metal band Seikima-II, whose name can be translated to "End of the Century." Either way, his observation leaves Arthur feeling cold.

Yata and Scop, page 174

Naturally, these creatures each have a name that is related to its species. "Yata"comes from *"yatagarasu,"* or "eight-span crow," a crow that, in Japanese mythology, was sent by the sun goddess to guide one of the first emperors. "Scop" comes from the Dutch word *"schop,"* which was adopted into the Japanese language as the name for small shovels, like spades and garden trowels. This mole was likely named for its shovel-like hands.

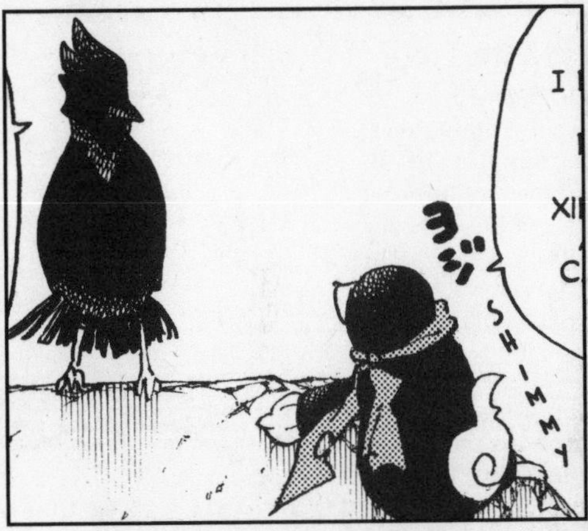
SHIMMY

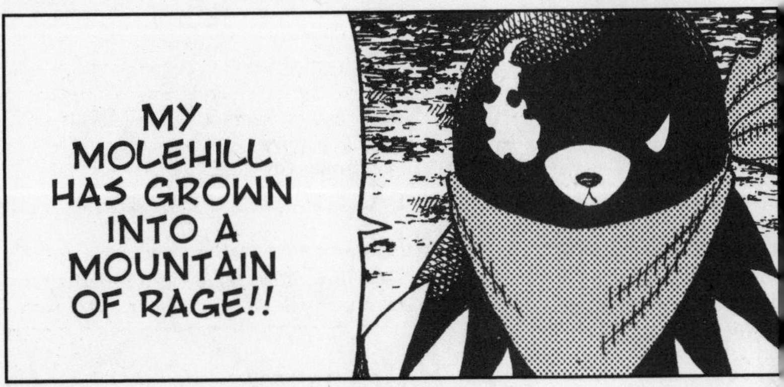
MY MOLEHILL HAS GROWN INTO A MOUNTAIN OF RAGE!!

Mountain of rage, page 177

The common Japanese word for mole is *"mogura,"* but another name for the creatures is doryū, which literally means "earth dragon." In the original text, Scop traded the kanji character meaning earth for one that is pronounced the same, but means anger. In other words, he is no longer a little earth dragon, because now he is a raging dragon. The translators attempted to capture the double meaning by using a familiar English expression.

Tabernacle, page 185

Strictly speaking, a tabernacle is a temporary dwelling, such as a tent, and nothing more. However, it is also used in religious contexts to refer an object or body in which a spirit or god dwells. This makes it a fitting translation for *"go-shintai,"* which literally means "divine body," and refers to objects that house gods.

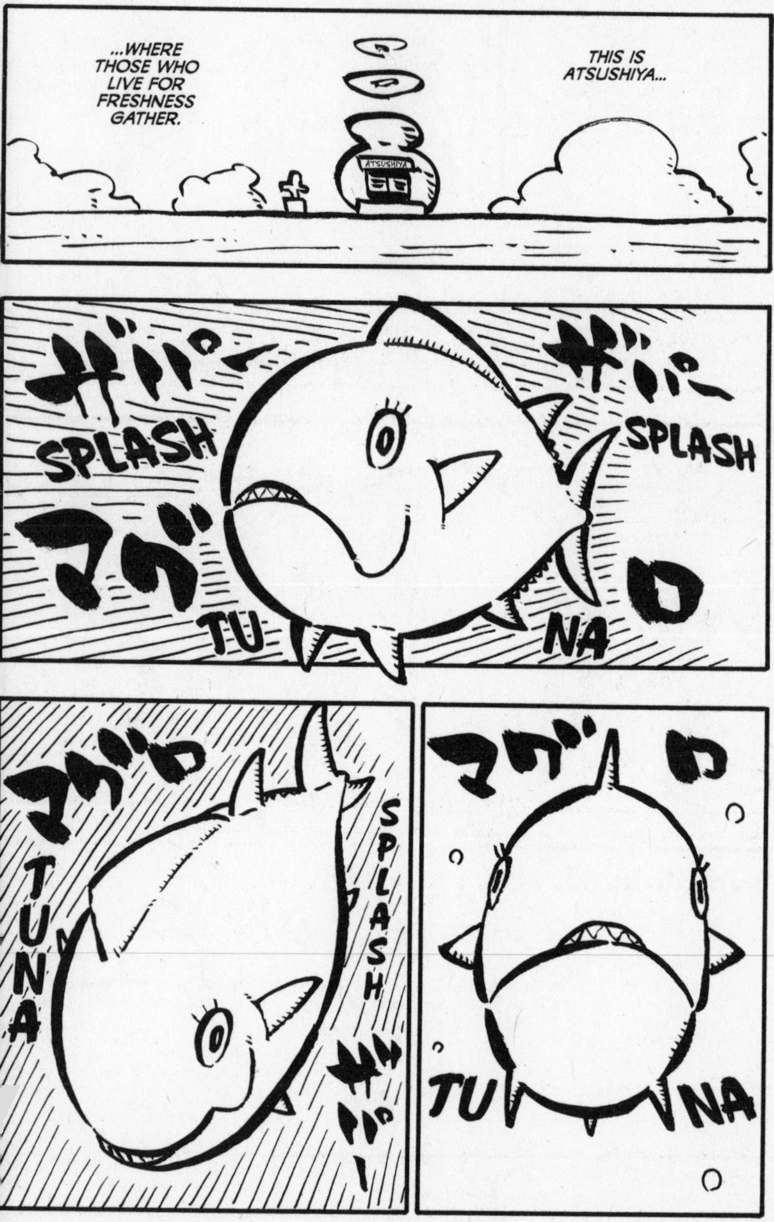
THIS IS ATSUSHIYA...
...WHERE THOSE WHO LIVE FOR FRESHNESS GATHER.
ATSUSHIYA
ザバー
SPLASH
ザバー
SPLASH
ロ
NA
マグ
TU
マグ ロ
TU
NA
SPLASH
ザバー
マグロ
TUNA

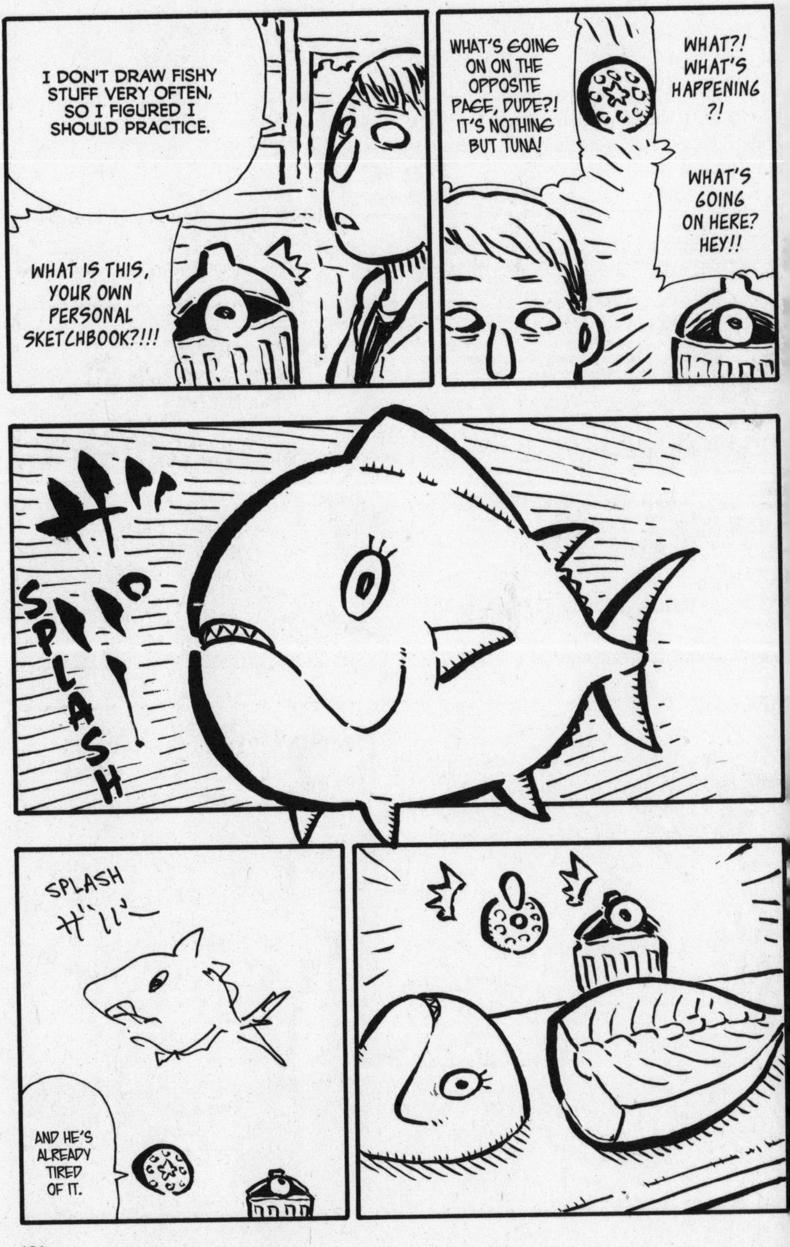

WHAT?! WHAT'S HAPPENING?!
WHAT'S GOING ON ON THE OPPOSITE PAGE, DUDE?! IT'S NOTHING BUT TUNA!
WHAT'S GOING ON HERE? HEY!!
I DON'T DRAW FISHY STUFF VERY OFTEN, SO I FIGURED I SHOULD PRACTICE.
WHAT IS THIS, YOUR OWN PERSONAL SKETCHBOOK?!!!
SPLASH
SPLASH
AND HE'S ALREADY TIRED OF IT.

A Kodansha Comics Trade Paperback Original.

Fire Force volume 13 copyright © 2018 Atsushi Ohkubo
English translation copyright © 2018 Atsushi Ohkubo

Published in the United States by Kodansha Comics, an imprint of Kodansha USA Publishing, LLC, New York.

Publication rights for this English edition arranged through Kodansha Ltd., Tokyo.

First published in Japan in 2018 by Kodansha Ltd., Tokyo.

ISBN 978-1-63236-664-1

Printed in the United States of America.

www.kodanshacomics.com

9 8 7 6 5 4 3 2

Translation: Alethea Nibley & Athena Nibley
Lettering: AndWorld Design
Editing: Alejandro Arbona and Lauren Scanlan
Kodansha Comics edition cover design: Phil Balsman